Social Change in Aegean Prehistory

edited by
Corien Wiersma
and Sofia Voutsaki

Oxford & Philadelphia

Published in the United Kingdom in 2017 by
OXBOW BOOKS
The Old Music Hall, 106–108 Cowley Road, Oxford OX4 1JE

and in the United States by
OXBOW BOOKS
1950 Lawrence Road, Havertown, PA 19083

© Oxbow Books and the individual contributors 2017

Paperback edition: ISBN 978-1-78570-219-8
Digital edition: ISBN 978-1-78570-220-4 (epub)

A CIP record for this book is available from the British Library

Library of Congress Cataloging-in-Publication Data

Names: Wiersma, Corien, 1983- editor of compilation. | Voutsaki, Sofia, editor of compilation.
Title: Social change in Aegean prehistory / edited by Corien Wiersma and Sofia Voutsaki.
Description: Oxford ; Philadelphia : Oxbow Books, 2016. | Papers from an international conference entitled Explaining Change in Aegean Prehistory, which was held in Groningen, the Netherlands, October 16-17, 2013. | Includes bibliographical references.
Identifiers: LCCN 2016036322 (print) | LCCN 2016036366 (ebook) | ISBN 9781785702198 (paperback) | ISBN 9781785702204 (ePub) | ISBN 9781785702204 (epub)
Subjects: LCSH: Prehistoric peoples--Greece--Congresses. | Bronze age--Greece--Congresses. | Social change--Greece--History--To 1500--Congresses. | Material culture--Greece--History--To 1500--Congresses. | Social archaeology--Greece--Congresses. | Excavations (Archaeology)--Greece--Congresses. | Greece--Antiquities--Congresses. | Aegean Sea Region--Antiquities--Congresses.
Classification: LCC GN815.A2 S66 2016 (print) | LCC GN815.A2 (ebook) | DDC 938--dc23
LC record available at https://lccn.loc.gov/2016036322

All rights reserved. No part of this book may be reproduced or transmitted in any form or by any means, electronic or mechanical including photocopying, recording or by any information storage and retrieval system, without permission from the publisher in writing.

Printed in the United Kingdom by Hobbs the Printers

Undertaken with the assistance of the Institute for Aegean Prehistory

For a complete list of Oxbow titles, please contact:

UNITED KINGDOM	UNITED STATES OF AMERICA
Oxbow Books	Oxbow Books
Telephone (01865) 241249, Fax (01865) 794449	Telephone (800) 791-9354, Fax (610) 853-9146
Email: oxbow@oxbowbooks.com	Email: queries@casemateacademic.com
www.oxbowbooks.com	www.casemateacademic.com/oxbow

Oxbow Books is part of the Casemate Group

Front cover: ©Learning Sites 2004. Provided courtesy of Learning Sites and the Nemea Valley Archaeological Project, directed by James C. Wright.

Contents

Abbreviations iv
Contributors v
Introduction: social change in Aegean prehistory vi

1. Pre-Mycenaean pottery shapes of the central Aegean:
   a new resource in development 1
   Walter Gauß and Michael Lindblom

2. The temporal slicing and dicing of Minyan Culture: a proposal for
   a tripartite division of a lengthier Greek Middle Bronze Age
   and the issue of nomadism at its beginning 16
   Jeremy B. Rutter

3. Early Helladic III: a non-monumental but revitalized social arena? 32
   Erika Weiberg

4. Reciprocity and exchange relationships: exploring the dynamics
   of Bronze Age social structures through feasting and hospitality 49
   Daniel J. Pullen

5. Domestic architecture: a means to analyse social change
   on the Bronze Age Greek mainland 69
   Corien Wiersma

6. Social change in Middle Helladic Lerna 98
   Sofia Voutsaki and Eleni Milka

7. Social complexity in Late Middle Bronze Age and Early Late
   Bronze Age Cyclades: a view from Ayia Irini 124
   Evi Gorogianni and Rodney D. Fitzsimons

8. Long-term developments in southern mainland settlement systems from Early
   Helladic to Late Helladic times as seen through the lens of regional survey 159
   John Bintliff

9. Middle Helladic reflections 168
   John F. Cherry

Abbreviations

EBA	Early Bronze Age		LH	Late Helladic
EH	Early Helladic		MBA	Middle Bronze Age
LBA	Late Bronze Age		MH	Middle Helladic

Contributors

JOHN BINTLIFF
Universities of Leiden and Edinburgh, Institute for History, Johan Huizingagebouw, Doelensteeg 16, 2311 VL Leiden, The Netherlands

JOHN F. CHERRY
Joukowsky Institute for Archaeology and the Ancient World, Brown University, Box 1837/60 George Street, Providence, RI 02912, USA

RODNEY D. FITZSIMONS
Ancient History and Classics, Trent University, Champlain College G 13, 1600 West Bank Drive, Peterborough, Ontario, Canada K9J 7B8

WALTER GAUß
Austrian Archaeological Institute, Leoforos Alexandras 26, GR-10683 Athens, Greece

EVI GOROGIANNI
Department of Anthropology, University of Akron, 246a Olin Hall, Akron, Ohio 44325-1910, USA

MICHAEL LINDBLOM
Department of Archaeology and Ancient History, Uppsala University, Box 626, 751 26 Uppsala, Sweden

ELENI MILKA
University of Groningen/Argolid Directorate of Antiquities, Groningen Institute of Archaeology, Poststraat 6, 9712 ER Groningen, The Netherlands

DANIEL J. PULLEN
Department of Classics, Florida State University, Tallahassee, Florida 32306-1510, USA

JEREMY B. RUTTER
Department of Classics, Dartmouth College, Hanover, NH 03755, USA

SOFIA VOUTSAKI
Groningen Institute of Archaeology, University of Groningen, Poststraat 6, 9712 ER Groningen, The Netherlands

ERIKA WEIBERG
Department of Archaeology and Ancient History, Uppsala University, Box 626, 751 26 Uppsala, Sweden

CORIEN WIERSMA
Groningen Institute of Archaeology, University of Groningen, Poststraat 6, 9712 ER Groningen, The Netherlands

Introduction: social change in Aegean prehistory

Corien Wiersma and Sofia Voutsaki

The volume before you is born out of the international conference entitled "Explaining Change in Aegean Prehistory", which was held in Groningen, the Netherlands on 16–17 October 2013. The aim of the conference was to explain processes of social, economic and cultural change from the Early Bronze Age III to the Late Bronze Age I period (ca. 2200–1600 BC) in the southern Aegean, but with special emphasis on the southern mainland. The beginning of this period (the end of the EBA) witnesses a severe crisis, but also the first tentative and uneven signs of recovery during the early phases of the MBA followed by the precipitation of social and cultural changes in the transition to the LBA. This specific timeframe enables us therefore to consider how mainland societies recovered from a "crisis" and how they eventually developed into the differentiated, culturally receptive and competitive social formations of the early Mycenaean period.

From EH III to LH I: problems and questions

The EH III–LH I period can be considered a period riddled with problems from several points of view. From a *material* perspective, the EH III and LH I periods pose the most problems. Across the southern mainland, only relatively small amounts of EH III material have been recovered. This can be attributed to several factors such as mainly population decline, but also ceramic regionalism and the possible continuation of EH II ceramic styles into the EH III period, or the dearth of diagnostic material in survey data. The latter problems also apply to the LH I period, during which ceramics in MH style are still being produced in some regions, and when new wares and imports are distributed unevenly across the different sites and regions. With respect to imported and/or valuable finds, the material record of the EH III and MH period is generally poor. Certain EB II objects-hallmarks, such as fine ware ceramics from the mainland (bowls and sauceboats), Cycladic marble figurines and stone vases, were widely traded and/or imitated in EB II. However, these objects disappeared by EB III, implying the discontinuation of ritual and sumptuary practices and concomitant changes in demand. The EH II trade network collapsed, became differently organized or shifted in directions, leading to a massive decline in imported objects during the EH III period, but also the appearance of new categories, *e.g.* those with Anatolian connections. It is difficult to understand patterns of interaction in this period, as different regions and different sites seem to be affected and to respond differently (Rutter 2001; Kiriatzi 2010). Technological advances may also have played a role during this unstable period: It has been suggested that the sailing ship was introduced in the Aegean at the end of the EBA and beginning of the early MBA (Broodbank 2000, 342). This must have revolutionized trade opportunities and interaction patterns, which were dynamic during EH III–MH II and are difficult to grasp (Kiriatzi 2010, 684). Interaction between the mainland and Aegina, the Cyclades and Crete slowly recovered during the MH period, especially across the eastern mainland and at coastal locations. The architectural record also indicates a regression: monumental EH II architecture, such as defensive walls and the so-called corridor buildings, disappear and it is only during the later MH period that fortifications and larger architectural structures are built again.

All these problems have much influenced our understanding of *social* relations and social change in the southern mainland. While (some of) the EH II communities were relatively complex and involved in an international trade network, the EH III and early MH communities are considered fairly simple, homogeneous and introvert. However, this has never been fully substantiated with in depth and systematic analyses of empirical data. It is during the later MH period, with the appearance of rich or monumental graves – especially the shaft graves at Mycenae – that more differentiated societies are once more reconstructed (see more recently Dickinson 2010; 2014). This again has affected the *research* perspective: little scholarly attention has been paid to the EH III and early MH periods. The later MH and LH I period have been investigated more intensively, but attention has focused almost exclusively on the mortuary data (Dietz 1982; 1991; Voutsaki 1999). However, how these social changes were rooted in the earlier MH period has not received systematic consideration, especially not outside the well-documented Argolid (in contrast to the situation in the Minoan world, see Schoep *et al.* 2012; for the Argolid, see Voutsaki 2010; Voutsaki *et al.* 2013).

A final problem concerns *chronology and periodization*. The Bronze Age is now partitioned into EH, MH and LH, and the sub-periods I, II and III. The EH II is further subdivided into EH IIA and EH IIB. In some cases cultural references are made to these periods. The EH IIA period is in some areas, such as the Corinthia, referred to as the Korakou Culture and EH IIB as the Lefkandi I Culture, while EH III is sometimes referred to as the Tiryns Culture in the Argolid (Renfrew 1972). Use of these terms seems not advisable since, being primarily based on ceramic data, they are of local rather than regional, let alone supra-regional relevance.

Problem 1:
a) The traditional ceramic sequence and tripartite periodization creates artificial divisions and units; historically speaking, the EH III period belongs more with MH

I–II than with EH II. The EH III to MH II period can be seen as a period of crisis, fragmentation and social regression though some signs of spasmodic and usually short-lived recovery can be seen here and there.
b) Historically speaking the same could be argued about MH III and LH I: this is a period of precipitation of social and cultural change and therefore decidedly different from the preceding period.
c) Should we then adopt a sub-division into EH III–MH I–MH II as separate from MH III–LH I, as heuristic divisions? Perhaps we should – as long as we do not reify these divisions into hermetic phases and as long as we examine changes also within and between these sub-phases.

Problem 2: Dating is based on the relative sequence and ceramic synchronisms. But these are fraught with problems because of the pronounced regional differences, but also the dearth of, first, well-preserved, well-excavated and well-published sequences (but see recently Gauß and Kiriatzi 2011) and, second, absolute dates (Gauß and Kiriatzi 2011, but see recently Voutsaki *et al.* 2006; 2009a; 2009b). Here we can only posit rather than solve this problem – but we take the opportunity to make a plea for more detailed publications of settlement material, and more radiocarbon dates from well stratified settlement deposits and/or tombs.

Although various aspects of the EH III–LH I period may be considered problematic, there is currently a wave of in interest in the MH period (Wright 2004; Philippa-Touchais *et al.* 2010; Whittaker 2009; 2014). Furthermore, restudy and/or re-evaluation of earlier excavated material is also taking place at various locations, such as Kolonna (Gauß and Smetana 2007), Aspis (Voutsaki *et al.* 2006; Triantaphyllou *et al.* 2006), Orchomenos (Sarri 2010), Brauron (Kalogeropoulos 2010) and Eleusis (Cosmopoulos 2010), and within larger projects such as the Middle Helladic Argolid Project (Voutsaki *et al.* 2012; 2013; Ingvarsson-Sundström *et al.* 2013; Milka 2006; 2010; forthcoming) and the Argos Tumuli Project (Voutsaki *et al.* 2007). These studies show a more complex picture of the development of social change during the EH III–LH I period. We therefore believe that the time has come for a thorough and systematic reconsideration of the EH III–LH I period, and especially of the social changes taking place and the changes in the material culture.

The explanation of social change in Aegean prehistory

A consideration of changes in society and material culture taking place from the EH III–LH I period is not a new theme, but is part of the ongoing discussion of the "emergence of civilization", or the emergence of social complexity in the prehistoric Aegean (*e.g.* Renfrew 1972; Barrett and Halstead 2004; Bintliff 2010; Wright 2010). Studies of social change have focused on possible causes (*Why did change take place?*) and possible mechanisms/strategies (*How did change take place?*). Of relevance for the period under study are discussions of: "External influences and diffusionist explanations", "Agricultural surplus and the intensification of production", "The physical environment", and "Interaction and conspicuous consumption". What follows is a brief summary of these discussions of social change, which is by no means a complete overview of the rich discussion on the emergence of complexity in the Aegean (for very interesting and closely related discussions, through centred exclusively on the Minoan world, see Schoep, Tomkins & Driessen 2012.

1. External influences and diffusionist explanations

In the early twentieth century change was usually attributed to external influences rather than to internal evolution. In Aegean studies migration and invasion, traditionally referred to as the "Coming of the Greeks", *i.e.* the arrival of Indo-European speaking people, were considered the primary causes of change during the EH II–III and EH III–MH period, especially on mainland Greece (Blegen 1928; Caskey 1960; Hood 1973; Howell 1973; Cadogan 1986; Hood 1986; Doumas 1996). Invading people were thought to have caused settlement destruction, desertion and depopulation, and to have introduced new material culture. On the other hand, the prevalent explanation for change during the late MH and early Mycenaean period has been Minoan Crete as a source of influence leading to "increased sophistication" of the mainland (*e.g.* Evans 1931; Dickinson 1977, 57; 1989, 136). Indeed Minoan societies were seen as infinitely more developed and sophisticated than their mainland counterparts – though of course the extent of Minoan influence and the role of the indigenous tradition have been hotly debated.

For decades, migrations and invasions have fallen out of fashion because of the justified critique of the processual approach (see Renfrew 1972 against the monolithic diffusionist explanations). However, internalist models (such as the one proposed by Renfrew himself) have also come under attack (Voutsaki 2005; Wright 2008; Maran 2011). Indeed it is becoming increasingly difficult to deny movements of populations during the EH/MH transition (Maran 2007), or the significance of external stimuli in the MH/LH transition (Parkinson and Galaty 2007).

2. Agricultural surplus and the intensification of production

In his seminal work on the emergence of civilization in the Aegean, Renfrew (1972) introduced the subsistence-redistribution model, in which the emergence of social complexity was attributed to a complex interplay of factors, but ultimately to subsistence changes. Simply put, the introduction of new cultivars, especially the olive and vine, to existing cereal-based subsistence strategies led to the intensification of agricultural production and the creation of surplus. The ecological diversity of the Mediterranean landscape made both diversification and specialization of production possible. The need to exchange agricultural resources led to the emergence of a redistributive elite who further enhanced their position by employing craft specialists and entering into exchange relations with other elites. The redistributive system therefore became the "locus for an emerging hierarchy of power and of wealth" (1972, 481).

The development of a general theoretical model to explain change was a significant innovation in Aegean archaeology. However, both the factual support for the individual components of the model (the introduction of the Mediterranean polyculture, agricultural specialization, etc.) as well as the causal relationships between them have been questioned (Runnels and Hansen 1986; Hansen 1988; Hamilakis 1996; Bintliff 2012, 84–85; Margaritis 2013). More recently, the critique is becoming more complex and focusses also on the methodological questions. For example, it has started to become clear that detecting the initial precondition on which the entire model is based, namely the domestication and large-scale cultivation of grapevines, is more complex than initially thought (Valamoti 2009, Chapter 7). By now the evidence points to a gradual diversification of resource base, including the introduction of the olive and vine, but the available evidence does not allow us to assess neither the scale of cultivation nor its effects on the social relations.

Halstead (Halstead and O'Shea 1982; Halstead 1981; 1988; 1994; 1995) intertwines the production of agricultural surplus with the physical environment and social relations. He attributes an important role to surplus production, while doing away with both specialization and redistribution. He argues that people were forced to produce surplus because of interannual variability. Depending on the ecological conditions, this surplus was harnessed differently, leading to different kinds of social developments. For example, he suggests that inequality existed in Thessaly during the Neolithic, while in southern Greece complexity emerged during the Early Bronze Age and explains this difference by arguing that the type of environment exploited (diverse versus marginal) led to different mechanisms to buffer periods of inter-annual fluctuations in agricultural yields. These different mechanisms affected social relations, as they could require households to share, pool or store agricultural surplus. Dickinson (1989) expressed critique of Halstead's model, arguing that there is no evidence at rising MH or LH I centres of them being more fortunate agriculturalists, or specialists in specific forms of stockbreeding or agriculture. Furthermore, there is no evidence of large-scale storage facilities, or administrative use of seals or script, which would be expected regarding the mobilization and redistribution of surplus (though by now some seals have been recovered in MH contexts). Halstead discusses EH II and LH material, but unfortunately omits the intermediate EH III and MH periods, while at the same time considering what was economically happening from EH II to LH onwards as a continuous development. This would require more research.

3. The physical environment

An increasing interest in cultural adaptation to environmental change was expressed already from the second half of the twentieth century (*e.g.* Fried 1967; Steward 1977). Environmental and ecological changes were used to explain cultural change, or to explain why contemporary and geographically close societies, such as Minoan Crete versus the mainland, could differ in social organization and complexity (Halstead

1994; Manning 1994). Several scholars have argued that ecology and environment may affect demographic changes and changes in land use (Bintliff 2012; Zangger 1993; 1994; Shriner and Murray 2003; Shriner *et al.* 2011; Weiberg *et al.* 2010). Consequently, different ecological settings may cause divergent social developments leading to different types of social organization. Land degradation due to over-exploitation and/or climate change, was suggested as the main cause of settlement decline and depopulation during the late EH II and EH III period (Renfrew 1972; van Andel *et al.* 1986; 1990; Zangger 1992; Manning 1997; Whitelaw 2000). Indeed there is some evidence for climate change in the wider Aegean and eastern Mediterranean area (Nüzhet Dalfes *et al.* 1997) during this period. However, the exact timing, extent and effect of these changes on the southern Greek mainland, let alone on specific regions and micro-environments have not really been studied and require systematic, interdisciplinary and problem-oriented research. The discussion so far has remained narrowly focused on methodological questions and the reliability of various proxy data – and the underlying issue, the interplay of anthropogenic, environmental and climatic factors, has only rarely been systematically explored. In addition, the repercussions that these changes may have had on social relations and their role in processes of social change are only rarely considered (as pointed out correctly by (Weiberg *et al.* 2010; Weiberg and Finné 2013).

4. Interaction and conspicuous consumption

By focussing on the physical environment, intensification of production, and the production of surplus, both Renfrew and Halstead have primarily taken internal factors into consideration. New models were developed in which the significance of interactions was reintroduced (*e.g.* Sherratt and Sherratt 1991; Parkinson and Galaty 2007).

Changing and increasing interaction patterns during MH and LH I played a role in social and material changes. Some scholars see the increasing interaction as a cause of internal change, while others seem to consider the increasing interaction to be a result of internal change, or a strategy to cope with internal change, as the mortuary record suggests a process in which households coalesced into kin groups or factions. Mortuary wealth increases progressively during the later MH period. Under influence of publications discussing gift giving in Archaic and simple societies (*e.g.* Mauss 1966; Sahlins 1972) the valuable goods in the shaft graves at Mycenae were considered gifts of the Minoan elite to the Mycenaean elite. Instead of interpreting the ostentatious burial gifts as a representation of elite status, Voutsaki sees them as a means to create status. People used mortuary display and conspicuous consumption as a strategy of exclusion and differentiation, to acquire status in the process of differentiation, and as a key weapon in social competition (Voutsaki 1995; 1997).

Wright sketches a possible scenario for the collection of means to acquire valuables. Wright (2004, 71) argued that leadership is a result of personal prowess, negotiation and manipulation. Leaders can create factions through the recruitment and maintenance of a group, based on the self-interest of the supporters. Wright (2001) proposes that several factions headed by emerging leaders operated within and among MH and early LH communities. Faction leaders continually had to build and maintain their group by means of ostentatious gestures like mortuary display or feasting. It seems that a larger social group could have pooled its resources to acquire valuable goods or to attract more followers, resulting in further expanding networks of (social) relations, alliances and exchange. Faction leaders subsequently manipulated external resources to benefit themselves and the faction. Competition could arise between leaders for access to distant resources (Wright 1995, 72).

Most recently, scholars have tried to attribute MH III–LH I change to a combination of internal and external processes. The acquisition of valuable resources and symbolic goods used in social competitions was partly caused by, but also led to, an intensification of interaction with other areas. Either way, a strict distinction between internal processes and external stimuli in a period of expanding horizons and increasing cultural receptivity becomes increasingly irrelevant.

Development of the debate in the last decade

During the EH II to LH I period we are faced with two horizons of social change:

a) Social regression during the late EH / MH period
b) social differentiation during the late MH / LH period

The causes of change during the late EH are likely to be pluriform. The traditional explanations have been rightly criticized, but not replaced with a coherent alternative. It is realized that we are dealing with complex processes, affecting different regions in different ways (Rutter 2001, 145). The concept of mobility and movement (Maran 2007) may be of use in formulating a new model for social and material change during EH III. But caution is needed, since the cause and effect of such concepts are not always clear or archaeologically traceable. For example, does mobility lead to social change, or vice versa? Does climate change lead to mobility, or was there already mobility?

Subtle changes occurring during the earlier MH have only recently been observed in, for example, the mortuary record (Voutsaki *et al.* 2013; Milka 2006; forthcoming; Voutsaki 2004). The period is considered as one in which some gradual growth took place. However, the influx of valuable goods and the sudden appearance of elite graves during the later MH suggest that more changes must have taken place during the earlier MH. Recently, it has been suggested that at Asine the first signs of emerging asymmetries are possibly already visible during MH II, and that some segments of the society demarcated themselves from the rest of the community by means of mortuary practices (Ingvarsson-Sundström *et al.* 2013). Further investigations of this period focus on changes in surplus production and, coupled to that, changes in household production and cooperation, as well as changes in the relationship between the community and the household (Wiersma 2014).

The causes of change occurring during the later MH and LH I are not entirely clear since we are dealing with complex processes, affecting different regions in different ways. Minoan Crete, the Cyclades, trade relations, the acquisition of valuables and social competition were significant factors in these processes, and these issues have received much scholarly attention. Future investigations may want to consider in more depth economic developments necessary in order to bear the costs of interaction and exchange, or consider different developments in inland and coastal areas. Coastal areas developed especially rapidly during MH, but some inland areas did too, yet these were seemingly less involved in external trade. It is with good reason that attempts are made to relate MH III–LH I changes to both internal developments and external stimuli (Voutsaki 2005). In addition, we need to gain a better understanding of changes occurring within specific areas, and throughout the EH III to LH I timeframe.

Fully solving the problem of material and social change on the EH III-LH I mainland is a very complex task which needs to take into account several factors. This volume is a further step towards solving this problem.

Outline of the book and the main themes addressed in the various papers

The focus of the papers in this volume is on the southern mainland, although we adopt a comparative approach and examine parallel (or divergent) processes in the surrounding islands. The variety of factors considered – demographic changes, reciprocal relations and sumptuary behaviour, household organization and kin structure, age and gender divisions, internal tensions, connectivity and mobility – attest to the liveliness of the debate. The emphasis is not only on the wider processes, but also on the variety of responses by different communities and social groups and even different individuals.

If we want to study social change first we need to have a clear, explicit and generally agreed upon method of periodization. An obvious place to start is a ceramic typology and sequence. The first paper, by Walter Gauß and Michael Lindblom, introduces a new tool to investigate ceramic change in the wider Aegean area. During their own studies of ceramic material from Kolonna and Lerna they both noticed the lack of an existing ceramic typology or classification system to deal with ceramic assemblages of products from different potting traditions and different dates. By adopting this more standardized terminology in a larger area of the Aegean, possibilities may open up for advances in ceramic studies, such as a better understanding of the appearance of shapes, individual potting traditions, variations within potting traditions, and production and consumption patterns of ceramics within households, settlements and regions. As such, this may become a valuable tool in investigating (ceramic) changes in the Aegean.

The paper of Jerry Rutter elaborates further on the problems of periodization and the correlation of ceramic sequences (on which the traditional chronological sub-divisions are based) with the social developments taking place in this period, *i.e.* the successive cycles of crisis, recovery and growth. A partitioning of the EH III–LH I period into three phases – EH III, MH I–II and MH III–LH I – is critically assessed. The paper focuses on the EH III period and discusses also the possibility of mobile population groups on the Greek mainland.

The next paper by Erika Weiberg offers a new and provocative interpretation of the causes and consequences of the severe crisis at the end of the EBA in relation to the absence of monumentality during the EH III period. She considers the meaning of monumentality, the pace of change, and interregional connectivity and argues for a change in social foci over time.

The following three papers examine different aspects of the evidence and different social practices in order to reconstruct and interpret social, economic and cultural changes during the period under discussion. Daniel Pullen considers the concepts of feasting and reciprocity and the dynamics of social organization through time to create a more coherent understanding of Aegean Bronze Age social structure and political economy. He discusses EH II and Mycenaean feasting practices, and expands this discussion by drawing a parallel with the Roman *convivium*. He then continues with a discussion of hospitality, feasting and reciprocity during the EH III and MH periods.

Domestic architecture and the organization of space are discussed in the paper of Corien Wiersma. The paper starts with a discussion of the domestic economy of simple societies, the concept of property and the possible meaning of material homogeneity and variety. This is followed by an overview of architectural developments and changes – observed at EH III–LH I settlements on mainland Greece – and how these relate to social change.

Sofia Voutsaki and Eleni Milka examine in detail funerary and domestic data in Lerna in order to discuss the rate and nature of social change during the MH period. They argue against the prevailing opinion which sees the MH societies as static, undifferentiated and homogeneous, and reconstruct a complex picture with changes taking place already in the earlier MH phases, but becoming intensified in the transition to the Mycenaean period. They also emphasize that these changes affected different social groups and communities in different ways; Lerna is perhaps considered as the MH type site, but the authors argue that it underwent a different trajectory than most contemporary communities in the Argolid.

The paper of Evi Gorogianni and Rodney D. Fitzsimons examines architectural changes in Ayia Irini, a highly interconnected harbour town in the Cyclades. In this way, the discussion includes different levels of analysis, different types of evidence and different trajectories across the southern Aegean.

The last paper by John Bintliff adopts a broader geographical view and examines processes of changing settlement systems on the Greek mainland. He offers some thoughts on what survey evidence provides for the mainland Bronze Age, and suggests models for interpreting these phenomena. The issue of regionalism, long ago set as a challenge by Oliver Dickinson, also appears an increasingly useful point for insights.

The volume is concluded by a sharp and insightful response by John Cherry, who reflects on the study of the period under discussion during the past decades.

* * * * *

To conclude, the international conference "Explaining Change in Aegean Prehistory", organized in October 2013 at the University of Groningen provided the opportunity to a group of specialists, but also to a wider group of interested scholars and students to reflect on cycles of social change through a long and turbulent period from the EH III to the LH I period on the basis of detailed and systematic analyses of the empirical evidence at different levels and from different angles.

We would like to thank the speakers, including Borja Legarra Herrero and Todd Whitelaw who were unable to contribute to this volume, and all the participants – both those who were physically present and those who followed the conference livestream – for their contribution to the conference. Our thanks also to Joost Crouwel, Oliver Dickinson, Jerry Rutter and Todd Whitelaw for chairing the discussions. We are grateful to Tamara Dijkstra, Heleen Duinker, Olivia Jones, Eleni Panagiotopoulou, Iris Rom and Theo Verlaan for their help with the organization and to Siebe Boersma for designing the conference material. We also thank the Audio-Visual Service of the University of Groningen for providing the conference with an excellent livestream and the INSTAP for financial help towards the publication of this volume.

Bibliography

Barrett, J. C., and P. Halstead, eds. 2004. *The Emergence of Civilisation Revisited*. Sheffield Studies in Aegean Archaeology 6. Oxford, Oxbow Books.

Bintliff, J. L. 2010. "The Middle Bronze Age through the Surface Survey Record of the Greek Mainland: Demographic and Sociopolitical Insights." In *Mesohelladika. The Greek Mainland in the Middle Bronze Age*, Bulletin de Correspondance Hellénique Supplement 52, edited by A. Philippa-Touchais, G. Touchais, S. Voutsaki, and J. Wright, 755–763. Athens, De Boccard.

Bintliff, J. 2012. *The Complete Archaeology of Greece: From Hunter-gatherers to the 20th Century AD*. Chichester/Malden, Wiley-Blackwell.

Blegen, C. W. 1928. "The Coming of the Greeks II. The Geographical Distribution of Prehistoric Remains in Greece." *American Journal of Archaeology* 32, 146–154.

Broodbank, C. 2000. *An Island Archaeology of the Early Cyclades*. Cambridge, Cambridge University Press.

Cadogan, G., ed. 1986. *The End of the Early Bronze Age in the Aegean*. Leiden, E.J. Brill.

Caskey, J. L. 1960. "The Early Helladic Period in the Argolid." *Hesperia* 29.3, 285–303.

Cosmopoulos, M. B. 2010. "The Middle Helladic Stratigraphy of Eleusis." In *Mesohelladika. The Greek Mainland in the Middle Bronze Age*, Bulletin de Correspondance Hellénique Supplement 52, edited by A. Philippa-Touchais, G. Touchais, S. Voutsaki, and J. Wright, 551–556. Athens, De Boccard.

Dickinson, O. T. P. K. 1977. *The Origins of Mycenaean Civilisation*, Studies In Mediterranean Archaeology 49. Göteborg, P. Åström.

Dickinson, O. T. P. K. 1989. "'The Origins of the Mycenaean Civilisation' Revisited." In *Transition. Le Monde Égéen du Bronze Moyen au Bronze Récent*, Aegaeum 3, edited by R. Laffineur, 131–136. Liège, University of Liège, Department of Art History and Archaeology of Ancient Greece.

Dickinson, O. T. P. K. 2010. "The 'Third World' of the Aegean? Middle Helladic Greece Revisited". In *Mesohelladika. The Greek Mainland in the Middle Bronze Age*, Bulletin de Correspondance Hellénique Supplement 52, edited by A. Philippa-Touchais, G. Touchais, S. Voutsaki, and J. Wright, 13–27. Athens, De Boccard.

Dickinson, O. T. P. K. 2014. "The Mainland Bronze Age: The Search for Patterns." *Pharos* 20.1, 143–159.

Dietz, S. 1982. *Asine II. Results of the Excavations East of the Acropolis, 1970-1974. Fasc. 1. General Stratigraphical Analysis and Architectural Remains*, ActaAth 4°, 24.1. Stockholm, P. Åström.

Dietz, S. 1991. *The Argolid at the Transition to the Mycenaean Age. Studies in the Chronology and Cultural Development in the Shaft Grave Period.* Copenhagen, National Museum of Denmark Department of Near Eastern and Classical Antiquities.

Doumas, C. G. 1996. "Early Helladic III and the Coming of the Greeks." *Cretan Studies* 5, 51–61.

Evans, A. 1931. *The Earlier Religion of Greece in the Light of Cretan Discoveries.* London, Macmillan.

Fried, M. H. 1967. *The Evolution of Political Society: An Essay in Political Economy.* New York, Random House.

Gauß, W. and E. Kiriatzi. 2011. *Pottery Production and Supply at Bronze Age Kolonna, Aegina: An Integrated Archaeological and Scientific Study of a Ceramic Landscape*, Ägina-Kolonna Forschungen und Ergebnisse V. Vienna, Austrian Academy of Sciences.

Gauß, W. and R. Smetana. 2007. "Aegina Kolonna, the Ceramic Sequence of the SCIEM 2000 Project." In *Middle Helladic Pottery and Synchronisms. Proceedings of the International Workshop held at Salzburg October 31st-November 2nd, 2004, Ägina-Kolonna Forschungen und Ergebnisse I/Österreichische Akademie der Wissenschaften Denkschriften der Gesamtakademie 42*, Aegaeum 19, edited by F. Felten, W. Gauß, and R. Smetana, 57–80. Vienna, Austrian Academy of Sciences.

Georgousopoulou, T. 2004. "Simplicity vs Complexity: Social Relationships and the MH I Community of Asine," In *The Emergence of Civilisation Revisited*, Sheffield Studies in Aegean Archaeology 6, edited by J. C. Barrett and P. Halstead, 207–213. Oxford, Oxbow Books.

Halstead, P. 1981. "From Determinism to Uncertainty: Social Storage and the Rise of the Minoan Palace." In *Economic Archaeology: Towards an Integration of Ecological and Social Approaches*, British Archaeological Report S96, edited by A. Sheridan and G. Bailey, 198–213. Oxford, Biritsh Archaeological Reports.

Halstead, P. 1994. "The North-South divide: Regional Paths to Complexity in Prehistoric Greece." In *Development and Decline in the Mediterranean Bronze Age*, edited by C. Mathers and S. Stoddart, 195–219. Sheffield, J. R. Collis.

Halstead, P. 1995. "From Sharing to Hoarding: The Neolithic Foundations of Aegean Bronze Age Society?" In *Politeia. Society and State in the Aegean Bronze Age. Proceedings of the 5th International Aegean Conference / 5e Rencontre égéenne internationale, University of Heidelberg, Archäologisches Institut, 10-13 April 1994*, Aegaeum 12, edited by R. Laffineur and W.-D. Niemeier, 11–20. Liège, University of Liège.

Halstead, P. 1988. "On Redistribution and the Origin of Minoan-Mycenaean Palatial Economies." In *Problems in Greek Prehistory: Papers Presented at the Centenary Conference of the British School of Archaeology at Athens, Manchester April 1986*, edited by E. B. French and K. A. Wardle, 519–530. Bristol, Bristol Classical Press.

Halstead, P. and J. O'Shea. 1982. "A Friend in Need is a Friend Indeed: Social Storage and the Origins of Social Ranking." In *Ranking, Resource and Exchange: Aspects of the Archaeology of Early European Society*, edited by C. Renfrew and S. Shennan, 92–99. Cambridge, Cambridge University Press.

Hamilakis, Y. 1996. "Wine, Oil and the Dialectics on Power in Bronze Age Crete: A Review of the Evidence." *Oxford Journal of Archaeology* 15.1, 1–32.

Hansen, J.M. 1988. "Agriculture in the Prehistoric Aegean: Data versus Speculation." *American Journal of Archaeology* 92.1, 39–52.

Hood, S. 1973. "Northern Penetration of Greece at the End of the Early Helladic Period and Contemporary Balkan Chronology." In *Bronze Age Migrations in the Aegean: Archaeological and Linguistic Problems in Greek prehistory: Proceedings of the First International Colloquium on Aegean Prehistory, Sheffield*, edited by R. A. Crossland and A. Birchall, 59–71. London, Duckworth.

Hood, S. 1986. "Evidence for Invasions." In *The End of the Early Bronze Age in the Aegean*, edited by G. Cadogan, 31–68. Leiden, Brill.

Howell, R. J. 1973. "The Origins of the Middle Helladic Culture." In *Bronze Age Migrations in the Aegean: Archaeological and Linguistic Problems in Greek prehistory: Proceedings of the First International Colloquium on Aegean Prehistory, Sheffield*, edited by R. A. Crossland and A. Birchall, 73–106. London, Duckworth.

Ingvarsson-Sundström, A., S. Voutsaki, and E. Milka, 2013. "People, Health and Social Differentiation in Middle Helladic Asine: A Bioarchaeological View." In *Diet, Economy and Society in the Ancient Greek World: Towards a Better Integration of Archaeology and Science*, Pharos Supplement 1, edited by S. Voutsaki and S. M. Valamoti, 149–161. Leuven, Peeters.

Kalogeropoulos, K. 2010. "Middle Helladic Human Activity in Eastern Attica: The Case of Brauron." In *Mesohelladika. The Greek Mainland in the Middle Bronze Age*, Bulletin de Correspondance Hellénique Supplement 52, edited by A. Philippa-Touchais, G. Touchais, S. Voutsaki, and J. Wright, 211–221. Athens, De Boccard.

Kiriatzi, E. 2010. ""Minoanising" Pottery Traditions in the Southwest Aegean during the Middle Bronze Age: Understanding the Social Context of Technological and Consumption Practice." In *Mesohelladika. The Greek Mainland in the Middle Bronze Age*, Bulletin de Correspondance Hellénique Supplement 52, edited by A. Philippa-Touchais, G. Touchais, S. Voutsaki, and J. Wright, 683–699. Athens, De Boccard.

Manning, S. W. 1994. "The Emergence of Divergence: Development and Decline on Bronze Age Crete and the Cyclades." In *Development and Decline in the Mediterranean Bronze Age*, edited by C. Mathers and S. Stoddart, 221–270. Sheffield, J.R. Collis.

Manning, S. W. 1997. "Cultural Change in the Aegean c. 2200 BC." In *Third Millennium BC Climate Change and Old World Collapse*, edited by H. N. Dalfes, G. Kukla and H. Weiss, 149–171. Berlin, NATO Scientific Affairs Division ASI Series Volume I.49.

Maran, J. 2007. "Seaborne Contacts between the Aegean, the Balkans and the Central Mediterranean in the 3rd Millennium BC: The Unfolding of the Mediterranean World." In *Between the Aegean and Baltic Seas: Prehistory Across Borders. Proceedings of the International Conference Bronze and Early Iron Age Interconnections and Contemporary Developments Between the Aegean and the Regions of the Balkan Peninsula, Central and Northern Europe, University of Zagreb, 11–14 April 2005*, Aegaeum 27, edited by I. Galanaki, H. Tomas, Y. Galanakis and R. Laffineur, 3–21. Liège, University of Liège, Department of Art History and Archaeology of Ancient Greece.

Maran, J. 2011. "Lost in Translation: The Emergence of Mycenaean Culture as a Phenomenon of Glocalization." In *Interweaving Worlds: Systemic Interactions in Eurasia, 7th to 1st Millennia BC*, edited by T. C. Wilkinson, S. Sherratt and J. Bennet, 282–294. Oxford, Oxbow Books.

Margaritis, E. 2013. "Distinguishing Exploitation, Domestication, Cultivation and Production: The Olive in the Third Millennium Aegean." *Antiquity* 87, 746–757.

Mauss, M. 1966. *The Gift: Forms and Gunctions of Exchange in Archaic Societies.* London, Routledge & Kegan Paul.

Milka, E. 2006. "From Cemeteries to Society: The Study of Middle Helladic (2000–1500 BC) Burials from the Argolid, Southern Greece." In *Symposium Onderzoek Jonge Archeologen Bundel 2005*, edited by M. Kerkhof, R. van Oosten, F. Tomas and C. van Woerdekom, 53–63. Leiden, Stichting Onderzoek Jonge Archeologen.

Milka, E. 2010. "Burials upon the Ruins of Abandoned Houses in the Middle Helladic Argolid." In *Mesohelladika. The Greek Mainland in the Middle Bronze Age*, Bulletin de Correspondance Hellénique Supplement 52, edited by A. Philippa-Touchais, G. Touchais, S. Voutsaki, and J. Wright, 347–355. Athens, De Boccard.

Milka, E. forthcoming. Diversity and Change in Middle Helladic Mortuary Practices: A Comparison of Lerna and Asine. PhD thesis, University of Groningen.
Nüzhet Dalfes, H., G. Kukla, and H. Weiss, eds. 1997. *Third Millennium B.C. Climate Change and Old World Collapse. Proceedings of a Workshop Held at Kermer, Turkey, Sept. 19–24, 1994*. Berlin, NATO Scientific Affairs Division ASI Series Volume I.49.
Parkinson, W. A. and M. L. Galaty. 2007. "Secondary States in Perspective: An Integrated Approach to State Formation in the Prehistoric Aegean." *American Anthropologist* 109.1, 113–129.
Philippa-Touchais, A., G. Touchais, S. Voutsaki, and J. C. Wright, eds. 2010. *Mesohelladika. The Greek Mainland in the Middle Bronze Age*, Bulletin de Correspondance Hellénique Supplement 52. Athens, De Boccard.
Renfrew, C. 1972. *The Emergence of Civilisation: The Cyclades and the Aegean in the Third Millennium B.C.* London, Methuen.
Runnels, C. and J. Hansen. 1986. "The Olive in the Prehistoric Aegean: The Evidence for Domestication in the Early Bronze Age." *Oxford Journal of Archaeology* 5.3, 299–308.
Rutter, J. B. 2001. "Review of Aegean prehistory II: The Prepalatial Bronze Age of the Southern and Central Greek Mainland and Addendum: 1993–1999" In *Aegean Prehistory: A Review*, edited by T. Cullen, 95–155. Boston, Archaeological Institute of America.
Sahlins, M. D. 1972. *Stone Age Economics*. New York, Aldine.
Sarri, K. 2010. *Orchomenos in der mittleren Bronzezeit*. München, Bayerische Akademie der Wissenschaften.
Schoep, I., P. Tomkins, and J. Driessen, eds. 2012. *Back to the Beginning. Reassesing Social and Political Complexity on Crete during the Early and Middle Bronze Age*. Oxford, Oxbow Books.
Sherratt, A. and S. Sherratt. 1991. "From Luxuries to Commodities: The Nature of Mediterranean Bronze Age Trading Systems." In *Bronze Age Trade in the Mediterranean*, edited by N. H. Gale, 351–386. Göteborg, P. Åström.
Shriner, C. M. and H. H. Murray. 2003. "The Application of Clay Mineralogical Analysis to the Reconstruction of a Greek Bronze Age Coastal Environment." In *Proceedings of the 12th international clay conference*, edited by E. Dominguez, C. Mas and F. Cravero, 163–170. Amsterdam, Elsevier.
Shriner, C. M., E. R. Elswick, E. M. Ripley, A. Schimmelman, and H. H. Murray. 2011. "Natural Environment as a Determinative Factor in Early Helladic Cultural Change on the Argive Plain." In *Helike IV. Ancient Helike and Aigialeia. Protohelladika. The Southern and Central Greek Mainland*, edited by D. Katsonopoulou, 233–247. Athens, Helike Society.
Steward, J. H. 1977. *Evolution and Ecology: Essays on Social Transformation*. Urbana, University of Illinois Press.
Triantaphyllou, S., M. P. Richards, G. Touchais, A. Philippa-Touchais, and S. Voutsaki. 2006. "Analyses of Middle Helladic Skeletal Material from Aspis, Argos, 2. Stable Isotope Analysis of Human Remains." *Bulletin de Correspondance Hellénique* 130.2, 627–637.
Valamoti, S. M. 2009. *I Archaiobotaniki Eureuna tis Diatrofis stin Proistoriki Ellada*. Thessaloniki, University Studio Press.
van Andel, T., C. Runnels, and K. Pope. 1986. "5000 Years of Land Use and Abuse in the Southern Argolid, Greece." *Hesperia* 55, 103–128.
van Andel, T., E. Zangger, and A. Demitrack. 1990. "Land Use and Soil Erosion in Prehistoric and Historical Greece." *Journal of Field Archaeology* 17, 379–396.
Voutsaki, S. 1995. "Social and Political Processes in the Mycenaean Argolid: The Evidence from the Mortuary Practices." In *Politeia. Society and State in the Aegean Bronze Age. Proceedings of the 5th International Aegean Conference / 5e Rencontre Égéenne Internationale, University of Heidelberg, Archäologisches Institut, 10-13 April 1994*, Aegaeum 12, edited by R. Laffineur and W.-D. Niemeier, 55–65. Austin, University of Texas at Austin, Program in Aegean Scripts and Prehistory.

Voutsaki, S. 1997. "The Creation of Value and Prestige in the Late Bronze Age Aegean." *Journal of European Archaeology* 5.2, 34–52.
Voutsaki, S. 1999. "Mortuary Display, Prestige and Identity in the Shaft Grave Era." In *Eliten in der Bronzezeit: Ergebnisse zweier Kolloquien in Mainz und Athen*, edited by I. Kilian and M. Egg, Monographien 43.1, 103–117. Mainz, Verlag der Römisch-Germanischen Zentralmuseums in Kommission bei Dr. Rudolf Habelt GmbH, Römisch-Germanisches Zentralmuseum Forschungsinstitut für Vor- und Frühgeschichte.
Voutsaki, S. 2004. "Age and Gender in the Southern Greek Mainland, 2000-1500 BC." *Ethnographisch-Archaologische Zeitung* 45, 339–363.
Voutsaki, S. 2005. "Social and Cultural Change in the Middle Helladic Period: Presentation of a New project." In *Autochthon. Papers Presented to O.T.P.K. Dickinson on the Occasion of his Retirement*, Britihs Archaeological Report S1432, edited by A. Dakouri-Hild & S. Sherratt, 134–143. Oxford, Archaeopress.
Voutsaki, S. 2010. "From the Kinship Economy to the Palatial Economy: The Argolid in the Second Millenium BC." In *Political Economies of the Aegean Bronze Age*, edited by D. J. Pullen, 86–111. Oxford, Oxbow Books.
Voutsaki, S., S. Dietz, and A. J. Nijboer. 2009a. "Radiocarbon Analysis and the History of the East Cemetery, Asine." *Opuscula. Annual of the Swedish Institutes in Athens and Rome* 2, 31–52.
Voutsaki, S., A. J. Nijboer, and C. W. Zerner. 2009b. "Middle Helladic Lerna: Relative and Absolute Chronologies." In *Tree-rings, Kings, and Old World Archaeology and Environment: Papers Presented in Honor of Peter Ian Kuniholm*, edited by S. W. Manning and M. J. Bruce, 151–161. Oxford, Oxbow Books.
Voutsaki, S., A. Ingvarsson-Sundström, and S. Dietz. 2012. "Tumuli and Social Status: A Re-examination of the Asine Tumulus." In *Ancestral Landscapes: Burial Mounds in the Copper and Bronze Ages*, edited by S. Müller Celka and E. Borgna, 445–461. Lyon, Travaux de la Maison de l'Orient.
Voutsaki, S., S. Triantaphyllou, E. Milka, and C. W. Zerner. 2013. "Middle Helladic Lerna: Diet, Economy, Society." In *Diet, Economy and Society in the Ancient Greek World: Towards a Better Integration of Archaeology and Science*, Pharos Supplement 1, edited by S. Voutsaki and S. M. Valamoti, 133–147. Leuven, Peeters.
Voutsaki, S., A. J. Nijboer, A. Philippa-Touchais, G. Touchais, and S. Triantaphyllou. 2006. "Analyses of Middle Helladic Skeletal Material from Aspis, Argos, 1. Radiocarbon Analysis of Human Remains." *Bulletin de Correspondance Hellénique* 130.2, 613–625.
Voutsaki, S., K. Sarri, O. T. P. K. Dickinson, S. Triantaphyllou, and E. Milka. 2007. "The Argos 'Tumuli' Project: A Report on the 2006 and 2007 Seasons." *Pharos* 15, 153–192.
Weiberg, E. and M. Finné. 2013. "Mind or Matter? People-environment Interaction and the Demise of Early Helladic II Society in the Northeastern Peloponnese." *American Journal of Archaeology*, 117.1, 1–31.
Weiberg, E., M. Lindblom, B. Leppänen Sjöberg, and G. C. Nordquist. 2010. "Social and Environmental Dynamics in Bronze and Iron Age Greece." In *The Urban Mind: Cultural and Environmental Dynamics*, edited by P. J. J. Sinclair, G. C. Nordquist, F. Herschend and C. Isendahl, 149–194. Uppsala, Department of Archaeology and Ancient History, Uppsala University.
Whitelaw, T. M. 2000. "Settlement Instability and Landscape Degradation in the Southern Aegean in the Third millennium BC." In *Landscape and Land Use in Postglacial Greece*, edited by P. Halstead and C. Frederick, 135–161. Sheffield, Sheffield Academic Press.
Whittaker, H. 2009. "Memory and Cultural Values in the Middle Helladic Period. Some Preliminary Thoughts." In *The Past in the Past: The Significance of Memory and Tradition in the Transmission of Culture*, British Archaeological Report S1925, edited by M. Georgiadis and C. Gallou, 5–15. Oxford, Archaeopress.
Whittaker, H. 2014. *Religion and Society in Middle Bronze Age Greece*. Cambridge, Cambridge University Press.

Wiersma, C. W. 2014. *Building the Bronze Age. Architectural and Social Change on the Greek Mainland during Early Helladic III, Middle Helladic and Late Helladic I*. Oxford, Archaeopress International Series.

Wright, J. C. 1995. "From Chief to King in Mycenaean Society." In *The Role of the Ruler in the Prehistoric Aegean. Proceedings of a Panel Discussion Presented at the Annual Meeting of the Archaeological Institute of America, New Orleans, Louisiana, 28 December 1992*, Aegaeum 11, edited by P. Rehak, 63-80. Liège, Universitey of Liège, Department of Art History and Archaeology of Ancient Greece.

Wright, J. C. 2001. "Factions and the Origins of Leadership and Identity in Mycenaean Society." *Bulletin of the Institute of Classical Studies of the University of London* 45, 182.

Wright, J. C. 2004. "The Emergence of Leadership and the Rise of Civilisation in the Aegean." In *The Emergence of Civilisation Revisited*, Sheffield Studies in Aegean Archaeology 6, edited by J. C. Barrett and P. Halstead, 64–89. Oxford, Oxbow Books.

Wright, J. C. 2008. "Early Mycenaean Greece." In *The Cambridge Companion to the Aegean Bronze Age*, edited by C. W. Shelmerdine, 230–257. Cambridge, Cambridge University Press.

Wright, J. C. 2010. "Towards a Social Archaeology of Middle Helladic Greece." In *Mesohelladika. The Greek Mainland in the Middle Bronze Age*, Bulletin de Correspondance Hellénique Supplement 52, edited by A. Philippa-Touchais, G. Touchais, S. Voutsaki, and J. Wright, 803–815. Athens, De Boccard.

Zangger, E. 1992. "Neolithic to Present Soil Erosion in Greece." In *Past and Present Soil Erosion*, edited by J. Boardman and M. Bell, 133-147. Oxford, Oxbow Books.

Zangger, E. 1993. *The Geoarchaeology of the Argolid*. Berlin, Mann.

Zangger, E. 1994. "Landscape Changes around Tiryns during the Bronze Age." *American Journal of Archaeology* 98, 189–212.

Chapter 1

Pre-Mycenaean pottery shapes of the central Aegean: a new resource in development

Walter Gauß and Michael Lindblom

Introduction

The purpose of this paper is to sketch the outlines of a new classification system in development for ceramics of the late Early Bronze Age to early Late Bronze Age. The necessity for such a tool crystallized some years ago, while the two authors were working jointly and individually on ceramic deposits at Kolonna on Aegina and Lerna in the Argolid. At the time, we were trying to isolate continuities and discontinuities in the ceramic repertoires used at the two settlements (*e.g.* Gauß and Smetana 2007; Lindblom 2007). Because of the intensive participation during the Bronze Age of these settlements in larger exchange networks, we were confronted with an extraordinarily rich array of ceramic products from different potting traditions in the Aegean. Among our publication responsibilities, we were also expected to deal with the ceramic transitions from the Early to Middle Helladic period at Kolonna and from the Middle to the Late Helladic period at both Kolonna and Lerna. Both of us noticed the lack of an existing ceramic typology accommodating these needs and we decided to join efforts and start developing a new classification system that could be applied on the entire Pre-Mycenaean ceramic dataset. This paper presents the first outcome of our efforts.

Previous research, some current obstacles and possible solutions

Starting with the ground-breaking excavations by Caskey at Lerna in 1952–1959 and augmented by ceramic finds at other places, a number of ceramic studies have demonstrated that two of the most significant ceramic breaks on the southern and central Greek mainland occurred between EH II and III (ca. 2200/2150 BC) and LH I and II (ca. 1575/1550 BC) respectively. This is not the place to discuss the nature of the ceramic changes; suffice to state that the former is most clearly manifested in the EH IIB fusion of shapes, many of which are wheel-thrown, of the Lefkandi I/Kastri assemblage with local, hand-built vessels (Rutter 1979; 1995). Together with larger societal forces, possibly involving fairly large scale dislocations of groups of people in the Central Aegean, the result was a relatively heterogeneous ceramic repertoire with a large number of distinct but partly overlapping potting traditions in the area. The situation remained basically the same under some six to seven centuries until new drinking and eating habits were introduced on the Greek mainland roughly up to the Spercheios in Phthiotis during LH II, this time under influence from Crete and some intermediary islands in the south. With new production centres being established on the northeast Peloponnese and in central Greece, the Mycenaean pottery rapidly replaced all drinking and pouring vessels and most of the storage, cooking and transport containers. In the Late MH and LH I is it possible to speak of a co-existence of native Helladic and alien Kytheran, Cycladic and Cretan ceramic traits in the mainland pottery production.

The close affinity between EH III and MH I in ceramic terms has been explored by scholars such as Howell (1974), Rutter (1983) and Spencer (2007; 2010) while Dickinson (1974), Davis (1979), Dietz (1991), Rutter (1990; forthcoming) and Zerner (2008), among others, have shown the gradual transition to the Late Bronze Age at places such as Korakou, Tsoungiza, Asine and Ayios Stephanos. Only at the beginning of LH II was the ceramic repertoire significantly altered with the massive spread of Mycenaean products in the central Aegean at the expense of other potting traditions. The ceramic EH III–LH I repertoire now appears so homogenous that some scholars argue for the enlargement of the MH period at the expense of EH III and LH I (Rutter, this volume). Interestingly, this suggestion accords well with the original perception of the Late Helladic period as expressed by Wace and Blegen (1917–1918). Most of the Mycenaean decorated sherds they made use of in their seminal article to illustrate the transition to the Late Bronze Age are in fact LH IIA in date (Dickinson 1972). In the last decade it has also become clear that the pottery often employed to define LH I on the northeast Peloponnese is slightly later in date than the locally produced LM IA/LH I pottery at Ayios Stephanos in Laconia and roughly equivalent to the volcanic destruction layer at Akrotiri (Zerner 2008; Lindblom and Manning 2011). The start of LH I has thus been pushed back in time twice since the publication by Wace and Blegen and this should perhaps have repercussions for the terminology used.

Over the last half century several relevant classifications systems have been devised to describe pottery shapes in the Aegean (Table 1.1). Most of these studies were well designed to answer the questions confronting scholars at the time, but from our perspective they are all too geographically and/or chronologically limited. In some cases this is because only a certain type of pottery is analysed, while in others it is due to how ceramic assemblages have been divided for publication.

Real or assumed transitions in the stratigraphic, ceramic or architectural sequences at settlements have traditionally resulted in a division of pottery for publication, and different scholars have defined different typologies to serve their own need. As a consequence, pottery even found within the same settlement but on different sides

1. Pre-Mycenaean pottery shapes of the central Aegean: a new resource in development

Table 1.1: Selected Aegean Bronze Age pottery shape typologies

Author	Material	Area	Period	Lacking for our purposes
Podzuweit 1979	Trojan pottery	Western Anatolia, Eastern Aegean	Anatolian EBA	Wrong area
Buck 1964	Middle Helladic matt painted pottery	Greek Mainland	Middle Helladic	One ceramic class; outdated
Dietz 1991	Argive MH II–LH I pottery	North-East Peloponnese	MH II–LH I	Ceramic classes and shapes not separated
Blegen et al. 1953	Troy VI pottery	Western Anatolia	Anatolian MBA	Wrong area
Caskey 1972	Ayia Irini pottery	Keos	EH/EC II–LH III	One settlement; MH I missing; outdated
Rutter 1995	Lerna IV pottery	South-Central Greek Mainland	EH III	Difficult to expand
Maran 1992	Pevkakia-Magula pottery	Volos Bay in Thessaly	Thessalian MBA	Southern Greek Mainland and Cyclades lacking
Furumark 1941	Mycenaean Decorated Pottery	South-Central Greek Mainland	LH I–III	One ceramic class; only LH I relevant
Barber 1974	Phylakopi pottery	Cyclades	MC-LC	Greek Mainland lacking; outdated
Lindblom 2001	Aeginetan potters' marks	Area of Aeginetan pottery distribution	MH I–LH IIIC	Limited to one potting tradition; not exhaustive

of a chronological transition is sometimes difficult to compare. This is true not only for how identical shapes are termed, but also which ceramic classes, or "wares" are identified. This is a known problem at many places of which the settlement at Lerna in the Argolid may serve as an example. Here the Pre-Mycenaean pottery assemblages were divided for publication according to settlement phases. While Rutter (1995) devised one classificatory system for the period IV vessels, Zerner (1979; 1993) arranged the ones from the succeeding period V differently (Fig. 1.1). Apart from some broad and general trends in the first and part of the second tiers, this division makes it very difficult to discern several continuities and discontinuities in the ceramic sequence at the place. Two examples by both systems may additionally illustrate this (Fig. 1.2): The first example is an EH III unpainted tankard from Kolonna which, with the Lerna IV system, would be classified as an unpainted (tier 1), fine (2), burnished (3), black surfaced (4) class. Assuming that the same form continues to be produced and used in the MH, it would be classified by the Lerna V system as an unpainted (tier 1), dark burnished (2), fine (3) class. A comparison even beyond tier 1 would be time-consuming and difficult.

The second example is a decorated MH bowl, again from Kolonna which by the Lerna V system is a painted (tier 1), pattern-painted (2), matt-painted (3), Gold Mica (4) class. If it would turn out that this vessel existed already in EH III, it would be

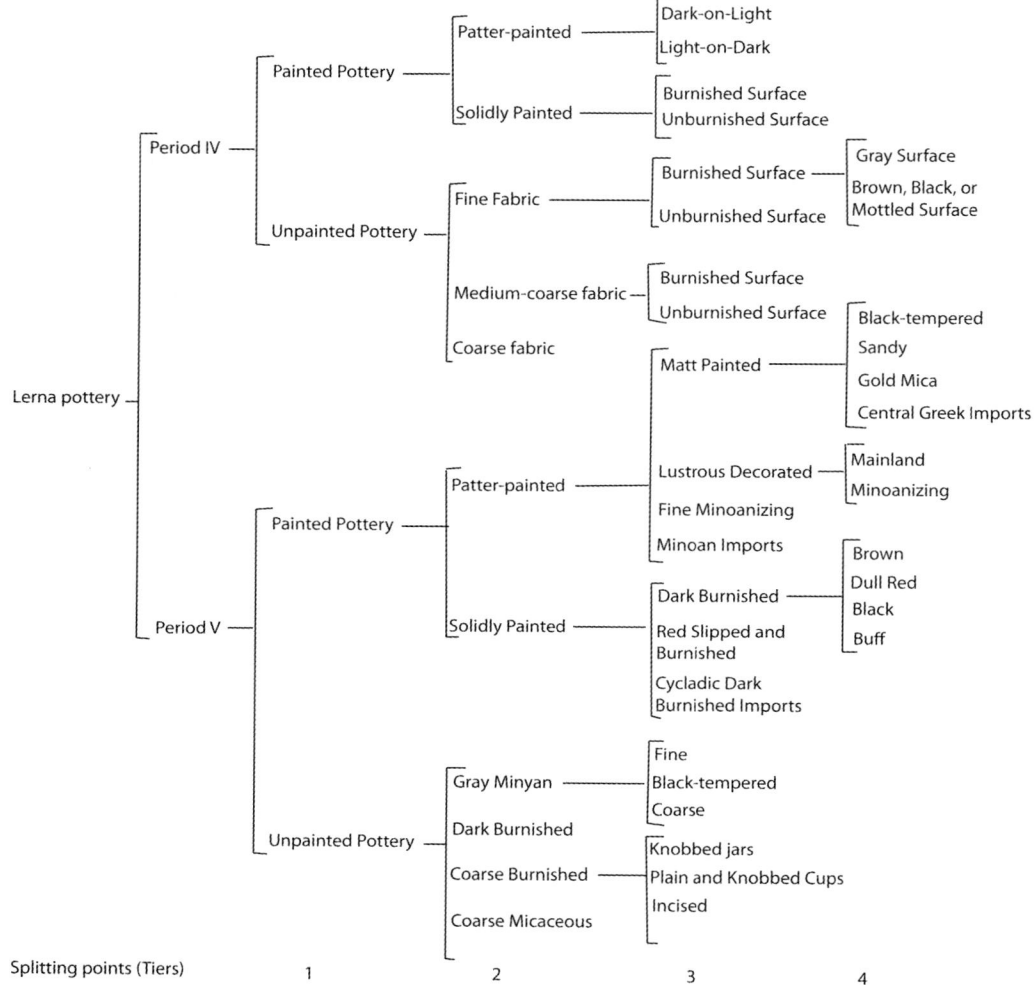

Fig. 1.1: Comparison of pottery divisions at periods IV-V at Lerna (based on Rutter 1986).

labelled according to the Lerna IV system as a painted (tier 1), pattern-painted (2), Dark-on-Light (3) example. Again, it would be almost impossible to easily verify trends of continuities and discontinuities beyond the second tier.

There is also an overwhelming array of terms in use to describe Pre-Mycenaean pottery (cf. Zerner 1993, 39). Concordances of nomenclature are needed just to relate groups of pottery in different publications, often in different languages. To this should also be added the more or less obligatory and usually bulky listing of parallels in shapes and motifs from various pottery assemblages found elsewhere. In order to overcome these obstacles, a standardized system to describe formal properties of the pottery is needed.

1. Pre-Mycenaean pottery shapes of the central Aegean: a new resource in development

Fig. 1.2: EH III tankard and MH matt-painted cup from Aegina Kolonna (photo W. Gauß).

For several years we were reluctant to introduce yet another system to document variations in shapes at Kolonna phases D–K and Lerna VI. Both of us tried, with limited success, to adapt the shape typology developed by Rutter (1995) for EH III Lerna IV to suit our needs. All attempts to extend his typology did, however, ultimately ruin its logic and user friendliness. Likewise it was not possible to use one of the existing shape typologies of the Middle Bronze Age and extend it backward to Early Bronze III and forward to Late Bronze I. The typology of Middle Bronze Age matt-painted pottery by Buck (1964) is sorely outdated by now and limited to only one type of pottery. The typology of shapes by Dietz (1991) covers the late Middle Bronze and Late Bronze I from a predominantly Argive perspective. However, it could not be used either, since it combines ceramic wares and shapes into the same system, whereas we insist to keep these properties apart. Finally, also the typology of decorated Mycenaean pottery by Furumark (1941) could not be extended backwards in time without rearranging his already established shapes beyond comprehension. Realizing that no existing system could accommodate our needs, we decided to develop a new tool, relevant specifically for our publication responsibilities.

Born out of a pragmatic need to process large amounts of pottery for publication, we decided to bring together all complete or largely restorable profiles from vessels in deposits of the period and arrange them in groups. Like many other typologies, the overarching principle would be similarities in form. There is nothing particularly striking in this, except perhaps that the range of imports at the two places soon made us realize that we were not doing a typology of Aeginetan or Argive pottery, but of a considerably larger area. With some additional input, we argued, mainly from settlements some distance from the Saronic Gulf and the Northeastern Peloponnese, this tool could be useful for other scholars as well. Encouraged by the appearance of several important publications of Pre-Mycenaean pottery, for example from Argos in the northeastern Peloponnese (*e.g.* Philippa-Touchais and Touchais 2011; 2009), Ayios Stephanos (Zerner 2008), Nichoria (Howell 1992), Orchomenos (Sarri 2010), Pevkakia

(Maran 1992) and Phylakopi (Renfrew *et al.* 2007), we went about the task to collect data from the whole central Aegean area. To help us surveying the number of sites which theoretically could enlarge the body of material and to better understand also its spatial distribution, we have made use of the information gathered by Syriopoulos (1995) in his massive, two-volume survey of prehistoric sites in Greece in tandem with Hope Simpson's and Dickinson's (1979) Gazetteer. In March 2014 we had assembled roughly 3800 vessels from 110 different sites and the database keeps growing. The area we aim to cover extends from the Volos Bay area in the north to the island of Kythera in the south, from the coast of Messenia in the west to the Cycladic islands in the east (Figs. 1.3–1.4). The map illustrated in Fig. 1.3 shows 713 EBA to LBA I sites

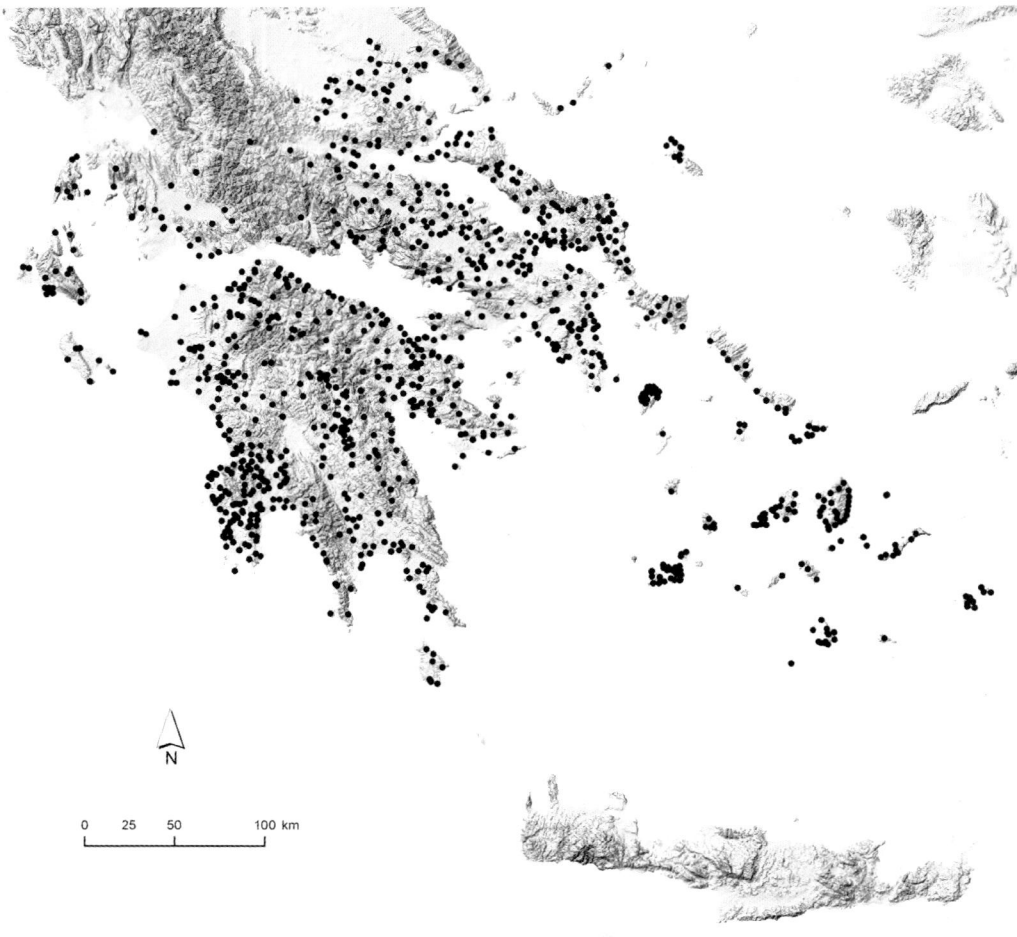

Fig. 1.3: Geographical scope of a new shape typology for the central Aegean area (based on Syriopoulos 1995 and Hope-Simpson and Dickinson 1979. Relief map of Greece and design Anavasis ©).

1. Pre-Mycenaean pottery shapes of the central Aegean: a new resource in development   7

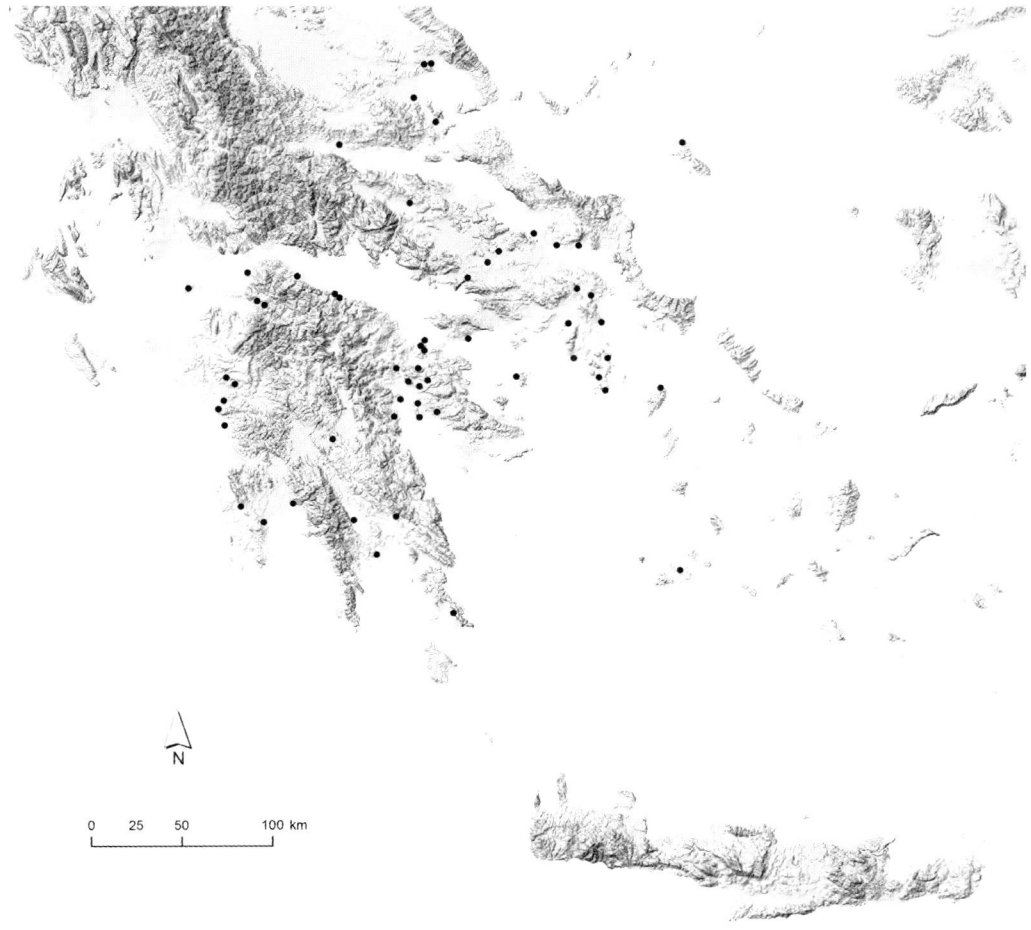

Fig. 1.4: Geographical scope of the 70 sites contributing to the new classification system (find spots based on Syriopoulos 1995 and Hope-Simpson and Dickinson 1979. Relief map of Greece and design Anavasis ©).

collected by Syriopoulos (1995) and Hope Simpson and Dickinson (1979) in the above defined geographical area, whereas Figure 1.4 highlights the 58 out of 110 sites thus far investigated that contributed complete or almost complete vessels. Certainly not all known find spots produced whole or largely preserved vessels, but in tandem the maps give an impression of the density and distribution of sites in the targeted area and of the geographical and research lacunas.

Ceramic assemblages from places in the eastern Aegean, western Anatolia, northern Aegean and Crete have not been included. With the exception of Crete, imports from these areas to the central Aegean, and especially to the Greek mainland, are rare. While ceramic imports from Crete are common from the Middle Bronze Age onwards in this area, the material is outside our academic comfort zones and we predict that few scholars dealing with Minoan pottery would use this resource anyway. Once again pragmatic considerations dictated the scope. A justifiable question would be why we have chosen to include the heavily minoanized pottery from Kastri on Kythera. The short answer is because the shape range overlaps with the one from Middle Helladic Ayios Stephanos in Laconia and there are numerous imports, presumably from both these areas, both at Kolonna and Lerna. The slightly more complex answer would include a discussion of where to draw the line between what we call "Minoan" and "minoanizing" pottery. Kolonna sees a period of local production of "minoanizing" pottery in MH II (Gauß and Smetana 2007, 63–65, figs. 7–8; Lindblom et al. 2015, 228–232), while the first Mycenaean pottery at Lerna is nothing but the northeast Peloponnesian version of Late Minoan IA pottery (Lindblom and Manning 2011). Additionally, a number of Middle Helladic shapes are imitations or adoptions of Minoan prototypes and the history of such shapes would not be well understood if relevant imports were not considered.

An overview of the proposed shape system

A new system to arrange Pre-Mycenaean pottery according to form should answer three basic needs. It should: (i) document variations in time and space in an easy and consistent way, (ii) offer a standardized terminology with transparent equivalences in English, Greek, German and French, and (iii) offer an expandable research tool for scholars and students interested in the analysis of Pre-Mycenaean pottery in the whole central Aegean. In order to establish a working platform (contrary to a cemented and final solution) for such a resource, much work must be devoted to the tedious collection and ordering of vessels in groups.

As a first tier, or splitting point, in the proposed system we use "open" and "closed" shapes as well as "lids" (Fig. 1.5). An open shape is a vessel with a larger rim diameter than height, excluding a possible pedestal or legs. A closed shape consequently has a greater height than rim diameter. Like always, there are exceptions to this rule; a few deep cups are presented as open shapes although they have a greater height than rim diameter (*e.g.* the EH III "Ouzo cup"). At the second tier we find eleven broad and generic types; five open and six closed ones. Splitting points within each type have been determined by the nature of the resting surface, the placement and orientation of the handle(s), the shape and curving of the rim, and, occasionally, the presence or absence of a carinated body. This procedure has resulted in roughly 80 forms. It is possible to do this rather mechanically, but the end result becomes strange in several cases and a reader would not feel comfortable with these divisions. For some forms a certain splitting point is therefore not used, while in other cases other points of divisions have been introduced. For example, bowls and jars are sometimes spouted, either with tubular, troughed or bridged spouts; many jugs have beaked or cutaway necks; lugs, sometimes in combination with handles, are frequently attested. These variations have to be accommodated for in the scheme as well. Sometimes very subtle

1. Pre-Mycenaean pottery shapes of the central Aegean: a new resource in development

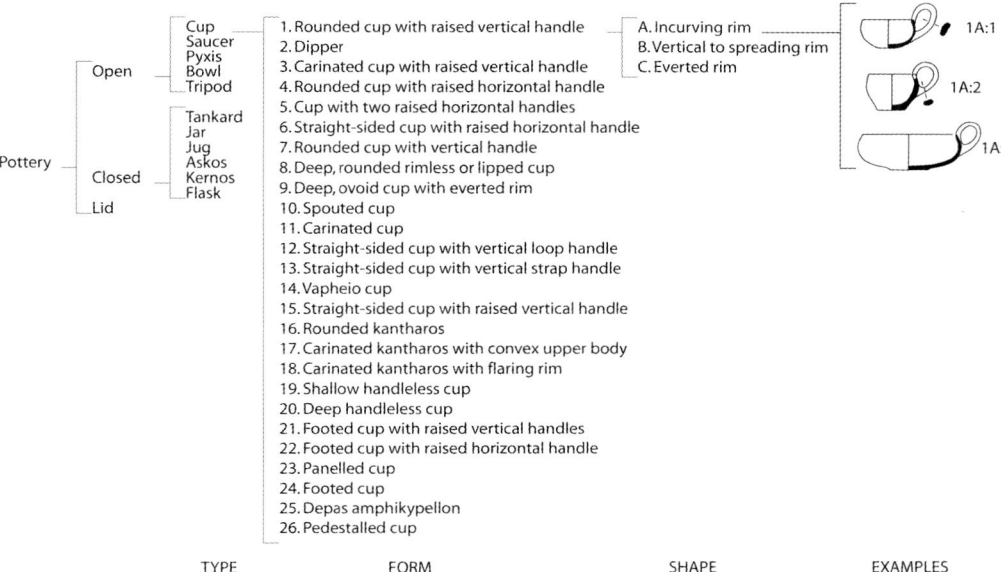

Fig. 1.5: Recognized Pre-Mycenaean types of pottery, forms of cups (1–26), shapes of rounded cups with raised vertical handle (1A–C) and individual examples of shape 1A with incurving rim (1A:1–3).

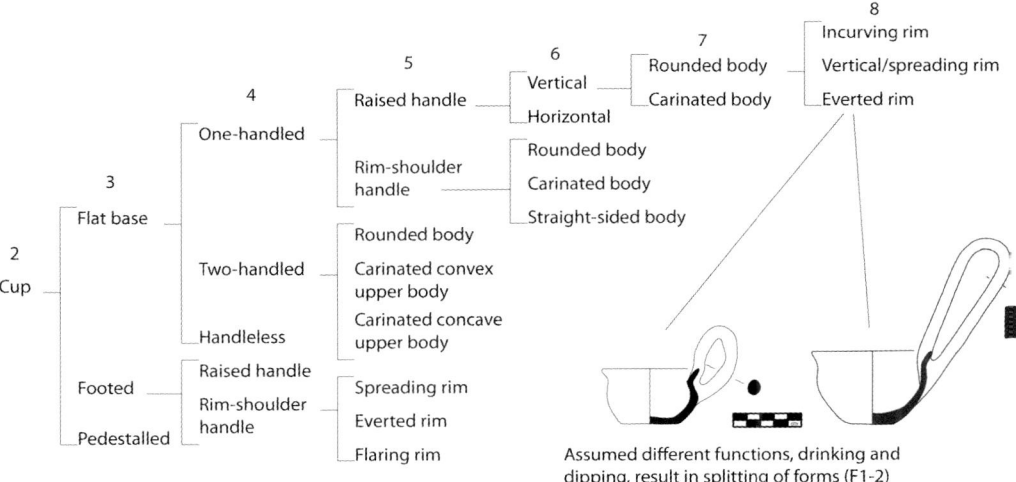

Fig. 1.6: Examples of second–eighth tiers division in the arrangement of ceramic forms. Note that even small differences, like the length of the handle, can have repercussions on the assumed function and thus the division.

variations have repercussions for our understanding of a form, as for instance the difference between small, open vessels designed for drinking and dipping (Fig. 1.6).

Fragmentary sherd material from excavations can usually only be identified with a certain degree of confidence to a specific form or shape and it should be possible to work with alternative terms that reflect this situation. There should thus be different levels of increasing detail in the way to refer to vessels or sherds of certain properties. The general type "Cup", for instance, is broken down into several discrete forms of which Form 20 is the deep, handleless cup (Fig. 1.7). Depending on differences in the base, body and rim, it is possible to distinguish four different shapes within the

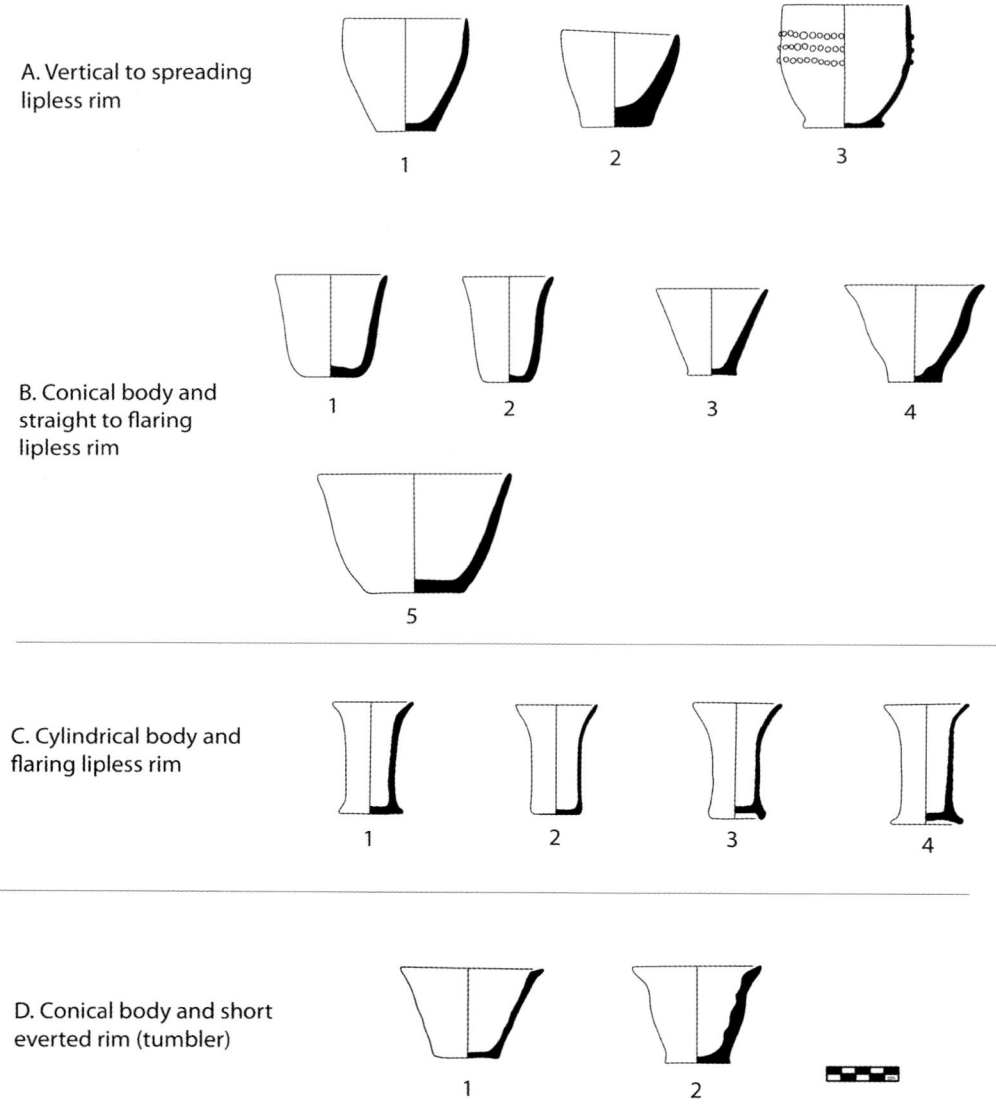

Fig. 1.7: Deep handless cup (Form 20) in four distinct shapes (20A–D) with individual examples showing the range of each shape.

form. Shape 20A, at the top, is the deep handleless cup with a vertical to spreading lipless rim. All vessels are unique however, and it is therefore appropriate to illustrate also a certain shape range. It is therefore exemplified by three vessels. The first is a Middle Cycladic specimen published by Barber (1974, 22, fig. 4, 169), the second an unpublished MH cup from Kolonna and the third an early Middle Minoan barboutine cup found at Lerna V (Zerner 1988, fig. 24, 3).

The Middle Helladic goblet – an example

When ceramic forms and shapes are structured in a consistent way and combined with other parameters, such as fabrics, decoration and geographical distribution, patterns begin to emerge. As an example, we want to draw your attention to one of the most emblematic forms of the Middle Helladic period, the goblet. We have selected three shapes which hold both chronological and regional variation (Fig. 1.8). The provisional

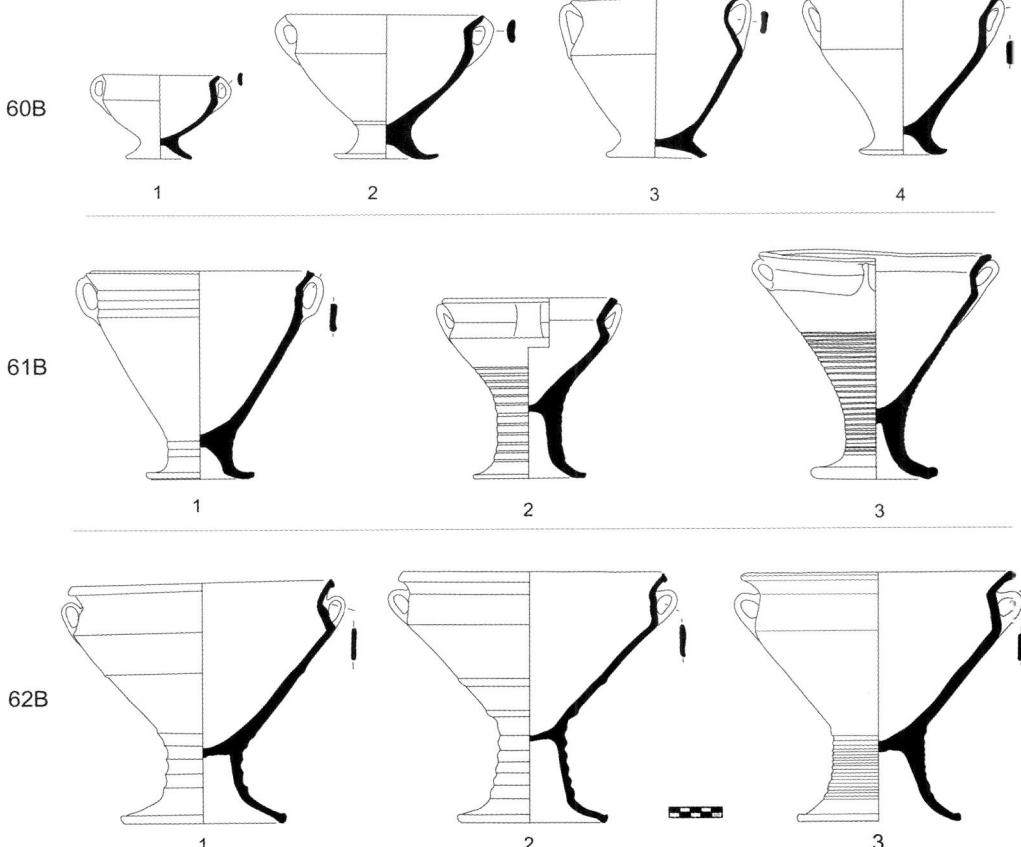

Fig. 1.8: Examples of three (out of eight) shapes of goblets: 60B Plain: 1. Lerna; 2. Kolonna; 3. Tsoungiza; 4. Asine. 61B Ribbed/Grooved: 1. Asine; 2. Asine; 3. Mycenae. 62B Lianokladhi: 1. Kolonna; 2. Orchomenos; 3. Pefkakia.

shape 62B in the lower register is the so-called Lianokladhi goblet with ribbed pedestal, thickened rim and edge of the base. The upper handle attachment is placed on the shoulder. As presently understood, it is invariably wheel-thrown and made of a fine gray fabric. Shape 61B in the middle row is similar, but the rim is either flattened or rounded, the upper handle attachment is placed on the exterior rim, the edge of the base is rounded and the pedestal is usually grooved rather than ribbed. It is handmade, has a more southerly distribution pattern and is produced in undecorated, matt painted and dark burnished varieties. Shape 60B at the top is the continuation of 61B and first appears at the closing decades of the Middle Helladic period. It is often smaller in size, has a single or no groove or rib and a considerably lower pedestal.

What we encounter here are the products of at least three distinguishable potting traditions, one located somewhere in central Greece (62B), another on the northeast Peloponnese (61B, 60B) and a third on Aegina and possibly also Keos (mainly 60B). At Kolonna, imports of shape 62B occurs in phase I (MH II), while shape 61B is usually associated with MH III on the Argive Plain, not least through their presence in the earlier shaft graves at Mycenae. In the LH I shaft graves at Lerna, shape 61B is absent while shape 60B is profusely attested both by local, undecorated and Aeginetan, solidly painted examples. An attractive explanation for the gradual reduction in size of the MH III–LH I goblet is a change in drinking practices either from the collective passing around of a single goblet to individualized drinking, or a switch in liquids normally served in them (*e.g.* diluted to undiluted wine).

A beginning – not the end. Expected benefits

Changes in the appearance and use of material culture inform us of altered behaviour, which in turn is indicative of social change when manifested on a large scale. In ceramic studies this typically entails divisions and groupings in the hope to infuse meaning into a fragmentary and often chaotic material record. Depending on the resolution we seek both patterns and anomalies within households, settlements or regions. These were partly preferential and based on a multitude of more or less articulated considerations like access, function, habit and desires, sometimes even contradictory. Shape variation in unexpected combinations with fabric and/or manufacturing techniques cry out for explanation.

Let us venture to suggest a few possible benefits that might come out if the new shape typology for EBA III–LBA I ceramics described above is used and, not least importantly, developed and maintained in a Geographical Information System (GIS): (i) By adopting a standardized terminology in pottery analysis, misunderstandings and confusion may be avoided in descriptive analysis; (ii) unless newly discovered anomalies motivate changes, there would be little necessity in comparative studies to repeat the pedigrees or contemporary parallels of single shapes; (iii) coupled with sets of radiocarbon dates from associated contexts, the first and last appearance of individual shapes would be much better understood (Voutsaki *et al.* 2009; Wild *et al.*

2010; Lindblom and Manning 2011); (iv) in tandem with chemical and/or petrographic analysis, our understanding of the repertoire and reach of individual potting traditions would increase (Gauß and Kiriatzi 2011); (v) shapes associated with individual pottery kilns and different local marking systems (*e.g.* on Aeginetan, Keian and Kytheran or Laconian pottery) would open up new avenues to discuss variations within the same potting tradition, possibly down to the individual household (Lindblom 2001); (vi) the relation between ceramic patterns and other quantified analyses of material culture available in a GIS can be more easily combined for comparisons and will eventually allow us to better understand the spread of imports and innovations or their rejection on the macro level to the division of specific features on a micro level; (vii) finally, provided that our efforts are successful one may even have the vision of an easy accessibly and regularly updated GIS based online research tool.

Bibliography

Barber, R. 1974. "Phylakopi 1911 and the History and the Later Cycladic Bronze Age." *Annual of the British School at Athens* 69, 1–53.

Buck, R. J. 1964. "Middle Helladic Mattpainted Pottery." *Hesperia* 33.3, 231–313.

Caskey, J. L. 1972. "Investigations in Keos: Part II: A Conspectus of the Pottery." *Hesperia* 41.3, 357–401.

Davis, J. L. 1979. "Late Helladic I Pottery from Korakou." *Hesperia* 48, 234–263.

Dickinson, O. T. P. K. 1972. "Late Helladic IIA and IIB: Some Evidence from Korakou." *Annual of the British School at Athens* 67, 103–112.

Dickinson, O. T. P. K. 1974. "The Definition of Late Helladic I." *Annual of the British School at Athens* 69, 109–120.

Dietz, S. 1991. *The Argolid at the Transition to the Mycenaean Age. Studies in the Chronology and Cultural Development in the Shaft Grave Period.* Copenhagen, National Museum of Denmark Department of Near Eastern and Classical Antiquities.

Furumark, A. 1941. *The Mycenaean Pottery. Analysis and Classification.* Stockholm, Svenska Institutet i Athen.

Gauß, W. and R. Smetana. 2007. "Aegina Kolonna, The Ceramic Sequence of the SCIEM 2000 Project." In *Middle Helladic Pottery and Synchronisms. Proceedings of the International Workshop held at Salzburg October 31st–November 2nd, 2004,* Ägina–Kolonna Forschungen und Ergebnisse I/Österreichische Akademie der Wissenschaften Denkschriften der Gesamtakademie 42, edited by F. Felten, W. Gauß, and R. Smetana, 57–80. Vienna, Austrian Academy of Sciences.

Gauß, W. and E. Kiriatzi. 2011. *Pottery Production and Supply at Bronze Age Kolonna, Aegina. An integrated Archaeological and Scientific Study of a Ceramic Landscape.* Vienna, Austrian Academy of Sciences.

Hope Simpson, R., and O. T. P. K. Dickinson. 1979. *A Gazetteer of Aegean Civilisation in the Bronze Age,* vol. 1: *The Mainland and the Islands,* Studies In Mediterranean Archaeology 52, Göteborg, Åströms.

Howell, R. J. 1974. "The Origins of the Middle Helladic Culture." In *Bronze Age Migrations in the Aegean. Archaeological and Linguistic Problems in Greek Prehistory,* edited by R. A. Crossland and A. Birchall, 73–106. Park Ridge, Noyes Press.

Howell, R. J. 1992. "Middle Helladic Settlement: Pottery." In *Excavations at Nichoria in Southwest Greece. Volume II. The Bronze Age Occupation,* edited by W. A. McDonald and N. C. Wilkie, 43–204. Minneapolis, University of Minnesota Press.

Lindblom, M. 2001. *Marks and Makers. Appearance, Distribution and Function of Middle and Late Helladic Manufacturers' Marks on Aeginetan Pottery,* Studies In Mediterranean Archaeology 128, Jonsered, Åströms.

Lindblom, M. 2007. "Early Mycenaean Mortuary Meals at Lerna VI With Special Emphasis on their Aeginetan Components." In *In Middle Helladic Pottery and Synchronisms. Proceedings of the International Workshop held at Salzburg October 31st–November 2nd, 2004*, Ägina–Kolonna Forschungen und Ergebnisse I/Österreichische Akademie der Wissenschaften Denkschriften der Gesamtakademie 42, edited by F. Felten, W. Gauß, and R. Smetana, 115–134. Vienna, Austrian Academy of Sciences.

Lindblom, M. and S. W. Manning. 2011. "The Chronology of the Lerna Shaft Graves." In *Our Cups Are Full: Pottery and Society in the Aegean Bronze Age. Papers Presented to Jeremy B. Rutter on the Occasion of his 65th Birthday*, BAR International Series 2227, edited by W. Gauß, M. Lindblom, R. A. K. Smith and J. C. Wright, 140–153. Oxford, Archaeopress.

Lindblom, M., W. Gauß, and E. Kiriatzi. 2015. "Some Reflections on Ceramic Technology Transfer at Bronze Age Kastri on Kythera, Kolonna on Aegina, and Lerna in the Argolid." In *The Transmission of Technical Knowledge in the Production of Ancient Mediterranean Pottery. Proceedings of the International Conference Held at the Austrian Archaeological Institute at Athens, 23rd-25th November 2012*, edited by W. Gauß, G. Klebinder-Gauß and C. v. Rüden, 225–37. Sonderschriften des Österreichischen Archäologischen Instituts 54. Wien. Österreichisches Archäologisches Institut.

Maran, J. 1992. *Die Deutschen Ausgrabungen auf der Pevkakia-Magula in Thessalien III. Die Mittlere Bronzezeit* (2 vols). Bonn, Dr Rudolf Habelt.

Philippa-Touchais, A. and G. Touchais. 2011. "Fragments of the Pottery Equipment of an Early Middle Helladic Household from Aspis, Argos." In *Our Cups Are Full: Pottery and Society in the Aegean Bronze Age. Papers Presented to Jeremy B. Rutter on the Occasion of his 65th Birthday*, BAR International Series 2227, edited by. W. Gauß, M. Lindblom, R. A. K. Smith and J. C. Wright, 203–216. Oxford, Archaeopress.

Philippa-Touchais, A. and G. Touchais. 2009. "Argos: L'Aspis." *Bulletin de Correspondance Hellénique* 133.2, 567–580.

Renfrew, C., N. Brodie, C. Morris and C. Scarre, eds. 2007. *Excavations at Phylakopi in Melos 1974-77*, Annual of the British School at Athens Supplement 42. London, British School at Athens.

Rutter, J. B. 1979. *Ceramic Change in the Aegean Early Bronze Age: the Kastri group, Lefkandi I, and Lerna IV: A Theory Concerning the Origin of Early Helladic III Ceramics*. Los Angeles, Institute of Archaeology, University of California.

Rutter, J. B. 1983. "Fine Gray–burnished Pottery of the Early Helladic III Period: The Ancestry of Gray Minyan." *Hesperia* 52.4, 327–355.

Rutter, J. B. 1990. "Pottery Groups from Tsoungiza of the end of the Middle Bronze Age." *Hesperia* 59, 375–458.

Rutter, J. B. 1995. *Lerna: A Preclassical Site in the Argolid III. The Pottery of Lerna IV*. Princeton, American School of Classical Studies at Athens.

Rutter, J. B. forthcoming. "Tsoungiza LH I–IIA". In *Nemea Valley Archaeological Project III: The Mycenaean Settlement on Tsoungiza Hill*, edited by J. C. Wright and M. K. Dabney.

Sarri, K. 2010. *Orchomenos IV: Orchomenos in der mittleren Bronzezeit*. Bayerische Akademie der Wissenschaften, Philosophisch-Historische Klasse, Abhandlungen Neue Folge 135. Munich, C. H. Beck.

Spencer, L. 2007. *Pottery technology and Socio-Economic Diversity on the Early Helladic III to Middle Helladic II Greek Mainland*. PhD dissertation, University of London.

Spencer, L. 2010. "The Regional Specialisation of Ceramic Production in the EH III through MH II Period." In *Mesohelladika. The Greek Mainland in the Middle Bronze Age*, Bulletin de Correspondance Hellénique Supplement 52, edited by A. Philippa-Touchais, G. Touchais, S. Voutsaki, and J. Wright, 669–681. Athens, De Boccard.

Syriopoulos, C. Th. 1995. *Η προϊστορική κατοίκησις της Ελλάδος και η γένεσις του Ελληνικού έθνους*, Library of the Archaeological Society at Athens 139, Athens, Archaeological Society.

Voutsaki, S., S. Dietz and A. J. Nijboer. 2009. "Radiocarbon analysis and the History of the East Cemetery, Asine." *Opuscula, Annual of the Swedish Institutes in Athens and Rome* 2, 31–56.

Wace, A. J. T. and C. W. Blegen. 1917–1918. "The Pre-Mycenaean Pottery of the Mainland." *Annual of the British School at Athens* 22, 175–189.

Wild, E. M., W. Gauß, G. Forstenpointner, M. Lindblom, R. Smetana, P. Steier, U. Thanheiser and F. Weninger. 2010. "^{14}C dating of the Early to Late Bronze Age Stratigraphic Sequence of Aegina Kolonna, Greece." *Nuclear Instruments and Methods in Physics Research* B 268, 1013–1021.

Zerner, C. 1979. *The Beginning of the Middle Helladic Period at Lerna*. PhD dissertation, University of Cincinnati.

Zerner, C. 1988. "Middle Helladic and Late Helladic I Pottery from Lerna: Part II. Shapes." *Hydra* 4, 1–10.

Zerner, C. 1993. "New Perspectives on Trade in the Middle and Early Late Helladic Periods on the Mainland." In *Wace and Blegen: Pottery as Evidence for Trade in the Aegean Bronze Age 1939–1939. Proceedings of the International Conference held at the American School of Classical Studies, Athens, Dec. 2-3, 1989*, edited by C. Zerner, P. Zerner and J. Winder, 39–56. Amsterdam, Brill.

Zerner, C. 2008. "The Middle Helladic pottery, with the Middle Helladic Wares from Late Helladic Deposits and the Potters' Marks." In *Ayios Stephanos: Excavations at a Bronze Age and Medieval Settlement in Southern Laconia*, Annual of the British School at Athens Supplement 44, edited by W. D. Taylour and R. Janko, 177–298. London, British School at Athens.

Chapter 2

The temporal slicing and dicing of Minyan Culture: a proposal for a tripartite division of a lengthier Greek Middle Bronze Age and the issue of nomadism at its beginning

Jeremy B. Rutter

Historical introduction

Ever since Blegen's pivotal excavations of 1915–1916 at Korakou (Blegen 1921) and his co-authoring with Wace of a tripartite schema for the mainland Greek Bronze Age based upon his findings there (Wace and Blegen 1918), the roughly six to seven centuries from ca. 2200/2150 to 1600 or 1500 BC have been subdivided into a series of archaeological phases assigned to the Early, Middle, and Late Helladic eras, as these three consecutive stages of the Bronze Age are termed on the mainland.[1] But a full generation later, Caskey's excavations of 1952–1959 at Lerna had an enormous impact on how the transitions from Early Helladic to Middle Helladic, and subsequently from Middle Helladic to Late Helladic, needed to be understood. For Caskey clearly demonstrated that the most important cultural break after the Helladic Bronze Age began occurred not between Early Helladic and Middle Helladic, but rather one or two centuries earlier between the phases that had been designated Early Helladic II and III (Caskey 1960). Moreover, still ongoing analysis of the rich pottery dumps found in the two Late Helladic I shaft graves Caskey excavated at Lerna have shown how closely related this initial Late Bronze Age phase is in ceramic terms to the Middle Helladic period that preceded it (Lindblom 2007). Together with growing evidence from other areas of the Greek mainland, this suggests that a more significant cultural shift may have separated LH I from LH IIA than what distinguished the end of the Middle Helladic era from LH I (Table 2.1).

---

[1] For the absolute duration of the archaeological phases under discussion here (Early Helladic III, all sub-phases of Middle Helladic, and Late Helladic I), see the range of suggestions in Dickinson 1997, 17–21, fig. 1.3; Rutter 2001, 106 and n. 39, table 2; Shelmerdine 2008, 3–6, figs. 1.1–2; Voutsaki 2010, 100–102, table 7.1; 2012, 164 table 7.1; Wild *et al.* 2010, 1020 table 3.

2. The temporal slicing and dicing of Minyan Culture

Table 2.1: Comparison of chronological schemata of Wace and Blegen (1918), Rutter (1995; 2001), and Wiersma (2013) vs. site-specific phases at Lerna (Zerner 1978; 1986; 1988) and Kolonna (Gauss and Smetana 2007) vs. novel terminology for EH III–LH I periods proposed by Rutter (this volume)

Wace and Blegen 1918	Howell 1974	Rutter 1995, 2001	Wiersma 2013	Zerner 1978, 1986, 1988 [Lerna]	Gauss and Smetana 2007 [Kolonna]	Approximate Calendar Years	Rutter Proposal at Groningen [October 2013]
Early Helladic II		EH II			Phase B	2700–2200 BCE	Early Helladic IIA
					Phase C		Early Helladic IIB
Early Helladic III	Protominyan	EH III: 1	EH III	EH III	Phase D	2200/2150–2050/2000 BCE	Middle Bronze Age A [MBAA]
		EH III: 2			Phase E		
		EH III: 3					
Middle Helladic	Early Minyan	MH I	MH I – MH II	Lerna IV/V Transitional	Phase F	2050/2000–1900 BCE	Middle Bronze Age B [MBAB]
				Lerna VA	Phase G		
				Lerna VB			
	Classical Minyan	MH II		Lerna VC	Phase H	1900–1750 BCE	
					Phase I		
	Late Minyan	MH III	MH III – LH I	Lerna VD	Phase J	1750–1680 BCE	Middle Bronze Age C [MBAC]
				Lerna VE			
Late Helladic I		LH I		Lerna VI	Phase K	1680–1640 BCE	

Already by 1970, the terminological problem caused by the identification of the major cultural break at the end of EH II had led scholars such as Howell to suggest that the distinctive Middle Helladic culture ought to be re-labeled with a new name (he suggested "Minyan") so that its closely related direct antecedent, the assemblage typical of the Early Helladic III phase, could be more transparently linked to it by being termed "Proto-Minyan"; recognized temporal sub-divisions of Middle Helladic, rather than being designated by Roman numerals (I–III), might then be given evolutionary labels such as Early, Classical, and Late Minyan (Table 2.1; Howell 1974, 81). Howell's re-christening of Middle Helladic culture as "Minyan" was popularized by Dickinson in his influential monograph, *The Origins of Mycenaean Civilisation*, although Dickinson substituted several differently named sub-divisions (such as Decorated, Mature, and Late Phase) for what Howell had called Classical and Late Minyan (Dickinson 1977, 17–24, figs. 1–2). In this same publication, Dickinson stressed how short, in his opinion, the Late Helladic I phase had been, as well as how much of the pottery of this brief phase was essentially Middle Helladic in character (Table 2.1; Dickinson 1977, 24–26).

Another full generation after the end of Caskey's excavations at Lerna, Forsén subjected the artefactual evidence that Caskey had cited in favour of at least one and perhaps even two migrations into the Argolid at the ends of the Early Helladic II and III periods, respectively, to a rigorous re-appraisal. Her analysis showed that Caskey's invasionist historical model could not be logically sustained: the new forms of material culture that Caskey had focused on were shown to have been introduced into southern Greece at a variety of different times, and had their origins in such disparate locales that interpreting them as appearing simultaneously in the northeastern Peloponnese as the baggage of putative northern invaders was simply not viable (Forsén 1992; 2010, 54; Rutter 2001, 115–116; Pullen 2008, 35–41). Yet even though Forsén's conclusion won general acceptance, the notion of a distinctly new material culture becoming prevalent in central and southern Greece toward the end of the third millennium BCE – a cultural assemblage that we may temporarily continue to refer to as "Minyan" – persisted, as did the employment of five or more inconsistently applied chronological labels, from Early Helladic III through various phases of Middle Helladic to Late Helladic I, to describe its stages of development.[2] In her recently completed doctoral thesis, Corien Wiersma has substituted for the five or more ceramically based phases a system of just three stages in the development of the domestic architecture of this cultural continuum (Table 2.1; Wiersma 2013, xxi–xxii, 191). My purpose here is to explore this tripartite division – one that was introduced by Sofia Voutsaki and the team she assembled to study Middle Helladic social and cultural change (Voutsaki 2005; Voutsaki et al. 2013; Ingvarsson-Sundström et al. 2013) – in terms of several of the principal characteristics of each phase.[3] I will argue that this three-part approach to Minyan culture makes far better sense of the data at our disposal than any of the traditional, more ceramically based schemes that I began this paper by reviewing.

The Peloponnese during the Early Helladic III period

Wiersma's first phase corresponds with what is ordinarily called Early Helladic III, Howell's "Protominyan" phase. The houses of this phase, especially early on within it, exhibit a number of features suggesting that their builders may have been accustomed to constructing their dwellings in materials other than the pisé or

---

[2] For a similar summary of the archaeological terminology applied to the material culture of the Greek mainland from ca. 2200–1700 BCE, see Spencer 2007, 12–15; 2010, 670. Spencer explicitly as well as logically omits consideration of the Shaft Grave era (MH III–LH I) from her study of the small-scale egalitarian societies that she views as prevalent during EH III, MH I, and MH II, phases that she combines under the heading of "LEMH" [= late Early and Middle Helladic]. By contrast, Wiersma (2013, xxi–xxii) includes the Shaft Grave era in her dissertation.
[3] These characteristics are helpfully collected and briefly described by Wiersma 2013, 241–242. For the distinction between the last two of Wiersma's stages, see Wolpert 2004; Voutsaki 2005, 2012; Spencer 2007, 15–23. For a discussion of social changes between the more numerous ceramically defined phases, see Voutsaki and Milka, this volume.

sun-dried mudbrick on a rubble stone socle that was standard practice locally in the preceding EH II period. For example, some of their buildings were built out of wattle and daub over a rough framework of wooden posts, or of mudbricks placed directly on the contemporary ground surface, without any stone socle to protect the unbaked brick from erosion by rainwater or minor flooding. The houses tend to feature a uniform plan – a longhouse with an apsidal back end and shallow porch at the front with an axially located doorway leading into its main, and often only, room. In settlements where significant numbers of individual dwellings have been cleared – for example, sites like Lerna, Tiryns, and Olympia – there seems to be no standard arrangement or organizing principle behind the disposition of such houses (Wiersma, this volume). This is perhaps most clearly evident in the phase plans that Elizabeth Banks has recently published for the architecture of Lerna stratum IV (Banks 2013, 34 plan 4, 112 plan 16, 162 plan 23). Although the state of preservation often leaves a good deal to be desired, it is clear enough that adjacent buildings often, although of course *not* invariably, faced in opposite directions. All were freestanding – that is, the use of party walls for two or more distinct groups of rooms is not attested. But the spaces left between these freestanding houses were often minimal, so that buildings in EH III settlements can legitimately be described as clumped, at least in the cases of Lerna and Tiryns.

Given the relatively short duration of the period as a whole – just 150 years or so – the number of distinct building horizons at any given location within the settlement of Lerna IV can be surprisingly high, in some cases as many as seven and often at least four or more. As can readily be imagined, these flimsily constructed residences usually had short lifetimes, on the order of between 15 and 30 years. What is particularly striking at Lerna, although as Wiersma has noted it is also attested at a number of other sites, in this as well as later stages of "Minyan" culture, is how often these structures were rebuilt almost directly on top of each other with much the same plan (Wiersma 2013, 20–21, 136, 140–141, 199–201, 238–240, 248–249). Exactly what all this signifies, of course, is debatable. But perhaps the simplest scenario to envision is that a particular building location (or plot) within the settlement was recognized as "belonging" in some sense to a particular social group – presumably a kin group, and most logically in view of the size and simplicity of these structures a nuclear family. When an individual house needed to be rebuilt – perhaps at the time of its principal occupant's demise – the structure would simply be demolished and re-erected on more or less the same plan by the previous occupant's primary heir.

Let me return to the implications of the flimsy nature of these buildings and the occasionally inappropriate construction methods used by their builders. These features have suggested to some scholars (*e.g.* Hielte 2004; Wiersma 2013, 17, 194–196, 222–225) that these buildings were those of a previously mobile population who were settling down in a single location – that is, becoming fully sedentary – for the first time in a fairly long time. How we might choose to label such a population – formerly nomadic, semi-nomadic, or freshly sedentary – is an interesting question in itself, the answer to which should depend on how much time the group was used to spending in one place and whether or not this period of residence was year-round or in some way intermittent. I have no fresh evidence to present on this subject, so will leave this labelling issue aside for scholars to debate in the future as the connections between nomadism and archaeology continue to be explored (*e.g.* Cribb 1991; Sellet, Greaves, and Yu 2006; Barnard and Wendrich 2008; Szuchman 2009; Anfinset 2010; Anthony 2016). What I am more interested in are some of the implications for the EH III period as a whole of population groups who pursued an occasionally or regularly nomadic lifestyle. I might expect some or all of the following:

(A) A dramatic decline in the evidence for settlements, since the portable architecture of the nomads would have been constructed in materials that would be light enough to carry, would be discarded or abandoned only if no longer useful, and thus would have virtually no survival potential for future archaeologists.
(B) The containers used by periodically or regularly nomadic groups would be made of materials that were as readily portable and unbreakable as possible – for example, of leather, basketry, or light woods, and certainly neither ceramic nor stone. Like their architecture, the containers of such groups would ordinarily not survive to be found by archaeologists several millennia later.
(C) Because of their itinerant lifestyle, moreover one which may not have had any recurring pattern to it (that is, not necessarily consisting of an annual round of stays at the same series of locations in some kind of regular annual rotation), such groups would be unlikely to bury their dead in particular places to which they could expect to return. As a consequence, they might well concoct some form of funerary behaviour that involved the permanent disposal of their dead in places or ways that precluded any return to the places of the bodies' disposal.

When such mobile population groups eventually did settle down somewhere, I might expect them to be steered to locations that had established records for having been hospitable to human inhabitants – that is, to previously or even presently occupied places rather than to entirely new site locations. I might expect the forms of their previously portable architecture to be translated quite speedily, though sometimes perhaps rather imperfectly, into more robust materials. It would not be at all surprising if the number of different architectural forms chosen for the newly sedentary groups' dwellings was extremely limited; after all, the groups were translating what had previously been little better than tents into their new pisé or mudbrick and timber houses. So I would expect a single form of building to predominate, but I would also expect each constituent social group (that is, nuclear family) to have its own structure, so that these would all be freestanding.

How these formerly migrant groups went about translating their containers from light and perishable materials into more robustly produced vessels in fired clay might have taken any number of different directions. Perhaps they would have been happy enough simply to have adopted the technology of terracotta vessel production and such aspects of this as local clay recipes from whomever of the region's previous occupants were still present to learn from, even if the newcomers insisted on their own shape preferences and their own decorative traditions, at least when it came to the syntax of the ornament and the general character of the motifs. How long it would have taken the newcomers to feel sufficiently at home in a new locale to begin to bury their dead in fixed locations and according to rites that resulted in the archaeological survival of the skeletal material is another question that is obviously not easy to answer. But it might not be surprising if an established tradition of body disposal that left no readily recoverable remains for archaeologists to identify persisted for several generations after the group became sedentary.

So what I am suggesting is that the Early Helladic III period, at least in the Peloponnese, may have been populated largely by mobile groups who only gradually and rather irregularly became sedentary over a period of some half-a-dozen generations in the regions that we presently know and understand best (that is, the Corinthia and the Argolid). Any suggestions as to what happened to the bulk of the earlier EH II population can only be speculative. Certainly some of them must have survived to become absorbed into settlements of the new arrivals: this was the situation at early EH III Tiryns, I think, where the numbers of these EH II survivors as a percentage of the total population appear to have been considerable. But most of these settlements were very small. It is difficult to imagine *any* later EH II settlement with a population of more than several hundreds of inhabitants.[4] So if the mobile groups of newcomers gradually drove out or even killed off these small EH II groups over a period of four to five generations, one wonders whether there would be much surviving evidence for such a gradual displacement scenario that would be indicative of what had happened.

So far, I have restricted my listing of the consequences of the intrusion of a new and mobile population into the Peloponnese to comments on their architecture, settlement pattern, repertoire of containers, and burial customs. Let us examine a few other aspects of EH III material culture. For example, under the heading of settlement histories we might draw attention to the fact that some EH III sites appear to be occupied and abandoned on more than one occasion within the period (*e.g.* Tsoungiza: Pullen 2011, 541–544, 907–909) or alternatively to have been substantially re-located at one and the same site (*e.g.* at Olympia, from the so-called New Museum site to the Altis site: Rambach 2004). This phenomenon, I would argue, is what we might recognize as a still detectable aspect of the larger process of initial sedentism following a period of high mobility: it might take a while for a group to agree on exactly *where* to settle down.

Discoveries of the past two decades in Boeotia have made it increasingly clear what was the region of origin of these mobile groups that filtered into the northeastern

---

[4] For population estimates of EH III and earlier MH settlements that seem rather high to my own way of thinking, see Spencer 2007, 52–53, fig. 2.10.

Peloponnese early in the last quarter of the third millennium BCE. In the process of expanding the Archaeological Museum in Thebes, Vasilis Aravantinos and his colleagues in the later 1990s exposed a large double-apsidal building adjacent to an Early Bronze fortification wall at the northern end of Thebes' prehistoric settlement on the Kadmeia (Alram Stern 2004, 685, 1255–1265; Aravantinos and Psaraki 2011a, 2011b). A mass burial of some fifteen individuals, both adults and children, in the ruins of this building preceded its burial under a tumulus of mudbricks. The pottery associated with this structure shows that it, like at least two other large EH apsidal buildings uncovered in Thebes, dates from the end of the EH II period, to a time when pottery characteristic of the so-called "Lefkandi I" horizon flourished in western Euboea, Boeotia, and coastal Locris and Thessaly. In 2007, an extraordinary settlement of large apsidal as well as possibly other building forms was partially revealed near the western end of the Kephisos valley at Latouphi Mavroneriou in a salvage excavation associated with the construction of a pipeline. The second phase of this short-lived, two-stage settlement had been destroyed in a sudden fire that left masses of mendable pottery on its house floors, including numerous large storage vessels (pithoi) full of carbonized agricultural produce, to be recovered by a small team directed by Kiki Psaraki working, again, under the overall supervision of Vasilis Aravantinos (Psaraki 2011; n.d.). The pottery again belongs to the "Lefkandi I" horizon and closely resembles that recovered from the apsidal buildings in Thebes just mentioned. These discoveries in what appears to have been a particularly densely occupied portion of the Early Helladic II and III mainland (Spencer 2007, 48–51, fig. 2.8), and the violent destructions that evidently brought these occupational episodes at Thebes and Latouphi to an end (and in the case of Latouphi, forever), show what may have been going on in this agriculturally rich portion of central Greece immediately before the EH III cultural assemblage appears in the northeastern Peloponnese. I suggested some 20 years ago, largely on the basis of ceramic evidence, that Boeotia was likely to have been the immediate source for many of the novelties in material culture that characterize the EH III period in the Corinthia and the Argolid (Rutter 1995, 648–650). Coupling the new finds of late EH II date in Boeotia with the evidence favouring a mobile way of life for many of the EH III inhabitants of the northern Peloponnese now makes sense not only of the observed changes in the pottery but also of those noted in the pattern of settlement, the domestic architecture, and the dearth of funerary evidence in EH III southern Greece: the mobile populations of the EH III Peloponnese were migrants from no further afield than Boeotia.

An even more recent discovery at the site of Karavas, on the west bank of the Eurotas river just a few kilometres north of Sparta, is also of interest in this connection. Although small numbers of potsherds identified as being of EH III date have been reported from a few sites in Laconia (Spencer 2007, 36–37), the absence of significant quantities of EH III material culture in Laconia despite numerous excavations and intensive as well as extensive surveys has been striking (Rutter 2001, 122–123; Cavanagh and Mee 2011). But in 2011, salvage excavations directed by Aris Papayiannis under the supervision of Adamantia Vasilogamvrou revealed EH III settlement remains at Karavas in connection with the construction of a bridge across the Eurotas to carry the new highway from Megalopolis to Sparta. I am extremely grateful to Aris Papayiannis for his permission to mention these findings here in advance of their preliminary publication in a paper he presented orally in the fall of 2012 (Papayiannis n.d.). Immediately below the remains of early LH IIIC houses on a series of low terraces were found dug into sterile soil a number of pits that contained pottery representing multiple phases of EH III ceramic development. No contemporary EH III architecture or living surfaces, however, were identified: these had either been completely eroded or else dug away during late Mycenaean terracing operations on the site's moderate slope down from the west towards the river. Of course, if the EH III buildings and associated floors had been as flimsily constructed as was much of the EH III architecture at Lerna, one can easily imagine that they would not have survived the 1000 years of weathering between EH III and LH IIIC times. Whatever were the specifics at Karavas, the point I am interested in making is simply that the apparent dearth of EH III remains in Laconia, and for that matter also for most of the period's duration in nearby Messenia (Rutter 2001, 123), may simply be due to the twin features of population mobility and architectural flimsiness that were apparently typical of Peloponnesian EH III culture.

The evidence from Karavas – namely, the identification of multiple phases of EH III occupation entirely from the contents of sub-surface pits or *bothroi* – brings to the fore another distinctive feature of EH III material culture, the frequency and ubiquity of *bothroi* (Strasser 1999; Banks 2013, 20–22). More than 200 of these pits were recorded in the excavated portions of Lerna IV, where they seem to have served a variety of possible functions: for storage, as cooking places, and as places of disposal, either for ordinary rubbish or for human waste. One wonders if this exceptional enthusiasm for *bothroi* may have been a local adaptation to the absence of pithoi in sufficient numbers for a population that had only recently chosen to become fully sedentary. Unfortunately, it is impossible to even guess at the number of pithoi recovered from EH III Lerna, due to the excessive discarding of coarse and cooking wares by the site's excavators prior to the final study for publication of the relevant pottery units. But the more recent excavations at Tsoungiza suggest that at least by the later stages of this period pithos production had become common enough (Pullen 2011, 538–540, 569–570, 727 fig. 6.66, 732 fig. 6.67, 733–736 fig. 6.68).

Distinguishing earlier Middle Helladic culture from that of Early Helladic III

Of course, without a fixed pattern of settlement, not only funerary behaviour but also evidence for interregional or intercultural exchanges – that is, what is often too casually referred to as trade – might also be expected to become less visible. So the often noted decline in recognized imports in EH III times is certainly intelligible enough, although it may be exaggerated.[5] It is also the case that the dramatic changes under the headings of both burial customs and external contacts that characterize the ensuing MH I and II phases – indeed, that effectively define how MH material culture is to be distinguished from its EH III predecessor at Lerna (Caskey 1960, 298–299; Zerner 1978) – are simple to understand if we simply recognize that a more stable pattern of settlement set in during the later EH III period, precisely when (for example) small settlements in Messenia such as Nichoria and Derizioti Aloni reappear for the first time since the end of EH II (Howell 1992, 16–18, 43–46, 70, 83–86 P2020–2082, figs. 3.1–4, pls. 3.1–3; Stocker 2003).

Until quite recently, the distinction between EH III and MH I material culture has been based largely on the findings at sites in the northeastern Peloponnese, especially Lerna but to a certain degree also at Asine and Berbati. Caskey's initial emphasis in 1960 on the appearance of burials within the settlement at Lerna, along with a dramatic increase in pottery recognized from its fabric or typology as, respectively, chiefly Aeginetan and either Minoan or Minoanizing (Zerner 1993) has been sustained by a generation's analyses of the finds (Zerner 1978; 1986; 1988; 1990; Nordquist 1987). But Zerner has explicitly stated that none of the earliest MH I burials at Lerna were those of adults, all of them being of either infants or young children, most of them buried in the same sort of wide-mouthed cooking jar as was used for the same purpose in contemporary infant burials at Olympia (Zerner 1990, 23–24, figs. 1–6, 8; for Olympia, Dörpfeld 1935, 94–96, figs. 15, 17, pl. 17). Thus the change from EH III to MH I burial customs at Lerna was relatively minor, since a small number of premature or neonate bodies, for the most part casually deposited in pits and *bothroi* without anything in the way of grave goods, were discovered in EH III levels at the site (Banks 2013, 419–420). Of the nine such bodies identified, just one dating from the latest EH III phase 3 was found within a container: a wide-mouthed cooking jar that serves as a local EH III precedent for what became much more common in the subsequent MH I phase (Banks 2013, 91 fig. 23, 367, 419).[6] Thus the transition in burial customs from EH III to MH I at Lerna was gradual rather than sudden and may not have involved any adult dead for an appreciable period of time. Much the same story of a gradual rather than sudden shift in material culture is evident from detailed analysis of the pottery, since Zerner was able to demonstrate a clear "transitional EH III/MH" stage of ceramic development that corresponded with a distinct stratigraphic horizon (Zerner 1978, 6–12, 22–25, 191–192; Rutter 1986, 29). Over the past decade, similarly detailed analyses of the ceramic

---

[5] Note that all imports in EH III contexts would necessarily have to come from settlement contexts and not from tombs, since effectively no EH III adult burials have been recognized.

[6] A possible burial of a potentially premature birth from near the west end of the main excavation area at Lerna may date to phase 1 of Lerna IV and may have been accompanied by as many as four decorated pots (Banks 2013, 103–105, fig. 28, plan 15). If these pots do in fact belong with the scattered bones that seem to represent a disturbed burial, Banks has suggested that this prematurely born infant may either have had some special social status or perhaps had links with the previous EH II inhabitants of the site or both.

development at Kolonna on Aegina and Lefkandi on Euboea have now provided us with comparable pictures of the contemporary ceramic transitions at two other sites far removed from the coastal Argolid (Gauß and Smetana 2007; Spencer 2007, 109–133). Very interestingly, both of these have revealed an EH III/MH transitional phase which, like that at Lerna, is characterized by novel shapes and aspects of decoration that seem to bear witness to a brief period of experimentation alien to the highly disciplined ceramic repertoires in the preceding as well as following periods (Zerner 1978, 6–12, 22–25, 191–192; Gauß and Smetana, 2007, 60, fig. 1 [Phase F]; Spencer 2007, 112–113, fig. 4.5 [Phases 2–3]). So something quite striking but with short-term effects appears to have influenced the evolution of material culture insofar as at least the three regions represented by these sites are concerned. What this may have been, and why it should have occurred within what appears to have been a relatively short timespan, is another subject that unfortunately lies beyond the bounds of this paper.

Most of the major differences that set early MH culture apart from that of the preceding EH III era – such phenomena as the gradually increasing robustness of settlement architecture (Wiersma 2013, 194–196, 205, 221), the vastly greater numbers of burials coupled with the increased visibility of a fair number of them in the form of above-ground tumuli (Müller 1989; Rambach 2007; Petrakis 2010; Merkouri and Kouli 2011; Papakonstantinou 2011; Voutsaki *et al.* 2011), and the establishment of regular interregional and intercultural exchanges, especially at the coastal locations where many of the more important sites of the MH I–II phases are situated (Rutter and Zerner 1984; Zerner 1993; Nikolakopoulou 2007) – are logical developments for a population that was gradually becoming more accustomed to full-time sedentism. The seemingly egalitarian nature of the earlier MH social order that has been inferred from the lack of established and ongoing hierarchies in either the funerary or domestic assemblages of this era is hardly new, but rather appears to be a clear continuation from the prevailing pattern during EH III times.[7]

The advent of the Shaft Grave Era of Middle Helladic III and Late Helladic I

What seems to bring the preceding cultural stage to an end is the introduction of a competition for status that manifests itself, most visibly in the funerary sphere, in the earliest shaft graves of the MH III period at Mycenae and the first tholoi in Messenia, but that is also visible in some fortification systems that may cluster in east-central

---

[7] The nature of MH I–II material culture and how it differs from that which defines the Shaft Grave era of MH III–LH I have been topics extensively covered by papers delivered at a Sheffield Round Table in 2002 (Wolpert 2004; Georgousopoulou 2004), two major international conferences held in Salzburg in 2004 (Felten, Gauß, and Smetana 2007) and Athens in 2007 (Philippa-Touchais, Touchais, Voutsaki, and Wright 2010), the research carried out by the Middle Helladic Argolid project directed by Sofia Voutsaki (Voutsaki 2005, Voutsaki and Milka, this volume), and the dissertations of Theodora Georgousopoulou (2003), Lindsay Spencer (2007), and now Corien Wiersma (2013).

Greece (*e.g.* Kiapha Thiti and Plasi in Attica) and that also appear elsewhere (*e.g.* Argos and perhaps Malthi). The vehicles chosen for this new interest in competitive display were not inventions of the mainlanders, being clearly derived from other regions within the Aegean. Moreover, the population resident at Mycenae for some reason managed to jump the gun and get a head start in this process that it would not relinquish for at least five centuries. The choice of the shaft grave form, of its placement on a site, and of the multiple emphases in its contents on warfare, hunting, and small-group consumption of what were presumably alcoholic beverages seems closely modeled after the later MH II burial of a warrior just outside the main gate of Kolonna on Aegina (Kilian-Dirlmeier 1997; Rutter 2012, 80–81; Harrell 2014). This same site, or possibly others located on nearby Cycladic islands such as Ayia Irini on Keos, provided the form of the fortification wall that caught on as a *communal* symbol of status not only in Attica but also at Argos and eventually even as far away as Malthi. But in the southern Peloponnese, and thus far most noticeably in Messenia, it was the tholos tomb, in my opinion adopted as a form from Crete, that turned out to be the architectural form through which the local elite competed. And so successful was this particular selection in a mainland Greek context that it ended up displacing the shaft grave at both Mycenae and Thorikos by the LH IIA period and perhaps at Corinth already by LH I (Kasimi 2013). Meanwhile, back in Messenia at Pylos, and once again taken over from the Minoans of central Crete rather than the Aeginetans, the mainlanders were building their earliest elite above-ground structures incorporating cut-stone masonry possibly even before the end of the MH period but certainly by LH I (Nelson 2001; 2007).

The motivations for what distinguishes the human behaviour of the terminal MH III–LH I stage of what I have been calling Minyan culture appear to be twofold: first, an impulse to emulate forms associated with elite classes in neighbouring regions; and second and far more important, an intense spirit of competition and interest in both establishing *and maintaining* social hierarchies that determine the directions taken by mainland Greek culture for the next half-a-millennium and indeed beyond (Wolpert 2004; Voutsaki 2005; 2012; Spencer 2007). Yet this agonistic pattern of behaviour appears to have been entirely lacking during the preceding half-a-millennium (ca. 2200–1700 BCE), so where did *this* come from and why was it so rapidly adopted and transmitted throughout the central and southern Greek mainland?

Conclusions

This paper has focused on two issues. First, the confusing chronological terminology for the periods traditionally designated as EH III, MH, and LH I that together constitute a clear continuum of cultural development rather than one to be chopped up into the three principal stages of the mainland Greek Bronze Age (Early, Middle, and Late Helladic). Let us at last acknowledge this unity of cultural development by substituting a new chronological schema that emphasizes continuity but that at the same time avoids any possible confusion with earlier terminological systems. I propose abandoning *both* the Helladic *and* the Minyan labels and substituting for them the terms Middle Bronze Age A (for EH III), B (for traditional Middle Helladic I–II), and C (for traditional MH III and LH I) (Table 2.1).[8] These terms correspond with the major divisions observed in settlement architecture by Wiersma and in burial customs by Voutsaki, and can also be easily correlated with the major ceramic distinctions being documented by Gauß and Lindblom in their shape analyses (Gauß and Lindblom, this volume).

My second focus was the problems posed by seeking to identify mobile population groups in the archaeological record during what I am calling Middle Bronze Age A (to be abbreviated MBAA). Another phase in the Greek mainland's lengthy history of continuous occupation that may likewise have witnessed what at first appears to be gross depopulation but may more likely be explicable as the consequence of a significant increase in mobile population groups in tandem with a substantial change in the overall settlement pattern is the Early Byzantine era of the seventh and eighth centuries CE (Bintliff 2012, 382–388). Roughly equivalent to the prehistoric MBAA phase in duration, this portion of the Early Byzantine era is known mostly from scrappy literary sources, coin hoards, and some lead seals, all deriving from a distant ruling authority which was unable to maintain control over anything but the local capital of Thessalonica, some major towns, and a number of coastal strips; the interior had fallen under the control of migrating Slavic tribes, themselves evidently quite diverse in terms of their material culture and their political and military allegiances (Curta 2006, 70–110; 2011, 97–134). Without the comparatively few surviving literary accounts and the evidence from scattered Byzantine fortresses located mostly on the islands – strongpoints from which the rulers in Constantinople maintained control through their navy – we would probably know a good deal less about life in the Peloponnese and central Greece from ca. 600 to 800 CE (often termed a "Dark Age") than we do about the same regions between 2750 and 3000 years earlier. As we seek in the future to explain what happened at the end of the EH IIB period to cause the nascent regionalism, radical change in settlement pattern, and substantial decline in the complexity of material culture that characterizes what I have termed the MBAA phase (*i.e.* the initial subdivision of a significantly longer than traditional Middle Bronze Age), we should perhaps consider the historic (though as yet very poorly documented archaeologically) example of Early Byzantine Greece as providing us with a potentially helpful comparandum for how mobile populations may have played a role in bringing the Early Bronze Age in these regions to a close.

---

[8] I would like to thank Walter Gauß and Jeannette Forsén for very helpful discussion and correspondence concerning this choice of terminology, without implying in any way that they are to be considered responsible for the changes proposed here.

Bibliography

Alram-Stern, E. 2004. *Die Ägäische Frühzeit: 2. Serie, Forschungsbericht 1975-2002* II, 2: *Die Frühbronzezeit in Griechenland mit Ausnahme von Kreta*. Vienna, Austrian Academy of Sciences.

Anfinset, N. 2010. *Metal, Nomads, and Culture Contact: The Middle East and North Africa*. London/Oakville, Equinox.

Anthony, D. W. 2016. "The Samara Valley Project and the Evolution of Pastoral Economies in the Western Eurasian Steppes." In *A Bronze Age Landscape in the Russian Steppes: The Samara Valley Project*, Monumenta Archaeologica 37, edited by D. W. Anthony, D. R. Brown, O. D. Mochalov, M. Khokhlov, and P. F. Kuznetsov, 3-36. Los Angeles, Cotsen Institute of Archaeology.

Aravantinos, V., and K. Psaraki. 2011a. "Οι Πρωτοελλαδικοί Τύμβοι της Θήβας." In *Ελίκη IV: Αρχαία Ελίκη και Αιγιαλεία. Πρωτοελλαδικά: Η Νότια και Κεντρική Ελλάδα*, edited by D. Katsonopoulou, 279–293. Athens, Helike Society.

Aravantinos, V., and K. Psaraki. 2011b. "Mounds over Dwellings: the Transformation of Domestic Spaces into Community Monuments in EH II Thebes, Greece." In *Ancestral Landscapes: Burial Mounds in the Copper and Bronze Ages*, edited by E. Borgna and S. Müller Celka, 401–413. Lyon, Travaux de la Maison de l'Orient.

Banks, E. C. 2013. *Lerna. A Preclassical Site in the Argolid* VI: *The Settlement and Architecture of Lerna IV*. Princeton, American School of Classical Studies at Athens.

Barnard, H., and W. Wendrich, eds. 2008. *The Archaeology of Mobility: Old World and New World Nomadism*, Cotsen Advanced Seminars 4. Los Angeles, Cotsen Institute of Archaeology.

Bintliff, J. 2012. *The Complete Archaeology of Greece: From Hunter-gatherers to the 20th Century AD*. Chichester/Malden, Wiley-Blackwell.

Blegen, C. W. 1921. *Korakou. A Prehistoric Settlement near Corinth*. Boston, American School of Classical Studies at Athens.

Caskey, J. L. 1960. "The Early Helladic Period in the Argolid." *Hesperia* 29, 285–303.

Cavanagh, W., and C. Mee. 2011. "Minding the Gaps in Early Helladic Laconia." In *Our Cups Are Full: Pottery and Society in the Aegean Bronze Age: Papers Presented to Jeremy B. Rutter on the Occasion of His 65th Birthday*, British Archaeological Report S2227, edited by W. Gauß, M. Lindblom, R. A. K. Smith, and J. C. Wright, 40–50. Oxford, Archaeopress.

Cribb, R. 1991. *Nomads in Archaeology*. Cambridge, Cambridge University Press.

Curta, F. 2006. *Southeastern Europe in the Middle Ages*. Cambridge, Cambridge University Press.

Curta, F. 2011. *The Edinburgh History of the Greeks, c. 500 to 1050: The Early Middle Ages*, Edinburgh, Edinburgh University Press.

Dickinson, O. T. P. K. 1977. *The Origins of Mycenaean Civilisation*, Studies In Mediterranean Archaeology 49. Göteborg, P. Åström.

Dörpfeld, W. 1935. *Alt-Olympia: Untersuchungen und Ausgrabungen zur Geschichte des ältesten Heiligtums von Olympia und der älteren griechischen Kunst*. Berlin, E. S. Mittler & Sohn.

Felten, F., W. Gauß, and R. Smetana, eds. 2007. *Middle Helladic Pottery and Synchronisms. Proceedings of the International Workshop held at Salzburg October 31st–November 2nd, 2004*, Ägina–Kolonna Forschungen und Ergebnisse I/Österreichische Akademie der Wissenschaften Denkschriften der Gesamtakademie 42. Vienna, Austrian Academy of Sciences.

Forsén, J. 1992. *The Twilight of the Early Helladics: A Study of the Disturbances in East-Central and Southern Greece towards the End of the Early Bronze Age*, Studies In Mediterranean Archaeology Pocket-book 116. Jonsered, Åström.

Forsén, J. 2010. "Early Bronze Age: Mainland Greece." In *The Oxford Handbook of the Bronze Age Aegean*, edited by E. Cline, 53–65. Oxford, Oxford University Press.

Gauß, W., and R. Smetana. 2007. "Aegina Kolonna, the Ceramic Sequence of the SCIEM 2000 Project." In *Middle Helladic Pottery and Synchronisms: Proceedings of the International Workshop held at Salzburg October 31st–November 2nd, 2004*, Ägina–Kolonna Forschungen und Ergebnisse I/Österreichische

Akademie der Wissenschaften Denkschriften der Gesamtakademie 42, edited by F. Felten, W. Gauß, and R. Smetana, 57–80. Vienna, Austrian Academy of Sciences.

Georgousopoulou, T. 2003. *The Negotiation of Identity in MH Asine*. Ph.D. dissertation, University of Sheffield.

Georgousopoulou, T. 2004. "Simplicity vs. Complexity: Social Relationships and the MH I Community of Asine." In *The Emergence of Civilisation Revisited*, Sheffield Studies in Aegean Archaeology 6, edited by J. C. Barrett and P. Halstead, 207–213. Oxford, Oxbow Books.

Harrell, K. 2014. "The Fallen and Their Swords: A New Explanation for the Rise of the Shaft Graves." *American Journal of Archaeology* 118, 3–17.

Hielte, M. 2004. "Sedentary versus Nomadic Lifestyles: The 'Middle Helladic People' in Southern Balkan (Late 3rd and First Half of the 2nd Millennium B.C.)." *Acta Archaeologica* 75, 27–94.

Howell, R. J. 1992. "The Origins of the Middle Helladic Culture." In *Bronze Age Migrations in the Aegean*, edited by R. A. Crossland and A. Birchall, 73–99. Park Ridge, Noyes.

Howell, R. J. 1974. "The Middle Helladic Settlement: Stratigraphy and Architecture" and "The Middle Helladic Settlement: Pottery." In *Excavations at Nichoria in Southwest Greece* II: *The Bronze Age Occupation*, edited by W. A. McDonald and N. C. Wilkie, 15–204. Minneapolis, University of Minnesota Press.

Ingvarsson-Sundström, A., S. Voutsaki, and E. Milka. 2013. "Diet, Health and Social Differentiation in Middle Helladic Asine: A Bioarchaeological View." In *Diet, Economy and Society in the Ancient Greek World: Towards a Better Integration of Archaeology and Science*, Pharos Supplement 1, edited by S. Voutsaki and S. M. Valamoti, 149–162. Leuven, Peeters.

Kasimi, P. 2013. "Ένας Πρώιμος Θολωτός Τάφος στην Αρχαία Κόρινθο." In *The Corinthia and the Northeast Peloponnese: Topography and History from Prehistoric Times until the End of Antiquity*, Athenaia 4, edited by K. Kissas and W.-D. Niemeier, 45–54. Munich, Hirmer.

Kilian-Dirlmeier, I. 1997. *Alt-Ägina* IV,3: *Das mittelbronzezeitliche Schachtgrab von Ägina*. Mainz on Rhine, Phillip von Zabern.

Lindblom, M. 2007. "Early Mycenaean Mortuary Meals at Lerna VI with Special Emphasis on their Aeginetan Components." In *Middle Helladic Pottery and Synchronisms: Proceedings of the International Workshop held at Salzburg October 31st–November 2nd, 2004*, Ägina–Kolonna Forschungen und Ergebnisse I/Österreichische Akademie der Wissenschaften Denkschriften der Gesamtakademie 42, edited by F. Felten, W. Gauß, and R. Smetana, 115–135. Vienna, Austrian Academy of Sciences.

Merkouri, C., and M. Kouli. 2011. "The Spatial Distribution and Location of Bronze Age Tumuli in Greece." In *Ancestral Landscapes: Burial Mounds in the Copper and Bronze Ages*, edited by E. Borgna and S. Müller Celka, 203–218. Lyon, Travaux de la Maison de l'Orient.

Müller, S. 1989. "Les tumuli helladiques: où? quand? comment?" *Bulletin de Correspondance Hellénique* 113, 1–42.

Nelson, M. C. 2001. *The Architecture of Epano Englianos, Greece*. Ph.D. dissertation, University of Toronto.

Nelson, M. C. 2007. "Pylos, Block Masonry and Monumental Architecture in the Late Bronze Age Peloponnese." In *Power and Architecture: Monumental Public Architecture in the Bronze Age Near East and Aegean*, edited by J. Bretschneider, J. Driessen, and K. van Lerberghe, 143–159. Leuven, Peeters.

Nikolakopoulou, I. 2007. "Aspects of Interaction between the Cyclades and the Mainland in the Middle Bronze Age." In *Middle Helladic Pottery and Synchronisms: Proceedings of the International Workshop held at Salzburg October 31st–November 2nd, 2004*, Ägina–Kolonna Forschungen und Ergebnisse I/Österreichische Akademie der Wissenschaften Denkschriften der Gesamtakademie 42, edited by F. Felten, W. Gauß, and R. Smetana, 347–359. Vienna, Austrian Academy of Sciences.

Nordquist, G. 1987. *A Middle Helladic Village: Asine in the Argolid*, Uppsala, Academia Ubsaliensis.

Papakonstantinou, M.-Ph. 2011. "Bronze Age Tumuli and Grave Circles in Central Greece: the Current State of Research." In *Ancestral Landscapes: Burial Mounds in the Copper and Bronze Ages*, edited by E. Borgna and S. Müller Celka, 391–400. Lyon, Travaux de la Maison de l'Orient.

Papayiannis, A. n.d. "Τα Πρωτοελλαδικά ΙΙ και ΙΙΙ Κατάλοιπα στον Καραβά Λακωνίας." Paper presented at *1st* International Conference "The Archaeological Work in the Peloponnese," Tripolis (Arcadia), November 2012.

Petrakis, V. P. 2010. "Diversity in Form and Practice in Middle Helladic and Early Mycenaean Elaborate Tombs: An Approach to Changing Prestige Expression in Changing Times." In *Mesohelladika. The Greek Mainland in the Middle Bronze Age*, Bulletin de Correspondance Hellénique Supplement 52, edited by A. Philippa-Touchais, G. Touchais, S. Voutsaki, and J. Wright, 403–416. Athens, De Boccard.

Philippa-Touchais, A., G. Touchais, S. Voutsaki, and J. Wright, eds. 2010. *Mesohelladika. The Greek Mainland in the Middle Bronze Age*, Bulletin de Correspondance Hellénique Supplement 52. Athens, De Boccard.

Psaraki, K. n.d. "Ενας άγνωστος Πρωτοελλαδικός Οικισμός στην Πεδιάδα του Μαυρονερίου." Lecture delivered at τηε N. P. Goulandris Museum, Athens, 11 April 2011.

Psaraki, K. forthcoming. "Νεότερα Στοιχεία για την Κατοίκηση στην Κοιλάδα της Χαιρώνειας την 3η Χιλιετία π.χ.: Η Εγκατάσταση στο Λατούφι Μαυρονερίου." In *4ο Αρχαιολογικό Έργο Θεσσαλίας και Στερεάς Ελλάδας 2009-2011. Από τους Προϊστορικούς στους Νεώτερους χρόνους, Βόλος 15-18 Μαρτίου 2012.*

Pullen, D. J. 2008. "The Early Bronze Age in Greece." In *The Cambridge Companion to the Aegean Bronze Age*, edited by C. W. Shelmerdine, 19–46. Cambridge, Cambridge University Press.

Pullen, D. J. 2011. *Nemea Valley Archaeological Project* I: *The Early Bronze Age Village on Tsoungiza Hill*. Princeton, American School of Classical Studies at Athens.

Rambach, J. 2004. "Olympia im ausgehenden 3. Jahrtausend v. Chr.: Bindeglied zwischen zentralem und östlichem Mittelmeerraum." In *Die ägäische Frühzeit: 2. Serie, Forschungsbericht 1975-2002 II, 2: Die Frühbronzezeit in Griechenland mit Ausnahme von Kreta*, edited by E. Alram-Stern, 1199–1254. Vienna, Austrian Academy of Sciences.

Rambach, J. 2007. "Investigations of Two MH I Burial Mounds at Messenian Kastroulia (near Ellinika, Ancient Thouria)." In *Middle Helladic Pottery and Synchronisms: Proceedings of the International Workshop held at Salzburg October 31st–November 2nd, 2004*, Ägina–Kolonna Forschungen und Ergebnisse I/Österreichische Akademie der Wissenschaften Denkschriften der Gesamtakademie 42, edited by F. Felten, W. Gauß, and R. Smetana, 137–150. Vienna, Austrian Academy of Sciences.

Rutter, J. B. 1986. "Some Comments on the Nature and Significance of the Ceramic Transition from Early Helladic III to Middle Helladic." *Hydra* 2, 29–57.

Rutter, J. B. 1995. *Lerna. A Preclassical Site in the Argolid* III: *The Pottery of Lerna IV*. Princeton, American School of Classical Studies at Athens.

Rutter, J. B. 2001. "Review of Aegean Prehistory II: The Prepalatial Bronze Age of the Southern and Central Greek Mainland" and "Addendum: 1993–1999" In *Aegean Prehistory: A Review*, edited by T. Cullen, 95–147 and 148–155. Boston, Archaeological Institute of America.

Rutter, J. B. 2012. "Migrant Drinking Assemblages in Aegean Bronze Age Settings." In *Materiality and Social Practice: Transformative Capacities of Intercultural Encounters*, edited by J. Maran and P. W. Stockhammer, 73–88. Oxford, Oxbow Books.

Rutter, J. B., and C. W. Zerner. 1984. "Early Hellado-Minoan Contacts" In *The Minoan Thalassocracy: Myth and Reality*, edited by R. Hägg and N. Marinatos, 75–83. Stockholm, Svenska Institutet i Athen.

Sellet, F., R. Greaves, and P.-L. Yu. 2006. *Archaeology and Ethnoarchaeology of Mobility*. Gainesville, University Press of Florida.

Shelmerdine, C. W. 2008. "Background, Sources, and Methods." In *The Cambridge Companion to the Aegean Bronze Age*, edited by S. Shelmerdine, 1–18. Cambridge, Cambridge University Press.

Spencer, L. C. 2007. *Pottery Technology and Socio-Economic Diversity on the Early Helladic III to Middle Helladic II Greek Mainland*. Ph.D. dissertation, University of London.

Spencer, L. C. 2010. "The Regional Specialization of Ceramic Production in the EH III through MH II Period." In *Mesohelladika. The Greek Mainland in the Middle Bronze Age*, Bulletin de Correspondance Hellénique Supplement 52, edited by A. Philippa-Touchais, G. Touchais, S. Voutsaki, and J. Wright, 669–681. Athens, De Boccard.

Stocker, S. R. 2003. "Pylos Regional Archaeological Project, Part V: Deriziotis Aloni: A Small Bronze Age Site in Messenia." *Hesperia* 72, 341–404.

Strasser, T. F. 1999. "Bothroi in the Aegean Early Bronze Age." In *Meletemata. Studies in Aegean Archaeology Presented to Malcolm H. Wiener as He Enters His 65th Year*, Aegaeum 20, edited by P. P. Betancourt, V. Karageorghis, R. Laffineur, and W.-D. Niemeier, 813–817. Liège/Austin, University of Texas at Austin.

Szuchman, J., ed. 2009. *Nomads, Tribes, and the State in the Ancient Near East: Cross-disciplinary Perspectives.* Chicago, Oriental Institute of the University of Chicago.

Voutsaki, S. 2005. "Social and Cultural Change in the Middle Helladic Period: Presentation of a New Project." In *Autochthon. Papers Presented to O. T. P. K. Dickinson on the Occasion of His Retirement*, edited by A. Dakouri-Hild and S. Sherratt, British Archaeological Report S1432, 134–143. Oxford, Archaeopress.

Voutsaki, S. 2010. "Middle Bronze Age: Mainland Greece." In *The Oxford Handbook of the Bronze Age Aegean*, edited by E. Cline, 99–112. Oxford, Oxford University Press.

Voutsaki, S. 2012. "From Value to Meaning, from Things to Persons: The Grave Circles of Mycenae Reconsidered." In *The Construction of Value in the Ancient World*, edited by G. Urton and J Papadopoulos, 112–137. Los Angeles, Cotsen Institute of Archaeology Press.

Voutsaki, S., A. Ingvarsson-Sundström, and S. Dietz. 2011. "Tumuli and Social Status: A Re-examination of the Asine Tumulus." In *Ancestral Landscapes: Burial Mounds in the Copper and Bronze Ages*, edited by E. Borgna and S. Müller Celka, 445–462. Lyon, Travaux de la Maison de l'Orient.

Voutsaki, S., E. Milka, S. Triantaphyllou, and C. Zerner. 2013. "Middle Helladic Lerna: Diet, Economy, Society." In *Diet, Economy and Society in the Ancient Greek World: Towards a Better Integration of Archaeology and Science*, Pharos Supplement 1, edited by S. Voutsaki and S. M. Valamoti, 133–148. Leuven, Peeters.

Wace, A. J. B., and C. W. Blegen. 1918. "The Pre-Mycenaean Pottery of the Greek Mainland." *Annual of the British School at Athens* 22, 175–189.

Wiersma, C. W. 2014. *Building the Bronze Age. Architectural and Social Change on the Greek Mainland During Early Helladic III, Middle Helladic and Late Helladic I*, Archaeopress International Series. Oxford, Archaeopress.

Wild, E. M., W. Gauß, G. Forstenpointner, M. Lindblom, R. Smetana, P. Steier, U. Thanheiser, and F. Weninger. 2010. "^{14}C Dating of the Early to Late Bronze Age Stratigraphic Sequence of Aegina Kolonna, Greece." *Nuclear Instruments and Methods in Physics Research Section B: Beam Interactions with Materials and Atoms* 268.7–8, 1013–1021.

Wolpert, A. 2004. "Getting Past Consumption and Competition: Legitimacy and Consensus in the Shaft Graves." In *The Emergence of Civilisation Revisited*, Sheffield Studies in Aegean Archaeology 6, edited by J. C. Barrett and P. Halstead, 127–144. Oxford, Oxbow Books.

Zerner, C. W. 1978. *The Beginning of the Middle Helladic Period at Lerna.* PhD dissertation, University of Cincinnati.

Zerner, C. W. 1986. "Middle Helladic and Late Helladic I Pottery from Lerna." *Hydra* 2, 58–73.

Zerner, C. W. 1988. "Middle Helladic and Late Helladic I Pottery from Lerna: Part II: Shapes." *Hydra* 4, 1–10.

Zerner, C. W. 1990. "Ceramics and Ceremony: Pottery and Burials from Lerna in the Middle and Early Late Bronze Ages." In *Celebrations of Death and Divinity in the Bronze Age Argolid*, edited by R. Hägg and G. C. Nordquist, 23–34. Stockholm, P. Åström.

Zerner, C. W. 1993. "New Perspectives on Trade in the Middle and Early Late Helladic Periods on the Mainland." In *Wace and Blegen: Pottery as Evidence for Trade in the Aegean Bronze Age, 1939–1989: Proceedings of the international conference held at the American School of Classical Studies at Athens, Athens, December 2–3, 1989*, edited by C., P. Zerner and J. Winder, 39–56. Amsterdam, Brill.

Chapter 3

Early Helladic III: a non-monumental but revitalized social arena?

Erika Weiberg

Monumental feats of the past are something that has always been of high interest within archaeological discourse. Some periods of Aegean prehistory can be defined as more "monumental" than others, *i.e.* more efforts were put, during these times, into the architectural appearance of space. The presence or absence of large scale building activities has been a trait often raised cross-culturally in relation to sociopolitical complexity (Alt 2010), such as in the list of traits indicative of urbanization put forward by Konsola (1986) for the Early Helladic (EH) period and often referred to since then. One result is a general stimulation of studies on certain periods, generally those with monumental features and other observable signs of societal complexity, and a shortage of studies on periods for which circumstances appear to be the opposite. In the following I will try to restore some identity to one period of the latter type, namely the final 100 years or so of the Early Bronze Age on the Greek mainland – the EH III period. Based on the degree of visibility and pervasiveness of the archaeological material, the centuries following the end of the EH II period on the Greek mainland could indeed be deemed rather insignificant. Beyond issues of monumentality and visibility, however, many things seem to have been stirring, indications of non-insignificant activity, even in areas such as the northeast Peloponnese where the differences from EH II appear especially stark. It is also clear that changes that did occur were not confined to the EH II–III transition but were played out during a much longer period of time. This fact puts new emphasis on regionally varying trajectories within the Greek mainland during the transitional period. The material contexts from the EH III mainland allows for discussions on issues of scale, human resourcefulness, innovation and the active reformulation of social agendas during times of change.

    One reason for the scarcity of studies on the EH III period specifically is likely to be found in the negative result of applying models for defining the level of societal complexity. The symbolic lacuna created by the discontinuation of the corridor houses, so distinctive for the late EH II period, must here be seen as significant. These buildings, as well as the fortifications, the use of sealings and a wide-reaching and relatively coherent ceramic repertoire have been portrayed as emblematic for the earlier period, and fit well with Konsola's morphological criteria for an urbanized society. Little can be said to be similarly representative for the succeeding period and as noted by Konsola (1986, 17): "most of the settlements of the period can lay no serious claim to urban status and seem to have reverted to a much simpler socio-economic and political organization, relapsing to a lower rank in the urban hierarchy."

The apsidal buildings, which by early EH III begin to replace the rectangular housing quarters as the most common architectural form (Wiersma, this volume), would by most be regarded as a rather poor replacement to the architectural refinement of the preceding period, regardless of the care taken in the construction of apsidals (Banks 2013, *e.g.* 92–93). Beyond the change in shape, the general but not all-inclusive conversion from rectangular to apsidal signifies also a change from agglomerate to freestanding structures. In EH II, the freestanding nature of the corridor houses was one aspect that set them apart from more ordinary agglomerative housing complexes; in EH III thus, the exception becomes the rule. If viewed along with other changes during the transitional period, it is possible to outline a general adjustment of the level of communal and individual organizations. Aspects of both will always be present, but the indications for a communal focus are certainly stronger for the EH II period than the EH III period. An emphasis on the community as a whole is expressed in the EH II period by the size of the settlements, the presence of extramural cemeteries, craft specialization, in the use of sealings, in the corridor houses – which I prefer not to view as residences of an elite but rather as a communally organized multipurpose buildings (Weiberg 2007, 52–57; cf. Peperaki 2004) – as well as in the combined efforts needed to accomplish these houses and other architectural undertakings of the EH II period.

Our knowledge of the EH III period suggests instead a growing focus on the household as the principal organizational level (Weiberg and Finné 2013, 24–27). Indications of this is the construction techniques and layout of the houses and settlements (Wiersma, this volume), a decreased level of craft specialization, increased scale of domestic storage, the use of intramural burial, and perhaps even more in the apparent absence of any recognizable extramural mortuary areas. These circumstances seem to go hand in hand with the material culture heterogeneity (Rutter 1988), or diversity, recognized for this period on a regional level, but stand in contrast to the relative and geographically widespread homogeneity recognized for the preceding period. On the individual level, however, the increased self-sufficiency of the household in the EH III period suggests a decreased number of definable social roles by which hierarchical, or heterarchical, socio-political structures could be formed (cf. Wiersma 2013, 233–234, 243–244). Although there are some signs of social differentiation in the EH III period (as suggested for example by the material recently published from EH III Lerna: Banks 2013; Wiersma 2013, 236–238), indications for formalized socio-political structures are much more numerous for the EH II period. The most obvious of these, of course, is the monumental corridor houses.

The meaning of monumentality

Monumentality is obviously a very relative concept. It can be measured in many ways, such as the work hours needed to accomplish the structures, the elaboration of the details, the durability over time, as well as of course in the actual size of the structures (cf. Fitzsimons 2011). Clearly, features defined as monumental in some contexts, would not be so in other. In this respect, monumentality is highly contextual and a framework for extraordinary accomplishments within specific settings.

In the large corpus, from the 1990s onwards, of cognitively based research on monuments and their place in landscapes (reviewed by Thomas 2012), the focus is generally on the capacity of monuments for harbouring socially construed conceptions of time and place, as mnemonic markers, in the centuries and millennia after their construction (*e.g.* Bradley 1998). Within Aegean archaeology, the focus has instead been primarily on the incentive for monumentality, that is the ideas and socio-political frameworks of their actual construction. It is thus generally implied that monuments should be seen as signs of a certain degree of complexity within the societies as well as a need for statements of socio-political cohesion and/or strength. These studies fall generally within two groups, those dealing with graves or those dealing with residential areas, respectively. Based on the Bronze Age material of the Greek mainland, it would seem that there is also a chronological aspect to this division. Although allowing for exceptions to any trend, it would thus seem that incentive to monumentality in the sepulchral domain is largely to be connected with societies with signs of accelerated processes of social manoeuvring and budding hierarchical structures. In the Early Bronze Age we have thus the EH I–IIA graves fields at Tsepi, Aghios Kosmas, Manika, and Kalamaki Elaiochorion (Weiberg 2007, 190–205, with references), but also some smaller concentrations of graves elsewhere. With more stable, and possibly less contested, socio-political circumstances, most demonstrations of socio-political power seem to move into the context of the settlements proper. In these cases, the focus seems to be on the architectural aggrandizement of the sphere of the living, such as the general architectural definition of the settlements throughout the EH II period and, more obvious perhaps, in the fortifications and large-scale buildings such as the corridor houses and the Tiryntian Rundbau in late EH II (a time for which graves are scarce).

Based on the Early Helladic period, we appear to have something of an either/or relationship between mortuary and domestic display in terms of the relative monumentality connected to these social arenas over time. A similar argument could be made for the Mycenaean period. In early Mycenaean times, just as in the first half of the Early Helladic period, the mortuary sphere was an important scene for socio-political positioning between competing parties in the societies, something that seems to be visible in the construction and furnishing of (new types of) graves (Fitzsimons 2011). The enhanced monumentality of the tholos tomb type, introduced in LH II, suggest socio-political competition on a regional level. Thereafter, we see a rechanneling of these efforts into non-funerary construction and the tholoi certain to be built in the Argolid after LH IIIA1 were limited to Mycenae itself (Fitzsimons 2011, 101–102). At that time, it would seem, tholoi were the prerogative of the ruling section of society, possibly to be seen as part and parcel of the palatial arena (rather than as a social arena of their own), and unique signs of success perhaps rather than continued competition. In the move from graves to the settlement, one could also see a gradual move from more or less individual statements towards one of communal, and perhaps regional, content. This is something that appears to be similarly valid for the Early Helladic period and Late Mycenaean times alike, and which should be seen as an important aspect and a complementing way to view the oscillations between the funerary scene and the settlement as main social arenas.

But what does the *lack* of monumentality really mean? Is the aspiration towards monumentality, and towards a certain long-term durability of this monumentality, to be seen as an inherent part of the human psyche and human interactions, if the means are available? If the presence of monumental features, whether in the domestic or mortuary sphere, symbolizes societies and/or individuals that could muster the needed resources and thus reflecting a certain degree of built up societal complexity, is the lack of monumental features a sign of the complete opposite? It would be easy to answer the latter two questions in the affirmative. In order to answer the first question, however, I believe it is needed to consider more carefully the human components, also in times when the most visible examples of human resourcefulness are lacking. The actions of individuals, or communities (smaller groups of individuals, equal or not to whole societies/settlements) should be equally central to discussions of the developments around the EH II–III transition as well as in the centuries that followed. I have argued elsewhere that the choice not to continue the tradition of corridor houses and the life styles we connect with these buildings would have been in the hands of individuals, just as their construction once was (Weiberg 2007, 178–181). Similarly, we should consider whether it is possible that the seemingly simplified life of the EH III period, in terms of the monumentality of its expressions, was in fact to some degree a matter of choice. In the following, I will bring forth some details and circumstances from the EH III period that could perhaps strengthen this argument.

Pace of change

One issue is the pace of change. The conventional time frame of the EH III period is 2200/2150–2050/2000 BC (Manning 1995, 173). This will give this last phase of the EBA the duration of 100–200 years. Recent radiocarbon analyses from the settlement of Kolonna on Aegina, have produced results that strongly indicate that the shorter time frame is to be preferred (Wild *et al.* 2010). These new data put the EBA/MBA transition to no later than 2100 BC, and possibly even as early as 2150 BC (the calibrated age range for the transition is 2183–2154 BC, with 68.2% probability). As the EH II–EH III transition seems to remain around 2200 BC, the duration of EH III, according to the Kolonna samples, should be revised to a 50–100 year timeframe. Recently published radiocarbon analysis from Dhaskalio-Kavos, Keros (Renfrew *et al.* 2012), gives an absolute chronology that pushes back the end of the EB III period as far as 2300 BC. So far, this result is difficult to correlate with known mainland sequences but it should be noted that also this sequence sets the duration of the EB III period to around a maximum of 100 years.

In addition to these absolute chronologies we have our relative chronologies. The ever more detailed ceramic sequencing at particular settlements gives good insights into the speed and particulars of ceramic change at particular settlements and glimpses of the social conditions within which these changes were formed and played out.

Looking thus at Kolonna, the EH III period has been divided into three ceramic phases (D–F), corresponding to the three architectural phases IV–VI (Walter and Felten 1981; Gauß and Smetana 2007; for absolute chronology: Wild *et al.* 2010). In comparison, for the preceding EH II period, encompassing roughly 500 years, only two ceramic phases have been distinguished. The same is also true for the succeeding MH I period, encompassing some 100–200 years. In the case of Lerna, EH II has been subdivided into four ceramic phases (Lerna III, phases A–D; Wiencke 2000) and EH III into three separate phases (Lerna IV, phases 1–3; Rutter 1995; Banks 2013), and in both cases they correlate to architectural phases with similar divisions.

That it has been possible to single out as many as three subdivisions for the 50–100 year long EH III period, in comparison with the two and four phases at Kolonna and Lerna, respectively, for the preceding 500 years of the EH II period, should I believe be seen as significant for an accelerated pace of change during the considerably shorter EH III period. Following the suggestion by Rutter (1995, 641), Lerna IV.3 would have been the longest and corresponding to the same number of years as the two earlier combined. This would equate roughly 25–50 years for the first two and 50–100 years for the last phase, following the conventional chronology. Considering the updated absolute chronology, the shorter time span now seems the more likely. This number of years equates a generation each for the two first phases, and 5–10 years each for their subphases (Table 3.1).

The pace of change is also evident in the architectural sequences. Based on the building techniques and the supposed duration of the architectural phases, it would seem that while in EH II the houses were built to last and were commonly adjusted over time, the EH III houses do not display the same intent. Instead, the building technique would seem to presuppose change and their use lives were indeed much

3. Early Helladic III: a non-monumental but revitalized social arena?

Table 3.1: Relative chronology with sub-phases and duration for Lerna and Kolonna

YEARS								
100	100	100	100	100	100	100	100	
PERIOD								
EH II					EH III		MH I	
KOLONNA Ceramics								
B			C		D	E	F	G	H
Architecture								
II			III/III Rebuild		IV	V	VI	VI	VII	VIII	VIIIA
LERNA Ceramics and Architecture								
A	B	C	D	1	2	3	1	2	3

shorter. Thus, at Lerna, phases IV.1 and IV.2 hold three subphases each and the final IV.3 phase incorporates four separate subphases (Banks 2013, plans 4, 16, and 23). As noted by Banks (in Rutter 1995, 10), the material from EH III Lerna attests to a more or less continuous building activity.

The architectural phasing does not in itself signify actual change in the daily life of the users. I would nevertheless argue that the ceramic and architectural stratigraphies from Kolonna and Lerna are at least signs of a significant degree of activity during the comparatively short duration of EH III. The detailed archaeological record for Lerna attests to an active and formative time, beginning in the late EH II period, intensifying in the first half of EH III and coming to more stable circumstances again later in the period. Corroborating evidence for this varying pace of change is the gradual development discernible also *within* the first two ceramic phases at EH III Lerna, a circumstance which stands in contrast to the final phase wherein very little development could be detected (Rutter 1995, 641). What can be traced is something of a reformulation of the social environment on the mound, from a communal/official milieu to a primarily domestic setting (Weiberg and Lindblom 2014). The change is reflected in the changing repertoire of drinking paraphernalia, from the very large number of saucers in late EH II (Wiencke 2000; Pullen 2011), to the ouzo cups of early EH III, to an "internally generated cultural reorganization" (Rutter 1995, 651) that would set the scene for the last half of the EH III period, when drinking had moved from the communal scene to one involving much smaller groups of people

(Rutter 2008). As argued by Pullen (this volume) this signifies a change from large scale, and community-wide feasting to a social situation favouring reciprocal exchange based on the principle of hospitality.

Material culture diversity

Further indications for ongoing processes of innovation during EH III are perhaps to be found if reviewing evidence for material culture diversity. In the accentuated trading climate indicative for the whole of EB I–II in the Aegean area (Renfrew 1972; Maran 1998; Broodbank 2000), a certain level of what might perhaps be called multiculturalism, or multivocality, would indeed seem to have been an obvious result. To a certain extent, this introduction of new practices and mixing of material culture traits were likely the result of non-local population elements (Rutter 1979; this volume; Banks 2013, 345) but the processes whereby the mix came about should not be simplified. A certain degree of variation within the material culture would have been present within as well as between settlements at all times. Based on the present material, some settlements, such as in Attika, Euboea and Boeotia, seem to have been multicultural environments already in late EH I. In all three regions, to a varying degree, we find signs of close interaction with the Cycladic sphere of influence, especially in material connected to the mainland mortuary sphere, and a mixing of traits more at home in the islands with ones commonly found on the mainland. One important example is the EH I grave field at Tsepi (Pantelidou-Gofa 2005). Although coloured by the different availability of resources – items usually fashioned from marble in the islands are at Tsepi represented in other types of stone or bone – the graves are very much "Cycladic" in structure and content. Pottery found outside the graves, however, such as in the remarkable deposit pit, is of household nature and fully at home within mainland Helladic traditions (Pantelidou-Gofa 2008). The pervasiveness of the mix is intriguing and materials such as this render the use of cultural designations highly questionable. It does further give ample opportunities for discussions on the complex nature of each settlement specific archaeological material.

In late EH II, "regimes of external dominance came increasingly to the fore" (Broodbank 2000, 320) and it seems that both the mainland and the Cycladic islands were involved on the receiving end of partnerships including also a third party. In Boeotia and on Aegina as well as in parts of the Cyclades, the new Kastri/Lefkandi I type of pottery did to some extent break up the ceramic *koiné* established some 100 years earlier. In small but likely sought after quantities, new wheel-thrown drinking utensils were introduced, probably as a result of a heightened integration of the central Aegean trade networks with eastern Aegean/Anatolian contemporaries through the southern extension of the 'Anatolian Trade Network' (Broodbank 2000, 313; Şahoğlu 2005; Kouka 2013). As argued by Rutter (1979; 1995), these new influences started a stylistic fusion, bringing together a mixture of ceramic traditions into what we define as the EH III repertoire of shapes and types. During this same time, at Thebes, the corridor house went out of use and large scale apsidal buildings were built (Aravantinos 2004) – well before the onset of EH III – suggesting an environment of change, incorporating not only the ceramic repertoire. In other regions and settlements, such as at Olympia and Lerna, a more complete EH II ceramic *koiné* remained until the end of the EH II period, possibly a result of the lack of direct involvement in the trade with the western Anatolian littoral (Şahoğlu 2005, 353–354). For some important parts of material culture *koiné*, such as the corridor houses, the fortifications and the use of sealings (which were all found also in the Peloponnese), parallel ideas can be found beyond the Greek mainland (Maran 1998; Şahoğlu 2005; Aruz 2008). It is certain that the histories of origin for these late EH II characteristics were to a large extent grounded in local or regional processes (*e.g.* Shaw 1987, for the corridor houses; Weiberg 2010, for seal use). It seems also clear, however, that these special features were forged within an international climate based on long-distance contact networks.

These networks would have connected the Greek mainland with the world beyond and are generally considered to have been wider and more active in the EH II period. Maran (1998) recognized a restructuring of the maritime trading networks in late EBA Mediterranean, with the communities on the Greek mainland thereafter taking on more peripheral roles within a trading climate of otherwise steady or even increased intensity. Even so, it could be argued that the history of multivocality continued also on the Greek mainland. The enhanced regionalism of the EH III period should be seen as one issue to be raised to support this argument. It is clear that some of the features earlier thought to have made their first appearance on the Greek mainland at around the EH II–III transition were in fact in place earlier (Forsén 1992), but it is equally clear that come the EH III period their numbers multiply. Ceramically, the EH III period is defined by several new styles without any clear local backgrounds. Fine Gray Burnished ware, Dark-on-Light ware, and Fine Incised and Impressed ware, are all new aspects of the EH III ceramic repertoire and they appeared over large parts of the Greek mainland around the same time, often in small but nevertheless distinct quantities (Forsén 1992, tables 11–13). The antecedents of these traditions have been traced to southwest Anatolia (Rutter 1983), northeastern Aegean (Rutter 1988), and northwestern Balkans (Rutter 1982; Maran 1998), respectively. People from the latter were by Maran (1998, 311–355) singled out as key actors in the early EH III *Kulturwandel*. Based on the presence of pottery with clear parallels to Cetina culture pottery, this is the most credible instance of the presence of people from foreign lands in Early Helladic settings.

The main issue here, to my mind, is not in the end whether or not the EBA settlements were multicultural environments – most communities are so at some level, as few communities are fully self-sufficient. The main point is neither if they came about through the actual mixing of people from different origin or by the subsuming of trends spread indirectly over shorter or longer distances and from any one or several geographical areas. It is neither a matter of how well connected different regions of the mainland were within the current contact networks (whether by sea or by land). Instead, we should ask ourselves what was the general *impact* of these circumstances. It is clear that the answer would need to vary with the region, as there seems to have been a varying acceptance of innovation in material culture (Maran 1998, 273–274). In all, however, more homogenizing forces would seem to have been active in EH II, especially when considering the geographical reach of some component of the material culture koiné, while heterogenizing ones were more prominent in EH III. If allowing for a certain degree of choice, it would seem that in the EH III period, diversity was more accepted and perhaps even promoted.

A very local example of the mixing of material culture traditions comes, not surprisingly, from Lerna. In the recent publication of EH III Lerna, Banks (2013, 350) suggests that people of two different origins occupied the north and south parts respectively of the excavated area on the Lernean mound throughout phases IV.1–2 (*i.e.* the first half of the EH III period). The suggestion is based on architecture and diagnostic pieces of pottery. One of these groups is thus defined by its trapezoidal buildings and an emphasis on Anatolian-derived drinking practices, and in Lerna IV.2 also by the tradition of especially marked-out bothroi (Banks 2013, 348–350, 355). The other group is defined mainly on the basis of the apsidal architectural tradition – the apsidal long-houses W-1 and W-36 given to the need of housing for a village headman to replace the corridor houses (Banks 2013, 349–350, 355). Although there are considerable problems with the direct equation of material cultural diversity with ethnic diversity, this example presents an interesting mix of material culture traits. The differences may be ethnic, functional or otherwise preferential, but they underline what was once concluded by Jeremy Rutter (1993, 28–29), that the cultural norms in EH III "appear to have been significantly more relaxed than they had been in the Korakou culture."

Interregional connectivity

How does this mixing of material culture traits and the accelerating pace of change compare with the negative image of the EH III period as one of simplification and depopulation? There is further an apparent imbalance between certain low-key regions of the mainland, such as the Argolid, and other, seemingly more progressive ones close by, such as Aegina and the settlement of Kolonna, which comprise evidence that seem to signify a greater degree of entrepreneurship than most other communities at the time. How should we assess these discrepancies?

The late EBA history of Kolonna is unique in many ways in mainland Helladic terms and does in some sense compare better with the societies on Crete than with those on the nearby Greek mainland. The material from Kolonna gives witness of expansion rather than simplification at the end of the Early Bronze Age (Walter and Felten 1981; Gauß and Smetana 2007). Given the large-scale architectural undertakings and technological sophistication evidenced from Kolonna, such as the early EH III metal furnace (inside a partly dismantled corridor house) and the somewhat later fortifications, the economic progress was not halted, even though the corridor house fell out of use. It could easily be argued that the inhabitants of Kolonna benefited from the key geographical location of their island and the sociopolitical transformations in nearby areas such as the Argolid, and used it to their own advantage, in order to expand their sphere of influence (cf. Maran 1998) – that is, progress at the expense of former friends and neighbours. But was this necessarily so? EH III Kolonna was, as far as the presence of imports goes, without ties to either the Minoan or the Cycladic sphere of interaction (Gauß and Smetana 2007; Wild *et al.* 2010, table 3: the only EH III Cycladic imports belonging to EB III–MB I transitional phase). This circumstance need not mean that no contacts existed (cf. Broodbank 2000, concerning the visibility of Cycladic-Minoan contacts and the direction of trade routes) but it is noteworthy still as a contrast to the close resemblances that have been identified between Kolonna and Lerna. Even though there was a gradually changing form repertoire in late EH II suggestive of a growing interest in the northeastern Aegean, at the expense of Peloponnesian contacts (Berger 2004, 1101), it would seem that this trend was reversed again in early EH III.

Rather than plainly judging settlements such as Kolonna as superior to other, less monumental settlements, it could also be argued that the apparent prosperity of some settlements would not have formed if not in intense interaction with their surroundings. The mere presence of clear EB III styles on the south-central mainland indicate that the people of these regions were not lacking initiative but were actively reforming the appearances of life. In doing so they were also essential in the forming of the Middle Bronze Age settings. Analyses of EH III–MH II ceramic technologies (Spencer 2010), however, suggest that we should allow for different dynamics within south-central Greek mainland. Based on the frequencies of locally produced wheel-thrown pottery, the material from the central Greek mainland, including Euboea, show continued signs of close interaction and a common trend of steadily increasing ceramic specialization and homogeneity in the pottery assemblages. Further south we have other signs for active interaction between communities. One such example is the mid-EH III evidence for close connections between Lerna and Kolonna (Rutter 1995, 642–643), based on the fact that 85% of the whole or largely restorable vessels from City V in Kolonna have close parallels in Lerna IV. Wiersma (2013, 93) has also emphasized the great resemblance between assemblages indicative of drinking ceremonies at these two settlements, assemblages defined by the presence of giant jars and tankards in combination with a few small drinking cups. As far as the quality and appearance of these drinking assemblages, the assemblages at Lerna, and not the ones from Kolonna, come forth as superior due to the greater elaboration of the vessels and their decoration.

The ceremonies within which the over-sized vases were likely used are those outlined by Rutter (2008; this volume; see also Pullen, this volume) on the basis of two ceramic assemblages from IV:2 Lerna: W-52 and W-84, a trapezoidal and a D-shaped structure, respectively. The contrast – in quantitative terms – between the content of these EH III assemblages and the ceremonial assemblages put forward for the EH II period (Pullen 2011) is indeed striking. The qualitative differences, however, do not noticeably favour the earlier period. On the contrary, while the number of the vessels certainly was greater in EH II, the EH III examples do often display a greater elaboration of both shape and decoration. This would seem to be valid regardless of the size of the vessels. While most common shapes in EH II ceremonial assemblages come forth as rather simple and primarily utilitarian (for a modern eye at least), many EH III examples of ouzo cups, kantharoi, giant jars and giant tankards, seem to signify a greater degree of care and specific intentions as well as attention to detail. These differences seem to mirror the changing focus from a communal to an individual or household agenda noted for other aspects of the two societies. Following the assessments by Rutter and Pullen regarding the size of the parties involved in these EH III ceremonies, it would seem that also the ritualized drinking had withdrawn from the communal sphere to the household arena. Neither of these circumstances, however, needs to reverse the picture of continued connectivity between settlements and regions as suggested by the similarities between Lerna and Kolonna. The fact that the trapezoidal shape of the structure within which one of the Lernaean ceremonial assemblages were found (W-52) is connected by Banks (2013, 349) to the house complexes along the fortification wall at Kolonna, may also be significant (as may also a few possibly direct imports to EH III Lerna: Rutter 1995, 649). All this seems to tie at least these two settlements together beyond the limits of their closest environment; at least it ties them both to the same sphere of interaction in the early EH III period. The presence of sherds of similar types of giant vessels also elsewhere in northern Peloponnese – but interestingly not in central Greece (Rutter 2008, 466–467) – suggest further that the social networks were of interregional relevance and made up from communities following similar social codes, but, also that beyond this geographical area, the drinking ceremonies may have been differently organized.

Altered social arenas

The material culture heterogeneity evidenced in both the number of ceramic traditions, their regionally varying expressions, and in the co-mingling of different architectural styles, could be used to argue a greater degree of independence or even reclusiveness of certain regions during EH III. In this scenario, each region would follow fully endogenous trajectories, unknowing of the outside world. But, it could also be seen as identity markers in a time of change and in the formation of new ideas and values, reflecting a high degree of interaction, now with less rigid ideas of how things should look. I have argued elsewhere that it was the inflexibility of the late EH II way of life that in the end caused the discontinuation of the features seen as characteristic for that period (Weiberg and Finné 2013). That way of life seems also to have lingered on longer in the northeastern Peloponnese than further north, possibly as a result of the determination of key groups of people in that region. This calls to question also the viability of the relative chronologies we use, or at least the way we use them, often supposing geographically wide-reaching concordance rather than specific choices of traditionalism or progressivism and favouring abrupt change over more gradual ones (Broodbank 2000, 332; Cavanagh and Mee 2011, 48).

As argued initially by Jeanette Forsén (1992), the features characteristic of EH III were not introduced as a package around 2200 BC but were introduced gradually over a longer period, starting in EH II. Similarly, I believe, it should be emphasized that the features characteristic of EH II were not *discontinued* as a package but went out of use or were gradually reformed under a longer period from the second half of the EH II period onwards. Thus, a nucleated settlement pattern was likely established already in late EH II (Wiencke 1989; Weiberg and Finné 2013). The corridor house at Thebes, as well as the proposed one at Zygouries (Pullen 1986), were chronological parallels to Building BG at Lerna, and were as such also abandoned before the end of the EH II period (Maran 1998; Shaw 2007). Unlike at Lerna, we know of no successor buildings at either Thebes or Zygouries and at these settlements the corridor houses were a feature of mid-EH II. So, beyond the monumental expressions of the late EH II societies, the impetus for change would already have been established. The gradual character of the transition is further emphasized at locations such as Tiryns, where the survival of EH II ceramic styles continued to the very end of the EH III period (Weisshaar 1983, figs. 8–11; Rutter 1995, 646; Weiberg and Lindblom 2014). Evidence from southern Peloponnesian locations suggests further that the changes may have been even more protracted in these regions where early EH III style pottery is largely lacking (Rutter 1979; 2001, 123; Cavanagh and Mee 2011; but see Rutter, this volume, for suggestive results from new excavations in Laconia).

Other similar indications come from the Cyclades, where the proposed solution of the EB III gap in the island region is based on the chronological stretching out of the Kastri and Phylakopi I material culture traditions, to have them converge within the EB III period (Manning 1995, 66–72; Broodbank 2000, 331–335, fig. 113; 2013). The appearances on the mainland as well as the Cycladic islands of Minoan contacts in MB I is another "abrupt" change that should likely be better characterized in more gradual terms, in parallel with the deconstruction of the MM I(B) emergence horizon of the Minoan palaces (Tomkins 2012). The (late) MH I onset of the export of pottery from the Kolonna workshop should likely also be seen in the light of pre-established contact networks (Zerner 1993). In all, we seem the end up with several good cases for gradual processes of societal reformulation in late EBA–early MBA Aegean. Late EB II–early EB III were unquestionably transformative times in the Aegean – a "Wendezeit" as it was defined by Maran (1998, 140–146). The spirit of change, however, seems to have persisted throughout the EH III period, as the essence of innovative processes that really set the scene for later Middle Bronze Age developments. Rather than suffering from the effects of "collapse", the peoples of the EH III were actively engaged in shaping the future (cf. Schwartz and Nichols 2006; McAnany and Yoffee 2010).

A matter of scale

The decrease in interregional ceramic congruence signifies lapsed intensity in long-distance contacts and a decreased need for mass-production. At the same time we can note the preservation of certain specialist skills in pottery production, such as the reduction firing needed for Fine Gray Burnished ware, the organization among potters in central Greece, and possibly even a heightened attention to details as evidenced by certain ceremonial vessels at least. We have thus a situation on the Greek mainland indicative of uprooted long-distance contact networks but many indications of preserved short term ones. The changing dynamics of the former was part of a larger scale alteration of trade networks elsewhere in the Aegean, through disruptions in the "Anatolian Trade Network" (Şahoğlu 2005; Kouka 2013), in parallel with similar processes in the Cycladic sphere (Broodbank 2000; 2013). In all cases, we have contemporary and significant socio-political transformations and the processes on the Greek mainland mirror the history in the eastern Aegean and western Anatolia (Kouka 2013). It may have been these events in the western Anatolian littoral – possibly due to similar processes in the Mesopotamian region causing disruption in metal driven trade routes through Anatolia – that caused further disruptions southwards along established trade routes, breaking up trade networks also in southern Aegean and socio-political transformation as a result.

This scenario supposes high relevance of long-distance linkages for socio-political structures in these regions during the EH II period. The chronological interconnectedness of similar processes in the Aegean makes this supposition plausible. In all, we may also theorize a structural interconnectedness between Aegean polities that with time would have made the network sensitive to disruptions. Kouka (2013, 578) has defined the processes in the eastern Aegean as signifying extroversion in the late EB II–EB IIIA, turning into introversion in the EB IIIB period. This is a definition that could also be applied to the Greek mainland and it is a definition that in my mind takes due notice of the socio-political changes without necessarily deactivating the Early Helladic inhabitants. Introversion in this case could be used to describe a time of socio-political flux that turned the societal focus towards the home region. The EH III period may then be seen as a time of reversed priorities, defined by the need for new socio-political structures. If allowing for a shift in scale – from the Aegean-wide arena to a more regionally defined one – we end up with a better ground for appreciating the socio-economic complexities of the EH III period. The suggested changes in drinking ceremonies, from the communal to the individual, can be raised to exemplify this transition.

Increase in material cultural diversity after socio-political transformations have been noted elsewhere (Nelson *et al.* 2006; 2011) and ties into an appreciation of the general positive effects of diversity for entrepreneurship and for the level of resilience within social-ecological systems (Holling 2001; cf. Weiberg and Finné 2013). In the case of the EH III period, we can add to the framework of material culture diversity the possibility of multicultural settings as a result of a new mixing of people with different cultural/geographical backgrounds, as well as a possibly increased diversity in land use with mobility as an alternative to full sedentism (Rutter 1988; this volume). However, whether or not we people the different material culture traditions in EH III with individuals of different origin, I believe there is cause to argue that the people and their communities were both reflective and inclusive while actively reforming their societies to more resilient forms of life. The indications are there for a revitalized social arena and communities unrestrained at that point by the strong and wide-reaching agenda of the EH II period that promoted concordance rather than individuality. We have a relatively less connected but revitalized social arena. If thus empowering the people of the EH III societies, it might be argued that the period was not only non-monumental but, in fact, demonumentalized. If expanding, or downscaling, the concept of monumentality to more moveable items, however, it could also be argued that with the giant jars and kantharoi, monumentality became a household matter. Monumentality in this case could help us to pinpoint prehistoric priorities and the changes in social foci over time.

Acknowledgements

I would like to warmly thank the organizers, Corien Wiersma and Sofia Voutsaki, for the invitation to participate in this workshop. Corien Wiersma, Sofia Voutsaki and Daniel Pullen also offered helpful comments on a draft of this paper. I further gratefully acknowledge the funding of the Swedish Research Council (grant number 421-2011–2014).

Bibliography

Alt, S. M. 2010. "Considering Complexity: Confounding Categories with Practices". In *Ancient Complexities. New Perspectives in Precolumbian North America*, edited by S. M. Alt, 1–7. Salt Lake City, University of Utah Press.

Aravantinos, V. 2004. "New Evidence about the EH II Period in Thebes: A New Architectural Complex and a Group Burial within the Kadmeia". In *Die Ägäische Frühzeit 2. Serie. Forschungsbericht 1975–2002. 2.2 Die Frühbronzezeit in Griechenland, mit Ausnahme von Kreta*, edited by E. Alram-Stern, 1255–1259. Vienna, Austrian Academy of Sciences.

Aruz, J. 2008. *Marks of Distinction. Seals and Cultural Exchange Between the Aegean and the Orient (ca. 2600–1360 B.C.)*. Corpus der minoischen und mykenischen Siegel, Beiheft 7. Mainz am Rhein, Philipp von Zabern.

Banks, E. C. 2013. *Lerna. A Preclassical Site in the Argolid* VI. *The Settlement and Architecture of Lerna IV*. Princeton, American School of Classical Studies at Athens.

Berger, L. 2004. "Ägina-Kolonna. Neue Ergebnisse zur FH II-Keramik aus der prähistorischen Innenstadt." In *Die Ägäische Frühzeit 2. Serie. Forschungsbericht 1975–2002. 2.2 Die Frühbronzezeit in*

Griechenland, mit Ausnahme von Kreta, edited by E. Alram-Stern, 1124–1126. Vienna, Austrian Academy of Sciences.

Bradley, R. 1998. *The Significance of Monuments. On Shaping the Human Experience in Neolithic and Bronze Age Europe*. London and New York, Routledge.

Broodbank, C. 2000. *An Island Archaeology of the Early Cyclades*. Cambridge, Cambridge University Press.

Broodbank, C. 2013. "'Minding the Gap': Thinking About Change in Early Cycladic Island Societies from a Comparative Perspective." *American Journal of Archaeology* 117.4, 535–543.

Cavanagh, W. and C. Mee. 2011. "Minding the Gaps in Early Helladic Laconia". In *Our Cups Are Full. Pottery and Society in the Aegean Bronze Age: Papers Presented to Jeremy B. Rutter on the Occasion of his 65th Birthday*, edited by W. Gauß, M. Lindblom, R. A. K. Smith and J. C. Wright, 40–50. Oxford, Archaeopress.

Fitzsimons, R. D. 2011. "Monumental Architecture and the Construction of the Mycenaean State." In *State Formation in Italy and Greece. Questioning the Neoevolutionist Paradigm*, edited by N. Terrenato and D. C. Haggis, 75–118. Oxford and Oakville, Oxbow Books.

Forsén, J. 1992. *The Twilight of the Early Helladics. A Study of the Disturbances in East-Central and Southern Greece Towards the End of the Early Bronze Age*. Studies in Mediterranean Archaeology Pocketbook 116. Jonsered, P. Åström.

Gauß, W. and R. Smetana. 2007. "Early and Middle Bronze Age Stratigraphy and Pottery from Aegina Kolonna." In *The Synchronisation of Civilisations in the Eastern Mediterranean in the Second Millennium B.C. III. Proceedings of the SCIEM 2000—2nd EuroConference, Vienna, 28th of May–1st of June 2003*, edited by M. Bietak and E. Czerny, 451–472. Österreichische Akademie der Wissenschaften Denkschriften der Gesamtakademie 37. Vienna, Austrian Academy of Sciences.

Holling, C. S. 2001. "Understanding the Complexity of Economic, Ecological, and Social Systems." *Ecosystems* 4.5, 390–405.

Konsola, D. 1986. "Stages of Urban Transformation in the Early Helladic Period." In *Early Helladic Architecture and Urbanization. Proceedings of a Seminar Held at the Swedish Institute in Athens, June 8, 1985*, Studies in Mediterranean Archaeology 76, edited by R. Hägg and D. Konsola, 9–19. Göteborg, P. Åström.

Kouka, O. 2013. "Against the Gaps: The Early Bronze Age and the Transition to the Middle Bronze Age in the Northern and Eastern/Western Anatolia." *American Journal of Archaeology* 117, 569–580.

Manning, S.W. 1995. *The Absolute Chronology of the Aegean Early Bronze Age*. Monographs in Mediterranean Archaeology 1. Sheffield, Sheffield Academic Press.

Maran, J. 1998. *Kulturwandel auf dem griechischen Festland und den Kykladen im späten 3. Jahrtausend v. Chr: Studien zu den kulturellen Verhältnissen in Südosteuropa und dem zentralen sowie östlichen Mittelmeerraum in der späten Kupfer- und frühen Bronzezeit*, 2 vols. Bonn, Habelt.

McAnany, P. A. and N. Yoffee, eds. 2010. *Questioning Collapse. Human Resilience, Ecological Vulnerability, and the Aftermath of Empire*. Cambridge and New York, Cambridge University Press.

Nelson, M. C., M. Hegmon, S. Kulow, and K. Gust. 2006. "Archaeological and Ecological Perspectives on Reorganization. A Case Study from the Mimbres Region of the U.S. Southwest". *American Antiquity* 71, 403–432.

Nelson, M. C., M. Hegmon, S. Kulow, M. A. Peeples, K. W. Kintigh, A. P. Kinzig. 2011. "Resisting Diversity. A Long-term Archaeological Study." *Ecology & Society* 16.1, 25.

Pantelidou-Gofa, M. 2005. Τσέπι Μαραθώνος. Το Πρωτοελλαδικό Νεκροταφείο. Library of Archaeological Society at Athens 235. Athens, Archaeological Society.

Pantelidou-Gofa, M. 2008. "The EH I Deposit Pit at Tsepi, Marathon. Features, Formation and the Breakage of the Finds." In *Horizon: A Colloquium on the Prehistory of the Cyclades*, edited by N. Brodie, J. Doole, G. Gavalas and C. Renfrew, 281–289. Cambridge, McDonald Institute for Archaeological Research.

Peperaki, O. 2004. "The House of the Tiles at Lerna: Dimensions of 'Social Complexity'". In *The Emergence of Civilisation Revisited*, Sheffield Studies in Aegean Archaeology 6, edited by J. C. Barrett and P. Halstead, 214–231. Oxford, Oxbow Books.

Pullen, D. J. 1986. "A 'House of Tiles' at Zygouries? The Function of Monumental Early Helladic Architecture". *Early Helladic Architecture and Urbanization: Proceedings of a Seminar Held at the Swedish Institute in Athens, June 8, 1985*, Studies in Mediterranean Archaeology 76, edited by R. Hägg and D. Konsola, 79–84. Göteborg, P. Åström.

Pullen, D. J. 2011. "Picking out Pots in Patterns: Feasting in Early Helladic Greece". In *Our Cups Are Full: Pottery and Society in the Aegean Bronze Age: Papers Presented to Jeremy B. Rutter on the Occasion of his 65th Birthday*, British Archaeological Report S2227, edited by W. Gauß, M. Lindblom, R. A. K. Smith and J. C. Wright, 217–226. Oxford, Archaeopress.

Renfrew, C. 1972. *The Emergence of Civilisation. The Cyclades and the Aegean in the Third Millennium B.C.* London, Methuen.

Renfrew, C., M. Boyd, and C. Bronk Ramsey. 2012. "The Oldest Maritime Sanctuary? Dating the Sanctuary at Keros and the Cycladic Early Bronze Age." *Antiquity* 86, 144–160.

Rutter, J. B. 1979. *Ceramic Change in the Aegean Early Bronze Age*. University of California at Los Angeles, Institute of Archaeology, Occasional Paper 5. Los Angeles, UCLA Institute of Archaeology.

Rutter, J. B. 1982. "A Group of Distinctive Pattern-decorated Early Helladic III Pottery from Lerna and its Implications." *Hesperia* 51.4, 459–488.

Rutter, J. B. 1983. "Fine Gray-Burnished Pottery of the Early Helladic III Period. The Ancestry of Gray Minyan." *Hesperia* 52.4, 327–355.

Rutter, J. B. 1988. "Early Helladic III Vasepainting, Ceramic Regionalism, and the Influence of Basketry." In *Problems in Greek Prehistory. Papers Presented at the Centenary Conference of the British School of Archaeology at Athens, Manchester, April 1986*, edited by E. B. French and K. A. Wardle, 73–89. Bristol, Bristol Classical Press.

Rutter, J. B. 1993. "Early Helladic Pottery. Inferences about Exchange and Production from Style and Clay Composition". In *Wace and Blegen. Pottery as Evidence for Trade in the Aegean Bronze Age, 1939-1989. Proceedings of the International Conference held at the American School of Classical Studies, Athens, Dec. 2-3, 1989*, edited by C. Zerner, P. Zerner and J. Winder, 19–37. Amsterdam, Brill.

Rutter, J. B. 1995. *Lerna. A Preclassical Site in the Argolid III. The Pottery of Lerna IV.* Princeton, American School of Classical Studies at Athens.

Rutter, J. B. 2001. "Review of Aegean Prehistory II: The Prepalatial Bronze Age of the Southern and Central Greek Mainland" and "Addendum: 1993-1999" In *Aegean Prehistory: A Review*, edited by T. Cullen, 95–147 and 148–155. Boston, Archaeological Institute of America.

Rutter, J. B. 2008. "The Anatolian Roots of Early Helladic III Drinking Behaviour." In *The Aegean in the Neolithic, Chalcolithic and the Early Bronze Age, October 13th-19th 1997, Urla-İzmir (Turkey)*, edited by H. Erkanal, H. Hauptmann, V. Şahoğlu and R. Tuncel, 461–481. Ankara, Ankara University Press.

Şahoğlu, V. 2005. "The 'Anatolian Trade Network' and the Izmir Region during the Early Bronze Age." *Oxford Journal of Archaeology* 24.4, 339–361.

Schwartz, G. M. and J. J. Nichols, eds. 2006. *After Collapse. The Regeneration of Complex Societies*. Tuscon, University of Arizona Press.

Shaw, J. W. 1987. "The Early Helladic II Corridor House. Development and Form." *American Journal of Archaeology* 91.1, 59–79.

Shaw, J. W. 2007. "Sequencing the EH II 'Corridor Houses'". *Annual of the British School at Athens* 102, 137–151.

Spencer, L. 2010. "The Regional Specialisation of Ceramic Production in the EH III through MH II Period". In *Mesohelladika. The Greek Mainland in the Middle Bronze Age*, Bulletin de Correspondance Hellénique Supplement 52, edited by A. Philippa-Touchais, G. Touchais, S. Voutsaki, and J. Wright, 669–681. Athens, De Boccard.

Thomas, J. 2012. "Archaeologies of Place and Landscape". In *Archaeological Theory Today. Second Edition*, edited by I. Hodder, 167–187. Cambridge and Malden, Polity Press.

Tomkins, P. 2012. "Behind the Horizon. Reconsidering the Genesis and Function of the 'First Palace' at Knossos (Final Neolithic IV–Middle Minoan IB)". In *Back to the Beginning. Reassessing Social and*

Political Complexity on Crete during the Early and Middle Bronze Age, edited by I. Schoep, P. Tomkins and J. Driessen, 32–80. Oxford and Oakville, Oxbow Books.

Walter, H. and F. Felten. 1981. *Alt-Ägina III:1. Die vorgeschichtliche Stadt. Befestigung, Häuser, Funde*. Mainz am Rhein, Philipp von Zabern.

Weiberg, E. 2007. *Thinking the Bronze Age. Life and Death in Early Helladic Greece*. Boreas. Uppsala Studies in Mediterranean and Near Eastern Civilisations 29. Uppsala, Uppsala University.

Weiberg, E. 2010. "Pictures and People: Seals, Figurines and Peloponnesian Imagery." *Opuscula. Annual of the Swedish Institutes at Athens and Rome* 3, 187–218.

Weiberg, E. and M. Finné. 2013. "Mind or Matter? People-environment Interactions and the Demise of the Early Helladic II Society in the Northeastern Peloponnese." *American Journal of Archaeology* 107.1, 1–31.

Weiberg, E. and M. Lindblom. 2014. "The Early Helladic II–III Transition at Lerna and Tiryns Revisited. Chronological Difference or Synchronous Variability?" *Hesperia* 83.3, 383–407.

Weisshaar, H. J. 1983. "Bericht zur frühhelladischen Keramik. Ausgrabungen in Tiryns 1981." *Archäologischer Anzeiger*, 329–358.

Wiencke, M. H. 1989. "Change in Early Helladic II." *American Journal of Archaeology* 93, 495–509.

Wiencke, M. H. 2000. *Lerna. A Preclassical Site in the Argolid IV: The Architecture, Stratification, and Pottery of Lerna III*. Princeton, American School of Classical Studies at Athens.

Wiersma, C. W. 2014. *Building the Bronze Age. Architectural and Social Change on the Greek Mainland During Early Helladic III, Middle Helladic and Late Helladic I*. Oxford, Archaeopress Archaeology.

Wild, E. M., W. Gauß, G. Forstenpointner, M. Lindblom, R. Smetana, P. Steier, U. Thanheiser, and F. Weninger. 2010. "^{14}C Dating of the Early to Late Bronze Age Stratigraphic Sequence of Aegina Kolonna, Greece." *Nuclear Instruments and Methods in Physics Research Section B: Beam Interactions with Materials and Atoms* 268.7–8, 1013–1021.

Zerner, C. W. 1993. "New Perspectives on Trade in the Middle and Early Late Helladic Periods on the Mainland." In *Wace and Blegen: Pottery as Evidence for Trade in the Aegean Bronze Age, 1939-1989. Proceedings of the International Conference held at the American School of Classical Studies, Athens, Dec. 2-3, 1989*, edited by C., P. Zerner and J. Winder, 39–56. Amsterdam, Brill.

Chapter 4

Reciprocity and exchange relationships: exploring the dynamics of Bronze Age social structures through feasting and hospitality

Daniel J. Pullen

In this paper I explore three strands of research that, I hope to show, can be intertwined into a more coherent understanding of Aegean Bronze Age social structure and political economy. One of these strands is feasting, a topic that seems to be of continual fascination to archaeologists. Here I wish to introduce the concept of "hospitality" or "hosting," that is the sharing of food and/or drink with a limited number of non-kin participants, in contrast to the usual crowds one often imagines by using the term "feasting"; this concept of hospitality, I argue, has great explanatory potential for social relationships. Another strand explored is the concept of reciprocity, one of several generalizing modes of exchange, along with redistribution and market exchange, that have undergone renewed scrutiny in the last couple of years by myself and others (see Galaty *et al.* 2011; Parkinson *et al.* 2013). Consideration of reciprocity is important in that it allows us to go behind the commensality of feasting and hospitality to the social dynamics of the exchange relationships involved in these acts. The third strand is the dynamics of social organization through time, specifically from the Early Bronze Age on the mainland to the beginnings of "palatial" society in the Late Bronze Age. By intertwining these three strands I examine feasting and hospitality diachronically from the Early Helladic to the Late Helladic to identify the changing nature of the exchange relationships generated and how those are manifested in the evolution of social structure.

Feasting
The archaeological study of feasting, by which we include the actions of eating and drinking, either together or individually, has become widespread since the appearance of Dietler's 1990 examination of how the native first millennium BC Gaulic elite manipulated imported Greek drinking paraphernalia and styles into political power

(Dietler 1990; see Dietler and Hayden 2001a). Within Aegean Neolithic and Bronze Age studies there have been a number of conference volumes devoted to the topic of feasting, such as *The Mycenaean Feast* (Wright 2004a), *Food, Cuisine and Society in Prehistoric Greece* (Halstead and Barrett 2004), *Cooking up the Past* (Mee and Renard 2007), and most recently *DAIS: The Aegean Feast* (Hitchcock et al. 2008), as well as many articles and papers not included in these volumes. This is a daunting amount of scholarship to digest, but much of it does not address what to my mind is the critical issue of *how* feasting relates to the reproduction or change of social relationships that characterize the Aegean mainland during the Bronze Age.

One of the goals of this conference, "Explaining Change in Aegean Prehistory From the Early Bronze III to the Late Bronze I," was to shed new light on a chronological period that on the mainland is greatly lacking in archaeological data. As one of my goals is to examine the changing dynamics of social structure over this arc of six to seven centuries, and how feasting relates to this, I first wish to review our beginning and end points – feasting and social structure in the Early Helladic II and in Late Helladic IIIB – about which we know a bit more before trying to tackle that which went on in between. I make use of cross-cultural models that take into account regional variability, as most scholars working in the Aegean now have accepted that a single model for social, economic, and political developments that can apply to both the Greek mainland and Crete is not possible. Though feasting is a prominent component of the mortuary sphere during many periods under consideration, I limit my discussion to feasting in the sphere of the living.

In several recent articles I have tried to identify feasting in Early Helladic contexts, either indirectly or as it relates to political economy (Pullen 2011a; 2011b; 2013). Thus I identified four contexts related to eating and drinking at Tsoungiza, and one at Lerna. One critique of this identification is the small number of vessels involved in several of the deposits discussed, and how one can differentiate between feasting and household consumption. This is a critically important question: how *do* we identify feasting in the archaeological record? Is the identification of feasting a methodological problem, for example a matter of scale, or is it a theoretical issue? To me, it is a theoretical issue, in that the identification of some drinking or eating assemblages in itself does not constitute feasting; we must consider what we mean by the term, and how we operationalize it in the social realm.

There are nearly as many definitions of feasting as there are scholars writing on the topic, but a very important point was made by Dietler and Hayden in the introduction to their ground-breaking 2001 volume (Dietler and Hayden 2001a) on feasts:

> "feasts are an extremely important aspect of social life on a worldwide scale, and ... understanding them is crucial for apprehending and comprehending many social and cultural processes in ancient societies". (Dietler and Hayden 2001b, 2)

The term feasting as used in the anthropological and archaeological literature incorporates a wide range of social and cultural phenomena. While Hayden would define a feast as "any sharing between two or more people of special foods ... in a meal for a special purpose or occasion" (Hayden 2001, 28), Wright has a narrower definition of feasting that is similar to definitions of feasting by others working in the Aegean:

> "as the formal ceremony of communal eating and drinking to celebrate significant occasions. I exclude the quotidian partaking of food and drink that is carried out for biological or fundamental social reasons, such as eating with family or casually with acquaintances, friends, and colleagues – activities that do not include any perceived reciprocity". (Wright 2004c, 133)

I question Wright's restrictions excluding certain circumstances, but I would reinforce the concept of reciprocity at work in a feasting situation. Wright's definition by its very formulation restricts feasting to large-scale events, and excludes what I believe is the critical category of small-scale events or situations. For this reason I employ the term hospitality for a more inclusive approach to the social consumption of food.

Hayden (2001) and Dietler (2001) each try to grapple with defining feasting, the reasons for and benefits of feasting, and the varieties of feasting. The range of occasions for which feasting of some sort is an integral component is wide and varied. Likewise the practical benefits of feasting can also be varied; according to Hayden (2001, 29–30), feasts

1. mobilize labour;
2. create cooperative relationships within groups or, conversely, exclude other groups;
3. create cooperative alliances between social groups (including political support between households);
4. invest surpluses and generate profits;
5. attract desirable mates, labour, allies, or wealth exchanges by advertising the success of the group;
6. create political power (control over resources and labour) through the creation of a network of reciprocal debts;
7. extract surplus produce from the general populace for elite use;
8. solicit favours; and
9. compensate for transgressions.

But most feasts involve primarily social relationships, whether their creation or their maintenance (Hayden 2001, 30). Reciprocity is a key component in that creation and maintenance, and allows us to move the discussion from the realm of the description of feasting to that of the social mechanisms behind feasting.

Early Helladic II feasting

Here I can give only a brief summary of some of the Early Helladic II evidence for feasting (see Pullen 2011a; 2011b). At Tsoungiza I identified three groups of ceramic vessels, used for food or drink consumption, whose deposition suggests that they were intended to be considered together, either as a set apparently made by the same hand or as a collection of similar vessels made by more than one hand. What distinguishes these groups is their limited number of vessel types in tableware dominated by small bowls for consumption but also including serving vessels such as basins and ladles or sauceboats, and their deposition in apparently single episodes of discard. In and of themselves these three contexts with their groups of pottery do not constitute direct evidence for feasting, but along with similar arguments for the recognition of ritualized drinking sets at Lerna by Wiencke (2011, 350–351), I do believe we can see archaeologically one component of feasting, specialized service sets.

More indicative of feasting *activities* are the two arenas for feasting I identified, one at Tsoungiza (see Pullen 2011a, 218–219 for details) and the other at Lerna. At Lerna an open public space in front of Building BG of Lerna III phase C (EH IIB early; see Fig. 4.1) continues in a more formally bounded manner in front of the House of the Tiles of Lerna III phase D (EH IIB late; Fig. 4.1). In Lerna III phase C the storage and preparation of food and the storage of large quantities of tableware took place in Room DM and House CA on the south side of the public space. In both locations was found evidence for sealing of pithoi, sometimes repeatedly, and figs and grains were prominent among the botanical remains. Several of the tableware vessels in DM had potter's marks (Wiencke 2000, 434–448), but Wiencke also notes the great variety of hands involved in making the tableware in both structures (Wiencke 2000, 135, 143), as well as the presence of several vessels of old-fashioned types, suggesting accumulation over a long period of time. In Lerna III phase D we have some evidence for a diacritical dimension to feasting, that is distinctions that could mark status or rank differences. Large storage pithoi were probably located outside the House of the Tiles on the south side (Wiencke 2000, 288; Pullen 2011a, 222) where is also found the entrance to Room XI, the small storage room containing over 60 small bowls and at least five sauceboats in contemporary use, and the archive of sealings. Elsewhere in the building was found very little; indeed only one jar out of 23 storage vessel fragments was preserved substantially enough that it *might* have been in use at the time of destruction (Wiencke 2000, 471–490, and 720, table 6a–b). Wiencke notes that the Room XI assemblage comprises three groups of small bowls totaling 38 of the 60 plus bowls, each made by a single hand. One of the small bowls has a potter's mark (Wiencke 2000, 480, no. 1062), perhaps of diacritical importance. The lack of storage vessels in Room XI, despite the large number of sealings that would have been affixed to such, is problematic unless these were removed after their use and only the sealings retained to record the exchanges. Using Peperaki (2004) and Weiberg's (2007) analyses of space in and around the House of the Tiles, we note the multiple locations where feasting could occur, from the large, well-finished Room XII to the open public space in front to the balcony on the second floor overlooking the space. Weiberg (2007, 49–50) suggests that the benches built against the long north and south flanks of the House of the Tiles, along with the narrower open spaces on those two sides, could also be used for

4. Reciprocity and exchange relationships

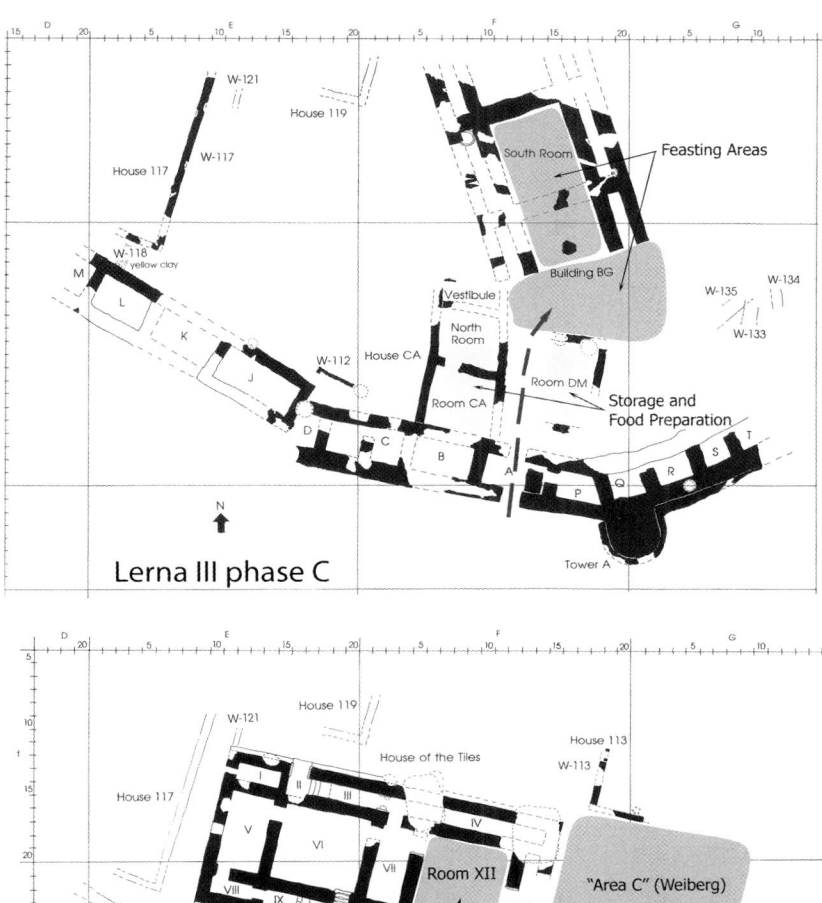

Fig. 4.1: Feasting locations at Early Helladic II Lerna (Lerna III). Top: Lerna III phase C, period of Building BG. Bottom: Lerna III phase D, period of the House of the Tiles (modified from Wiencke 2000, plans 7 and 8; courtesy of the Trustees of the American School of Classical Studies at Athens).

feasting. The large, double doorways of the House of the Tiles could be manipulated to include, exclude, or even just give a glimpse of participants in these various locations. Thus a potential diacritical dimension of feasting in Early Helladic society can be identified in the variation of seating for feasting, reinforcing the reconstruction of a ranked society. But at the same time, the large quantity of individual vessels in Room XI suggests that a large portion of the community could be feasted at one time. One wonders whether the few vessels decorated in different manners (the pot marks, the painted sauceboats) really would have stood out as another diacritical dimension; otherwise the great similarity in the vessels might indicate some equality among them.

Whereas I have suggested before that the sealings from Room XI are evidence for the participants having *contributed* towards the feasting, which is essentially following the redistributive model of exchange, I wonder whether the sealings might not be evidence of some other aspect of the gift-giving that is often a characteristic of feasting. That is, items mobilized by the sponsor of the feast from the community are recorded through the sealings, yet their presence in Room XI may be because those items have been disbursed to guests of the feast.

Mycenaean feasting

Perhaps the best known examples of feasting in the Aegean Bronze Age come from the Late Bronze Age Mycenaean palaces, especially the Palace of Nestor at Pylos with its Linear B archive as well as its archaeological record. The quantities of foodstuffs recorded are truly staggering (Nakassis 2010; Bendall 2004, 2008), and while the number of participants is never specified, it is assumed that these numbers too could be quite large, numbering even in the thousands of participants. Likewise, the quantity of ceramic vessels, presumably also for feasting, stored at the palace is quite large (Hruby 2006; 2010). The literature on Late Helladic feasts is immense, and cannot be reviewed here in any comprehensive manner, but I will discuss briefly the limited scholarship that deals with the social processes at work in these feasts.

Feasts were of great importance for the Late Helladic society and political economy, especially from the point of view of the palaces which are, of course, the source for the textual documentation. As in other areas of Mycenaean studies, there is often a myopic focus on the palace in discussions of Mycenaean feasts. Many scholars acknowledge that "banquets and festivals represented occasions for consolidation, manipulation and negotiation of social and political power" (Bendall 2008, 93), and Mycenaean feasts are seen as reinforcing the political hierarchy with the palace at the centre (Nakassis 2012, 23). Yet the mechanisms for these processes are often not discussed in any detail. Nakassis, citing Shelmerdine's important observations (2008; see also Wright 2004b, 125) that Mycenaean feasts are not all the same – they vary in scale, in location (even outside the palace), and in who provisions them – suggests that there might also be variation in the social processes and political strategies involved and argues for consideration of individual feasts (Nakassis 2012, 24). As scholars of feasting outside the Aegean have recognized, feasts are active arenas in which participants with differential access to resources create, maintain, manipulate, and legitimize social and political power through personal relationships, contributions of feasting material, and presence as consumers of the food and drink (Nakassis 2012). "Feasts and other ritualized practices," Nakassis declares, "are not merely reflections of Mycenaean political authority and society, but active forces in their creation" (Nakassis 2012, 25).

Wright (2004c) and Borgna (2004) each reconstruct the development of feasts in Mycenaean society from the Shaft Grave period through the palatial period. Both suggest that in the highly competitive early Mycenaean period, feasting and hospitality displays were exclusive and restricted to elite segments of society. Borgna, citing the evidence of vessels, especially metal ones, first found in tombs of late MH Argolid (see evidence compiled in Wright 2004c, 139, 141–143, tables 1–5), suggests that later feasting practices are founded in "the private sphere of elite social values, which emphasized generosity and hospitality in the framework of direct, reciprocal transactions" developed in the earlier periods (Borgna 2004, 261). With the emergence of more complex social stratification in the later Mycenaean period, feasting gained in importance and impacted larger groups of people in the community, whether as participants or as suppliers of food, materials, or labour. Borgna sees the large-scale feasts documented in the Linear B tablets as "instruments of social control by promoting inclusive ideological strategies and behaviour, including possibly open participation and the direct involvement of commoners" (Borgna 2004, 264), but as Wright shows, the sponsor of the feast was the big winner, for he demonstrated:

> "the ability to bring together large groups (through coalitions and alliances), to mobilize labour, and to command surplus and distribute it. The sponsor gains in prestige through these activities and advances his family, lineage, and allies both within and beyond the community". (Wright 2004c, 171)

These are good examples of the network strategies employed by the Mycenaean elites in their struggle for political power; these network strategies emphasize reciprocity in exchange relationships among the participants (see Parkinson and Galaty 2007).

This shift from more kin-related feasting of the early, Shaft-Grave period to the larger scale state-sponsored feasts of the later, palatial Mycenaean period, echoes the shifts in social structure that Sofia Voutsaki has outlined, from the "kinship economy" of early MH to the "palatial economy" in her examination of the process of political centralization in the Argolid (Voutsaki 2010). As Borgna has indicated, the key to how feasting and hospitality appeared before the Shaft Graves, and how they were utilized in social strategies, is to examine the "framework of direct, reciprocal transactions," that is reciprocal exchange relationships (Borgna 2004, 261). I now turn to the relationship between reciprocity and feasting.

Reciprocity and feasting

There are some allusions in the literature dealing with Aegean feasting besides Borgna and Wright to the processes by which alliances are generated, and the role feasting plays in these. Reciprocity is occasionally mentioned, but with few details provided. Indeed overall in Aegean studies there is a surprising lack of interest in reciprocity, despite the great interest in the subject on the part of Homeric scholars. Reciprocity has seen much less attention by Aegean archaeologists than other economic concepts such as redistribution, largely because of an assumption that reciprocity is characteristic of "egalitarian" or less developed societies and a related interest in political economies of more complex (palatial) societies assumed to be characterized by redistribution (see the articles in Parkinson *et al.* 2011). In Aegean archaeology consideration of reciprocity is usually limited to gift-exchange, either royal in the context of Late Bronze Age interactions with other societies in the eastern Mediterranean, or among elites in a Homeric model. For example, the chapter on the Aegean Bronze Age in the 2007 *Cambridge Economic History of the Greco-Roman World* (Bennet 2007) does not even mention the word "reciprocity"; "gift-exchange," the usual substitute (but not equivalent) expression, is mentioned once in the context of the Amarna tablets recording exchanges between political units. Yet reciprocity has great potential in understanding political economies and social organization of the Late Bronze Age Aegean.

Reciprocity is part of the larger concept of exchange within the discussion of political economy and social organization, and incorporates more than the concept of gift-exchange as generally used in Aegean archaeology. Reciprocity encompasses the social dynamics of any exchange between individuals and how these social relationships form the structure of social organization. The anthropological study of exchange began with Marcel Mauss' 1924 *Essai sur le don*, or *The Gift* in English (1924; 1990), in which he distinguished between gift-exchange, which establishes a social relationship between the participants, and commodity-exchange, in which the relationship is between the objects exchanged in a price-forming process. A gift creates a debt that must at some point be repaid; thus a gift-economy is a debt economy, and the object is to acquire gift-debtors, not a profit in the commercial sense (Gregory 1982, 19). One critical aspect of the exchange of gifts is the obligation to do so, and it is through these obligations that social relations of control and dominance emerge. Since Mauss the study of exchange (see Gregory 1982 for one of the most important discussions of gifts and commodities since Mauss), and especially the gift, has been of great interest to anthropologists such as Lévi-Strauss, who focused on the exchange of people in *Les Structures élémentaires de la parenté* (Lévi-Strauss 1949), and Marshall Sahlins.

Sahlins' (1972) *Stone Age Economics* is credited with formulating exchange not as a binary distinction between gifts and commodities, but rather as continuum of reciprocity with the axes of social or kinship distance and time elapsed between exchanges. It is this formulation that has had profound effect on archaeological studies of exchange. Sahlins (1972, 191–196) distinguishes three points on his continuum of reciprocity:

- generalized reciprocity, wherein the gift (or service) is given without the expectation of an immediate return or of one of equal value; thus there is a gift-debt incurred through gift-exchange;
- balanced reciprocity, wherein the obligation is immediately discharged or the return is of equal value; this is often equated with commodity exchange;
- negative reciprocity, wherein one "attempts to get something for nothing".

It is this last endpoint of the continuum that has seen modification by several scholars to a situation in which "the benefit accrues to only one participant in the exchange" (Lyons 2012, 13). Roller introduces the concept of hostile reciprocity whereby "the recipient may not want the object or service given, or its accompanying social obligation, nor may the giver always bestow a gift with the recipient's good in view" (Roller 2001, 133). Thus hostile reciprocity retains an element of personal relationship, whereas negative reciprocity according to Sahlins is impersonal. Another dimension to reciprocity that more recent work has drawn attention to is that of competitive generosity, as seen, for example, in the potlatch of some North American societies.

Of particular interest for me is how these standard categories of reciprocity, that is generalized (gift-exchange), balanced (trade or immediate discharge of debt), and negative (one-sided benefit), are manipulated through strategies such as competitive generosity and asymmetrical exchanges, leading to indebtedness of one exchange partner to the other, and how this indebtedness can be institutionalized into hierarchical social structures. Feasting plays a major role in many of these exchanges.

It is surprising how much more common the study of reciprocity is in Iron Age, Classical and Roman studies (*e.g.*, Lyons 2012; Gill *et al.* 1998; Roller 2001). Gift-giving is a central element in the construction of a Homeric hero and his interactions, often through feasting, with his peers and his leader (as in the case of Achilles and Agamemnon: Postlethwaite 1998; see articles in Gill *et al.* 1998). This is not the place to analyse the use of reciprocity in Homeric and Classical studies (see Cook 2016), but I do want to examine one of the most studied systems of reciprocity employed in the amassing of social and political power that we know of from the ancient world: the patronage system of Rome.

Patronage in Rome is again another large topic, and I cannot claim expertise in this field, but I find the reanalysis by Matthew Roller (Roller 2001) of patronage in terms of reciprocal exchange relationships to be very compelling. Not only does he show how exchange relationships are central to the establishment and maintenance of social relationships, in particular those relationships where power or status is unequal (Roller 2001, 130), but he does so within the context of the *convivium*, the Roman banquet or dinner party, arguing that this was the arena where power relationships were negotiated through a set of exchanges at all stages of the *convivium*

(Roller 2001, 134). As Roller notes, Roman writers describe the exchanges and their consequences in terms of the relationships between pairs of individuals (Roller 2001, 131 n. 1), giving us an agency-based account of power relationships in these exchanges.

Roller focuses on exchange rather than patronage in its classical sense, pointing to Saller's definition of patronage as:

> "ongoing personal relationships between social unequals, which are established and reproduced through the reciprocal exchange of goods and services; moreover, this exchange is typically asymmetrical, with the socially dominant party giving more than he receives". (Saller 1982, 1, picked up by Wallace-Hadrill 1989a, 3–4; Konstan 1995, 328; see Roller 2001, 130)

Such definitions that remove the terms patron and client, and all their accompanying baggage, from the discussion and focus instead on the exchanges and their transactors allow for analysis of other exchanges such as those that emphasize the ideological importance of not forming hierarchical relationships as well as instances in which exchanges are declined or resisted (hostile reciprocity as outlined above). A gift creates or reinforces a personal relationship between the two participants, but more specifically, it imposes a gift-debt, that is the obligation on the part of the recipient at some later time (but not immediately) to give a gift to the original giver. Most critically, the gift debt of the recipient makes the recipient inferior to the giver, and potentially subservient in social and political power (Roller 2001, 132). Only upon reciprocation at a level equal to or greater than the original gift can the gift-debt and consequent subordination be absolved.

As Roller (2001, 135–146) reconstructs it, the Roman *convivium* was the "arena in which social distinctions and power relations are established, confirmed, or challenged," all through dynamics of gift-exchange. This gift-exchange is actually a series of offerings and counter-offerings, beginning with the issuance of an invitation, its acceptance or rejection, the arrival, treatment, and placement of guests, the types of food and drink offered and to whom, and the presents given and received by the host. "A dinner invitation from a superior can reciprocate a wide variety of objects and services offered by an inferior," chief among them is subordination (Roller 2001, 137), and a higher status guest can confer the greater benefit by accepting the hospitality of a lower status host. These are but a few of the gift-exchange strategies employed by Romans in their competition for social and political power, but I maintain they are excellent demonstrations of the possibilities for using feasting and hospitality to acquire social and political power.

EH III hospitality and reciprocity

In returning to the Aegean Bronze Age I want to introduce the concept of hospitality, modelling it in part on the dynamics of the Roman system of reciprocity. As discussed previously, much of the Late Bronze Age feasting is focused on large-scale, palatial feasting. Though scale is one criterion often used in Aegean archaeology, and usually with the implication that feasting is large in scale, Jeremy Rutter has suggested that small-scale (*i.e.*, beyond the immediate family) consumption by a limited number of participants, even by as few as two individuals, can be indicative of the social consumption of food or drink, when utilizing specialized vessels or in certain definable contexts. This fits in very well with the anthropological concept of feasting, as well as the Roman *convivium*. Ultimately we must remember that feasting, the communal consumption of food and drink, and hospitality, the sharing of food and drink among a limited number of participants, are *social* activities that involve the social dynamics of exchange between individuals beyond the bounds of the immediate kin group.

At Lerna IV in the EH III period, Rutter (2008) has identified an EH III drinking assemblage that consists of very large, usually highly decorated containers in only two shapes, the narrow-necked jar, sometimes with three necks, and the shoulder-handled tankard, and very small drinking vessels usually plain or simply decorated (Fig. 4.2). The decoration of the narrow-necked jars in the earlier portion of Lerna IV (phases 1 and 2) combines pattern-painted decoration and relief bands that can form curvilinear elements, while in the later portion of Lerna IV (phase 3) they are decorated with one mode or the other. The lower half of the large narrow-necked jars is painted on the interior. The large tankards, appearing in the earlier portion of Lerna IV have only pattern-painted decoration, and are replaced by giant kantharoi in the later portion of Lerna IV. When these vessels appear in bothroi, there is only one restorable giant example, in addition to a few normal sized mendable pots (Rutter 2008, 463). More informative are buildings W-52 (Banks 2013, 114–122) and W-84 (Banks 2013, 154–158), both of Lerna IV phase 2, in which examples of these giant vessels are found with other vessels (see Fig. 4.3 for locations).

From an earlier phase of structure W-52 came a giant tankard and the famous triple-neck "Hydra of Lerna," small tankards (in lieu of the standard ouzo drinking cup), and pairs of shapes such as askoi, pyxides, smaller narrow-necked jars, and sets of small tankards (Rutter 2008, 464). Slightly later, the odd apse-shaped building W-84 was also destroyed by fire and an even larger deposit was found, apparently originally housed on shelves. Several giant vessels, including two pairs of narrow-necked jars, were found, as well as a quantity of drinking vessels such as ouzo cups and rim-handled cups (as opposed to the small tankards of W-52). There seem to be only four small cups for every large container. Pithoi were found, but cooking pottery and bowls were very rare, unlike regular domestic contexts. Of particular interest are the few examples of Lefkandi I vessel types (Rutter 2008, 465).

This EH III drinking assemblage, then, consists of these very large, usually highly decorated containers in only two shapes (narrow-necked jars and shoulder-handled tankards), and very small drinking vessels (ouzo cups, rim-handled cups, or small tankards), usually plain or simply decorated (Fig. 4.2). Apparently not part of this EH III drinking assemblage are jugs, askoi, strainers, and dippers; when jugs and askoi do appear with the assemblage they are usually plain, not decorated. Rutter draws attention to the near lack of these highly decorated giant vessels and ouzo cups in central Greece, yet their occurrence at nearly all sites in the northern Peloponnese

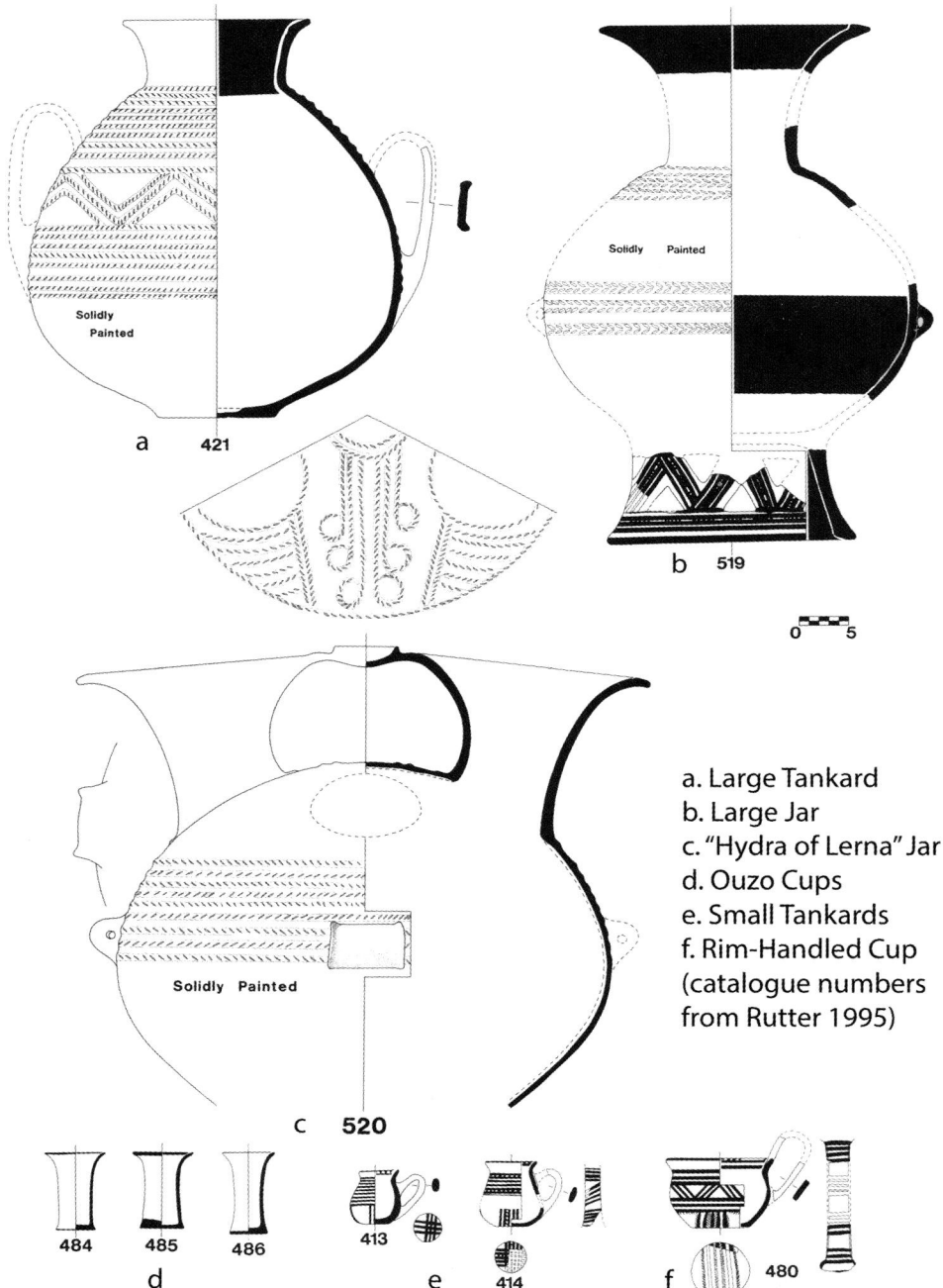

Fig. 4.2: Early Helladic III drinking assemblage vessel types: a) large tankard; b) large jar; c) the "Hydra of Lerna" large jar; d) ouzo cups; e) small tankards; f) rim-handled cup (catalogue numbers and illustrations from Rutter 1995; courtesy of the Trustees of the American School of Classical Studies at Athens).

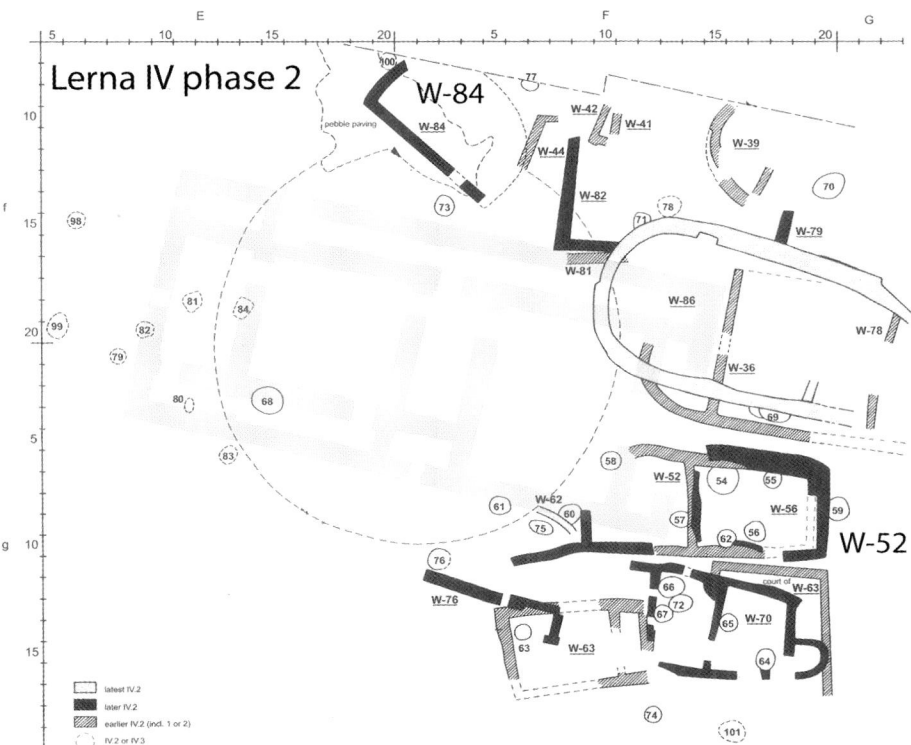

Fig. 4.3: Locations of drinking assemblages at Early Helladic III Lerna (Lerna IV phase 2) (modified from Banks 2013, plan 16; courtesy the Trustees of the American School of Classical Studies at Athens).

and Aigina (Rutter 2008, 466). He links this EH III Peloponnesian drinking assemblage with the eastern Aegean through the derivation of the small cups from prototypes found in western Anatolia and northeastern Aegean; the multiple thin taenia bands in curvilinear and horizontal patterns deriving from Kastri Group practices in EH IIB; and the parallels of the triple-necked "Hydra of Lerna" with the quadruple-necked vessels from Karataş Semayük and Aphrodisias in southwestern Anatolia (Rutter 2008, 466). The liquid consumed is unknown, but wine, some type of fermented barley drink, or even beer has been proposed. Banks (2013, 120) doubts that the liquid consumed from the "Hydra" was wine or other grape-derived liquid, due to the lack of grape finds before late Lerna IV.3,[1] and suggests some liquid fermented from barley, plentiful quantities of which were found on the floor of W-52. Rutter (2008, 468) too, while accepting the possibility of wine, suggests some other distilled beverage, noting that the pithoi in building W-84 suggest long-term storage of wine or distilled liquids, and

---

[1] Note that modern flotation techniques were not used to recover organic materials during the excavations at Lerna, and grape finds would be preserved only if subjected to fire, a rare situation unlike for cereals.

the absence of strainers, and precludes short term fermented liquids such as beer. And, he suggests that instead of the straws used in Mesopotamian or traditional African cultures, the small cups were used because of the potency of the liquid.

Rutter (2008, 469) builds on these contexts and the relative quantities of the limited shapes to suggest that perhaps there were only two participants in the drinking ceremony represented by these vessels, a host and a guest. The pairing of identical vessel forms, but not in fact identical in decoration, in these deposits is also suggestive of a ritual involving only two. But whether indeed there are two or four individuals involved, the most important point is that the elaborate drinking ritual is limited to only a few participants, and is not meant to be community-wide as perhaps was the case in EH II. By many definitions of feasting used in the Aegean this drinking activity at Lerna IV would not be included, yet it features virtually all the usual criteria except for scale. For this reason I wish to use the term hospitality to reinforce the social nature of the drinking activity represented here. In contrast to the more communal-oriented feasting that may be characteristic of EH II, in EH III we see pairs of individuals in a reciprocal exchange of hosting and guesting. Would some of the pairs of vessels be split and one portion given to the guest upon his departure, only to form a new pair back at his home? The elaborate decoration of the vessels, without direct duplication, might suggest that each vessel was unique, was identifiable by its patterning, and given as part of reciprocal exchange at a drinking ritual; the vessel was thus imbued with special significance, with a narrative if you would, and its discard was carefully controlled in a bothros along with other similar vessels.

Feasting and reciprocity in the Middle Helladic

While we have little direct evidence for feasting in the Middle Helladic period, the pairing of vessels has been identified by Nordquist (1999) as a part of the social behaviour of eating and drinking, with an emphasis on drinking by a limited number of participants. In particular she notes that often these pairs of vessels were not identical, similar to the situation of the pairs of vessels at Lerna in EH III. In the MH period, groups of drinking vessels are found in the tombs of both males and females, as well as in the tombs of children and even infants, pointing to an elite ideology of social drinking behaviour and the ability to host or sponsor a drinking event. In other words, hospitality is reinforced in the elite ideology as a proper social behaviour. In the later MH there is an increase in the numbers of vessels (almost always in multiples of two) found in graves, but these later tombs tend to have multiple burials and are extramural. Nordquist argues, on the basis of this development in the mortuary context, for an increasing emphasis on group identity, especially of an elite of "socially defined upper class" (Nordquist 2002, 133). These MH drinking ceremonies and rituals were part of the symbolic behaviour of the elite that was amplified in the Late Helladic period; whereas the EH and (earlier) MH drinking rituals may have been small scale, perhaps even just between two people, by the palatial period they were large scale

(Nordquist 1999, 572–573). The presence of larger groups of drinking vessels in rich late MH graves is seen by Nordquist to be "an intermediate stage, when individuals of the elite are attempting to extend their social and political influence over larger groups of the population, retainers, or clients" (Nordquist 1999, 573), a conclusion similar to those of Borgna and Voutsaki discussed above.

Thus we see in the later MH period a situation whereby the old guest-host relationship of two individuals in a drinking ritual (such as we see in EH III) is expanded to larger scale drinking and feasting within an elite ideology as a means for that elite to extend social and political power. The addition of metal vessels to the mortuary sphere, as seen in the Shaft Graves at Mycenae, reinforces the importance of feasting, and especially drinking, for early Mycenaean society, in not only increasing the scale of hospitality but also more prominently marking distinctions among the participants.

Manipulation of reciprocity is a key component in this transformation of the guest-host relationship in the emergence of elite power in early Mycenaean society. As a gift-debt is incurred in a guest-host relationship between two persons, a person who can maintain multiple guest-host relationships, resulting in multiple gift-debt obligations to him or her, will accrue increased social standing, economic power, and political influence. As in the case of the Roman *convivium*, by making it nearly impossible to reciprocate at the same level, for instance, by using metal drinking vessels as seen in the Shaft Graves, the host can transform the multiple gift-debt obligations into social and political power by making the guests his subordinates, as they cannot reciprocate in the same manner. Instead, the indebted guest reciprocates through pledging loyalty, support, or fealty to the host.

Michael Lindblom (2007) has drawn our attention to the large quantity of ceramics, with a very high frequency of Aeginetan painted pottery, in the fill of the two LH I Shaft Graves at Lerna. He suggests that these are the remains of funerary meals attended by hundreds of participants, a part of the long history of hospitality in the MH period as discussed above. More specifically, Lindblom argues that the deliberate destruction of so many Aeginetan vessels (along with other vessels at the mortuary feast) is an ostentatious display of the social and economic connections of the deceased (and his family) with exchange networks outside of the Argolid, namely with Kolonna, perhaps the largest and most important polity outside of Neopalatial Crete at this time (Gauß 2010). The family of the deceased buried in the Shaft Graves at Lerna emphasized their knowledge of the outside world (undoubtedly through maritime capabilities), their connections with elites from elsewhere, and their ability to amass hundreds of foreign objects, but did so within the traditional setting of the funerary feast that "emphasized continuity, reciprocity, hosting, and feast provision" (Lindblom 2007, 126). Lindblom also argues that the funerary feast reinforced the social obligations of the guests and hosts, and perhaps was even the setting to recognize the transferral of rights in these obligations to an heir, in a precursor to the political offices recognized in the later Mycenaean period (Lindblom 2007, 126).

The importance to elites of the late MH and Shaft Grave period in mainland Greece of establishing contacts with foreign elites has recently been emphasized by Steel (2013), who argues that the elites at Mycenae in particular were attempting to participate in the exchange networks of the eastern Mediterranean world, whether directly or through intermediaries (Steel 2013, 50–63; see also Parkinson 2010, the papers in Parkinson and Galaty 2009, and Burns 2010 for the importance of long distance exchange networks for the development of Aegean Bronze Age states). These long distance connections are the source not only for raw materials and exotic goods, but also for new social practices and ideas, all of which provide the local elites with prestige, social and cultural capital as they strive to distinguish themselves from others (Steel 2013, 52). Of particular relevance here is Steel's reiteration of the importance for creating social relationships through gift exchange in its many forms, how events of ceremonial and other exchanges involve feasting or drinking, and how hospitality and generosity play roles in that feasting and drinking.

Conclusions

With this model of reciprocity in the EH III–early LH period through drinking rituals and gifting we can see how social relationships would be formed, and how they could be manipulated into asymmetrical relationships of power dominance through strategies of competitive exchange and gift-debt. But at the same time, the *lack* of a clear hierarchy in EH III society (*e.g.*, Banks 2013, 355, 367; Wiersma 2013, 243–244) suggests a strong egalitarian ideology at work to counter asymmetrical exchange relationships. As suggested above, the (re-) introduction of metal vessels later in the MH period coincides with the emergence of elite families and powerful individuals, leading to the inclusion of these metal vessels in burials of individuals who have succeeded in establishing their power through reciprocal relationships with others as a signal of that success. In a similar manner, the large quantities of imported Aeginetan pottery discarded at the funeral represent the successful forging of exchange relationships by the elite with foreign elites.

Voutsaki has argued that there is little evidence of differentiation in either the mortuary sphere or the domestic sphere within MH I–II settlements in the Argolid (Voutsaki 2010, 91). She notes that there is, however, more manufactured or imported goods in settlements than in cemeteries, and suggests these manufactured and imported items were meant to circulate among households within the settlement, and not be accumulated by one individual or family and deposited in houses or tombs. Especially noteworthy is that imported pottery appears in most households at Asine without a concentration in any particular one, indicating that, as Voutsaki puts it, people "acquired pottery in order to exchange" (Voutsaki 2010, 92), and that the maintenance of exchange relationships both within the community and outside was what mattered. Thus, Voutsaki argues, material culture was not used to construct status or other differences among individuals, and instead social organization was based on kin relationships. The pairing of vessels in EH III and MH drinking rituals as outlined above fits well with this argument. This did not prevent individuals, or more likely their kin groups, from attempting to promote themselves through manipulation of exchange relations but these were not leveraged into permanent structures of dominance and status differentiation (Voutsaki 2010, 91–92 gives the example of the Minoan storage jars around Lerna House 98A). Wiersma (2013, 243–247), too, argues for a lack of clear hierarchical distinctions between houses throughout the EH III and earlier MH periods.

By the time of the Shaft Graves, though, it is clear that some kin groups in the Argolid were able to leverage these exchange relationships into great wealth and status differentiation, and the burial or destruction of this wealth in ostentatious ways was a "key weapon in social competition" (Voutsaki 2010, 96–97; also Lindblom 2007). It is surely significant that an important component of this wealth was vessels, both metal and imported ceramic, connected with feasting, as Wright and Lindblom have shown (Wright 2004c, 139–144, tables 1–6; Lindblom 2007). This evidence also indicates that feasting, wealth acquisition, and ostentatious display were most likely restricted to elite kin groups throughout the Argolid, and perhaps primarily at Mycenae. The hosting of drinking events or feasts with a display of conspicuous consumption is a way for an individual to demonstrate his wealth, power, status, and prestige, or at least his claims to such, by manipulating exchanges into a series of asymmetrical relationships. The institutionalization of these asymmetrical relationships, in the form of gift-debts of obligations, resulted in the stratified society we know of from the Linear B tablets of the Mycenaean palaces.

Acknowledgements

I would like to thank Corien Wiersma and Sofia Voutsaki for the invitation to the conference "Explaining Change in Aegean Prehistory From the Early Bronze III to the Late Bronze I," and for the hospitality shown to us during our time in Groningen. I would also like to thank Dimitri Nakassis, Jeremy Rutter, and Erika Weiberg for their comments on this paper.

Bibliography

Banks, E. C. 2013. *Lerna VI: The Settlement and Architecture of Lerna IV*. Princeton, American School of Classical Studies at Athens.

Bendall, L. M. 2004. "Fit for a King? Hierarchy, Exclusion, Aspiration and Desire in the Social Structure of Mycenaean Banqueting." In *Food, Cuisine and Society in Prehistoric Greece*, Sheffield Studies in Aegean Archaeology 5, edited by P. Halstead and J. C. Barrett, 105–135. Oxford, Oxbow.

Bendall, L. M. 2008. "How Much Makes a Feast? Amounts of Banqueting Foodstuffs in the Linear B Records of Pylos." In *Colloquium Romanum. Atti del XII colloquio internazionale di micenologia, Roma, 20-25 febbraio 2006*, Pasiphae 1, edited by A. Sacconi, M. Del Freo, L. Godart, and M. Negri, 77–101. Rome, Fabrizio Serra.

Bennet, J. 2007. "The Aegean Bronze Age." In *The Cambridge Economic History of the Greco-Roman World*, edited by W. Scheidel, I. Morris, and R. Saller, 175–210. Cambridge, Cambridge University Press.

Borgna, E. 2004. "Aegean Feasting: A Minoan Perspective." In *The Mycenaean Feast. Papers of a Colloquium at the General Meeting of the Archaeological Institute of America, Philadelphia, January 2001*, Hesperia 73, 2, edited by J. C. Wright, 127–159. Princeton, American School of Classical Studies at Athens.

Burns, B. E. 2010. *Mycenaean Greece, Mediterranean Commerce, and the Formation of Identity*. Cambridge, Cambridge University Press.

Cook, E. 2016. "Homeric Reciprocities." In Reciprocity in Aegean Palatial Societies: Gifts, Debt, and the Foundations of Economic Exchange, edited by D. Nakassis, M. L. Galaty, and W. A. Parkinson. *Journal of Mediterranean Archaeology* 29.1, 94–104.

Dietler, M. 1990. "Driven by Drink: The Role of Drinking in the Political Economy and the Case of Early Iron Age France." *Journal of Anthropological Archaeology* 9, 352–406.

Dietler, M. 2001. "Theorizing the Feast: Rituals of Consumption, Commensal Politics, and Power in African Contexts." In *Feasts: Archaeological and Ethnographical Perspectives on Food, Politics, and Power*, edited by M. Dietler and B. Hayden, 65–114. Washington, Smithsonian Institution Press.

Dietler, M., and B. Hayden, eds. 2001a. *Feasts: Archaeological and Ethnographical Perspectives on Food, Politics, and Power*. Washington, Smithsonian Institution Press.

Dietler, M., and B. Hayden. 2001b. "Digesting the Feast–Good to Eat, Good to Drink, Good to Think: An Introduction." In *Feasts: Archaeological and Ethnographical Perspectives on Food, Politics, and Power*, edited by M. Dietler and B. Hayden, 1–20. Washington, Smithsonian Institution Press.

Galaty, M. L., D. Nakassis, and W. A. Parkinson, eds. 2011. "Redistribution in Aegean Palatial Societies." *American Journal of Archaeology* 115, 175–244.

Gauß, W. 2010. "Aegina Kolonna." In *The Oxford Handbook of the Bronze Age Aegean*, edited by E. H. Cline, 737–751. Oxford, Oxford University Press.

Gill, C., N. Postlethwaite, and R. Seaford, eds. 1998. *Reciprocity in Ancient Greece*. Oxford, Oxford University Press.

Gregory, C. A. 1982. *Gifts and Commodities*. London, Academic Press.

Halstead, P., and J. C. Barrett, eds. 2004. *Food, Cuisine, and Society in Prehistoric Greece*, Sheffield Studies in Aegean Archaeology 5. Oxford, Oxbow Books.

Hayden, B. 2001. "Fabulous Feasts: A Prolegomenon to the Importance of Feasting." In *Feasts: Archaeological and Ethnographical Perspectives on Food, Politics, and Power*, edited by M. Dietler and B. Hayden, 23–64. Washington, Smithsonian Institution Press.

Hitchcock, L. A., R. Laffineur, and J. Crowley, eds. 2008. *DAIS: The Aegean Feast. Proceedings of the 12th International Aegean Conference, University of Melbourne, Centre for Classics and Archaeology, 25-29 March 2008*, Aegaeum 29. Liège, University of Liège, Department of Art History and Archaeology of Ancient Greece.

Hruby, J. 2006. *Feasting and Ceramics: A View from the Palace of Nestor at Pylos*. Ph.D. dissertation, University of Cincinnati.

Hruby, J. 2010. "Mycenaean Pottery from Pylos: An Indigenous Typology." *American Journal of Archaeology* 114, 195–216.

Konstan, D. 1995. "Patrons and Friends." *Classical Philology* 90, 328–342.

Lévi-Straus, C. 1949. *Les Structures élémentaires de la parenté*. Paris, Presses universitaires de France.

Lindblom, M. 2007. "Early Mycenaean Mortuary Meals at Lerna VI with Special Emphasis on their Aeginetan Components." In *Middle Helladic Pottery and Synchronisms. Proceedings of the International Workshop held at Salzburg October 31st-November 2nd, 2004*, Ägina-Kolonna Forschungen und Ergebnisse I/Österreichische Akademie der Wissenschaften Denkschriften der Gesamtakademie 42, edited by F. Felten, W. Gauß, and R. Smetana, 115–135. Vienna, Austrian Academy of Sciences.

Lyons, D. J. 2012. *Dangerous Gifts: Gender and Exchange in Ancient Greece*. Austin, University of Texas Press.

Mauss, M. 1924. "Essai sur le don. Forme et raison de l'échange dans les sociétés archaïques." *L'Année Sociologique* (nouvelle série) 1, 30–186.

Mauss, M. 1990. *The Gift: The Form and Reason for Exchange in Archaic Societies*, trans. by W. D. Halls, foreword by M. Douglas. London, Routledge.

Mee, C., and J. Renard, eds. 2007. *Cooking up the Past: Food and Culinary Practices in the Neolithic and Bronze Age Aegean.* Oxford, Oxbow Books.

Nakassis, D. 2010. "Reevaluating Staple and Wealth Finance at Mycenaean Pylos." In *Political Economies of the Aegean Bronze Age: Papers from the Langford Conference, Florida State University, Tallahassee, 22-24 February 2007*, edited by D. J. Pullen, 127-48. Oxford, Oxbow Books.

Nakassis, D. 2012. "Prestige and Interest: Feasting and the King at Mycenaean Pylos." *Hesperia* 81, 1-30.

Nordquist, G., 1999. "Pairing of Pots in the Middle Helladic Period." In *Meletemata. Studies in Aegean Archaeology presented to Malcolm H. Wiener as he enters his 65th year*, Aegaeum 20, edited by P. P. Betancourt, V. Karageorghis, R. Laffineur, and W.-D. Niemeier, vol. 2, 569-573. Liège/Austin. University of Texas at Austin.

Nordquist, G. 2002. "Pots, Prestige, and People. Symbolic Action in Middle Helladic Burials." *Opuscula Atheniensia Annual of the Swedish Institute at Athens* 27, 119-135.

Parkinson, W. A. 2010. "Beyond the Peer: Social Interaction and Political Evolution in the Bronze Age Aegean." In *Political Economies of the Aegean Bronze Age, Papers from the Langford Conference, Florida State University, Tallahassee, 22-24 February 2007*, edited by D. J. Pullen, 11-34. Oxford, Oxbow Books.

Parkinson, W. A., and M. L. Galaty. 2007. "Secondary States in Perspective: An Integrated Approach to State Formation in the Prehistoric Aegean." *American Anthropologist* 109, 113-129.

Parkinson, W. A., and M. L. Galaty, eds. 2009. *Archaic State Interaction: The Eastern Mediterranean in the Bronze Age.* Santa Fe, SAR Press.

Parkinson, W. A., D. Nakassis, and M. L. Galaty, eds. 2013. Crafts, Specialists, and Markets in Mycenaean Greece. *American Journal of Archaeology* 117, 413-459.

Peperaki, O. 2004. "The House of the Tiles at Lerna: Dimensions of 'Social Complexity'." In *The Emergence of Civilisation Revisited*, Sheffield Studies in Aegean Archaeology 6, edited by J. C. Barrett and P. Halstead, 214-231. Oxford, Oxbow Books.

Postlethwaite, N. 1998. "Akhilleus and Agamemnon: Generalized Reciprocity." In *Reciprocity in Ancient Greece*, edited by C. Gill, N. Postlethwaite, and R. Seaford, 93-104. Oxford, Oxford University Press.

Pullen, D. J. 2011a. "Picking out Pots in Patterns: Feasting in Early Helladic Greece." In *Our Cups Are Full: Pottery and Society in the Aegean Bronze Age. Papers presented to Jeremy B. Rutter on the occasion of his 65th birthday*, British Archaeological Report S2227, edited by W. Gauß, M. Lindblom, R. A. K. Smith, and J. C. Wright, 217-226. Oxford, Archaeopress.

Pullen, D. J. 2011b. "Before the Palaces: Redistribution and Chiefdoms in Mainland Greece." In Redistribution in Aegean Palatial Societies, edited by D. Nakassis, W. A. Parkinson, and M. L. Galaty, *American Journal of Archaeology* 115, 185-195.

Pullen, D. J. 2013. "'Minding the Gap:' Bridging the Gaps in Cultural Change Within the Early Bronze Age Aegean." *American Journal of Archaeology* 117, 545-553.

Roller, M. B. 2001. *Constructing Autocracy: Aristocrats and Emperors in Julio-Claudian Rome.* Princeton, Princeton University Press.

Rutter, J. B. 2008. "The Anatolian Roots of Early Helladic III Drinking Behaviour." In *The Aegean in the Neolithic, Chalcolithic and the Early Bronze Age: Proceedings of the International Symposium, Urla-Izmir, October 13-19, 1997*, Ankara University Research Center for Maritime Archaeology Publication 1, edited by H. Erkanal, H. Hauptmann, V. Şahoğlu, and R. Tuncel, 461-481. Ankara, Ankara University Press.

Sahlins, M. D. 1972. *Stone Age Economics.* Chicago, Aldine.

Saller, R. P. 1982. *Personal Patronage under the Early Empire.* Cambridge, Cambridge University Press.

Shelmerdine, C. W. 2008. "Host and Guest at a Mycenaean Feast." In *DAIS: The Aegean Feast. Proceedings of the 12th International Aegean Conference, University of Melbourne, Centre for Classics and Archaeology, 25-29 March 2008*, Aegaeum 29, edited by L. A. Hitchcock, R. Laffineur, and J. Crowley, 401-410. Liège, University of Liège, Department of Art History and Archaeology of Ancient Greece.

Steel, L. 2013. *Materiality and Consumption in the Bronze Age Mediterranean*. Routledge Studies in Archaeology 7. New York and London, Routledge.

Voutsaki, S. 2010. "From the Kinship Economy to the Palatial Economy: The Argolid in the Second Millennium BC." In *Political Economies of the Aegean Bronze Age: Papers from the Langford Conference, Florida State University, Tallahassee, 22-24 February 2007*, edited by D. J. Pullen, 86–111. Oxford, Oxbow Books.

Wallace-Hadrill, A., ed. 1989. *Patronage in Ancient Society*. London, Routledge.

Weiberg, E. 2007. *Thinking the Bronze Age. Life and Death in Early Helladic Greece* In *Boreas, Uppsala Studies in Ancient Mediterranean and Near Eastern Civilisations.* Acta Universitatis Upsaliensis 29. Uppsala, Uppsala University.

Wiencke, M. H. 2000. *Lerna IV: The Architecture, Stratification and Pottery of Lerna III*. Princeton, American School of Classical Studies at Athens.

Wiencke, M. H. 2011. "Ceremonial Lerna." In *Our Cups Are Full: Pottery and Society in the Aegean Bronze Age. Papers presented to Jeremy B. Rutter on the occasion of his 65th birthday*, British Archaeological Report S2227, edited by W. Gauß, M. Lindblom, R. A. K. Smith, and J. C. Wright, 345–354. Oxford, Archaeopress.

Wiersma, C. W. 2014. *Building the Bronze Age. Architectural and Social Change on the Greek Mainland During Early Helladic III, Middle Helladic and Late Helladic I*. Oxford, Archaeopress Archaeology.

Wright, J. C., ed. 2004a. *The Mycenaean Feast. Papers of a Colloquium at the General Meeting of the Archaeological Institute of America, Philadelphia, January 2001*, Hesperia 73, 2. Princeton, American School of Classical Studies at Athens.

Wright, J. C. 2004b. "The Mycenaean Feast: An Introduction." In *The Mycenaean Feast. Papers of a Colloquium at the General Meeting of the Archaeological Institute of America, Philadelphia, January 2001*, Hesperia 73.2, edited by J. C. Wright, 121–132. Princeton, American School of Classical Studies at Athens.

Wright, J. C. 2004c. "A Survey of Evidence for Feasting in Mycenaean Society." In *The Mycenaean Feast. Papers of a Colloquium at the General Meeting of the Archaeological Institute of America, Philadelphia, January 2001*, Hesperia 73.2, edited by J. C. Wright, 133–178. Princeton, American School of Classical Studies at Athens.

Chapter 5

Domestic architecture: a means to analyse social change on the Bronze Age Greek mainland

Corien Wiersma

In the past decades an increasing scholarly interest has been expressed in domestic architecture (Nanoglou 2001; 2008; Souvatzi 2008; Glowacki and Vogeikoff-Brogan 2011), as well as the Middle Helladic period (*e.g.* Voutsaki 2005; Philippa-Touchais *et al.* 2010). For several reasons, the domestic architecture of the Early Helladic III, Middle Helladic and early Late Helladic periods has received only little attention. EH III and MH architecture is a few times generally discussed in the context of overviews of architectural developments, whereby the overall impression is that houses as well as the social organization were of a simple nature (*e.g.* Overbeck 1963; Sinos 1971; Pullen 1985; Werner 1993). Indeed, compared to the EH II period, which could boast a few settlements with monumental architecture such as defensive structures and/or "Corridor houses", the domestic architecture of the EH III and MH periods has been considered and dismissed as simple.

However, although the EH III and MH societies did not produce complex architecture, this does not necessarily also imply that social relationships were simple and did not develop over time. Evidence for the development of social differentiation during the earlier MH period is actually slowly increasing, while that of the later MH and LH I period is being more qualified and quantified (Voutsaki 2004; Voutsaki and Milka this volume; Voutsaki *et al.* 2013; Ingvarsson-Sundström *et al.* 2013; Milka 2006; forthcoming). Except for this recent research, the focus of research on social differentiation during this period has mainly been on the mortuary data of the MH III–LH I period. During this phase, we see the development of more elaborate funerary architecture reflected in the appearance of extramural cemeteries, grave circles, large cist graves and funerary stelai. In addition, more (valuable) gifts were deposited with the death, such as golden and silver table ware, stone vases and imported vessels. Some cemeteries or graves contained excessively valuable finds, indicating the rise of an elite at some settlements. Opposed to the mortuary context, the domestic context and household have barely been considered in the discussion about the rise of social differences during the MH and LH I period (but see Philippa-Touchais 2010, Voutsaki 2010). This lack seems almost strange as it can be expected that to achieve more interaction and to be able to exhibit differences between people through the increasing deposition of valuable grave gifts and the construction of elaborate graves, changes need to take place in the household and especially in the household economy as pointed out already by Voutsaki (2010). Concepts of property and ownership should be examined more closely, as Halstead (1995; see also Halstead and O'Shea 1982; Halstead 1989; 1999; 2006) has done for the Neolithic households in Greece. The social and economic dependency of households on one another and the community needs to be analysed as well as possible effects on actions undertaken by the household.

The aims of this article are twofold: first, to outline how analysis of "simple" domestic architecture can lead to a better understanding of social and economic change, thereby especially focusing on the concept of property. Secondly, to present the main results of my analysis of EH III, MH and LH I domestic architecture, to illustrate this approach. In this way, social change in Aegean prehistory is being addressed from a new perspective. First it is outlined how a simple domestic economy is organized, what kind of circumstances can lead to changes in the concept of property and in which ways architectural characteristics can change accordingly. This discussion is not meant to be exhaustive since others have more elaborately discussed various aspects of the theory (*e.g.* Kent 1990; Samson 1990; Carsten and Hugh-Jones 1995; Steadman 1996; Cutting 2006). Also, the architectural characteristics that are brought forward are especially applicable to the Helladic architecture under discussion. Different characteristics may be focused on while researching other types of houses.

The domestic economy in egalitarian societies

Sahlins (1972) posed that the economy tends to be under-productive in small-scale and largely egalitarian societies. Land and food are available in sufficient quantities. As a result people experience an economy of affluence and they only produce as much as they need. This has several repercussions: labour and land are underused and people do not have a sense of property. Depending for example on yields and labour input substantial household variation can exist in the amount of food possessed. However, the domestic economy forces households to share their stock in case of need, based on reciprocity. Within this economic and social context, the household is an independent production unit but is simultaneously submerged in the community. This creates a continuous dilemma between satisfying the domestic wellbeing of the household without endangering broader kinship commitments that force members to share their resources (Sahlins 1972, 127). In such an economy, the development of household differentiation is not possible. It is not unlikely that the EH III domestic economy may have been structured in a more or less similar way, as will be argued below.

Flannery (1972) suggests that in societies where the individual household is the basic production unit more opportunities and incentives emerge for intensification of production once sharing takes place more selectively. It can therefore be argued that economic and social changes need to take place before differences between households can develop. Production needs to be increased, an incentive is needed for the increase of production and the sharing of foodstuffs must be less of an obligation. This last process is elaborated on now because once sharing becomes less of an obligation, households will have an incentive to intensify their production: a surplus will benefit themselves, rather than other households or the community.

The availability of land and resources affects the relationship between people and social groups but also affects concepts of property and the development of social differences (Sanders and Webster 1978). For example, in places where exploitable land is abundant, people tend to have no concept of property. High mobility in addition to the abundant availability of land is likely to render the concept of property superfluous (see for examples Goody 1976; Bloch 1984). However, under pressured circumstances, the concept of property will become important. In case of a scarcity of land, people will try to stay in possession of the land they already have (Meggitt 1965, 218). Land or resources can become scarce due to, among other things, increasing population, invasions, war or climate change. A stronger sense of ownership over resources can also develop when more labour needs to be invested, for example, the construction of drainage systems (see again Bloch 1984 for an example). When scarcity of resources occurs, people are likely to change rules of sharing. We may expect a decreasing commitment towards sharing, and as a result the development of an increasing sense of property. Households will now keep their resources largely to themselves, but since they are not likely to be entirely self-sufficient some sharing will still take place. Halstead (1995) has argued a similar development for Greek households. In order to cope with more chronic and widespread scarcity of land and resources during the later Neolithic, households became an independent economic unit and started to isolate themselves from the community at large, to withdraw from community obligations to share food.

Decreasing commitments toward the community may also result from increasing commitments towards a smaller social group. An increasing population at a settlement can render decision-making processes difficult. To resolve this, part of a community can decide to fission and form a new community. However, when fissioning does not take place, new mechanisms have to be put in place. Vertical and/or horizontal political subdivision may be necessary (Bintliff 2010). Horizontal subdivisions may involve either the enlargement of social groups, for example, the enlargement of a nuclear family to an extended family, or the enlargement of a kin group (Knappett 2009, 16–18). Vertical subdivisions include the rise of some social groups, such as households, families or kin groups, over others. When a community is increasingly subdivided into social groups, households may become more committed towards the group they are a member of. Decreasing sharing commitments towards the community can stimulate increasing household production, as the excess produce will be of benefit to the household or its social group. Especially large households are likely to benefit from such a situation (Netting 1982). Eventually, some households can economically rise over others, which can subsequently lead to social differences and inequalities.

We are aware of an increase in settlement size and settlement numbers during the later MH period, and an increasing population of marginal areas (*e.g.* Wright 2004a; Zavadil 2010). Furthermore, groupings (whatever their exact composition) begin to appear in the mortuary record during the MH period. Changes in community commitment may have been a result of these processes. An analysis of domestic architecture may give insights into such changes.

Property and architecture

The economic and social changes outlined above can to some extent be reflected in the archaeological and architectural record. For example, we could make inferences about the extent of affluence or pressure people experienced based on population numbers, settlement densities and size, signs of threat or war reflected in the construction of circumference or defensive walls. We can look for signs or evidence of sharing or hoarding of resources. For example, storage buildings or communal hearths may indicate economic cooperation and sharing, while private storage areas and enclosed hearths may indicate household focused or private consumption practices (Halstead 1995; Peperaki 2010). A systematic analysis of such aspects has never been carried out on EH III–LH I domestic architecture.

It may be easier to look for signs of (the demarcation of) property. For example, boundaries can be constructed to demarcate property. Boundaries may be tangible, such as walls, ditches or defensive walls constructed to demarcate and protect land or the settlement. It seems that such walls were increasingly being constructed during the later MH and LH I period (Wiersma 2014). Such structures can also function as a symbolic boundary between the insiders (the community) and the outsiders (other communities). Especially in cases where demarcation is not a physical obstacle, such as rubbish ditches, symbolic interpretations are plausible (Brück 2000, 286–287). Other means of demarcating space can, for example, be the construction of extramural cemeteries, which were increasingly constructed during the later MH period. Also houses can be built in such a way as to communicate isolation and achieve more privacy, as has been pointed out for Greek Neolithic houses (Nanoglou 2001).

Once property is demarcated, it also becomes important to ensure it remains in the family or social group. Marriage rules can be such a means, but archaeologically this is difficult to identify. However, what can be identified in the archaeological record are claims on the past and references to descent and ancestors. For example, rebuilding a house on the exact same location can be a mechanism to transmit property within the family or social group. The act of rebuilding a house is an act of demarcating property and communicating claims on land, based on the ancestry of the house and the household (Nanoglou 2001; 2008; Chapman 1990; Borić 2002). Rebuilding of houses has been pointed out for the EH II and EH III period (Peperaki 2010; Weiberg 2007).

Other means of transmission could be the intramural burial of people, especially in direct relation to houses, which has been argued for the MH period (Voutsaki *et al.* 2013, 139; Georgousopoulou 2004, 207–213). The intimate relation between the built environment of the house and (presumably) its past inhabitants would also function as a continuous reference to ancestors and descent and could therefore strengthen claims on property.

Architectural homogeneity and variation

Changes in the domestic economy and social relations can also affect other architectural aspects. In a closed economy households can become richer through collaboration with other households in their community. In such communities, there is a need for greater social cohesion because households are to some extent dependent on one another (see Wilk 1983, 112–113 for a description of such a situation at the Kekchi Maya). Even when economic differences and inequalities exist these are not exhibited. Instead, solidarity is emphasized, for example through architectural homogeneity, or other forms of homogenizing behaviour (Goodman 1999, 151; Blanco-Gonzales 2011, 404). In an open economy households can become wealthier through collaboration with entities outside their own community. Within such communities, there is less need for social cohesion because the households are less dependent on one another. As a result, households are able to exhibit differences and inequalities and more architectural variety such as elaborate houses or monumental architecture may be expected (see Wilk 1983, 112–113 for the description of such a situation at the Mopan Maya).

A social aspect of dependency, namely intermarriage, should also be considered. Intermarriage may to some extent be affected by settlement size. Wobst (1974; 1976) argued that in social groups of 400–500 individuals or less (which could approximately equal settlements of ca. 2 ha or less) the human health could be affected by inbreeding of the gene pool. Communities of such size may be exogamous, meaning that they may try to find suitable marriage partners outside their own community. The cultivation of relationships between small neighbouring communities must as a result be significant (Bintliff 2010, 758), and may involve earlier mentioned homogenizing forms of behaviour. Settlements larger than 2 ha have a more varied gene pool. Endogamy, meaning intermarriage between people living in the same community, is therefore more likely to happen. As a result, relationships with neighbouring communities could be less significant, while relationships with households within one's own community could be more significant. It is not likely that settlements as a whole are strictly exogamous or endogamous as marriage rules and arrangements may vary among social groups.

EH III–LH I domestic architecture and social change

The following analysis shows how developments regarding the domestic economy, dependency, the concept of property and the transmission of property are actually reflected in domestic architecture of the EH III–LH I period. The discussion focusses on three sub-periods, each marked by different developments. The EH III period (ca. 2200–2000 BC) is discussed separately from the MH period for several reasons: this period is characterized by settlement destructions and overall depopulation (Forsén 1992; Maran 1998) as well as increasing isolation or introversion. The material record is poor and different trade routes existed. Ceramic assemblages are different from MH, characterized especially by Pattern Painted wares, Fine Grey Burnished wares and tankards (Rutter 1982; 1983a; 1988; 1995; Nakou 2000). Only a few intramural burials of possible EH III date have been uncovered so far (Forsén 1992, fig. 17).

The domestic architecture of the MH I–II period (2000–1800 BC) is also separately analysed. This period sees a slow and uneven increase in population and settlement numbers (Zavadil 2010). Trade relations increased between the mainland and Crete, Aegina and the Cyclades (various articles in Philippa-Touchais *et al.* 2010; Rutter and Zerner 1984; Lambropoulou 1991; Zerner 1993; Felten, Gauß and Smetana 2007). New ceramic wares were introduced such as Grey Minyan and Matt painted wares (*e.g.* Buck 1964; Zerner 1986; Sarri 2010; Pavuk and Horejs 2012). Many intramural graves have been uncovered so far, as well as a few extramural graves or cemeteries (Blackburn 1970; Cavanagh and Mee 1998).

The MH III–LH I period (1800–1600 BC) is a time of rapid developments: settlement numbers rapidly increased (Wright 2004a; Zavadil 2010) and interaction with other areas, especially with Crete, further intensified (Dietz 1991; 1998; Graziadio 1991; Cadogan and Kopaka 2010). Ceramic developments took place as well, but most noticeable were changes in mortuary practices which became more elaborate and complex (Voutsaki 1999). These developments set the MH III period apart from MH II (see Voutsaki and Milka, this volume for a slightly different view on this point). The integration of LH I with MH III are based on three considerations. Although lately improvements have been made in the dating of LH I ceramics (Lindblom 2007; Pruckner 2011; Mathioudaki 2010a, 2010b (*non vidi*), 2014), problems do remain in several geographical areas, especially because MH ceramic wares continued to be produced well into the LH period. Some material dated to MH III could therefore actually be LH I in date. Secondly, houses dated to LH I tend to be comparable to MH III in terms of architecture, and, thirdly, also the mortuary practices indicate that this is a coherent period.

By choosing this specific time frame we can consider how society recovered from a 'crisis' and eventually developed into a society that was, seemingly, socially differentiated. This period encloses approximately 600 years during which variation and differentiation did exist. It is not possible to expand on this in detail in this short article (see for details Wiersma 2014).

The following regions from the central to southern mainland were selected for analysis: southern Thessaly, Phthiotis, Phocis, Euboea, Boeotia, Attica, the Corinthia, Argolid, Achaia, Arcadia, Laconia, Messenia and Elis. The wide geographical scope compensates to some extent for the problems concerning the quality and quantity of architectural data available. Settlement organization and the appearance of houses are discussed for each period, followed by a discussion of architectural signs of the cooperation of households and communities, architectural variety and homogeneity and indications of the demarcation and transmission of property. Examples are provided to illustrate the architectural patterns and developments. Possible causes of change are put forward, also by referring to other developments on the mainland and in the wider Aegean.

EH III domestic architecture

EH III settlements were small, overall unorganized and few investments were made in the built environment since few to no large scale communal works were carried out. Settlement size does not seem to affect spatial organization. However, settlements located on slopes or 'magoulas', such as Kolonna and Pevkakia Magula, show sometimes signs of planning, reflected in the construction of terraces.

EH III houses were generally freestanding and relatively simple. Houses were usually one or two roomed (Fig. 5.1) and approximately 40 m^2 in overall size (Fig. 5.2). Many houses were indeed apsidal in layout, but some houses were rectangular, D-shaped or irregular shaped (Fig. 5.3). Many houses were freestanding and axial in design, but a few exceptions did exist, such as the room complexes at Tiryns, Kolonna and Helike (Kilian 1983, figs. 39–40; Walter and Felten 1981, fig. 22 and plan vii; Katsonopoulou 2011, fig. 3).[1] We can therefore observe during EH III slight differences in house layout, shape, size and number of rooms. These differences can be seen more clearly in the better documented sites, such as Lerna in the Argolid (Banks 2013. Fig. 5.4) and Argissa in Thessaly (Figs. 5.5 and 5.6). Buildings usually had one entrance. In combination with the freestanding nature, it seems that as a result most houses communicated a certain sense of isolation.

EH III households seem to have been largely economically self-sufficient, at least concerning the basic resources. Evidence of the economic cooperation of households may be seen at Lerna, where building W-84 contained many coarse ware storage

---

[1] The room complexes at Tiryns and Helike could be considered EH II remnants because they seem to have been erected during EH II and may have continued to be inhabited during EH III. In addition, a debate exists on the settlement continuity at Helike and the exact dating of the remains. Most of the remains were dug while in the mud or almost underwater, with little consistent control for stratigraphy. At Tiryns, the exact dating of the remains and the continuity of habitation are also not entirely certain. The excavation of the EH III remains was carried out in artificial levels rather than in natural stratigraphic layers.

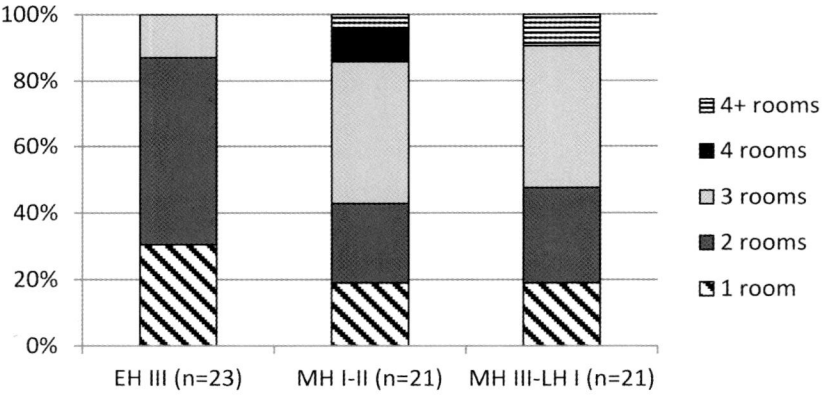

Fig. 5.1: Development of number of rooms created inside houses.

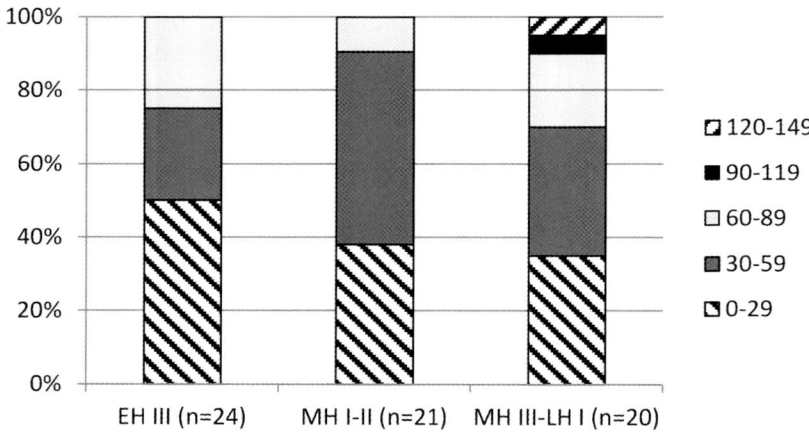

Fig. 5.2: Development of house size.

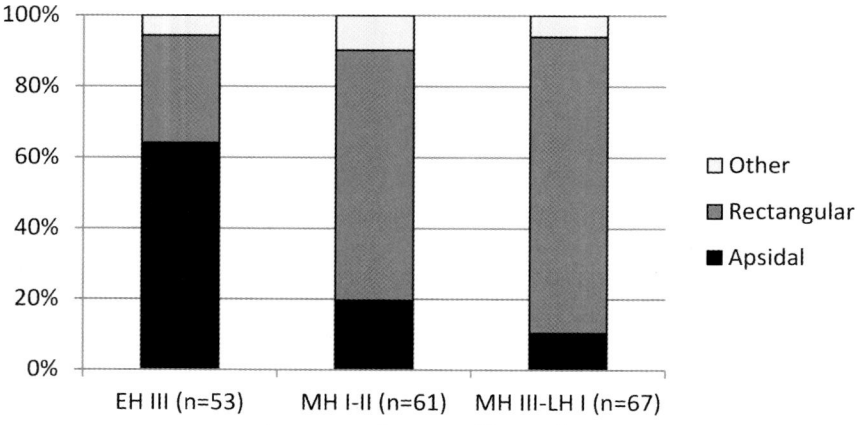

Fig. 5.3: Development of house shape.

Fig. 5.4: Lerna. EH III phase 2 (author, modified after Rutter 1995, plan iv).

vessels and therefore may have functioned as a storage facility (Banks 2013, 154–158; Rutter 2008).[2] But it remains unclear if this was used by the whole community or only part of the community (Banks 2013, 157–158, 358). Signs of economically cooperating households were not seen at other EH III settlements. However, houses were fairly small and open space around the houses must have been used for other, perhaps more communal and certain less private, activities.

---

[2] Building W-84 is dated to Lerna IV:2. The building is not visible in Figure 5.4, but was located partly on the northern side of the tumulus.

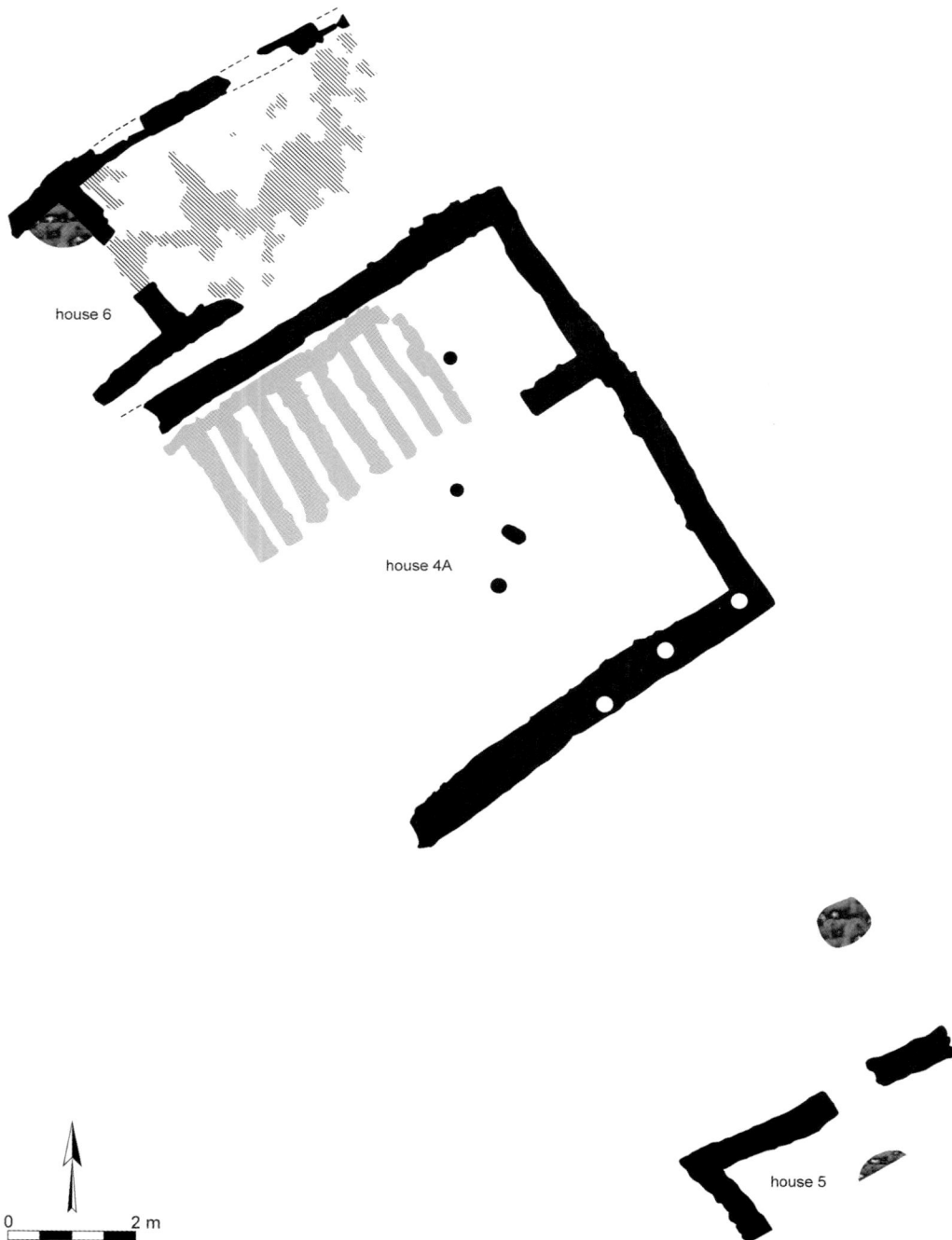

Fig. 5.5: Argissa. Later EH III (architectural phase MBA 2) (author, modified after Hanschmann and Bayerlein 1981, Tafel F).

5. Domestic architecture

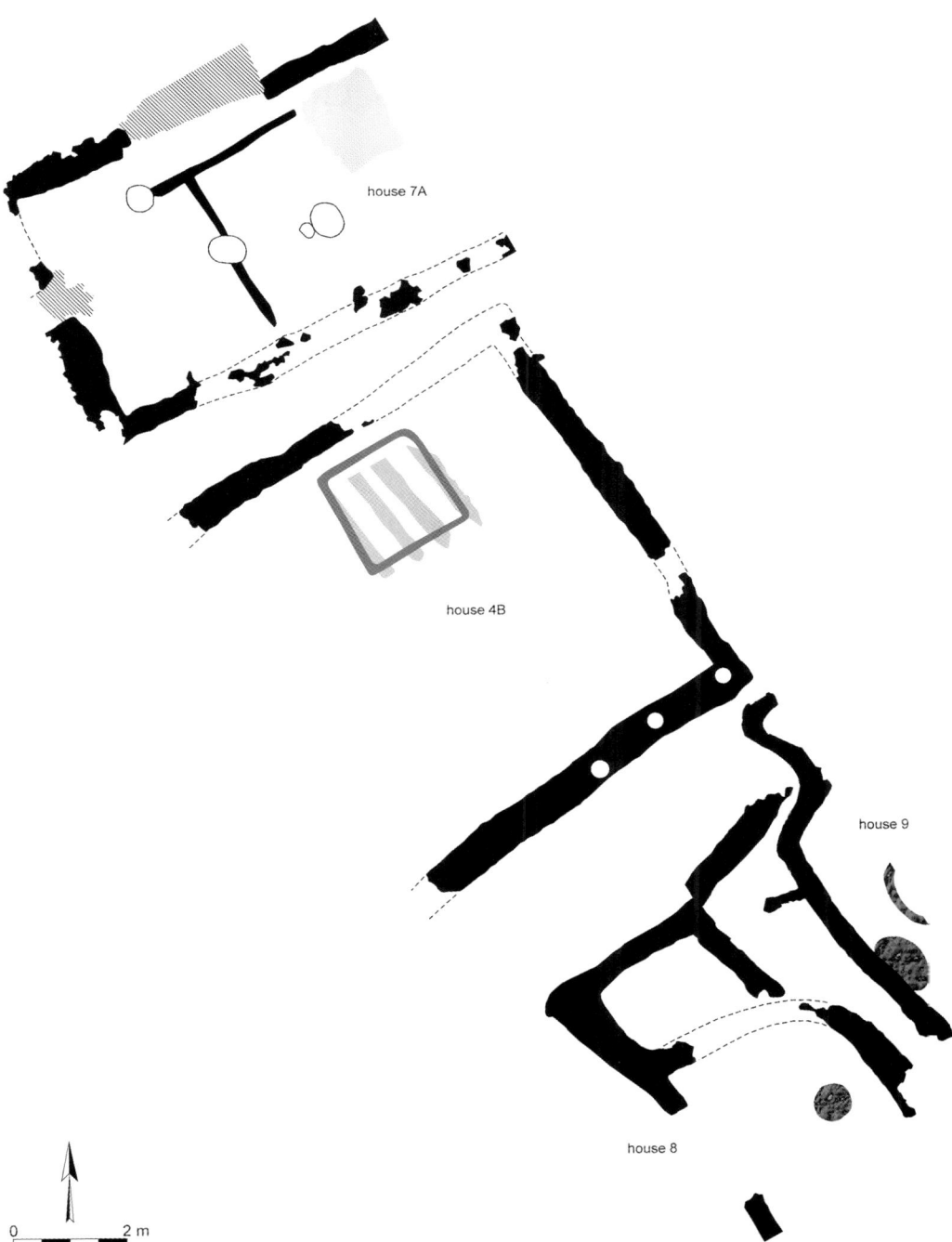

Fig. 5.6: Argissa. Later EH III (architectural phase MBA 3) (author, modified after Hanschmann and Bayerlein 1981, Tafel E).

So far, no evidence has been found of the demarcation of space or property, but some houses were rebuilt on the same location. Two-third of the houses were simply built upon by new structures after desertion or destruction, while approximately one-third was rebuilt. Rebuilding may have been a means to transmit property as has been argued by others. For example, in some Greek Neolithic settlements it seems that transmission was ensured by accentuating relations with ancestors. By being rebuilt on the same location, the Neolithic houses became a mnemonic device which related both physically and symbolically to the past (Nanoglou 2001; 2008). The impression of continuity can allow the inhabitants of the house to construct a narrative of a permanent social group with a fixed place in space and time (Gerritsen 2007, 163). The emphasis on the individual household becomes as such also a physical and symbolical means to communicate a shift away from reciprocal communality (Kotsakis 1999). Differences exist in the accurateness of rebuilding (see for example houses 2.1 and 2.3 in Figure 5.4, and houses 4A and 4B in Figures 5.5 and 5.6), but there are no clear signs that this was of special meaning. House rebuilding on the same spot is not clearly correlated with settlement size, house size, shape or number of rooms although it seems that it occurred especially at settlements with continuity of habitation (but the data are incomplete). Since rebuilding took also place during EH II, we may see this practices as evidence of continuity from EH II to EH III. Micromorphological data are needed to further investigate the rebuilding or modification of houses over time (Karkanas and Van de Moortel 2014). For example, data are lacking on the time passed between the desertion of a house and the subsequent rebuilding of the house, or on the time passed between the replastering of floors and walls.

Social change in the EH III period

The EH III domestic architecture is very different from that of EH II (see Harrison 1995 and Weiberg 2007 for a discussion of (aspects of) EH II domestic architecture). Monumental constructions were built during EH II such as defensive walls and corridor houses. The arrangement of houses into blocks located along streets gave some settlements an organized appearance. Some settlements were large, such as Manika estimated at 40 ha, though most EH III settlements were only a few hectares in size. EH II houses were freestanding and rectangular or apsidal in layout, but also agglomerated rooms forming houses or household were constructed. How do we explain and interpret the disappearance of monumental constructions, the overall absence of settlement organization and the transformation to almost solely freestanding houses during EH III?

It was mentioned earlier that the EH III period is characterized by a so-called 'crisis', consisting of settlement destructions, depopulations, decrease in settlement size, the loss of site hierarchy and the absence of monumental architecture (see Weiberg this volume for a different approach to the EH III crisis). I would like to suggest that the changes seen in the domestic architecture during EH III reflect a fragmentation of the social body. Communities were broken up and dispersed already during the later EH II period. Small settlements were left in which the household was seemingly the most important social unit, emphasized by the freestanding house. The household must also have been important during EH II, but it seems that at some settlements also larger social groups were of social significance. These larger groups are for example reflected in the clustering of graves, agglomerations of rooms and possibly the corridor houses (*e.g.* Pullen 1985; Weiberg 2007; Harrison 1995). The emphasis on a smaller social group during EH III is also indicated by small-scale drinking assemblages (Rutter 2008), compared to larger-scale EH II drinking assemblages (Wiencke 2000; 2011; Peperaki 2004; 2010; Pullen 2011a; 2011b; this volume). The uniform EH III architecture could have been a means to strengthen community relationships. These relationships were needed because households as well as settlements remained to some extent dependent on one another, especially considering the small size of settlements. It appears that property and ownership were not very relevant notions for most communities. Only in cases of more permanence of habitation does it seem that some consideration is given to the conveyance of property, reflected in rebuilding practices.

MH I–II domestic architecture

MH I–II settlements were barely spatially organized and only a few investments were made in the built environment. For example, paved streets seem to have occurred more frequently than during EH III and remained in long use, for example at Lerna, Kolonna and Eutresis, sometimes evidenced by renewed paving. Drains were constructed at some, especially MH II, settlements, namely Kastraki, Krisa and Ayios Stephanos. A few households start to appropriate settlement space, by means of the construction of outdoor facilities or enclosure walls (Figs. 5.7 and 5.8).

Houses remained freestanding, but were partitioned into more rooms (Fig. 5.1) and expanded in size (Fig. 5.2). As a result, a few houses with multiple axes were constructed and the apsidal house shape was slowly replaced by the rectangular house shape (Fig. 5.3). Therefore, increasing variation was visible in the shape, size and segmentation of houses although the overall appearance of houses remained homogenous. Depending on the preservation of the finds and internal structures, it was possible to indicate the performance of specialized activities to a few partitioned rooms. For example, room C of Krisa house A was probably used for cooking and storage activities (Fig. 5.7). Two pi-shaped structures of small stones set in clay were located here. The floor of these structures consisted of clay mixed with small pieces of animal bones. Furthermore, a considerable amount of ashes was found and lots of coarse wares were uncovered near the structures.

At some settlements outdoor auxiliary structures for storage and cooking were constructed. In some cases such auxiliaries were associated with specific houses, but

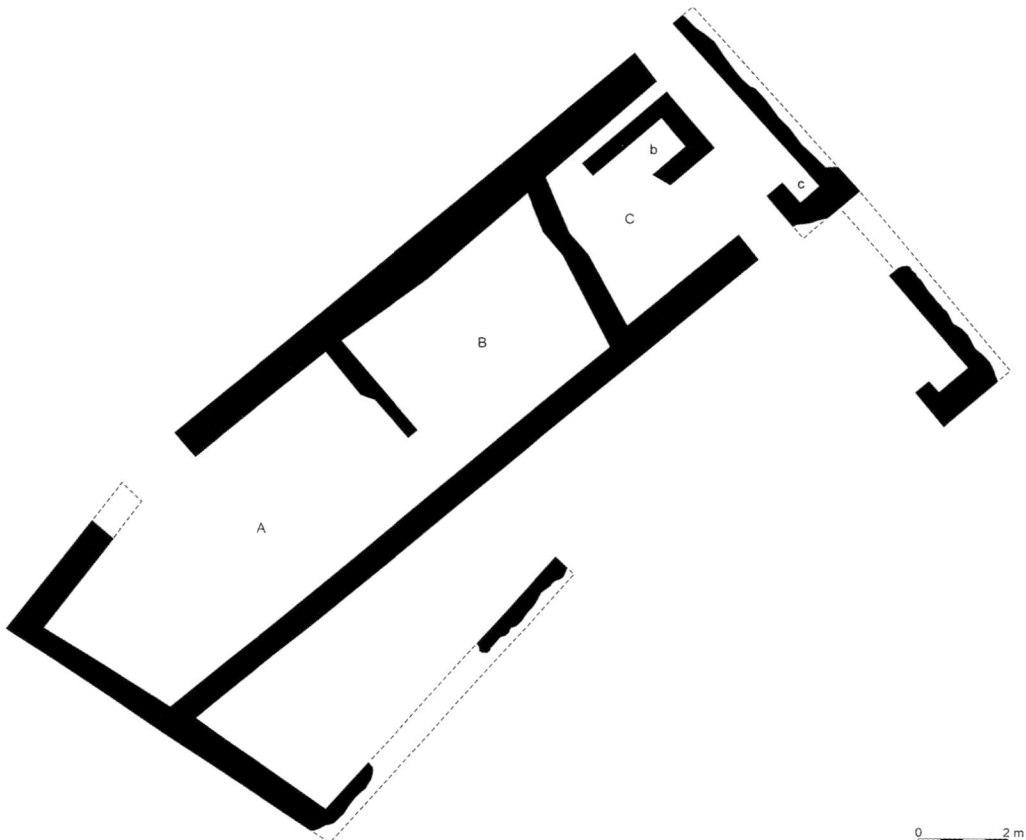

Fig. 5.7: Krisa. House A (author, modified after Jannoray and Van Effentere 1937, fig. 3).

in other cases a communal function seems more likely. For example, auxiliary rooms 44 and 45 at Lerna (Fig. 5.8), used for cooking and storage, were clearly part of house 98 (Zerner 1978, 42–45). The small apsidal structure D at Krisa was filled with pithoi and a pit (Jannoray and Van Effenterre 1937, 306–308). The structure is not clearly associated with a house and may have been of communcal use. At Argissa several outdoor storages structures were built (Hanschmann and Bayerlein 1981). Some of these, but perhaps not all, were closely associated with a house. The construction and use of storage structures, possibly by several households or the whole community, suggests increasing economic cooperation. Therefore, the social body seems less fragmented but more coherent at some settlements. It is also during MH II that at Kolonna large-scale consumption practices took place (Gauß *et al.* 2011) indicating cooperation of several households or the whole community.

Besides the suggested increased economic collaboration between some households, also signs of increased separation of some households are observed. It was already

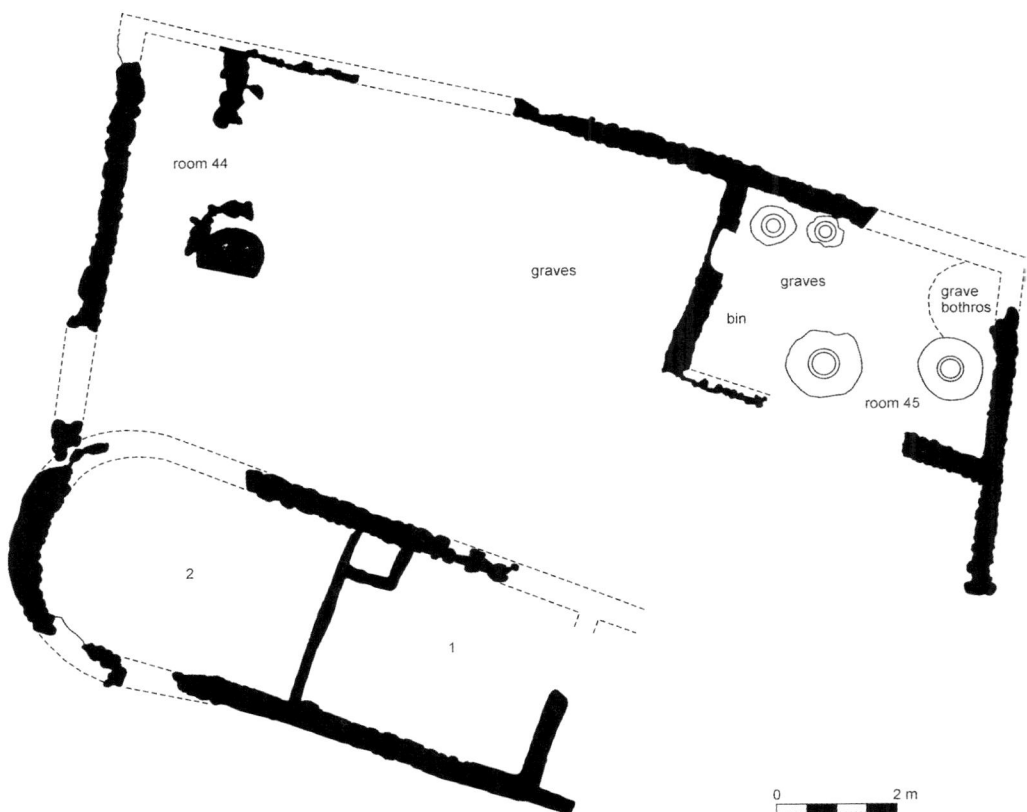

Fig. 5.8: Lerna. Room complex (author, modified after Zerner 1978, fig. vii).

mentioned above that a few households at Krisa (Fig. 5.7) and Lerna[3] (Fig. 5.8) fenced off an area beside the house. This area was in some cases used for cooking or storage activities, rendering the impression that some economic activities of these households were visibly shielded from the larger community. The two suggested economic developments of increased cooperation and seperation seem contrasting, but they could reflect the same process of some households moving away from commitments to share resources with the community.

Approximately one-third of the MH I–II houses were rebuilt, but it seems that compared to EH III rebuildings were carried out less meticulously and that slightly more modifications took place. Human burial took place among the houses (Milka 2006; 2010; forthcoming) while extramural cemeteries and/or tumuli appeared more

---

[3] Remains of two possible contemporary court complexes were only partly uncovered: houses BI and BS in area B seem to form a complex. The second example is apsidal house 55 with rooms AR and AM in area DE, of which no details are published (Voutsaki et al. 2013, 139; Caskey 1957, 146–148).

often. We can therefore conclude that the concepts of descent and ancestors became more present and visible in the settlement as well as the mortuary context.

MH I–II social change

It is suggested above that some households started to move away from commitments to share their resources with the community. At the same time more, but still minor, architectural variation becomes visible. In addition, a rising importance of ancestors and descent is seen both in the settlement and mortuary context. I shall argue below that a combination of increasing population and interaction may have partly caused these developments.

Although it is hard to pin-point settlement density and size, the observed architectural changes were especially attested at settlements of two or more hectares and social groups at these settlements may therefore have been endogamous. Perhaps pressure for or competition over resources resulted in less sharing with the community. Increasing population numbers (see above) could have led to social (re)organization at the level of the household and social group. Reorganization or enlargement of social groups could have been an incentive for households to share less with the community, but more or only with their specific social group. The suggested increasing economic and social intertwining of households may have slowly changed the expression of transmission: it seems that the expression of transmission, both symbolical and physical, was slowly shifted from the settlement context to the mortuary context (see also Voutsaki and Milka, this volume). It should be re-emphasized here that the earlier MH period is the period in which the first signs of some slight differences are seen in the mortuary record.

More interaction took place with the wider Aegean during the earlier MH period. This increase may be related to the introduction of the sailing boat, the development of towns on Cycladic islands, the growth of Kolonna on Aegina, as well as to the increasing influence of Minoan Crete in the wider Aegean (*e.g.* Dabney and Wright 1990; Wright 1995; Voutsaki 1993; 1999; 2001; Broodbank 2000; Maran 2011; Alberti 2012; Bintliff 2012). Increasing interaction may have stimulated economic cooperation among households, social groups and settlements, which subsequently may have given rise to a slight increase in architectural differences. Indeed, developments on the mainland can be considered simple and uninteresting especially when compared to the Cyclades and Crete. However, something is clearly stirring among mainland communities.

MH III–LH I domestic architecture

Research on LH I domestic architecture has focused more on settlements than on houses, due to the overall poor preservation or limited uncovering of house remains. Building activties of the later LH period have obliterated or covered up many early LH structures, and knowledge about this period is mainly derived from mortuary data (Shelton 2010, 140). An additional problem is the identification of LH I in survey material, which is further complicated by the earlier mentioned continuous production and use of MH-type ceramics during LH I (Rutter 1983b, 138; Wright 2008, 230–231). This last problem especially applies to areas where Mycenaean influence did not permeate rapidly, such as central Greece and Thessaly.

The population increased which led to the habitation of inland and marginal areas (Wright 2004a; Zavadil 2010). Easily defensible locations, such as slopes and hill tops, were preferred for the founding of settlements. Dietz (1991, 294, 325) suggests that during this transitional period, social and economic conditions became altered. Maran (1995) also observes that during the Shaft Grave period resettlement and expansion into marginal areas took place, and that there was a specific concern for defence, considering the construction of defensive walls and the positioning of settlements at defensible locations. However, at the same time a discontinuity of settlement took place, whereby the settled area was turned into a burial ground. These discontinuities are related by some to a restructuring and reorganization of settlements, which arose out of a polarization of social differences within society (Maran 1995, 72 and note 25). An increasing number of settlements were surrounded by defensive or circumference walls (Table 5.1). This development is attested at both coastal and inland sites, implying that hostilities took place among mainland communities. When this development exactly started is not yet clear, as several such walls cannot be accurately dated within MH. Defensive and circumference walls are especially observed in Attica and the Saronic Gulf, areas of intense (maritime) interaction.

The architectural data available indicate that some settlements were larger, better organized and that more investments were made in the organization of space. House density increased but overall it does not seem that this resulted in a better spatial organization of houses. Drains were uncovered at a few settlements and a large-scale system, possibly for the collection and storage of water, was constructed at Midea (Demakopoulou and Divari-Valakou 2010). It seems therefore that water management became more elaborate and technically complex at a few settlements. The architectural changes, although minor and gradual, show that development did take place. Argos is the best illustration of a well-planned settlement of this period (Fig. 5.9). Houses were arranged in a concentric circle around the summit of the hill and on several reinforced terraces (Philippa-Touchais 2010; Touchais 1998; Philippa-Touchais and Touchais 2008).

The number of rooms created inside houses continued to increase during MH III–LH I (Fig. 5.1), as well as the overall size of houses (Fig. 5.2).[4] Architectural differences

---

[4] Several large and multi-roomed houses were only partly preserved or uncovered and therefore not included in the figures. The increase in number of rooms is as a result not clearly reflected in Figure 5.1, while the increase in house size was actually stronger than indicated in Figure 5.2.

Table 5.1: MH defensive, circumference or perimeter walls

Region	Settlement	Description	Date
Thessaly	Dimini	Mud-brick perimeter wall	Near the end of the MBA
Boeotia	Davlose Megalo Kastraki	Peribolos wall	MH
Euboea	Eretria	Large retaining wall that, due to its heavy construction, is reminiscent of a defensive wall	Later MH
Attica	Brauron	Cyclopean walls and retaining wall	First dated to MH, but may be later?
Attica	Kiapha Thiti	Defensive wall	Late MH–LH
Attica	Plasi	Prehistoric fortification	Of possible EH date, but not later than MH
Attica	Thorikos	Remains of a defensive wall	Late MH/Pre-Mycenaean (?)
Attica	Sklavos	Possible defensive wall	MH II–III (?)
Attica	Kolonna	Fortifications, entrance system	EH III, MH, LH I
Argolid	Argos	Although technically not a defensive wall, the circular arrangement of houses gives an impression of defence and control over access	MH III
Argolid	Megali Magula	Defensive wall, and bounded access road	MH
Messenia	Malthi	Defensive wall	LH?
Messenia	Ano Englianos	Circuit wall	Possibly constructed in LH I
Laconia	Geraki	Repair of EH II enceinte	MH
Elis	Pisa	Circumference or defensive wall	MH III

became more pronounced, and were especially reflected in the layout and appearance of houses. Many houses continued to be freestanding and axially designed, but houses with multiple axes increased in number, possibly to accommodate the increasing number of rooms. Figure 5.9, showing the house remains at Argos, illustrates the construction of freestanding and axially designed houses, but also shows axially designed houses sharing the front or rear wall with another houses. Also houses consisting of two axes or possibly one axis and a fenced court beside the house are visible on the top of the hill. The construction of houses with multiple axes is best illustrated by house remains from Asine (Fig. 5.10). Clearly, architectural variation increased. A possible repercussion of the construction of houses with multiple axes was the slow disappearance of the apsidal house shape (Fig. 5.3).

Demarcation of property next to the house is barely seen during MH III–LH I. Perhaps this area was now becoming part of the built house, hence the increase in house size. Only at Kirrha, which can be characterized as an extended settlement,

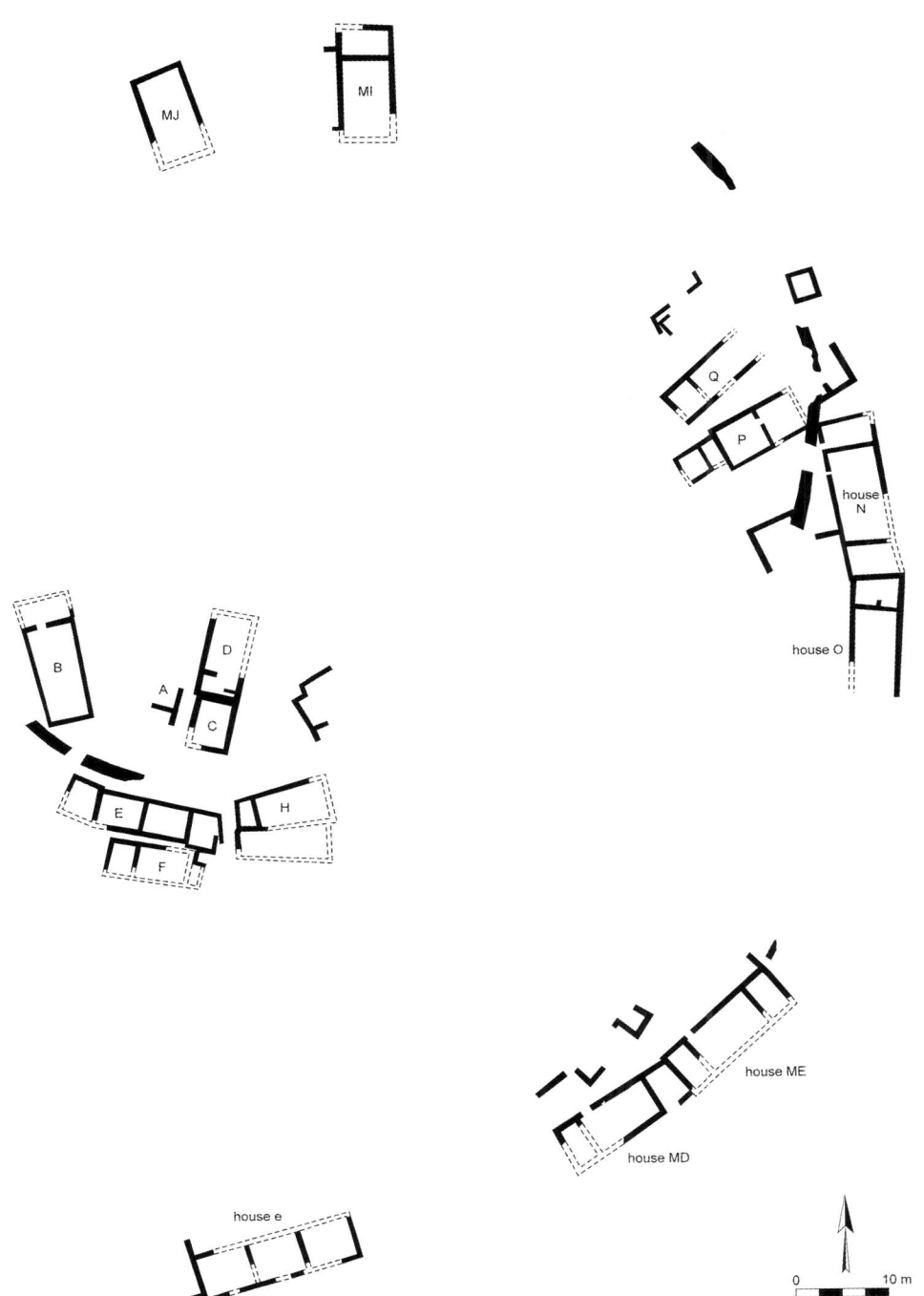

Fig. 5.9: Argos. MH IIIB–LH IA settlement remains on the Aspis (author, modified after Philippa-Touchais 2010, fig. 10).

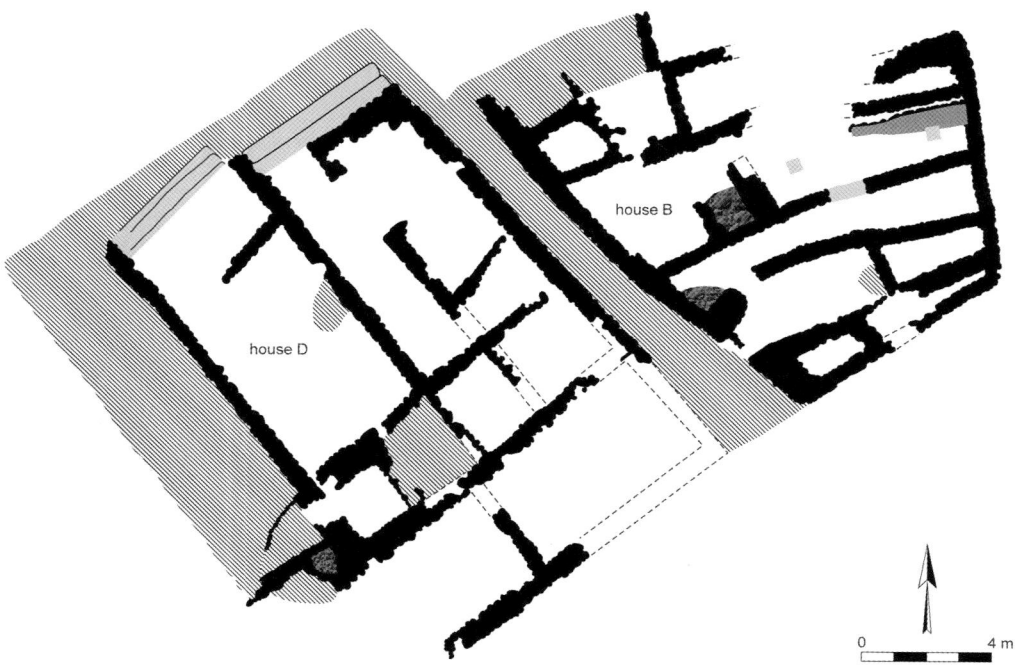

Fig. 5.10: Asine. MH III–LH I remains in the Lower Town (author, modified after Nordquist 1987, fig. 14).

do we see signs of demarcation of space between the houses, perhaps for the use of stock gardens or animal pens (Philippa-Touchais 2010; Fig. 5.11).

The increasing size and segmentation of houses suggest changes in cooperation and/or activities that were performed. For example, based on an analysis of MH houses at Asine in the Argolid, Voutsaki (2010) suggested that multiple households may have inhabited late MH houses B and D (Fig. 5.10), and may have cooperated economically. Additional explanations for the increase in house size could be the enlargement of the household, the performance of an increasing number of specialized tasks, or the simultaneous performance of more tasks in the house (Wilk and Rathje 1982). Unfortunately it proved difficult to reconstruct activities performed inside the different rooms, due to a lack of data on furnishings and finds.

It seems that the act of rebuilding houses ceased during this period, but the data are limited. Internal modifications or additions to the house were more frequently attested. Therefore, the decrease in rebuilding and increase in modification of houses tentatively pointed out for MH I–II may have further intensified during MH III–LH I. Mortuary practices reflect an increasing concern for kinship and descent, considering the reburial of remains, the clustering of burials and the burial of multiple people in the same grave.

Fig. 5.11: Kirrha. MH III–LH I remains in trench D (author, modified after Dor et al. 1960, pl. xii and Philippa-Touchais 2010, fig. 4).

MH III–LH I social change

The described MH III–LH I developments can be summarized as rapid intensifications of changes observed for the earlier MH. What caused these developments to happen may be various external and internal factors and their interaction: increase in population and settlement size, more intensive and far-reaching trade contacts, increasing interaction between local and regional spheres and increasing competition and threats of warfare. Most of these factors were already present during the earlier MH, but less intensely than during MH III–LH I. The rise of the palaces on Minoan Crete and the increasingly far-reaching cultural influence of the Minoans in the Aegean may have accelerated or intensified some of these developments. Increasing interaction took place on a local scale as a result of the increase in settlement numbers, and on a regional scale considering the increasing strength and influence of Minoan Crete. These circumstances may have led to increasing local competition, threat and tensions (see also Wright 2004b; 2010) and the construction of circumference and defensive walls. The depictions of warriors on ships on Aeginetan ceramics, on funerary steles and on the Late Cycladic miniature fresco at Akrotiri (also depicting a great fleet, sea battle and falling soldiers) are of significance in this context.

Increasing settlement size may also have been a cause of change at the level of the community specifically. The outlined economic changes were especially observed at settlements of 2 ha or larger, as was also observed for the MH I–II period. When settlements expand, new social mechanisms are needed to cope with the growing population, otherwise problems may occur in for example decision making processes (see under heading "developing a concept of property"). The enlargement of a social group could have been an incentive for the household to specifically share more with its own social group and less with the community at large. Cooperation of households would likely lead to more economic stability of individual households and the social group. This, in combination with less sharing with the community at large, may have created incentives for the production of surplus. The extra produce could have been used to strengthen the position of the household and of the social group. The suggested increasing importance of larger social (and economic) groups may have caused the eventual cessation of house rebuilding. The end of this practice seems to coincide with earlier mentioned changes in mortuary practices that indicate an increasing concern for ancestors and descent. Therefore, I would like to suggest that the mortuary sphere gradually became the most important domain for communicating transmission, instead of the domestic sphere. A similar argument is also made by Voutsaki (1997) based on changes in the mortuary practices, such as the introduction of multiple inhumations in tombs, re-use, secondary treatment and in general the increasing elaboration of the mortuary practices. The mortuary sphere is very suited for the expression of the emphasis on descent, continuity and transmission and may have been more malleable than the domestic sphere. After all, household relationships, alliances and status could have altered during one's lifetime, and domestic architecture may not have offered enough possibilities to continuously give expression to such fluctuating relationships.

Domestic architecture and social change

The results of the analysis of EH III, MH I–II and MH III–LH I domestic architecture have added some new perspectives to the social developments taking place on the Greek mainland. The analysis of EH III domestic architecture has to some extent confirmed what was already known. Houses were indeed fairly simple, small and overall homogenous in appearance. However, the analysis has nuanced these observations, something that had not been done before, and has shown that minor architectural differences did exist. A new perspective is suggested for some of the changes taking place on the mainland during EH III: The social body is more fragmented compared to EH II. The fragmentation is reflected in a decreasing importance of communal economic (and ceremonial?) activities and in an increasing emphasis on the house(hold) and the transmission of resources. The use of the apsidal house shape and rebuilding practices may be seen as evidence of continuity from EH II to EH III, though further research is needed here. The analysis of MH I–II domestic architecture has to some extent underwritten the general impression of houses as fairly simple, small and homogenous in appearance, but in addition architectural developments have also been pointed out. The rectangular house shape became more popular, house size increased, more rooms were created inside houses, settlement space was in a few instances more segmented and auxiliary structures were built. This geographically broad and comprehensive analysis reinforces earlier suggestions that changes may have taken place in household size and activities and that some households may have cooperated economically. A decreasing dependence on the community at large may have resulted in the slight increase in architectural variation. The analysis of MH III–LH I domestic architecture further substantiates these notions, as it showed an intensification of changes observed for the MH I–II period. It is important to realize that the MH III–LH I architectural changes were embedded in the earlier MH period and that the architectural changes and developments differed locally and were generally limited in nature.

In the foregoing, I have tried to show that domestic architecture, and especially simple domestic architecture, can be a valuable source of information when researching social change. Domestic architecture can render information about the household, sharing and hoarding of resources, the concepts of property or ownership and the transmission of this within the social group. For the EH III–LH I period specifically, the data on house architecture are finally providing something of a counterbalance for the scholarship available on mortuary practices.

Bibliography

Alberti, M. E. 2012. "Aegean Trade Systems. Overview and Observations on the Middle Bronze Age." In *Exchange Networks and Local Transformations. Interactions and Local Changes in Europe and the Mediterranean from the Bronze to the Iron Age*, edited by M. E. Alberti and S. Sabatini, 22–43. Oxford, Oxbow Books.

Banks, E. C. 2013. *Lerna. A Preclassical Site in the Argolid VI: The Settlement and Architecture of Lerna IV.* Princeton, American School of Classical Studies at Athens.

Bintliff, J. L. 2010. "The Middle Bronze Age through the Surface Survey Record of the Greek Mainland: Demographic and Sociopolitical Insights." In *Mesohelladika. The Greek Mainland in the Middle Bronze Age*, Bulletin de Correspondance Hellénique Supplement 52, edited by A. Philippa-Touchais, G. Touchais, S. Voutsaki, and J. Wright, 755–763. Athens, De Boccard.

Bintliff, J. 2012. *The Complete Archaeology of Greece: From Hunter-gatherers to the 20th Century AD*. Chichester/Malden, Wiley-Blackwell.

Blackburn, E. T. 1970. *Middle Helladic Graves and Burial Customs with Special Reference to Lerna in the Argolid*. PhD dissertation, University of Cincinnati.

Blanco-Gonzales, A. 2011. "From Huts to 'the House': The Shift in Perceiving Home Between the Bronze Age and the Early Iron Age in Central Iberia (Spain)." *Oxford Journal of Archaeology* 30.4, 393–410.

Bloch, M. 1984. "Property and the End of Affinity." In *Marxist Analyses and Social Anthropology*, edited by M. Bloch, 203–228. New York, ASA Studies, Travistock Publications.

Broodbank, C. 2000. *An Island Archaeology of the Early Cyclades*. Cambridge, Cambridge University Press.

Brück, J. 2000. "Settlement, Landscape and Social Identity: The Early–Middle Bronze Age Transition in Wessex, Sussex and the Thames Valley." *Oxford Journal of Archaeology* 19.3, 273–300.

Buck, R. J. 1964. "Middle Helladic Mattpainted Pottery." *Hesperia* 33.3, 231–313.

Cadogan, G. and K. Kopaka. 2010. "Coping with the Offshore Giant: Middle Helladic Interactions with Middle Minoan Crete." In *Mesohelladika. The Greek Mainland in the Middle Bronze Age*, Bulletin de Correspondance Hellénique Supplement 52, edited by A. Philippa-Touchais, G. Touchais, S. Voutsaki, and J. Wright, 847–858. Athens, De Boccard.

Carsten, J. and S. Hugh-Jones, eds. 1995. *About the House: Lévi-Strauss and Beyond*. Cambridge, Cambridge University Press.

Caskey, J. L. 1957. "Excavations at Lerna: 1956." *Hesperia* 26.2, 142–162.

Cavanagh, W. G. and C. Mee. 1998. *A Private Place: Death in Prehistoric Greece*. Jonsered, Paul Åströms.

Cutting, M. 2006. "More Than One Way to Study a Building: Approaches to Prehistoric Household and Settlement Space." *Oxford Journal of Archaeology* 25, 225–246.

Dabney, M.K. and J.C. Wright. 1990. "Mortuary Customs, Palatial Society and State Formation in the Aegean Area: A Comparative Study." In *Celebrations of Death and Divinity in the Bronze Age Argolid: Proceedings of the Sixth International Symposium at the Swedish Institute at Athens, 11–13 June 1988*, edited by. R. Hägg and C. G. Nordquist, 45–52. Stockholm, P. Åström.

Demakopoulou, K. and N. Divari-Valakou. 2010. "The Middle Helladic Settlement on the Acropolis of Midea" In *Mesohelladika. The Greek Mainland in the Middle Bronze Age*, Bulletin de Correspondance Hellénique Supplement 52, edited by A. Philippa-Touchais, G. Touchais, S. Voutsaki, and J. Wright, 31–44. Athens, De Boccard.

Dietz, S. 1991. *The Argolid at the Transition to the Mycenaean Age. Studies in the Chronology and Cultural Development in the Shaft Grave Period*. Copenhagen, National Museum of Denmark Department of Near Eastern and Classical Antiquities.

Dietz, S. 1998. "The Cyclades and the Mainland in the Shaft Grave Period – A Summary." In *Proceedings of the Danish Institute at Athens 2*, edited by S. Dietz and S. Isager, 9–35. Athens, Danish Institute at Athens.

Felten, F., W. Gauß and R. Smetana, eds. 2007. *Middle Helladic Pottery and Synchronisms. Proceedings of the International Workshop Held at Salzburg, October 31st-November 2nd, 2004*, Ägina–Kolonna Forschungen und Ergebnisse I/Österreichische Akademie der Wissenschaften Denkschriften der Gesamtakademie 42. Vienna, Austrian Academy of Sciences.

Flannery, K. V. 1972. "The Origins of Village as a Settlement Type in Mesoamerica and the Near East: A Comparative Study." In *Man, Settlement and Urbanism: Proceedings of a Meeting of the Research Seminar in Archaeology and Related Subjects Held at the Institute of Archaeology, London University*, edited by P. J. Ucko, R. Tringham and G. W. Dimbleby, 25–53. London, Duckworth.

Forsén, J. 1992. *The Twilight of the Early Helladics: A Study of the Disturbances in East-Central and Southern Greece towards the End of the Early Bronze Age*, Studies In Mediterranean Archaeology Pocket-book 116. Jonsered, P. Åström.

Gauß, W., M. Lindblom and R. Smetana. 2011. "The Middle Helladic Large Building Complex at Kolonna. A preliminary view." In *Our Cups Are Full: Pottery and Society in the Aegean Bronze Age:*

Papers Presented to Jeremy B. Rutter on the Occasion of His 65th Birthday, British Archaeological Report S2227, edited by W. Gauß, M. Lindblom, R. A. K. Smith, and J. C. Wright, 76–87. Oxford, Archaeopress.

Georgousopoulou, T. 2004. "Simplicity vs. Complexity: Social Relationships and the MH I Community of Asine." In *The Emergence of Civilisation Revisited*, Sheffield Studies in Aegean Archaeology 6, edited by J. C. Barrett and P. Halstead, 207–213. Oxford, Oxbow Books.

Gerritsen, F. 2007. "Relocating the House: Social Transformations in Late Prehistoric Northern Europe." In *The Durable House: House Society Models in Archaeology*, edited by R. A. Beck, 154–174. Carbondale, Center for Archaeological Investigations, Southern Illinois University.

Glowacki, K. and N. Vogeikoff-Brogan, eds. 2011. *Stega: The Archaeology of Houses and Households in Ancient Crete*. Princeton, New Jersey, American School of Classical Studies at Athens.

Goodman, M. 1999. "Temporalities of Prehistoric Life: Household Development and Community Continuity." In *Making Places in the Prehistoric World: Themes in Settlement Archaeology*, edited by J. Bruck and M. Goodman, 145–159. London, Routledge.

Goody, J. 1976. *Production and Reproduction. A Comparative Study of the Domestic Domain*. Cambridge, Cambridge University Press.

Graziadio, G. 1991. "The Process of Social Stratification at Mycenae in the Shaft Grave Period: A Comparative Examination of the Evidence." *American Journal of Archaeology* 95, 403–440.

Halstead, P. 1989. "The Economy Has a Normal Surplus: Economic Stability and Social Change Among Early Farming Communities of Thessaly, Greece." In *Bad Year Economics: Cultural Responses to Risk and Uncertainty*, edited by P. Halstead and J. O'Shea, 68–80. Cambridge, Cambridge University Press.

Halstead, P. 1995. "From Sharing to Hoarding: The Neolithic Foundations of Aegean Bronze Age society?" In *Politeia. Society and State in the Aegean Bronze Age. Proceedings of the 5th International Aegean Conference / 5e Rencontre égéenne internationale, University of Heidelberg, Archäologisches Institut, 10-13 April 1994*, Aegaeum 12, edited by R. Laffineur and W.-D. Niemeier, 11–20. Liège, University of Liège.

Halstead, P. 1999. "Neighbours from Hell? The Household in Neolithic Greece." In *Neolithic Society in Greece*, Sheffield Studies in Aegean Archaeology 2, edited by P. Halstead, 77–97. Sheffield, Sheffield Academic Press.

Halstead, P. 2006. *What's Ours is Mine? Village and Household in Early Farming Society in Greece*, G.H Kroon Memorial Lecture 28. Amsterdam, University of Amsterdam.

Halstead, P., and J. O'Shea. 1982. "A Friend in Need is a Friend Indeed: Social Storage and the Origins of Social Ranking." In *Ranking, Resource and Exchange: Aspects of the Archaeology of Early European Society*, edited by C. Renfrew and S. Shennan, 92–99. Cambridge, Cambridge University Press.

Hanschmann, E., and P. M. Bayerlein. 1981. *Die deutschen Ausgrabungen auf der Argissa-Magula in Thessalien. Die mittlere Bronzezei*. Bonn, Rudolf Habelt.

Harrison, S. 1995. "Domestic Architecture in Early Helladic II: Some Observations on the Form of Non-Monumental Houses." *Annual of the British School at Athens* 90, 23–40.

Ingvarsson-Sundström, A., S. Voutsaki and E. Milka. 2013. "People, Health and Social Differentiation in Middle Helladic Asine: A Bioarchaeological View." In *Diet, Economy and Society in the Ancient Greek World: Towards a Better Integration of Archaeology and Science*, Pharos Supplement 1, edited by S. Voutsaki and S. M. Valamoti, 149–161. Leuven, Peeters.

Jannoray, J., and H. Van Effenterre. 1937. "Fouilles de Krisa (Phocide)." *Bulletin de Correspondance Hellénique* 61, 299–326.

Karkanas, P., and A. Van de Moortel. 2014. "Micromorphological Analysis of Sediments at the Bronze Age Site of Mitrou, Central Greece: Patterns of Floor Construction and Maintenance." *Journal of Archaeological Science* 43, 198–213.

Katsonopoulou, D. 2011. "A Proto-Urban Early Helladic Settlement Found on the Helike Delta." In *Helike IV. Ancient Helike and Aigialeia. Protohelladika. The Southern and Central Greek Mainland*, edited by D. Katsonopoulou, 63–88. Athens, Helike Society.

Kent, S., ed. 1990. *Domestic Architecture and the Use of Space. An Interdisciplinary Cross-Cultural Study.* Cambridge, Cambridge University Press.

Kilian, K. 1983. "Ausgrabungen in Tiryns 1981. Bericht zu den Grabungen." *Archäologischer Anzeiger,* 277–328.

Knappett, C. 2009. "Scaling Up: From Household to State in Bronze Age Crete." In *Inside the City in the Greek World. Studies of Urbanism from the Bronze Age to the Hellenistic Period*, edited by S. Owen and L. Preston, 14–26. Oxford, Oxbow Books.

Kotsakis, K. 1999. "What Tells can Tell: Social Space and Settlement in the Greek Neolithic." In *Neolithic Society in Greece*, Sheffield Studies in Aegean Archaeology 2, edited by P. Halstead, 66–76. Sheffield, Sheffield Academic Press.

Lambropoulou, A. 1991. *The Middle Helladic Period in the Corinthia and the Argolid: An Archaeological Survey.* PhD dissertation, Bryn Mawr College.

Lindblom, M. 2007. "Early Mycenaean Mortuary Meals at Lerna VI with Special Emphasis on their Aeginetan Components." In *Middle Helladic Pottery and Synchronisms. Proceedings of the International Workshop held at Salzburg October 31st-November 2nd, 2004*, Ägina–Kolonna Forschungen und Ergebnisse I/Österreichische Akademie der Wissenschaften Denkschriften der Gesamtakademie 42, edited by F. Felten, W. Gauß, and R. Smetana, 115–135. Vienna, Austrian Academy of Sciences.

Maran, J. 1995. "Structural Changes in the Pattern of Settlement During the Shaft Grave period on the Greek Mainland." In *Politeia. Society and Dtate in the Aegean Bronze Age. Proceedings of the 5th International Aegean Conference / 5e Rencontre Égéenne Internationale, University of Heidelberg, Archäologisches Institut, 10-13 April 1994*, Aegaeum 12, edited by R. Laffineur and W.-D. Niemeier, 67–72. Liège, Université de Liège.

Maran, J. 1998. *Kulturwandel auf dem griechieschen Festland und den Kykladen im späten 3. Jahrtausend v. Chr.* Bonn, Habelt.

Maran, J. 2011. "Lost in Translation: The Emergence of Mycenaean Culture as a Phenomenon of Glocalization." In *Interweaving Worlds: Systemic Interactions in Eurasia, 7th to 1st Millennia BC*, edited by T. C. Wilkinson, S. Sherratt and J. Bennet, 282–294. Oxford, Oxbow Books.

Mathioudaki, I. 2010a. ""Mainland Polychrome" Pottery: Definition, Chronology, Typological Correlations." In *Mesohelladika. The Greek Mainland in the Middle Bronze Age*, Bulletin de Correspondance Hellénique Supplement 52, edited by A. Philippa-Touchais, G. Touchais, S. Voutsaki, and J. Wright, 621–633. Athens, De Boccard.

Mathioudaki, I. 2010b. Η *«Ηπειρωτική Πολύχρωμη» Κεραμεική στην Ηπειρωτική Ελλάδα και στο Αιγαίο.* PhD dissertation, University of Athens.

Mathioudaki, I. 2014. "Shifting Boundaries: The Transition from the Middle to the Late Bronze Age in the Aegean Under a New Light." *Aegean Studies* 1, 1–20.

Meggitt, M. J. 1965. *The Lineage System of the Mae-Enga of New Guinea.* New York, Barnes and Noble.

Milka, E. 2006. "From Cemeteries to Society: The Study of Middle Helladic (2000–1500 BC) Burials from the Argolid, Southern Greece." In *Symposium Onderzoek Jonge Archeologen Bundel 2005*, edited by M. Kerkhof, R. van Oosten, F. Tomas and C. van Woerdekom, 2–12. Leiden, Stichting Onderzoek Jonge Archeologen.

Milka, E. 2010. "Burials Upon the Ruins of Abandoned Houses in the Middle Helladic Argolid." In *Mesohelladika. The Greek Mainland in the Middle Bronze Age*, Bulletin de Correspondance Hellénique Supplement 52, edited by A. Philippa-Touchais, G. Touchais, S. Voutsaki, and J. Wright, 347–355. Athens, De Boccard.

Milka, E. forthcoming. Diversity and Change in Middle Helladic Mortuary Practices: A Comparison of Lerna and Asine. PhD dissertation, University of Groningen.

Nakou, G. 2000. "Metalwork, Basketry and Pottery in the Aegean Early Bronze Age: A Meaningful Relationship." In *Dorima: A Tribute to the A.G. Leventis Foundation on the Occasion of its 20th Anniversary*, edited by A. Serghidou, 27–57. Nicosia, A. G. Leventis Foundation.

Nanoglou, S. 2001. "Social and Monumental Space in Neolithic Thessaly, Greece." *European Journal of Archaeology* 4.3, 303–322.

Nanoglou, S. 2008. "Building Biographies and Households." *Journal of Social Archaeology* 8.1, 139–160.

Netting, R. M. 1982. "Some Home Truths on Household Size and Wealth." *American Behavioral Scientist* 25.6, 641–662.

Overbeck, J. C. 1963. *A Study of Early Helladic Architecture*. PhD dissertation, Ann Arbor, University of Cincinnati.

Pavuk, P., and B. Horejs. 2012. *Mittel- und spätbronzezeitliche Keramik Griekenlands*. Vienna, Austrian Academy of Sciences Press.

Peperaki, O. 2004. "The House of the Tiles at Lerna: Dimensions of 'Social Complexity'." In *The Emergence of Civilisation Revisited*, Sheffield Studies in Aegean Archaeology 6, edited by J. C. Barrett and P. Halstead, 214–231. Oxford, Oxbow Books.

Peperaki, O. 2010. "Models of Relatedness and Early Helladic Architecture: Unpacking the Early Helladic II Hearth Room." *Journal of Mediterranean Archaeology* 23.2, 245–264.

Philippa-Touchais, A. 2010. "Settlement Planning and Social Organisation in Middle Helladic Greece." In *Mesohelladika. The Greek Mainland in the Middle Bronze Age*, Bulletin de Correspondance Hellénique Supplement 52, edited by A. Philippa-Touchais, G. Touchais, S. Voutsaki, and J. Wright, 781–801. Athens, De Boccard.

Philippa-Touchais, A., and G. Touchais. 2008. "The Rise to Complexity of a Pre-Palatial Society: The MH Settlement of Aspis at Argos." *Bulletin of the Institute of Classical Studies of the University of London* 51, 193–194.

Philippa-Touchais, A., G. Touchais, S. Voutsaki, and J. C. Wright, eds. 2010. *Mesohelladika. The Greek Mainland in the Middle Bronze Age*, Bulletin de Correspondance Hellénique Supplement 52. Athens, De Boccard.

Pruckner, K. 2011. "Vollständig und bichrom bemalte äginetische Keramik des späten MH bis frühen SH aus Ägina-Kolonna." In *Österreichische Forschungen zur Ägäischen Bronzezeit 2009*, edited by. F. Blakolmer, C. Reinholdt, J. Weilhartner and G. Nightingale, 241–252. Vienna, Institut für Klassische Archäologie.

Pullen, D. J. 1985. *Social Organization in Early Bronze Age Greece: A Multi-Dimensional Approach*. PhD dissertation, Ann Arbor, University of Cincinnati.

Pullen, D. J. 2011a. "Before the Palaces: Redistribution and Chiefdoms in Mainland Greece." *American Journal of Archaeology* 115, 185–195.

Pullen, D. J. 2011b. "Picking out Pots in Patterns: Feasting in Early Helladic Greece." In *Our Cups are Full: Pottery and Society in the Aegean Bronze Age. Papers Presented to Jeremy B. Rutter on the Occasion of his 65th Birthday*, British Archaeological Report S2227, edited by. W. Gauß, M. Lindblom, R. A. K. Smith and J. C. Wright, 217–226. Oxford, Archaeopress.

Rutter, J. B. 1982. "A Group of Distinctive Pattern-Decorated Early Helladic III Pottery from Lerna and its Omplications." *Hesperia* 51. 4, 459–488.

Rutter, J. B. 1983a. "Fine Gray-Burnished Pottery of the Early Helladic III Period. The Ancestry of Gray Minyan." *Hesperia* 52.4, 327–355.

Rutter, J. B. 1983b. "Some Thoughts on the Analysis of Ceramic Data Generated by Site Surveys." In *Archaeological Survey in the Mediterranean Area*, British Archaeological Report S155, edited by D. R. Keller and D. W. Rupp, 137–142. Oxford, British Archaeological Reports.

Rutter, J. B. 1988. "Early Helladic III Vasepainting, Ceramic Regionalism, and the Influence of Basketry." In *Problems in Greek Prehistory. Papers Presented at the Centenary Conference of the British School of Archaeology at Athens, Manchester, April 1986*, edited by E. B. French and K. A. Wardle, 73–89. Bristol, Bristol Classical Press.

Rutter, J. B. 1995. *Lerna a Pre-classical Site in the Argolid. Results of the Excavations Conducted by the American School of Classical Studies at Athens. Volume III. The Pottery of Lerna IV*. Athens, American School of Classical Studies.

Rutter, J. B. 2008. "The Anatolian Roots of Early Helladic III Drinking Behavior." In *The Aegean in the Neolithic, Chalcolithic, and Early Bronze Age*, edited by H. Erkanal, H. Hauptmann, V. Şahoğlu and R. Tuncel, 461–481. Ankara, Ankara University Research Center for Maritime Archaeology.

Rutter, J. B., and C. W. Zerner. 1984. "Early Hellado-Minoan Contacts." In *The Minoan Thalassocracy: Myth and Reality. Proceedings of the Third International Symposium at the Swedish Institute in Athens, 31 May–5 June, 1982*, edited by R. Hägg and N. Marinatos, 75–83. Athens, Swedish Institute of Athens.

Sahlins, M. D. 1972. *Stone Age Economics*. New York, Aldine.

Samson, R., ed. 1990. *The Social Archaeology of Houses*. Edinburgh, Edinburgh University Press.

Sanders, W. T., and D. Webster. 1978. "Unilinealism, Multilinealism, and the Evolution of Complex Societies." In *Social Archaeology: Beyond Subsistence and Dating*, edited by C. L. Redman, M. J. Berman, E. V. Curtin, W. T. Langhorne Jr, N. W. Versaggi and J. C. Wanser, 249–302. New York, Academic Press.

Sarri, K. 2010. "Minyan and Minyanizing Pottery. Myth and Reality About a Middle Helladic Type Fossil." In *Mesohelladika. The Greek Mainland in the Middle Bronze Age*, Bulletin de Correspondance Hellénique Supplement 52, edited by A. Philippa-Touchais, G. Touchais, S. Voutsaki, and J. Wright, 603–613. Athens, De Boccard.

Shelton, K. 2010. "Late Bronze Age. Mainland Greece." In *The Oxford handbook of the Bronze Age Aegean*, edited by E. H. Cline, 139–148. Oxford, Oxford University Press.

Sinos, S. 1971. *Die Vorklassischen Hausformen in der Ägäis*. Mainz on Rhine, Philipp von Zabern.

Souvatzi, S. 2008. *A Social Archaeology of Households in Neolithic Greece. An Anthropological Approach*. Cambridge, Cambridge University Press.

Steadman, S. R. 1996. "Recent Research in the Archaeology of Architecture: Beyond the Foundations." *Journal of Archaeological Research* 4, 51–93.

Touchais, G. 1998. "Argos à l'époque mésohelladique: Un habitat ou des habitats?" In *Argos et l'Argolide. Topographie et Urbanisme. Actes de la table ronde internationale. Athènes-Argos*, edited by A. Pariente and G. Touchais, 71–78. Athens, Ecole Française d'Athènes.

Voutsaki, S. 1993. *Society and Culture in the Mycenaean World: An Analysis of Mortuary Practices in the Argolid, Thessaly and the Dodecanese*. PhD dissertation, University of Cambridge.

Voutsaki, S. 1997. "The Creation of Value and Prestige in the Late Bronze Age Aegean." *Journal of European Archaeology* 5.2, 34–52.

Voutsaki, S. 1999. "Mortuary Display, Prestige and Identity in the Shaft Grave Era." In *Eliten in der Bronzezeit: Ergebnisse zweier Kolloquien in Mainz und Athen*, edited by I. Kilian and M. Egg, Monographien 43.1, 103–117. Mainz, Verlag der Römisch-Germanischen Zentralmuseums in Kommission, Römisch-Germanisches Zentralmuseum Forschungsinstitut für Vor- und Frühgeschichte.

Voutsaki, S. 2001. "The Rise of Mycenae: Political Interrelations and Archaeological Evidence." *Bulletin of the Institute of Classical Studies of the University of London* 45, 183–184.

Voutsaki, S. 2004. "Age and Gender in the Southern Greek Mainland, 2000–1500 BC." *Ethnographisch-Archäologische Zeitung* 45, 339–363.

Voutsaki, S. 2005. "Social and Cultural Change in the Middle Helladic Period: Presentation of a New Project." In *Autochthon. Papers Presented to O.T.P.K. Dickinson on the Occasion of His Retirement*, British Archaeological Reports S1432, edited by A. Dakouri-Hild and S. Sherratt, 134–143. Oxford, Archaeopress.

Voutsaki, S. 2010. "The Domestic Economy in Middle Helladic Asine." In *Mesohelladika. The Greek Mainland in the Middle Bronze Age*, Bulletin de Correspondance Hellénique Supplement 52, edited by A. Philippa-Touchais, G. Touchais, S. Voutsaki, and J. Wright, 765–779. Athens, De Boccard.

Voutsaki, S., S. Triantaphyllou, E. Milka, and C. W. Zerner. 2013. "Middle Helladic Lerna: Diet, Economy, Society." In *Diet, Economy and Society in the Ancient Greek World: Towards a Better Integration of Archaeology and Science*, Pharos Supplement 1, edited by S. Voutsaki and S. M. Valamoti, 133–147. Leuven, Peeters.

Walter, H., and F. Felten. 1981. *Alt-Ägina III,1. Die vorgeschichtliche Stadt: Befestigungen, Häuser, Funde, Fasc. 1*. Mainz am Rhein, Philipp von Zabern.

Weiberg, E. 2007. *Thinking the Bronze Age. Life and Death in Early Helladic Greece*. PhD dissertation, Uppsala University, Stockholm.

Werner, K. 1993. *The Megaron During the Aegean and Anatolian Bronze Age: A Study of Occurrence, Shape, Architectural Adaptation, and Function*. Jonsered, P. Åström.

Wiencke, M. H. 2000. *Lerna a Preclassical Site in the Argolid. Results of the Excavations Conducted by the American School of Classical Studies at Athens. Volume IV. The Architecture, Stratification and Pottery of Lerna III*. Princeton, New York, American School of Classical Studies at Athens.

Wiencke, M.H. 2011. ""Ceremonial Lerna." In *Our Cups are Full: Pottery and Society in the Aegean Bronze Age. Papers Presented to Jeremy B. Rutter on the Occasion of his 65th Birthday*, British Archaeological Reports S2227, edited by W. Gauß, M. Lindblom, R. A. K. Smith and J. C. Wright, 345–354. Oxford, Archaeopress.

Wiersma, C. W. 2014. *Building the Bronze Age. Architectural and Social Change on the Greek Mainland During Early Helladic III, Middle Helladic and Late Helladic I*. Oxford, Archaeopress International Series.

Wilk, R. R. 1983. "Little House in the Jungle: The Causes of Variation in House Size Among Modern Kekchi Maya." *Journal of Anthropological Archaeology* 2, 99–116.

Wilk, R. R., and W. L. Rathje. 1982. "Household Archaeology." *American Behavioral Scientist* 25.6, 617–639.

Wobst, H .M. 1974. "Boundary Conditions for Paleolithic Social Systems." *American Antiquity* 39, 147–178.

Wobst, H. M. 1976. "Locational Relationships in Palaeolithic Society." *Journal of Human Evolution* 5, 49–58.

Wright, J. C. 1995. "From Chief to King in Mycenaean society." In *The Role of the Ruler in the Prehistoric Aegean. Proceedings of a Panel Discussion Presented at the Annual Meeting of the Archaeological Institute of America, New Orleans, Louisiana, 28 December 1992*, Aegaeum 11, edited by P. Rehak, 63–80. Liège, University of Liège, Department of Art History and Archaeology of Ancient Greece.

Wright, J. C. 2004a. "Comparative Settlement Patterns during the Bronze Age in the Northeastern Peloponnesos, Greece." In *Side-by-Side Survey: Comparative Regional Studies in the Mediterranean World*, edited by S. E. Alcock and J. F. Cherry, 114–131. Oxford, Oxbow Books.

Wright, J. C. 2004b. "The Emergence of Leadership and the Rise of Civilisation in the Aegean." In *The Emergence of Civilisation Revisited*, Sheffield Studies in Aegean Archaeology 6, edited by J. C. Barrett and P. Halstead, 64–89. Oxford, Oxbow Books.

Wright, J. C. 2008. "Early Mycenaean Greece." In *The Cambridge Companion to the Aegean Bronze Age*, edited by C. W. Shelmerdine, 230–257. Cambridge, Cambridge University Press.

Wright, J. C. 2010. "Towards a Social Archaeology of Middle Helladic Greece." In *Mesohelladika. The Greek Mainland in the Middle Bronze Age*, Bulletin de Correspondance Hellénique Supplement 52, edited by A. Philippa-Touchais, G. Touchais, S. Voutsaki, and J. Wright, 803–815. Athens, De Boccard.

Zavadil, M. 2010. "The Peloponnese in the Middle Bronze Age: An Overview." In *Mesohelladika. The Greek Mainland in the Middle Bronze Age*, Bulletin de Correspondance Hellénique Supplement 52, edited by A. Philippa-Touchais, G. Touchais, S. Voutsaki, and J. Wright, 151–163. Athens, De Boccard.

Zerner, C. W. 1978. *The Beginning of the Middle Helladic Period at Lerna*. PhD dissertation, University of Cincinnati.

Zerner, C. W. 1986. "Middle Helladic and Late Helladic I Pottery from Lerna." *Hydra* 2. 58–73.

Zerner, C. W. 1993. "New Perspectives on Trade in the Middle and Early Late Helladic Periods on the Mainland." In *Wace and Blegen: Pottery as Evidence for Trade in the Aegean Bronze Age, 1939-1989*, edited by C. and P. Zerner and J. Winder, 39–56. Amsterdam, Brill.

Chapter 6

Social change in Middle Helladic Lerna

Sofia Voutsaki and Eleni Milka

The problem: social change in the MH period

The Middle Helladic period is caught between two peaks of economic prosperity, social differentiation and cultural connectivity, the Early Helladic and Mycenaean periods. In addition, the MH mainland has suffered from comparison with the Minoan palatial societies and the maritime polities of the Aegean (Rutter 2001, 32). As a result, the MH period is generally considered as undifferentiated, backward and stagnant and has until recently received little attention. For most of the twentieth century research concentrated on the origins of the MH civilization or on typological sequences, although studies by Dickinson (1977), Zerner (1978), Nordquist (1987) and papers in the Journal *Hydra* laid the foundations for subsequent research. The last decades have seen a renewed interest in the period spurred by Rutter's excellent synthesis (Rutter 2001) and two recent conferences on the MH period (Felten *et al.* 2007; Philippa-Touchais *et al.* 2010) which have brought together recent research across the mainland. Seminal new publications have appeared (*e.g.* Pefkakia: Maran 1992); investigations have started anew at important sites (*e.g.* Kolonna: Gauß and Smetana 2010; Aspis: Piérart and Touchais 1996; Philippa-Touchais 2010; Kirrha: Skorda and Zürbach 2011); old data have been re-examined (MH Argolid: Voutsaki 2005; Voutsaki *et al.* 2013; Ingvarsson-Sundström *et al.* 2013; Argos "tumuli" cemeteries: Voutsaki *et al.* 2007; Orchomenos: Sarri 2010; pre-Mycenaean finds from Ano Englianos: Davis and Stocker 2010); new regional syntheses have been published (Argolid and Corinthia: Lambropoulou 1991; central Greece: Gorogianni 2002, Phialon 2011; Laconia: Boyd 2002; Messenia: Zavadil 2013); ceramic (Pavuk and Horejs 2012) and bioarchaeological studies have appeared (Kolonna: Kanz *et al.* 2010; Lerna: Triantaphyllou *et al.* 2008a, Kovatsi *et al.* 2009, Voutsaki *et al.* 2013; Aspis: Triantaphyllou *et al.* 2008b; Asine: Ingvarsson-Sundström *et al.* 2009; Koufovouno: Lagia and Cavanagh 2010); and finally, broader syntheses have been attempted (Kilian-Dirlmeier 1997; Whittaker 2014). These investigations and discussions have cast doubt on the traditional perception of MH societies as static, backward, isolated and largely homogenous (as pointed out already by Rutter 2001, 132). It is now generally accepted that already the MH III period witnessed pervasive social, political and cultural changes that lead to the formation of the early Mycenaean polities and the later palatial states.

Much as these new studies have transformed our understanding of the MH mainland, the core of the problem, the timing and nature of social change during the MH period, has been raised (Rutter 2001 and this volume; Dickinson 2010; Wright 2004; 2010), but not addressed systematically, in contrast to the vibrant discussion surrounding Early Minoan and Middle Minoan Crete (Schoep *et al.* 2012). We still lack systematic, problem-oriented and theoretically informed analyses of empirical data from the MH mainland.[1] We still need to address the following questions: What changes do we observe in the material record, and when exactly do they occur? How does the rate of change fluctuate through time? How is change manifested in different spheres of life (and death)? How are different social (age, gender, status and kin) groups, or different communities affected by the changes taking place during the MH period, and how do they respond to the new conditions?

This paper attempts to address these questions by carrying out a systematic contextual analysis of mortuary and domestic data from Lerna.[2] The choice is not fortuitous: Lerna is the only site in the southern mainland with a well-documented and accurately dated sequence of both graves and houses.[3] In terms of its material culture, Lerna is still considered to be the type site of the MH mainland (see Rutter 2007). However, in this paper we will actually question whether Lerna can be considered a representative case and whether the entire Argolid undergoes a uniform social development. Reconstructing social change in Lerna therefore allows us to directly confront the question: *How static and undifferentiated, but also how homogenous were the societies of the MH mainland?*[4]

The analysis of the data

We will start our discussion with a systematic analysis of mortuary practices in Lerna. It is generally thought that MH mortuary practices are simple and uniform, and indeed

---

[1] The studies which present the results of the *Middle Helladic Argolid Project* and Wiersma 2014 constitute the sole exceptions.
[2] Eleni Milka has carried out the contextual analysis of the mortuary practices, though Sofia Voutsaki (with assistance from Francis Koolstra) has re-analysed the evidence in order to make finer observations on change between the different sub-phases of the MH period and variation between social groups. Sofia Voutsaki has analyzed the evidence from the houses, on the basis of unpublished data, kindly made available by Carol Zerner (see n. 3).
[3] The MH graves and the small finds have been published by Blackburn (1970) and Banks (1967) respectively. The pottery and houses of MH Lerna remain unpublished; an article on the houses is now in preparation (Voutsaki and Zerner forthcoming). For our analyses we have been given full access to the Lerna Archive, for which we would like to thank Carol Zerner, Martha Wiencke and the American School of Classical Studies.
[4] This article should be read together with Voutsaki 2016, which contains a more extensive theoretical discussion.

the majority of the burials consist of single, contracted inhumations accompanied by few, if any grave goods. However, subtle variation underlies this apparent homogeneity: cemeteries may be extramural or intramural; they may be "flat" cemeteries or tumuli, or both; tombs may be cists or pits of different size and construction, while jar burials and *pithoi* are also found; double or multiple burials occur, though they are rare, and secondary treatment is sometimes attested. Most descriptions of MH mortuary practices (see Cavanagh and Mee 1998, 23–40) limit themselves to this kind of general statement, which is in many ways correct – but it does obscure both changes through time and variation between regions and sites. If we take the first point, the prevailing opinion is that MH I–II mortuary practices are simple, homogenous and conservative, and that real changes only set in during the MH III–LH I period with the appearance of more complex practices and elaborate tomb types. A closer look[5] at the evidence from Lerna reveals this general statement to be erroneous.

If we look at fluctuations in tomb numbers through time (Figs. 6.1), we see a steady increase from EH III to MH II. The pattern may denote demographic growth (which could indicate a recovery from the EH/MH crisis), but it also reveals changes in the inclusion of different age groups: All EH III burials belong to sub-adults, while from MH I onwards all age groups, adults included, receive burial in or among houses (contra Rutter, this volume). The possible growth in the number of burials in MH III–LH I[6] can at first sight be taken as an indication of further population growth, but in the case of Lerna it also denotes the gradual transformation of the settlement into an intramural cemetery and anticipates its virtual abandonment after LH I–II (Wiencke 1998).

A quick look at Figure 6.2 shows us that we can also observe significant changes in tomb types through time: While in EH III we only find burials in pits and jars, in MH I or MH II[7] cists are introduced and their number increases in MH III, while jar burials disappear. Finally, in LH I the two shaft graves are built, while the proportion between cists and pits remains effectively unchanged. The evidence suggests a gradual increase in tomb size and complexity of construction, with changes setting in already in MH I–II. The dearth of well-dated early MH burials elsewhere does not allow us to check if these observations are valid in other MH settlements.[8] It is well-

---

[5] The mortuary evidence from Lerna is very well documented: Blackburn (1970) has published the graves in a preliminary manner, and the date and stratigraphic associations of the individual tombs has been revised by Carol Zerner as part of the Lerna Publication Project. Eleni Milka has carried out the contextual analysis of the mortuary practices (Milka in Voutsaki *et al.* 2007; Milka forthcoming). As part of the *Middle Helladic Argolid Project*, the skeletal assemblage has been re-examined by Sevi Triantaphyllou (Triantaphyllou 2010), while radiocarbon analysis (Voutsaki *et al.* 2009b), stable isotope analysis (Triantaphyllou *et al.* 2008a) and ancient DNA analysis (Kovatsi *et al.* 2009) of the human remains have been carried out.

[6] We use the chronological system introduced by Carol Zerner. The Shaft Grave era (SGE) comprises the period from the transition from the MH III to the LH I period to the very beginning of the LH IIA period.

[7] The date of the few (uncertain or atypical) MH I cists has not as yet been revised by Carol Zerner; she believes (pers. comm.) that cists are introduced in MH II.

[8] In both Ayios Stephanos (Taylour and Janko 2008) and Asine (Nordquist 1987), the only published and well-documented MH "intramural" cemeteries used throughout the period, few graves can be accurately

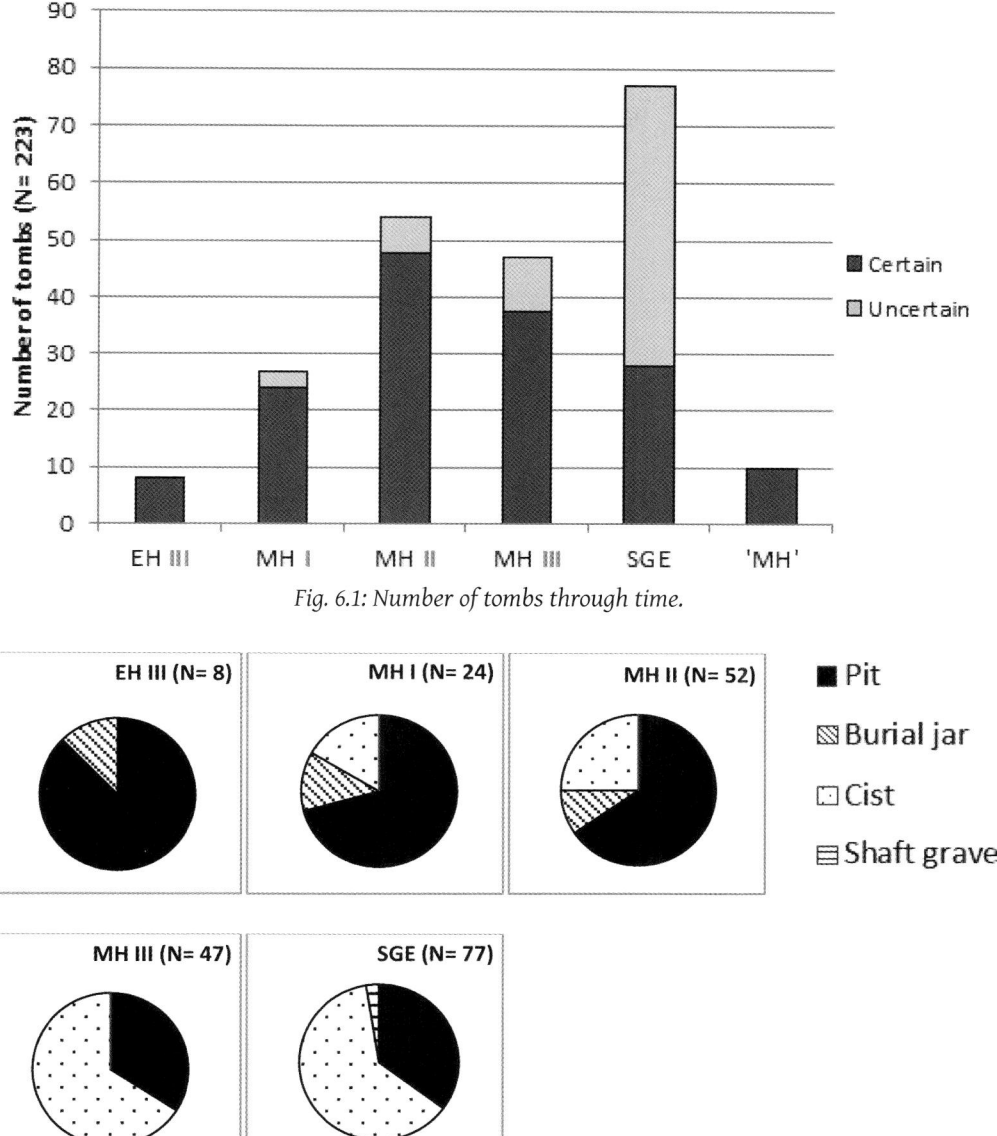

Fig. 6.1: Number of tombs through time.

Fig. 6.2: Tomb types through time.

known that a pervasive transformation of the mortuary practices takes place in MH III–LH I across the southern mainland: This period sees the introduction of larger and

dated because of the scarcity of offerings, or their undiagnostic character. A systematic comparison between Lerna and Asine is undertaken by Milka (forthcoming).

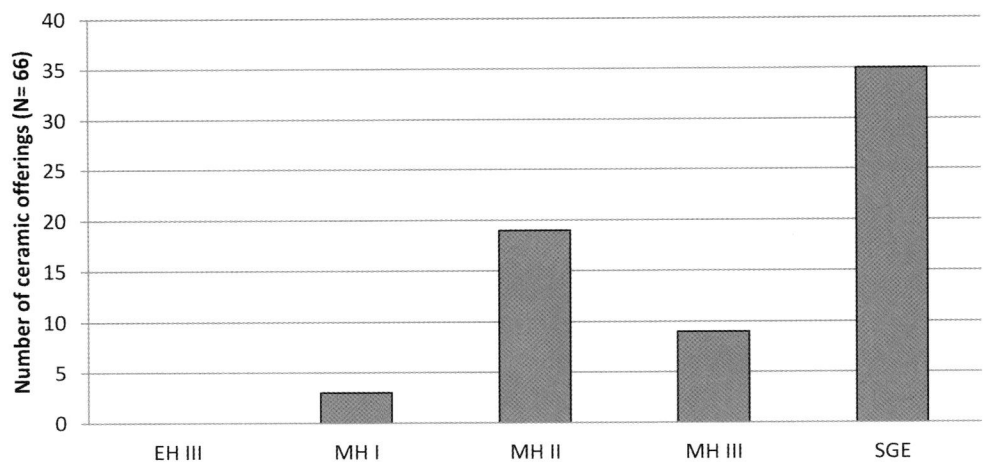

Fig. 6.3: Deposition of ceramic offerings through time.

more elaborate graves (elaborate cists, built graves, shaft graves and various hybrid types), but also of tholos and chamber tombs. Lerna is, however, less affected by these changes than the neighbouring cemeteries in Argos, Asine and, of course, Mycenae.[9] We could attribute this to the fact we are dealing with "intramural"[10] burials – but the extramural cemetery in Myloi (Dietz and Divari-Valakou 1990) does not have large or rich tombs either. We will return to this point later – for the time being, it suffices to note that Lerna seems to deviate from the general trends.

Figure 6.3 confirms that important changes are observed already in the early phases: the MH II period in particular sees a fairly marked increase in the deposition of ceramic offerings, which seems to drop in MH III and take off again in MH III/LH I–LH I. We have to point out that the graph does not include the large amounts of fine pottery found in the two LH I shaft graves, as it has been argued convincingly by Lindblom (2007) that these represent the remains of funerary feasting rather than offerings as such.

However, if we examine the deposition of non-ceramic offerings (Fig. 6.4) we see a rather different pattern: While we observe once more a sharp increase in MH II, the situation changes little between MH III and LH I with minor fluctuations between the different categories. We should keep in mind that offerings are modest throughout the period and consist mostly of simple bone, clay or stone tools and ornaments, though a couple of silver ornaments and one uncertain iron fragment have been found in MH III–LH I. Of course, the shaft-graves have been robbed and emptied, but there is no indication that they ever contained rich or exotic items. As far as we can

---

[9] Where built tombs, tumuli, large elaborate shaft graves and chamber tombs are found (Argos: Protonotariou-Deilaki 1980; Voutsaki *et al.* 2009a; Sarri and Voutsaki 2012; Asine: Dietz 1980; Milka 2006; Milka forthcoming; Voutsaki *et al.* 2012; Ingvarsson-Sundstrom *et al.* 2013; Mycenae: Schliemann 1878; Mylonas 1973; Alden 2000).

[10] See Milka's (2010) reservation about the term "intramural".

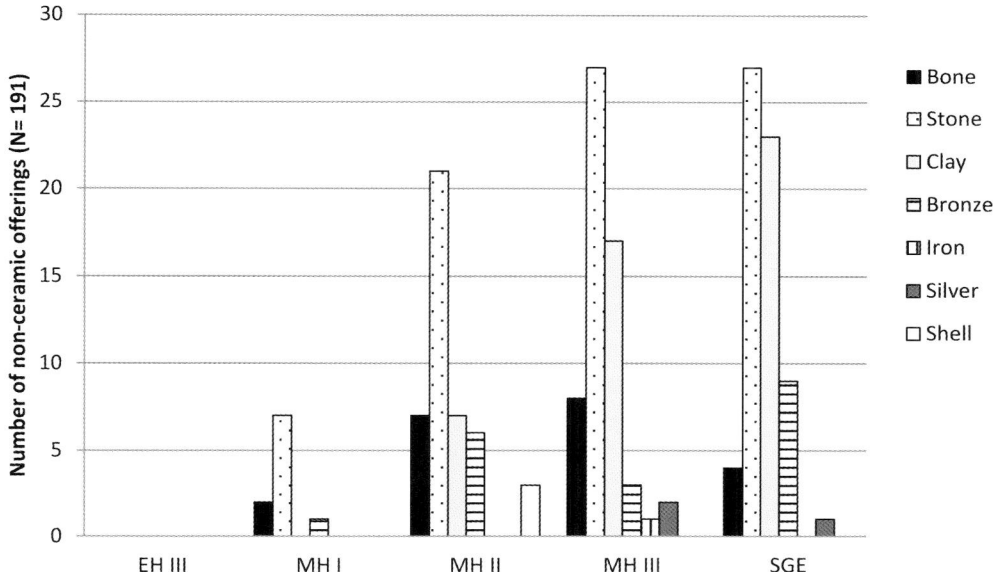

Fig. 6.4: Deposition of non-ceramic offerings through time.

say (and admittedly the evidence is problematic), the emphasis in LH I Lerna seems to be more on collective feasting than on personal distinction. Therefore Lerna does not seem to follow the general trend of increasing mortuary wealth at the transition to the Mycenaean period.[11] Once more Lerna deviates from the general pattern.

Let us summarize the observations so far: We certainly observe change through time, *e.g.* with the appearance of cists and later of shaft graves, but this is not really reinforced by a marked increase in the deposition of offerings. If we look in more detail and correlate different aspects of the mortuary practices, or examine them against age and gender, the picture becomes even more nuanced and complex. For instance, the few burials in EH III all belong to infants and neonates in pits or jars, and are all unfurnished. In MH I adults (both sexes) are also buried among the houses; the first vases are deposited, but they are rare (offerings are found in 2–3 adult graves) and they never exceed one vase per grave; the first bone or stone tools are also deposited. In MH II we observe new changes: Cists may be introduced in this period for the first time.[12] In addition, more graves contain vases, more vases are deposited with individual burials and vases are now also found with sub-adults, and ornaments or simple weapons are also deposited with the dead. In MH III the number of cists

---

[11] In contrast to *e.g.* Argos (Voutsaki *et al.* 2009a, 178–179; Sarri and Voutsaki 2012), Asine (Milka 2006; forthcoming; Voutsaki *et al.* 2012; Ingvarsson-Sundstrom *et al.* 2013), Midea (Demakopoulou and Divari-Valakou 2010), and of course Mycenae (Voutsaki 1999). For a more extended discussion on differences between Lerna and the other sites in the Argolid, see Voutsaki 2010b.

[12] See n. 7.

increases, while the number of pits declines. In general, more adults are buried in cists, and more sub-adults in pits, but this is merely a tendency rather than a rule. No differences between the sexes can be observed. We have already seen that there is no marked increase in the offerings – but we have to keep in mind that by LH I large parts of the settled area seem to be abandoned and turned over to a cemetery, mostly used for sub-adult burials. In contrast, adult burials in cists predominate in the extramural cemetery in neighbouring Myloi.[13] By LH I cists predominate also among the "intramural" burials; in the same period the two shaft graves are built, but there is hardly an increase in offerings.

We therefore do observe changes through time: In some aspects there is a certain "scaling up" through time, but important changes can be observed already in MH I–II when grave numbers increase, adults are included in the intramural graves, cists are introduced, and more offerings, including non-ceramic goods, are placed with the dead. Changes are also observed in the later phases, *e.g.* with the adoption of extramural cemeteries or the appearance of shaft graves, but these are not accompanied by an increase in (valuable) offerings. In fact, the moment we begin to correlate the different aspects of the mortuary practices – for instance, if we examine tomb types against offerings, or both against age/gender – we realize that the use of general measures, *e.g.* "tomb elaboration" or "wealth", let alone the abstract notion of "energy expenditure", obscure the complexity and unevenness of developments across the burial community – whose composition also changes through time.

We can reach two important conclusions: First, change in mortuary practices in Lerna is neither linear, nor cumulative, and second, the changes affect different (age, gender, kin and status) groups in varying degrees.

Let us now address a slightly different question: If we see changes during MH I–II, does this imply that there is differentiation already in this period? And does differentiation become more pronounced in MH III–LH I, or not? Before we discuss this, we need to define what we mean by differentiation. When we archaeologists examine social differentiation on the basis of mortuary practices, we are accustomed to think primarily about status differences. However, social status is only one aspect of personal identity, and in most pre-modern societies it cannot be discussed separately from other aspects, notably from age, gender and kin position.

Age

We have already observed significant differences between age groups. We have pointed out that the proportional representation of age groups changes through time: In EH III the only burials found belong to neonates and infants, while in MH I–II all age groups are buried in the settlement area.[14] The situation changes in

---

[13] We see a similar phenomenon in other extramural cemeteries, *e.g.* in Prosymna (Blegen 1937), in the East Cemetery in Asine, or in the North Cemetery in Ayios Vasilios, Laconia (Voutsaki *et al.* in press).
[14] As observed also in Asine by Ingvarsson-Sundström 2008; Nordquist and Ingvarsson-Sundström 2005, 156–174, and by Pomadère 2010.

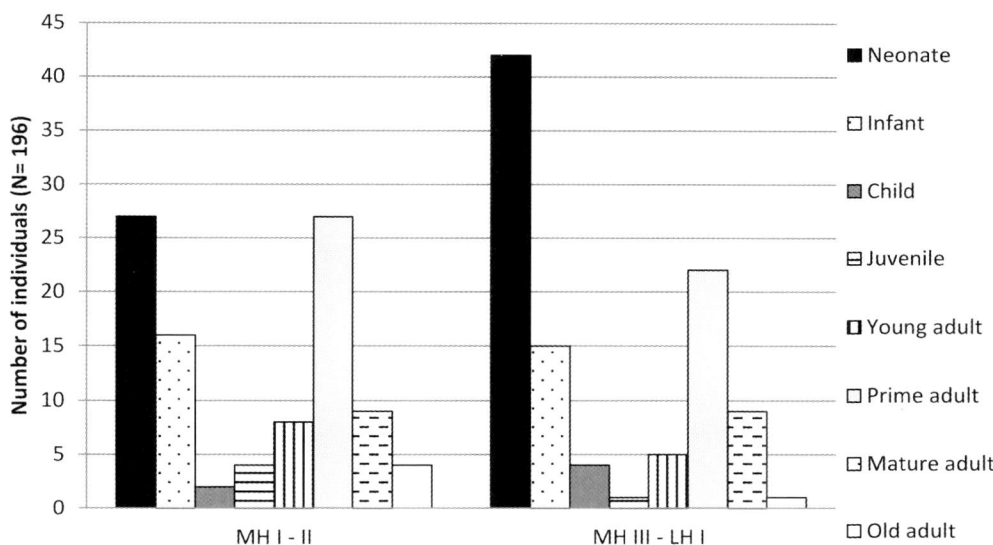

Fig. 6.5: Demographic profile through time. Neonate = 0-1 yrs; Infant = 1-6 yrs; Child = 6-12 yrs; Juvenile = 12-18 yrs; YA = Young Adult (18-30 yrs); PA = Prime Adult (30-40 yrs); MA = Mature Adult (40-50 yrs); OA = Old Adult (50+ yrs).

MH III/LHI, and especially in LH I when parts of the settlement seem to be abandoned and turned over to burial areas, used primarily for sub-adults, especially neonates (Fig. 6.5; see also Voutsaki *et al.* 2013, 135). As we pointed out above, the extramural cemetery in Myloi contains primarily adult burials. Age differentiation is therefore important throughout the period, but seems to become more pronounced in MH III–LH I. This conclusion is reinforced by other observations, as specific practices were seemingly used by certain age categories: for instance, with one exception, only adults are buried in extended position,[15] while the very limited evidence we have from the shaft graves[16] tentatively suggests that they were also used (primarily?) for adults.[17]

Differences can also be observed in the location of graves, as neonates and infants are sometimes placed in graves under houses in use, while adults are as a rule buried in ruined or abandoned houses (Milka in Voutsaki *et al.* 2006, 107; Milka 2010). We also see differentiation in tomb types: jar burials are used only for neonates, infants and more rarely for child burials. While cists and pits are used by both adults and sub-adults, the situation changes through time and pits are increasingly used for sub-adults in MH III–LH I (see Fig. 6.6). Age-related variation can also be observed in the

---

[15] The only exception is perhaps the burial in grave DC 2, where a two-year-old infant (148 Ler) may have been buried extended on its back and was accompanied by rich offerings (Blackburn 1970, 174).
[16] Only few foot bones of an adult were recovered from shaft grave 2.
[17] As indeed was the case in the Grave Circles of Mycenae where adult burials predominate: Angel 1973; Triantaphyllou in Voutsaki *et al.* 2007, 90–91; Papazoglou-Manioudaki *et al.* 2010; Voutsaki 2004.

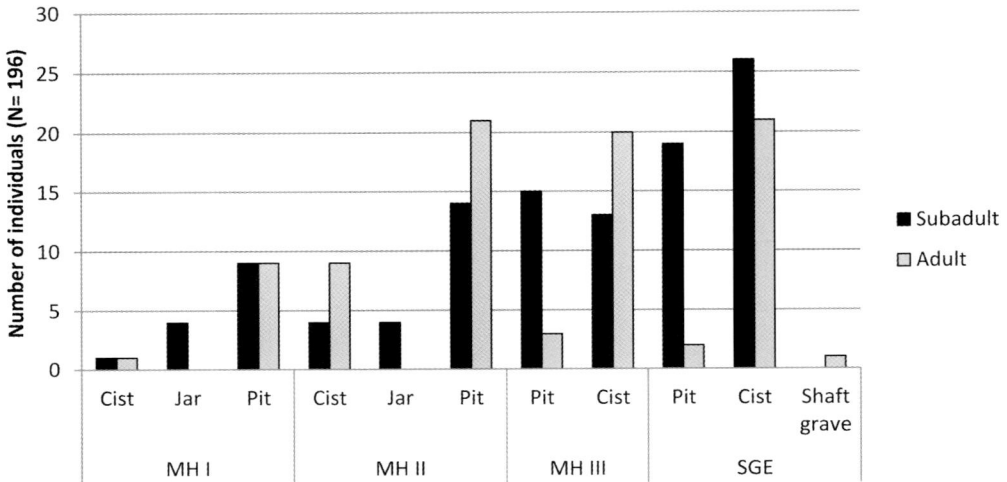

Fig. 6.6: Tomb types against age categories through time.

offerings: throughout the period non-ceramic objects, and ornaments in particular, are found predominantly in sub-adult burials.

Finally, dietary differences have also been attested between the adult and sub-adult population (Voutsaki *et al.* 2013, 135): The study of oral pathologies suggests that the sub-adult segment of the population consistently consumed soft and processed foodstuffs already in MH I–II.

To conclude: age remains an important principle of differentiation throughout the period and becomes more pronounced in the later phases.

Gender

In contrast to age, gender differences are not really pronounced in MH Lerna, though the situation changes slightly in MH III–LH I. We should first point out that more men than women are buried in the Lerna graves throughout the period and the discrepancy becomes even more marked in MH III–LH I (see Fig. 6.7) – a pattern which remains difficult to explain. Throughout the period females tend to be buried on their left, and males on their right side (Nordquist 1979, 17; Ruppenstein 2010). If we examine burial position through time, we see that the difference becomes clearer in MH II and persists into the later phases (Fig. 6.8).

Some subtle differentiation in grave goods can also be observed, but it is difficult to observe changes through time because of the small number of graves with offerings. Through time slightly more tools have been found in male (14 tools) than in female graves (12 tools). Ornaments (for the first time deposited in MH II) are found often, but not always, with female (juvenile) burials.[18] (Simple)

---

[18] The majority are found in grave H 1.

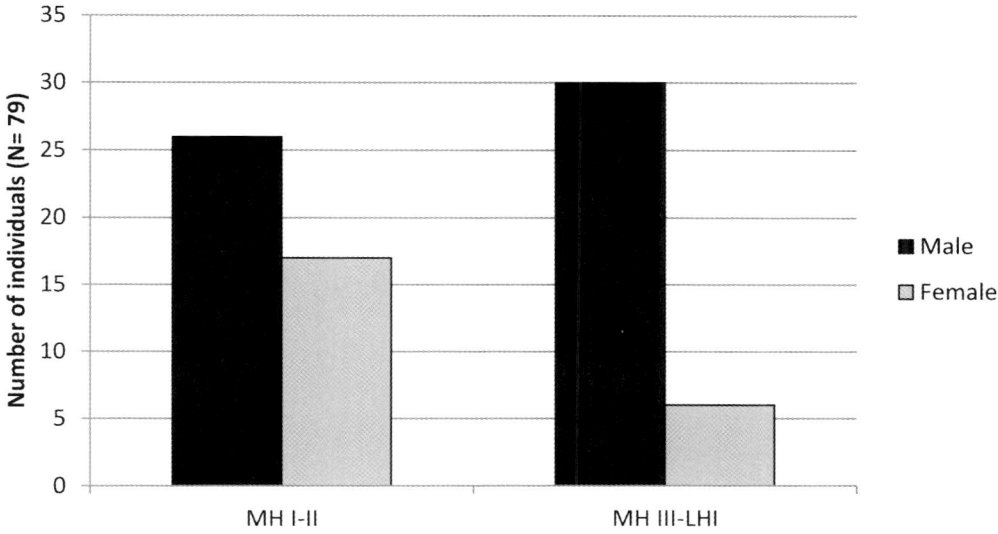

Fig. 6.7: Men and women through time.

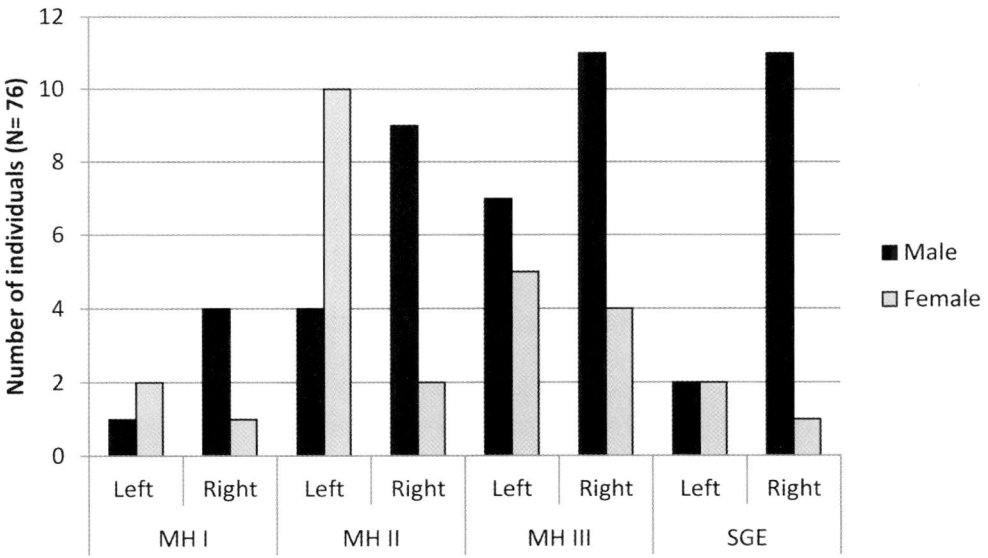

Fig. 6.8: Burial position against sex through time.

weapons[19] are found only in male graves, while single male burials contain ornaments only exceptionally[20] (Voutsaki 2004, 356; Milka in Voutsaki et al. 2007, 65).

---

[19] Such as arrowheads or pellets; no metal weapons have been found in the Lerna graves, with the exception of the razor blade or knife in grave J 4B which may have been used as a weapon (see below).
[20] Grave DE 45, Blackburn 1970, 139–140 (grave 180).

The osteological evidence points to some kind of division of labour, or different life-styles already in MH I–II:[21] While both sexes show high rates of skeletomuscular lesions and non-specific infections which imply that they engaged in heavy manual work, women also had higher rates of anaemia and enamel hypoplasia, and must have been more exposed to malnutrition and poorer living conditions. In addition, men consistently show a slightly higher incidence of non-specific infections, which may suggest more frequent exposure to pathogenic agents, perhaps due to external contacts. However, in both cases the differences are small. In MH III–LH I differences in health status and diet show a slight increase, though they remain statistically insignificant due to the small sample size.

Finally, the stable isotope analysis shows that differences in diet were not pronounced, though the dental microwear analysis suggests that women ate softer foodstuffs than men (Triantaphyllou *et al.* 2008a; Voutsaki *et al.* 2013, 135–136) – but again the sample sizes are very small.

"Wealth" and "social status"

Social status is often reconstructed on the basis of the number, provenance or quality of offerings, or the type, size and construction of the grave. However, theoretical objections against the equation between wealth or tomb elaboration and social status have been voiced since the early 1980s (Hodder 1982; Parker Pearson 1982). It is now generally accepted that mortuary practices are a form of self-representation, which may reveal the main structuring principles of social life (Morris 1992), but do not necessarily mirror social divisions.

In the early MH period in particular, wealth and status are not really meaningful categories. Small differences in the quality, quantity and diversity of offerings exist, but they do not correlate with grave type, size or construction.[22] For instance, H 1,[23] the MH II burial of an adolescent girl, among the "richest" burials in Lerna, which was accompanied by a jug, an armband consisting of beads and shells and a few loose shells,[24] was found in a simple pit. It is very likely that differences in offerings reflect personal preferences, beliefs and circumstances or emotional attachment – at least the fact that offerings in this period do not form standard sets and associations point to this direction.

There is perhaps one exception: MH II grave J 4B[25] contains the extended burial of a man in a cist accompanied by two sets of vases (drinking cup plus pouring jug or jar, including one Minoan import) and a bronze razor blade or knife. In this grave not only do different aspects of the mortuary practices correlate; it also displays several innovative features (the use of a semi-cist, the extended position, the deposition of

---

[21] See Voutsaki *et al.* 2013 for a more extensive discussion on this point.
[22] Elsewhere (Voutsaki *et al.* 2013) we have argued that the (minimal) differences in mortuary treatment do not correlate with diet, pathologies or stress levels.
[23] Blackburn 1970, 116–117 (grave 136).
[24] Four stone or paste beads, six shells and two crystals were found near the girl's left arm.
[25] Blackburn 1970, 81–82 (grave 84).

more offerings, notably in sets) which will gradually become the norm in the following periods. In addition, the tomb was re-used; a male skeleton (J 4A[26]) in contracted position, accompanied by a bowl was placed on top of the earlier burial, disturbing it and displacing some of its bones. Interestingly, the burial indicates some external contacts: apart from the presence of a Minoan jar, the composition of the funerary assemblage seems to be a (poorer) imitation of contemporary rich graves, *e.g.* the built grave in Kolonna (Kilian-Dirlmeier 1997).

Either way, we see that the first "richer" graves appear already in MH II. As we have pointed out above, in MH III we observe a very modest increase in mortuary deposition. The situation does not really change much in LH I – the two shaft graves were admittedly emptied at a later period, but there is no indication that they contained precious offerings.[27] A few other burials in Lerna and in the neighbouring extramural cemetery in Myloi received some more offerings than had been the norm in previous periods, though, as pointed out above, neither their quantity nor their quality is impressive. On the other hand, in this period correlations between different aspects of the mortuary treatment become slightly stronger (though still not statistically significant). Extended skeletons, for instance, are usually found in larger cists (and presumably in the shaft graves?) and are accompanied by more offerings. Differentiation is therefore more consistent – though in Lerna it never becomes pronounced. We have already stressed that the relative poverty of Lerna becomes even more striking when compared with neighbouring Argos or Asine and of course with Mycenae.

It is therefore difficult to identify ostentatious burials (Kilian-Dirlmeier 1997) or aggrandizing leaders (Wright 2004) before the LH I shaft graves. One possible exception is J 4B which, however, is distinguished more by its innovative practices than by wealth or ostentation. We will return to this point below.

Kinship relations

At first sight, kinship and descent are not emphasized in the intramural burial in Lerna: practices such as the re-use of graves or secondary treatment remain rare even in the MH III–LH I period. However, multiple use and the secondary treatment of earlier burials[28] characterize extramural cemeteries rather than intramural graves. Indeed secondary burials are rare also in other intramural cemeteries, *e.g.* in Ayios Stephanos in Laconia.

However, this first impression is misleading. A different picture emerges if we approach the evidence in a different way – *i.e.* if we analyse not only differentiation

---

[26] Blackburn 1970, 81–82 (grave 84).
[27] Blackburn 1970, 168–173. See also Lindblom 2007 for a recent discussion on the nature of the assemblage from the shaft graves.
[28] It has been argued elsewhere that the re-use of graves and the introduction of new grave types especially designed for multiple interments – such as the shaft grave, the tholos and chamber tomb – designates an increased emphasis on kinship and descent in a period when status divisions become important (Voutsaki 2010b).

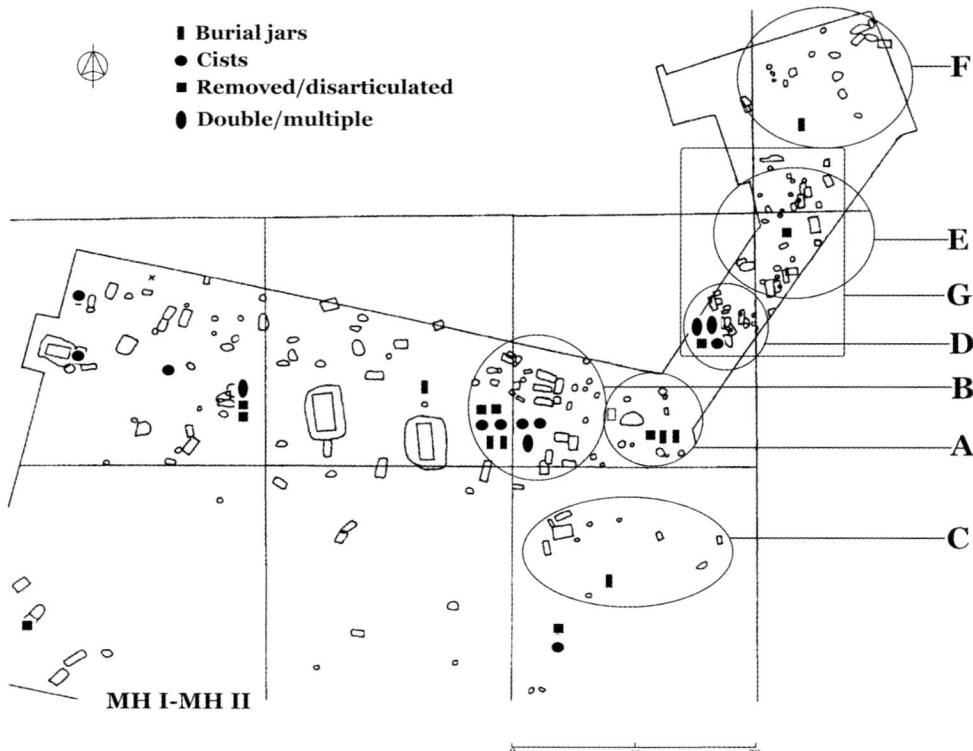

Fig. 6.9: Differentiation between groups of graves. MH I-MH II: Mortuary treatment in the different grave groups.

between *individual graves* but also differentiation *between groups of graves*, and if we analyse the graves also in relation to the houses (Milka in Voutsaki *et al.* 2007, 66–68; Milka 2010; Voutsaki *et al.* 2013). Indeed intramural graves in Lerna form groups which consist of graves located close together and are associated with the same house, or house plot through time.[29] Since these groups contain men, women and children, it is reasonable to infer that they represent households or "families". This conclusion is strengthened by the similarities within the groups (Figs. 6.9–6.12): For instance, ceramic, imports and non-ceramic offerings (Figs. 6.10 and 6.12), cists (the new tomb type) and jar burials, but also double and multiple, or removed and disarticulated burials (Figs. 6.9 and 6.11) are found in higher frequencies in certain grave groups, in what seems to be the most prominent part of the settlement, near the tumulus erected over the House of Tiles. Most importantly, these differences persist throughout

---

[29] As demonstrated by Milka 2010, the use of specific plots alternates between burial and domestic use, as graves are cut into the ruins of abandoned or destroyed houses, and these graves are in their turn built over by a new house built more or less in the same location.

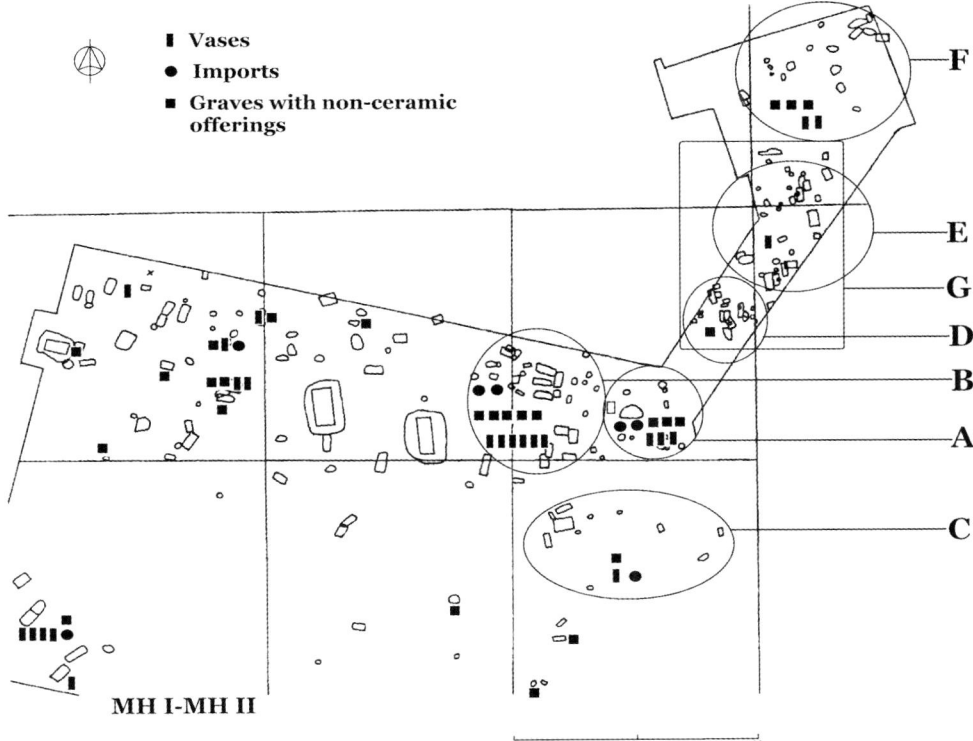

Fig. 6.10: Differentiation between groups of graves. MH I-MH II: The distribution of offerings across the different grave groups.

the period (see Figs. 6.9–6.10 versus Figs. 6.11–6.12); in fact, the LH I shaft graves are cut in the same general area, into and next to the tumulus.

This persisting pattern implies that kinship divisions remain important throughout the MH period.[30] This conclusion speaks against the presence of fluid *ad hoc* groups such as factions formed and dissolved by aspiring leaders according to the exigencies of the moment (Wright 2001). We have already remarked that it is difficult to identify aggrandizing leaders in the mortuary record before the LH I shaft graves. Mortuary practices in Lerna seem to be characterized throughout the MH period by restraint and austerity. This conclusion is strengthened by another observation: If we examine the occurrence of craft products and/or valuables in MH Lerna (Table 6.1), we observe that all categories, with the exception of beads, are found more often in settlement layers than in graves. This implies that more goods circulated in real life than we find deposited in the graves. We can conclude that during the MH period the emphasis

---

[30] For an extended discussion on kinship, descent and the transmission of resources within the family, see Voutsaki 2016.

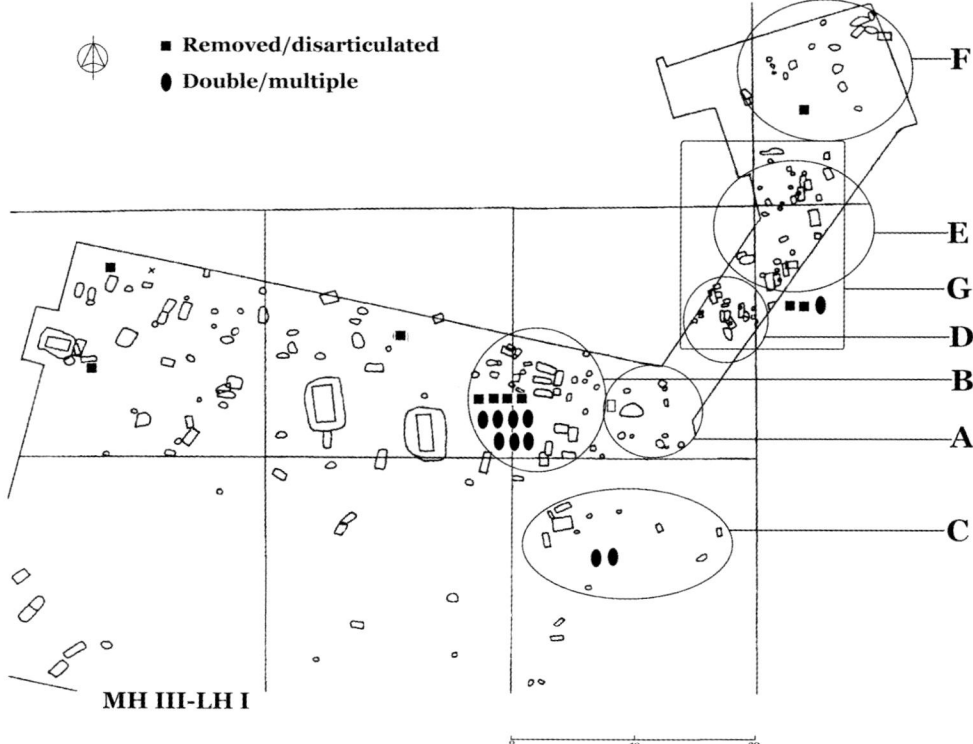

Fig. 6.11: Differentiation between groups of graves. MH III–LH I: Mortuary treatment in the different grave groups.

must have been on sharing and reciprocity rather than on accumulation and display (Voutsaki 2016).

Therefore, the working hypothesis with which we started the *Middle Helladic Argolid Project* seems to be largely confirmed by our analyses: *The main structuring principle underlying mortuary patterning in the MH I–II period is kinship rather than social status; that as authority was inscribed and embedded in kin relations, it did not require elaborate practices and material distinctions for its legitimation* (Voutsaki 2005, 137; Voutsaki 2010b, 92). However, we also need to qualify our hypothesis: We have already observed that subtle changes take place already in the earlier phases, especially in MH II. It is worth noting that the two graves that can be said to stand out in MH II (H 1 and especially J 4B) do not belong to any of the groups in the centre of the settlement. It is tempting to see here the beginnings of a tension between the traditional kinship-based order where personal status is defined by kinship and descent, and new ideas where status is claimed and performed by practices diverging from the norm. Caution is of course necessary, as the argument is based mostly on grave J 4B, whose context is rather unclear. However, a similar tension between kinship and personal distinction, or

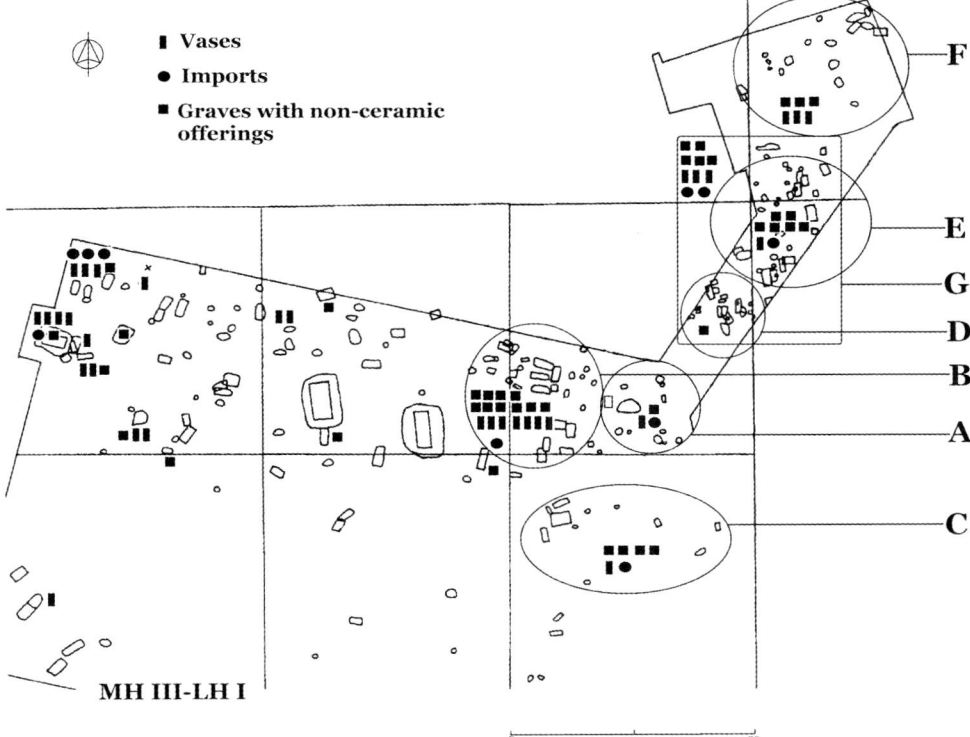

Fig. 6.12: Differentiation between groups of graves. MH III-LH I: The distribution of offerings across the different grave groups.

between tradition and innovation can also be detected in the LH I shaft graves: They are larger and more complex, and their use was accompanied by a festive meal to which a large group must have participated – but there is no evidence for rich offerings and they were placed in the traditional, "intramural" setting, on or near the tumulus and the (abandoned) houses.

Before we place the mortuary data in the settlement context, we should briefly summarize the discussion so far: Against the prevailing opinion, there is differentiation in the Lerna (burial) community throughout the period, and changes in mortuary practices are observed already in MH I-II. However, status differences are not emphasized. The general austerity of the mortuary practices and the persistent differences between grave groups indicate a society organized along kin divisions; age is another import criterion of categorization, while gender differences exist, but are less marked, at least in the mortuary sphere. In LH I there is some evidence for status differentiation, which however remains very modest when compared to other sites in the Argolid. Changes are therefore observed throughout the period, but are neither linear, nor cumulative.

Table 6.1: Deposition of non-ceramic and/or valuable items in MH Lerna

		Offerings in graves	Found in settlement deposits
Bone	Awls	3	259
	Pins	3	199
	Needles	—	18
	Combs	—	4
	Whorls	—	5
	Beads	—	2
	Pendants	—	2
	Amulets	1	6
Stone	Arrowheads	3	41
	Seal	—	1
	Mould	—	1
	Cup	—	2
	Pommel	—	1
	Beads	20	9
	Amulets	—	7
Glass paste	Beads	38	—
Ivory		1	1
Bronze	Weapons	—	2
	Knife	1	2
	Awl	—	1
	Pins	3	16
	Rings	8	2
	Beads	9	—
Silver		3	2

Let us now look at the evidence from houses. By definition, a discussion on social change cannot be based solely on the mortuary practices, which do not necessarily offer an accurate reflection of social processes. In an intramural context, integrating mortuary with settlement data, *i.e.* with observations on domestic architecture and assemblages, is even more necessary. We have already seen that in MH Lerna graves are cut in or around the ruins of abandoned or destroyed houses which are later built over by a new house in more or less the same location. This alternation between graves and houses starts in MH II, and implies a growing emphasis on the demarcation and continuity of the household and the safeguarding and transmission of resources.

Our discussion will start with the same questions we posited on the funerary data: Do we see variation between houses, and is this the case already in MH I–II? Do we detect changes through time, both in the earlier and the later periods?

Houses in MH I–II Lerna are predominantly self-standing, small and apsidal (see Wiersma 2014, 137–141). The absence of an organized settlement lay-out and the limited evidence of collective works implies an emphasis on the individual domestic unit, *i.e.* the household rather than the extended kin group or the community.[31] The two EHIII/MH I apsidal houses 68A and 99E are typical for this early period: one- or two-roomed, with evidence of cooking and storage indoors and of basic manufacturing activities both indoors and in the narrow lane between them. Both houses were replaced in late MH I by a house complex which differs from earlier (and contemporary) houses:[32] It occupies a larger plot demarcated by an enclosure, which contains a rather small apsidal house (98A), a courtyard with a hearth and two auxiliary rooms (44 and 45).[33] The house complex has impressive storage capacity, including a large number of imported Minoan jars, indicating the accumulation of surplus and participation in exchange networks.[34] It has been interpreted as "the chief's house" implying social differentiation already in this early period.[35] However, the house was not particularly rich in other respects:[36] The usual assemblage of tools and small finds, implying basic manufacturing activities, was recovered from it, though nothing that could be termed valuable.[37] In addition, no valuable or exceptional finds came from the graves that were dug into its ruins after its destruction in late MH II. In this case, therefore, surplus does not seem to have stimulated the manufacture of valuables or the employment of craft specialists, nor did it lead to a wealth differential. Most importantly, the domestic assemblage shows no evidence for ostentatious practices, such as feasting. Nor is this complex unique: Carol Zerner's re-examination of the evidence revealed that at least two other such compounds may have existed, though both are partly preserved and poorly documented.[38]

Most MH II houses are poorly preserved, but in any case the house complexes are destroyed or fall out of use at the end of the period. Although the situation is not much better in MH III due to the erosion of the upper settlement layers, some definite changes can be seen: A few (very fragmentary) MH III houses in area DE are larger, and have a more complex and organized lay-out with some evidence for duplication

---

[31] See Wiersma 2014, and for the social implications Voutsaki 2016.

[32] In contrast, no differentiation is observed among MH I–II houses in Asine. See Voutsaki 2010a; Wiersma 2014, 121–128.

[33] Caskey 1956, 159. For a more detailed analysis, see Voutsaki and Zerner forthcoming.

[34] According to Carol Zerner, this period represents the peak of Minoan imports in Lerna. It is unfortunately impossible to study the distribution of Minoan imports across the settlement, as not all ceramic material was kept.

[35] Wright 2001; 2004, 70ff.

[36] It should be added that the house complex was destroyed in a violent fire and became covered by accumulated debris which sealed its contents.

[37] *I.e.* ground stone, obsidian and chert tools, bone pins, bone tools, clay whorls, etc. It should be mentioned here that metal tools, simple ornaments, or bronze pins have been found elsewhere in MH II Lerna (Banks 1967, passim).

[38] These are apsidal house 55 with rooms AR, AM in area DE (in the area of grave group A) and apsidal house BI with room BS in area D (grave group F).

of functions (*e.g.* double entrance, more than one cooking installations or storage areas, etc.). These houses resemble the large, multi-roomed houses B, D, E in Asine (Nordquist 1987; Voutsaki 2010a; Wiersma 2014, 121–128)[39] which seem to be composed of megaron-shaped units joined together, with different entrances, and usually more than one oven, hearth or cooking area. In the transition to the LH period, therefore, the self-standing, simple and relatively small MH houses become transformed to the larger, more complex multi-roomed and diversified Mycenaean houses (Darcque 2005). This phenomenon indicates changes in the size and composition of the domestic unit, but also a shift away from the individual household to the wider kin group. We have suggested elsewhere that (possibly related) families moved together, perhaps in order to enlarge their work force, pool resources and thereby improve their position in exchange networks (see Voutsaki 2010a; Voutsaki 2016; for a general discussion, see Wiersma 2014, 245–246, this volume). To conclude, kinship relations remain important throughout the period, but undergo a transformation through the MH period from the household to the extended kin group.

Concluding discussion

The main aim of our paper was to reconstruct processes of social change in MH Lerna by means of a contextual analysis of mortuary and settlement data. An indirect aim was also to critically assess prevailing opinion on the MH mainland and to examine how static, undifferentiated and homogeneous the societies of the MH mainland *really* were.

Our analysis has demonstrated that social life in MH Lerna was far from static. To start with, the changing composition of the burial group indicates shifting criteria of inclusion throughout the period, but possibly also demographic growth in MH I-II. Our contextual analyses have also revealed that mortuary practices underwent changes, and that forms and practices were adopted or abandoned throughout the period. Several horizons of change can be reconstructed: In EH III the new practice of intramural burial is adopted, at first only for neonates and infants, but from MH I onwards also for adults. Cists seem to be introduced in MH II, when jar burials are abandoned. In MH I vases accompany the dead for the first time, while in MH II non-ceramic objects are also deposited. In MH III few changes can be observed among the intramural burials, but the first extramural cemeteries seem to come to use. In LH I, the two shaft graves are opened in the most prominent part of the settlement. Their use must have been accompanied by a funerary feast – but the settlement as a whole seems to become largely abandoned and to be used mostly for the burial of sub-adults.

While changes occur throughout the period, their rate, nature and extent also change. In MH II the rate intensifies: In the mortuary practices we observe experimentation

---

[39] Similar houses are known from other sites (*e.g.* Lambda house II in Ayios Stephanos in Laconia, see Wiersma 2014, 160).

and a certain "scaling up", although we only rarely (in the case of the man buried in J 4B) see overt or consistent differentiation. In the domestic sphere, the appearance of house complexes for the first time indicates differences between households. These developments need to be placed in their wider context: This period sees the peak of Minoan imports in Lerna and increasing interaction across the Aegean (Zerner 1993; Alberti 2013). In addition, important changes take place in the neighbouring important centre, Kolonna in Aegina: Both the Large Building Complex (with evidence for feasting) and the built grave with the rich male burial date to this period. It is very likely that these developments exert some influence on the Lerna community – we have already pointed out the similarities between the Kolonna burial and J 4B.

The important question is whether these changes lead to a process of gradual and incremental growth. We have already remarked that the accumulation of surplus and imports in (at least one of) the house complexes did not lead to a wealth differential nor to the adoption of ostentatious practices. Either way, the house complexes fall out of use by the end of MH II, and mortuary practices in MH III are characterized by conservatism and continuing austerity. Individual status in Lerna was not emphasized before the beginning of the LH period, and differences between individual members of the community were minimal. However, differences between households and kin groups existed. Indeed kinship seems to have been the basic principle structuring social relations, as manifested by the clustering of graves and their association with specific houses, but also the shared features within burial groups and their persistence through time. We have also concluded that age and to a lesser extent gender divisions were also important – age and gender are of course closely connected with kin roles. We can therefore conclude that kinship remains the main structuring principle in Lerna throughout the MH period. Having said that, the introduction of novel practices by J 4B (or strictly speaking by his survivors and/or family members), implies that despite the weight of traditional structures and norms, the possibility for innovation, departure from the norm and individual agency existed.

The introduction of shaft graves in LH I – which clearly imitate the Mycenae shaft graves – indicates that personal status emerged as a new criterion for social categorisation. However, the positioning of the shaft-graves in the area of the tumulus and abandoned houses implies that descent and continuity retain their importance. Feasting practices associated with the use of the graves indicate that the support of the wider community, or at least of some selected groups was deemed necessary. The shaft graves therefore seem to encapsulate the dilemma between personal distinction and social obligations, between aggrandizing claims on status and the traditional kin-based order, or – to put it differently – between innovation and tradition.

We therefore would like to suggest that the developments in the earlier part of the period do not set in motion an evolutionary and irreversible process of growing complexity. But is Lerna representative of the entire Argolid, let alone of the entire southern mainland? Throughout the paper, we have suggested that Lerna follows a different social trajectory than the other sites in the Argolid. Although a systematic comparison with other sites lies beyond the scope of this paper,[40] we would like to conclude our discussion with some related remarks. Lerna undergoes a period of growth during the early MH period, receives a larger number of Minoan imports and shows more prosperity than the only other well-documented site in the Argolid, Asine (Zerner 1993, Nordquist 1987). While the complex excavation history and the poor preservation or documentation at Mycenae and Argos do not allow us to reconstruct the early phases of these important settlements, the data for the later part of the period are much more abundant: We can say with relative certainty that Lerna seems to decline in the later part of the period and that it falls into relative obscurity during the Mycenaean period. We have argued elsewhere (Voutsaki 2010b) that the decline of Lerna is part of the political realignments that led to the rise of Mycenae. We cannot reproduce the entire argument here; for the purposes of the present discussion it is sufficient to retain that Lerna follows a different trajectory than other sites, and that social developments in the MH period are not uniform.

To return to our initial question: The societies of the MH mainland are not static, but undergo subtle changes throughout the period; they are not undifferentiated, but are organized along kin, age and gender divisions, while status becomes important in the transition to the Mycenaean era; finally, different communities undergo different trajectories towards the new, Mycenaean world.

Acknowledgements

We would like to thank the Netherlands Organization for Scientific Research (NWO) for its generous funding of the *Middle Helladic Argolid Project*; the University of Groningen for providing matching funding and INSTAP for additional Research Grants. We would like to express our thanks to the successive Directors of the Argolid Directorate of Classical and Prehistoric Antiquities, Mrs Zoi Aslamatzidou, Mrs Anna Banaka and Dr Alkistis Papadimitriou, the Department of Conservation at the Greek Ministry of Culture, the American School of Classical Studies, and Dr M. Wiencke, Dr C. Zerner and Dr E. Banks for granting us permission to study and sample the Lerna skeletons. We would also like to acknowledge the assistance of the staff at the Argolid Directorate. The personnel in the Museum of Argos have been extremely helpful throughout our stay in Argos; we thank them all. Sofia Voutsaki would like to thank Francis Koolstra for his assistance during the preparation of this paper.

Bibliography

Alberti, M. E. 2013. "Aegean Trade Systems: Overview and Observations on the Middle Bronze Age." In *Exchange Networks and Local Transformations: Interaction and Local Change in Europe and the Mediterranean from the Bronze Age to the Iron Age*, edited by M. E. Alberti and S. Sabatini, 22–43. Oxford, Oxbow Books.

---

[40] A systematic comparison between Lerna and Asine is undertaken by Milka (forthcoming).

Alden, M. 2000. *The Prehistoric Cemetery: Pre-Mycenaean and Early Mycenaean Graves*. Well-Built Mycenae. The Helleno-British Excavations within the Citadel at Mycenae, 1959–1969, fasc. 7 Oxford, Oxbow Books.

Angel, J. L. 1973. "Human skeletons from Grave Circles at Mycenae." In *Ο Ταφικός Κύκλος Β' των Μυκηνών*, edited by G. Mylonas, 379–394. Library of the Archaeological Society at Athens 73. Athens, Archaeological Society.

Blegen, C. W. 1937. *Prosymna: The settlement Preceding the Argive Heraeum*. Cambridge, Cambridge University Press.

Blackburn, E. T. 1970. *Middle Helladic Graves and Burial Customs with Special Reference to Lerna in the Argolid*. PhD Dissertation, University of Cincinnati.

Banks, E. C. 1967. *The Early and Middle Helladic Objects from Lerna*. PhD Dissertation, University of Cincinnati.

Boyd, M. J. 2002. *Middle Helladic and Early Mycenaean Mortuary Practices in the Southern and Western Peloponnese*. Oxford, Archaeopress.

Caskey, J. L. 1956. "Excavations at Lerna, 1955." *Hesperia* 25, 147–173.

Cavanagh, W., and C. Mee. 1998. *A Private Place: Death in Prehistoric Greece*. Studies in Mediterranean Archaeology 125. Jonsered, P. Åström.

Darcque, P. 2005. *L'habitat mycénien: formes et fonctions de l'espace bâti en Grèce continentale à la fin du IIe millllénaire avant J.-C*. Athens, École française d'Athènes/De Boccard.

Davis, J.L., and S. Stocker. 2010. "Early Helladic and Middle Helladic Pylos: The Petropoulos Trenches and Pre-Mycenaean Remains on the Englianos Ridge." In *Mesohelladika. The Greek Mainland in the Middle Bronze Age*, Bulletin de Correspondance Hellénique Supplement 52, edited by A. Philippa-Touchais, G. Touchais, S. Voutsaki, and J. Wright, 101–106. Athens, De Boccard.

Demakopoulou, K., and N. Divari-Valakou. 2010. "The Middle Helladic Settlement on the Acropolis of Midea." In *Mesohelladika. The Greek Mainland in the Middle Bronze Age*, Bulletin de Correspondance Hellénique Supplement 52, edited by A. Philippa-Touchais, G. Touchais, S. Voutsaki, and J. Wright, 31–44. Athens, De Boccard.

Dickinson, O. T. P. K. 1977. *The Origins of Mycenaean Civilisation*. Studies in Mediterranean Archaeology 49. Göteborg, P. Åström.

Dickinson, O. T. P. K. 2010. "The 'Third World' of the Aegean? Middle Helladic Greece Revisited." In *Mesohelladika. The Greek Mainland in the Middle Bronze Age*, Bulletin de Correspondance Hellénique Supplement 52, edited by A. Philippa-Touchais, G. Touchais, S. Voutsaki, and J. Wright, 13–27. Athens, De Boccard.

Dietz, S. 1980. *The Middle Helladic Cemetery, the Middle Helladic and Early Mycenaean Deposits*. Asine II. Results of the Excavations East of the Acropolis 1970–1974, fasc. 2. Acta Instituti Atheniensis Regni Sueciae 4, 24.2. Stockholm, Skrifter utgivna av Svenska instituteti Athen.

Dietz, S., and N. Divari-Valakou 1990. "A Middle Helladic III/Late Helladic I Grave Group from Myloi in the Argolid (Oikopedon Manti)." *Opuscula Atheniensia* 18, 4, 45–62.

Felten, F., W. Gauß, and R. Smetana, eds. 2007. *Middle Helladic Pottery and Synchronisms. Proceedings of the International Workshop held at Salzburg October 31st-November 2nd, 2004*, Ägina–Kolonna Forschungen und Ergebnisse I/Österreichische Akademie der Wissenschaften Denkschriften der Gesamtakademie 42. Vienna, Austrian Academy of Sciences.

Gauß, W., and R. Smetana 2010. "Aegina Kolonna in the Middle Bronze Age." In *Mesohelladika. The Greek Mainland in the Middle Bronze Age*, Bulletin de Correspondance Hellénique Supplement 52, edited by A. Philippa-Touchais, G. Touchais, S. Voutsaki, and J. Wright, 165–174. Athens, De Boccard.

Gorogianni, E. 2002. *Middle Helladic Period in Boiotia: A Study of Social Organization*. MA Dissertation, University of Cincinnati.

Hodder, I. 1982. "The Identification and Interpretation of Ranking in Prehistory: A Contextual Perspective." In *Ranking, Resource and Exchange*, edited by C. Renfrew and S. Shennan, 150–154. Cambridge, Cambridge University Press.

Ingvarsson-Sundström, A. 2008. *Children Lost and Found: A Bioarchaeological Study of Middle Helladic Children in Asine with a Comparison to Lerna*. Asine III: Supplementary Studies on the Swedish Excavations 1922–1930, fasc. 2. Stockholm, Swedish Institute at Athens.

Ingvarsson-Sundström, A., M. P. Richards and S. Voutsaki. 2009. "Stable Isotope Analysis of the Middle Helladic Population from the Two Cemeteries at Asine: Barbouna and the East Cemetery." *Mediterranean Archaeology and Archaeometry* 9.2, 1–14.

Ingvarsson-Sundström, A., S. Voutsaki, and E. Milka. 2013. "People, Animals and Social Diversity in Middle Helladic Asine: A Bioarchaeological View". In *Diet, Economy and Society in the Ancient Greek World: Towards a Better Integration of Archaeology and Science*, Pharos Supplement 1, edited by S. Voutsaki and S.M. Valamoti 149-162. Leuven, Peeters.

Kanz, F., K. Grossschmidt, and J. Kiesslich. 2010. "Subsistence and More in MBA Aegina Kolonna: An Anthropology of Newborn Children." In *Mesohelladika. The Greek Mainland in the Middle Bronze Age*, Bulletin de Correspondance Hellénique Supplement 52, edited by A. Philippa-Touchais, G. Touchais, S. Voutsaki, and J. Wright, 479–487. Athens, De Boccard.

Kilian-Dirlmeier, I. 1997. *Das mittelbronzezeitliche Schachtgrab von Ägina*. Kataloge vor- und frühgeschichtlicher Altertümer 27, Alt-Ägina 4.3. Mainz am Rhein, Philipp von Zabern.

Kovatsi, L., D. Nikou, S. Triantaphyllou, S. N. Njau, S. Kouidou, and S. Voutsaki. 2009. "DNA Repair Enables Sex Identification in Genetic Material from Human Teeth." *Hippokratia* 13.3, 165–168.

Lagia, A., and W. Cavanagh. 2010. "Burials from Kouphovouno, Sparta, Lakonia." In *Mesohelladika. The Greek Mainland in the Middle Bronze Age*, Bulletin de Correspondance Hellénique Supplement 52, edited by A. Philippa-Touchais, G. Touchais, S. Voutsaki, and J. Wright, 333–346. Athens, De Boccard.

Lambropoulou, A. 1991. *The Middle Helladic Period in the Corinthia and the Argolid: An Archaeological Survey*. PhD Dissertation, Bryn Mawr College.

Lindblom, M. 2007. "Early Mycenaean mortuary meals at Lerna VI with special emphasis on their Aeginetan components." In *Middle Helladic Pottery and Synchronisms. Proceedings of the International Workshop held at Salzburg October 31st-November 2nd, 2004*, Ägina–Kolonna Forschungen und Ergebnisse I/Österreichische Akademie der Wissenschaften Denkschriften der Gesamtakademie 42, edited by F. Felten, W. Gauß, and R. Smetana, 115–135. Vienna, Austrian Academy of Sciences.

Maran, J. 1992. *Die Deutschen Ausgrabungen auf der Pevkakia-Magula in Thessalien III. Die Mittlere Bronzezeit*. Bonn, Rudolf Habelt.

Milka, E. 2006. From Cemeteries to Societies. The Study of the Middle Helladic (2000–1500 BC) Burials from the Argolid, Southern Greece. In *Symposium voor Onderzoek door Jonge Archeologen (SOJA) Bundel 2005*, edited by M. Kerkhof, R. van Oosten, F. Tomas and C. van Woerdekom, 53–63. Leiden, Stichting Onderzoek Jonge Archeologen.

Milka, E. 2010. "Burials upon the Ruins of Abandoned Houses in the MH Argolid." In *Mesohelladika. The Greek Mainland in the Middle Bronze Age*, Bulletin de Correspondance Hellénique Supplement 52, edited by A. Philippa-Touchais, G. Touchais, S. Voutsaki, and J. Wright, 433–443. Athens, De Boccard.

Milka, E. forthcoming. *Diversity and Change in Middle Helladic Mortuary Practices: A Comparison of Lerna and Asine*. PhD Dissertation, University of Groningen.

Morris, I. 1992. *Death Ritual and Social Structure in Classical Antiquity*. Cambridge, Cambridge University Press.

Mylonas, G. 1973. *Ο Ταφικός Κύκλος Β' των Μυκηνών*. Library of the Archaeological Society at Athens 73. Athens, Archaeological Society.

Nordquist, G. C. 1979. *Dead Society. A Study of the Intramural Cemetery at Lerna*. MA Dissertation, University of Southampton.

Nordquist, G. C. 1987. *A Middle Helladic Village. Asine in the Argolid*. Boreas, Uppsala Studies in Ancient Mediterranean and Near Eastern Civilisation, fasc. 16. Uppsala, Acta Universitatis Upsaliensis.

Nordquist, G. C. and A. Ingvarsson-Sundström. 2005. "Live Hard, Die Young: Middle and Early Late Helladic Mortuary Remains of Children from the Argolid in Social Context" In *Autochthon. Papers*

Presented to O. T. P. K. Dickinson on the Occasion of his Retirement, British Archaeological Report International S1432, edited by A. Dakouri-Hild and S. Sherratt, 156–174. Oxford, Archaeopress

Papazoglou-Manioudaki, L., A. Nafplioti, J. H. Musgrave, and A. J. N. W. Prag. 2010. "Mycenae Revisited Part 3. The Human Remains from Grave Circle A at Mycenae. Behind the Masks: A Study of the Bones of Graves I–V." *Annual of the British School at Athens* 105, 157–224.

Parker Pearson M. 1982. "Mortuary Practices, Society and Ideology: An Ethnoarchaeological Study." In *Symbolic and Structural Archaeology*, edited by I. Hodder, 99–113. Cambridge, Cambridge University Press.

Pavúk, P. and B. H. Horejs. 2012. *Mittel- und Spätbronzezeitliche Keramik Griechenlands. Sammlung Fritz Schachermeyr 3*. Österreichische Akademie der Wissenschaften Philosophisch-Historische Klasse Denkschriften 439, Veröffentlichungen der mykenischen Kommission 31. Vienna, Austrian Academy of Sciences.

Phialon, L. 2011. *L'émergence de la civilisation mycénienne en Grèce centrale*. Aegaeum 32. Leuven, Peeters.

Philippa-Touchais, A., G. Touchais, S. Voutsaki, and J. Wright. 2010. *Mesohelladika. The Greek Mainland in the Middle Bronze Age*, Bulletin de Correspondance Hellénique Supplement 52. Athens, De Boccard.

Philippa-Touchais, A. 2010. "Settlement Planning and Social Organisation." In *Mesohelladika. The Greek Mainland in the Middle Bronze Age*, Bulletin de Correspondance Hellénique Supplement 52, edited by A. Philippa-Touchais, G. Touchais, S. Voutsaki, and J. Wright, 781–801. Athens, De Boccard.

Pierart, M., and G. Touchais. 1996. *Argos: une ville grecque de 6000 ans*. Paris, Paris-Méditérrannée.

Pomadère, M. 2010. "De l'indifférenciation à la discrimination spatiale des sépultures? Variété des comportements à l'égard des enfants morts pendant l'HM-HR I." In *Mesohelladika. The Greek Mainland in the Middle Bronze Age*, Bulletin de Correspondance Hellénique Supplement 52, edited by A. Philippa-Touchais, G. Touchais, S. Voutsaki, and J. Wright, 433–443. Athens, De Boccard.

Protonotariou-Deilaki, E. 1980. Οι Τύμβοι του Αργους. PhD Dissertation, University of Athens.

Ruppenstein, F. 2010. "Gender and Regional Differences in Middle Helladic Burial Customs." In *Mesohelladika. The Greek Mainland in the Middle Bronze Age*, Bulletin de Correspondance Hellénique Supplement 52, edited by A. Philippa-Touchais, G. Touchais, S. Voutsaki, and J. Wright, 431–439. Athens, De Boccard.

Rutter, J. B. 2001. "The Prepalatial Bronze Age of the Southern and Central Greek Mainland." In *Aegean Prehistory: A Review*, edited by T. Cullen, 95–147. Boston, Archaeological Institute of America.

Rutter, J. B. 2007. "Reconceptualizing the Middle Helladic 'Type Site' from a Ceramic Perspective: Is 'Bigger' Really 'Better'?" In *Middle Helladic Pottery and Synchronisms: Proceedings of the International Workshop held at Salzburg October 31st–November 2nd, 2004*, Ägina–Kolonna Forschungen und Ergebnisse I/Österreichische Akademie der Wissenschaften Denkschriften der Gesamtakademie 42, edited by F. Felten, W. Gauß, and R. Smetana, 35–44. Vienna, Austrian Academy of Sciences.

Sarri, K. 2010. *Orchomenos IV: Orchomenos in der mittleren Bronzezeit*. Bayerische Akademie der Wissenschaften, Philosophisch-Historische Klasse, Abhandlungen, Neue Folge 135. Munich, Bavarian Academy of Sciences.

Sarri, K., and S. Voutsaki. 2012. "The Argos 'Tumuli'. A Re-examination." In *Ancestral Landscapes: Burial Mounds in the Copper and Bronze Ages*, edited by E. Borgna and S. Müller Celka, 433–443. Lyon, Travaux de la Maison de l'Orient.

Schliemann, H. 1878. *Mykenae: Bericht über meine Forschungen und Entdeckungen in Mykenae und Tiryns*. Leipzig, Brockhaus.

Schoep, I., P. Tomkins, and J. Driessen. 2012. *Back to the Beginning: Reassessing Social and Political Complexity on Crete during the Early and Middle Bronze Age*. Oxford, Oxbow Books.

Skorda, D., and J. Zürbach 2011. "Kirrha (Phocide)." *Bulletin de Correspondance Hèllenique* 135.2, 535–539.

Taylour, W. D., and R. Janko. 2008. *Ayios Stephanos: Excavations at a Bronze Age and Medieval Settlement in Southern Laconia*. Annual of the British School at Athens Supplement 44. London, British School at Athens.

Triantaphyllou, S. 2010. "Prospects for Reconstructing the Lives of Middle Helladic Populations in the Argolid: Past and Present of Human Bone Studies." In *Mesohelladika. The Greek Mainland in the Middle Bronze Age*, Bulletin de Correspondance Hellénique Supplement 52, edited by A. Philippa-Touchais, G. Touchais, S. Voutsaki, and J. Wright, 553–565. Athens, De Boccard.

Triantaphyllou, S., M. P. Richards, C. Zerner, and S. Voutsaki. 2008a. "Isotopic Dietary Reconstruction of Humans from Middle Bronze Age Lerna, Argolid, Greece." *Journal of Archaeological Science* 35, 3028–3034.

Triantaphyllou, S., M. P. Richards, G. Touchais, A. Philippa-Touchais, and S. Voutsaki. 2008b. "Stable Isotope Analysis of Human Bone from Middle Helladic Aspis." *Bulletin de Correspondance Héllenique* 130.2, 627–637.

Voutsaki, S. 1999. "The Shaft Grave Offerings as Symbols of Power and Prestige." In *Eliten in der Bronzezeit: Ergebnisse zweier Colloquien in Mainz und Athen*, edited by I. Kilian-Dirlmeier and M. Eggs, Monographien 43.1, 103–117. Mainz, Verlag der Römisch-Germanischen Zentralmuseums in Kommission, Römisch-Germanisches Zentralmuseum Forschungsinstitut für Vor- und Frühgeschichte.

Voutsaki, S. 2004. "Age and Gender in the Southern Greek Mainland, 2000–1500 BC." *Ethnographisch-Archäologische Zeitung*, 46.2–3, 339–363.

Voutsaki, S. 2005. "Social and Cultural Change in the Middle Helladic Period: Presentation of a New Project." In *Autochthon. Papers Presented to O. T. P. K. Dickinson on the Occasion of his Retirement*, British Archaeological Report S1432. edited by A. Dakouri-Hild and S. Sherratt, 134–143. Oxford, Archaeopress.

Voutsaki, S. 2010a. "The Domestic Economy in Middle Helladic Asine." In *Mesohelladika. The Greek Mainland in the Middle Bronze Age*, Bulletin de Correspondance Hellénique Supplement 52, edited by A. Philippa-Touchais, G. Touchais, S. Voutsaki, and J. Wright, 765–779. Athens, De Boccard.

Voutsaki, S. 2010b. "From the Kinship Economy to the Palatial Economy: The Argolid in the 2nd Millennium BC." In *Political Economies in the Aegean Bronze Age: Papers from the Langford Conference, Florida State University, Tallahassee*, edited by D. J. Pullen, 86–111. Oxford, Oxbow Books.

Voutsaki, S. 2016. "From Reciprocity to Centricity: The Middle Bronze Age in the Greek Mainland." In *Reciprocity in Aegean Palatial Societies: Gifts, Debt, and the Foundations of Economic Exchange*, edited by M. Galaty, D. Nakassis and W. Parkinson, American Journal of Archaeology Forum.

Voutsaki, S., S. Triantaphyllou, A. Ingvarsson-Sundström, S. Kouidou-Andreou, L. Kovatsi, A. J. Nijboer, D. Nikou, and E. Milka. 2006. "Project on the Middle Helladic Argolid: A Report on the 2005 Season." *Pharos* XIII, 93–117.

Voutsaki, S., S. Triantaphyllou, A. Ingvarsson-Sundström, K. Sarri, M. P. Richards, A. J. Nijboer, S. Kouidou-Andreou, L. Kovatsi, D. Nikou, and E. Milka. 2007. "Project on the Middle Helladic Argolid: A Report on the 2006 Season." *Pharos* XIV, 59–99.

Voutsaki, S., K. Sarri, O. Dickinson, S. Triantaphyllou, and E. Milka. 2009a. "The Argos Tumuli Project: A Report on the 2006 and 2007 Seasons." *Pharos* XV (2007), 153–192.

Voutsaki, S., A. J. Nijboer, and C. Zerner. 2009b. "Middle Helladic Lerna: Relative and Absolute Chronologies." In *Tree-rings, Kings, and Old World Archaeology and Environment: Papers Presented in Honour of Peter Ian Kuniholm*, edited by S. W. Manning and M. J. Bruce, 151–161. Oxford, Oxbow Books.

Voutsaki, S., A. Ingvarsson-Sundström, and S. Dietz. 2012. "Tumuli and Social Status: A Re-examination of the Asine Tumulus." In *Ancestral landscapes: Burial mounds in the Copper and Bronze Ages*, edited by S. Müller Celka and E. Borgna, 445–461. Lyon, Travaux de la Maison de l'Orient.

Voutsaki, S., E. Milka, S. Triantaphyllou, and C. Zerner. 2013. "Middle Helladic Lerna: Diet, Economy and Society." In *Diet, Economy and Society in the Ancient Greek World: Towards a Better Integration of Archaeology and Science*, Pharos Supplement 1, edited by S. Voutsaki and S. M. Valamoti, 133–148. Leuven, Peeters.

Voutsaki, S., I. Moutafi, A. Vasilogamvrou, D. Kondyli, and V. Hachtmann. In press. "Ayios Vasilios, Sparta – The North Cemetery. A Preliminary Report of the Seasons 2010–2011." *Hesperia*.

Voutsaki, S., and C. Zerner. Forthcoming. "Houses and Households in Middle Helladic Lerna." *Hesperia*.

Whittaker von Hofsten, H. 2014. *Religion and Society in Middle Bronze Age Greece*. Cambridge, Cambridge University Press.

Wiencke, M. H. 1998. "Mycenaean Lerna." *Hesperia* 67, 125–214.

Wiersma, C. W. 2014. *Building the Bronze Age. Architectural and Social Change on the Greek Mainland During Early Helladic III, Middle Helladic and Late Helladic I*. Oxford, Archaeopress International Series.

Wright, J. C. 2001. "Factions and the Origins of Leadership and Identity in Mycenaean Society." *Bulletin of the Institute of Classical Studies* 45, 182.

Wright, J. C. 2004. "The Emergence of Leadership and the Rise of Civilisation in the Aegean." In *The Emergence of Civilisation Revisited*, Sheffield Studies in Aegean Archaeology 6, edited by J. C. Barrett and P. Halstead, 64–89. Oxford, Oxbow Books.

Wright, J. C. 2010. "Towards a Social Archaeology of Middle Helladic Greece." In *Mesohelladika. The Greek Mainland in the Middle Bronze Age*, Bulletin de Correspondance Hellénique Supplement 52, edited by A. Philippa-Touchais, G. Touchais, S. Voutsaki, and J. Wright, 803–815. Athens, De Boccard.

Zavadil, M. 2013. *Monumenta: Studien zu mittel- und späthelladischen Gräbern in Messenien*. Mykenische Studien 33, Österreichische Akademie der Wissenschaften Philosophisch-Historische Klasse Denkschriften 450. Vienna, Austrian Academy of Sciences.

Zerner, C. W. 1978. *The Beginnings of the Middle Helladic Period at Lerna*. PhD Dissertation, Ann Arbor, University of Cincinnati.

Zerner, C. W. 1993. "New Perspectives on Trade in the Middle and Early Late Helladic Periods on the Mainland." In *Wace and Blegen: Pottery as Evidence for Trade in the Aegean Bronze Age 1939–1989*, edited by C. Zerner, P. Zerner, and J. Winder, 39–56. Amsterdam, J.C. Gieben.

Chapter 7

Social complexity in Late Middle Bronze Age and Early Late Bronze Age Cyclades: a view from Ayia Irini

Evi Gorogianni and Rodney D. Fitzsimons

Introduction

In this paper, we present the results of a preliminary examination of the manifestations of social complexity in the archaeological record of the Middle Bronze Age and the early phases of the Late Bronze Age at Ayia Irini, on Kea (Fig. 7.1). Ayia Irini is a logical candidate and a *sine qua non* for a study of social change in this period. First and foremost, Ayia Irini is one of the most thoroughly published Aegean sites with ample archaeological remains dating to the periods in question (Coleman 1977; Bikaki 1984; Cummer and Schofield 1984; Caskey *et al.* 1986; Davis 1986; Georgiou 1986; Overbeck 1989; Petruso 1992; Wilson 1999; Schofield 2011). Moreover, Ayia Irini, along with Phylakopi on Melos and Akrotiri on Thera, seem to have been important nodes in an environment of sustained and intensified inter-regional contact and exchange (Davis 1979; Davis *et al.* 1983; Broodbank 2004; Knappett and Nikolakopoulou 2005; 2008; Whitelaw 2005; Berg 2007a; Broodbank and Kiriatzi 2007; Davis and Gorogianni 2008; Gorogianni 2016; Gorogianni *et al.* 2016b; Fitzsimons and Gorogianni forthcoming). Strangely, even though the special character of these Cycladic communities that participated in this connected environment has been discussed thoroughly in the literature, their internal social composition has rarely been considered (for a notable exception, see Whitelaw 2005), especially when compared to the interest that their Early Bronze Age counterparts have attracted (Broodbank 1989; 1993; 2000; Whitelaw 2004; Gorogianni 2011). Thus, this paper lays the groundwork for a nuanced picture of social variability displayed at Ayia Irini, one of the sites that played a very significant role as a mediator in the socio-cultural landscape of the Aegean, and a locus where local and inter-regional social identities were negotiated. However, it does not offer straightforward answers.

7. Social complexity in Late Middle Bronze Age and Early Late Bronze Age Cyclades 125

Fig. 7.1: Ayia Irini and the Aegean World (by B. Trail).

One may rightly ask what we hope to accomplish by such an evaluation. A cursory look at these polities perhaps is enough to classify them as pre-state societies based on their size. Moreover, they were located in geographic proximity to the state-level societies of Crete and later emerging states on the mainland, and have been considered to maintain a relationship with these powers, a relationship that has been described in terms of its 'special-ness' (Davis 1979; Schofield 1982) both by those who accept the existence of actual colonies (Branigan 1981; 1984; Wiener 2013, 166) and those who do not (Davis and Gorogianni 2008; Knappett and Nikolakopoulou 2008). Therefore, what does this relationship (whatever its degree) mean for their internal socio-political landscapes? Are we to perceive these communities as microcosms of the palatial societies, equally hierarchical? At first glance, this might seem a reasonable assumption, especially if one accepts these sites as colonies and thus belonging to larger social and political units. Such hierarchies are implied by the identifications of the Pillar Rooms Complex at Phylakopi in City II (Whitelaw 2005, 54–60) and of House A at Ayia Irini during Period VII (Cummer and Schofield 1984, 1) as mansions, differentiated from other buildings by their size, central location, distinguished finds, and concentration of Minoan-inspired features. However, in the case of Ayia Irini, even if we accept unreservedly the pre-eminence of House A in Period VII and equate it with one pre-eminent family or group, this does not inherently justify the assumption for the same hierarchical relationships during previous phases of the site's life. Moreover, recent scholarship has shown that in every society there are tensions

Table 7.1: Chronological concordances in the Aegean. Absolute dates after Manning (2010, 23, tab. 2.2)

	Relative chronology	Approximate absolute dates	Ayia Irini
Final Neolithic	FN	3500–3000 BC	Period I
Early Bronze Age	EB I	3000–2650 BC	Hiatus
	EB II	2650–2200 BC	Period II
	EB III	2200–2000 BC	Period III
Middle Bronze Age	MB I	2000–1900 BC	Hiatus
	MB II	1900–1800 BC	Period IV
	MB III	1800–1700 BC	Period V
Late Bronze Age	LB I	1700–1600 BC	Period VI
	LB II	1600–1400 BC	Period VII
	LB III/LH IIIA	1400–1300 BC	Period VIII
	LB III/LH IIIB	1300–1200 BC	
	LB III/LH IIIC	1200–1100 BC	

between egalitarian and hierarchical relations (Brumfiel and Fox 1994; Ehrenreich *et al.* 1995; Chapman 2003, 71–76), hence no society is truly one or the other. In the same vein, there are cases of communities (*e.g.*, kibbutzes) emphasizing egalitarian relationships even when integrated into a larger social system based on hierarchical and stratified social interactions (Donner 1988; Keene 1991).

With these parameters in mind, this paper surveys the archaeological record of Ayia Irini in search of all the "usual" indices of inequality or ranking (Wason 1994). The periods of interest for this paper are Ayia Irini Periods IV, V, VI, and VII, which span ca. 1900 to 1400 BC, or the middle phase of the Middle Bronze Age to Late Bronze Age II, a time during which a number of communities on the Greek mainland were in the process of developing into state-level societies themselves (Fitzsimons 2011) (Table 7.1). The treatment of these periods, and the resultant observations, are inherently uneven because of differing degrees of preservation and intensity of research. Hence, the description of the potential rise of socio-economic differentiation for Periods IV and V is by necessity more homogenizing in style, whereas for Periods VI and VII there is a focus on attitudes toward differential consumption in the various areas of the site. The data and analysis draw heavily on current research conducted in the Northern Sector and Area B.[1] It is our contention that distinct areas, at least

---

[1] The Northern Sector has been investigated and is being published by the Ayia Irini Northern Sector Archaeological Project, co-directed by the authors (Gorogianni 2016; Gorogianni *et al.* 2015, 2016a; Gorogianni and Abell forthcoming). Area B has been investigated by Abell (Abell 2014a). The ceramic data that are quoted in this paper have been discussed in Gorogianni and Abell (forthcoming) and pertain to proportion of imported macroscopic categories of material relative to the total assemblage of imported ceramics. This

during the main phases of the site, represent different social groups and that the archaeological record of Ayia Irini preserves evidence that could be used to elucidate the changing dynamics among these groups, dynamic relationships that were not always predominantly hierarchical.

Period IV

Overbeck and Crego have claimed that the settlement of Ayia Irini during the Middle Bronze Age (Table 7.1) was the product of a deliberate colonization expedition that took place sometime after the beginning of the period, an expedition that sought to establish an emporium for the facilitation of trade and exchange (Overbeck 1982; Overbeck and Crego 2008; Crego 2010) (Fig. 7.2 and Table 7.1).[2] Settlers from elsewhere chose this location, probably attracted to the significant advantages in terms of access to coveted resources, i.e., the Lavrion ores on the opposite shore (Gale and Stos-Gale 2008), the nearby fresh-water spring (Overbeck 1989b, 122; Schofield 2011, 53), and the immediate proximity to maritime pathways that criss-cross the Aegean (Agouridis 1997; Broodbank 2000, 92–96, esp. fig. 21).

The settlement that was established featured a fortification wall with at least one horseshoe-shaped tower and a gate accessible via an earthen ramp, and freestanding buildings that were probably used as residences. The connections of this settlement's inhabitants with the outside world were remarkable. Crego, commenting on the earliest settlement (IVa), argued that the settlement represents the "first comprehensive linking of the Helladic, Cycladic, and Minoan exchange networks" (Crego 2010, 841) since from the very beginning, there is evidence for imports from Central Greece, Aegina, the Southern Cyclades, and the Minoan world (Overbeck 1982, 1984b; Overbeck and Crego 2008; Crego 2010). Overall, it seems that about a quarter of the assemblage (from all phases of Period IV) was imported from other parts of the Aegean (Gorogianni and Abell forthcoming, tab. 2; Abell 2014a, 364–365) (Table 7.2); of this, over half of the imports may have come from Crete, while a significant percentage came from the mainland, including central Greece, and perhaps the Peloponnese, while other

---

methodology was deemed appropriate because of the nature of the archaeological record preserved from Caskey's excavations, which has been compromised in a sense by discarding of "uninformative" material. Thorough descriptions of the archaeological process as well as assessments of its impact on the archaeological record and knowledge have been discussed elsewhere (Gorogianni 2008, 88–115; 2013; Gorogianni and Abell forthcoming; Gorogianni in progress); nevertheless, it is sufficient to say in this context that the distinctiveness of the local fabric aided in the selection (and preservation) of a large volume of imported materials. As a result the assumption inherent in the analyses of the ceramic material from the site here and elsewhere is that the relative percentages of imports present in the extant material represent past realities more or less accurately (for more details on the differential effects of the discarding process in various periods see Gorogianni and Abell forthcoming, table 2).

[2] For recent treatments of colonization of the Mediterranean, as well as for problematization of traditional views on the colonization process, see Malkin 1998; Dietler 2005; Hodos 2006; Broodbank 2013; Dawson 2013.

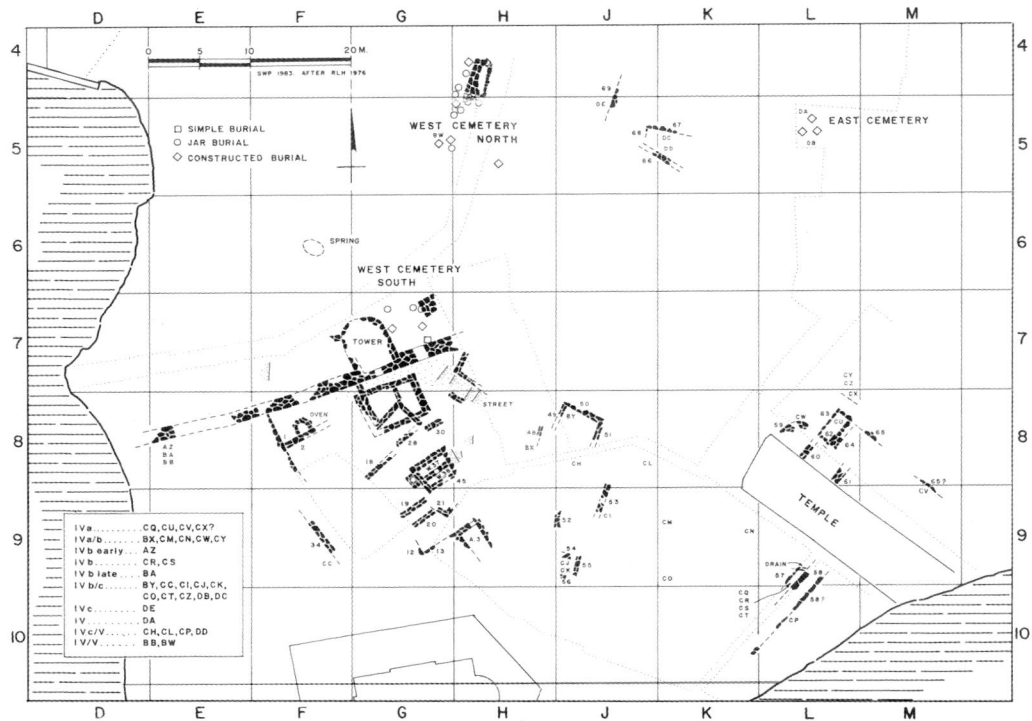

Fig. 7.2: Period IV settlement and cemeteries (Overbeck 1989b, pls. 10–11).

vessels were imported from the Cyclades, including Melos and/or Thera, Aegina, and possibly Kythera, in addition to other, unknown production centres.[3]

The composition of the first generation of settlers has been of interest recently. The site (and therefore the community) was not much larger than its EBA predecessor, which was probably a village-sized community of no more than 200 residents (Davis 1984a, 20, n. 17; Broodbank 2000, 218, n. 2). Overbeck and Crego have suggested that the origin of these settlers can be traced back to places such as Central Greece (Overbeck 1982; Overbeck and Crego 2008) and Aegina (Crego 2010) on the basis of parallels in ceramics as well as on the architectural layout of the settlement and the fortification wall. Moreover, Crego hypothesized that there were few women in the first group based on the limited quantities of weaving and spinning equipment that have been found associated with the earliest phase of Period IV (Crego 2010). Nevertheless, in a recent reassessment of the question Abell argues persuasively that the settler population was more diverse than previously believed and included both

---

[3] For the methodology of these analyses, see note 54 and Gorogianni and Abell forthcoming. The percentages reported here for Area B are somewhat different from Overbeck and Crego's published estimations (Overbeck 1989b; Overbeck and Crego 2008), which might be due to different analytical categories (Abell 2014a, 364–365).

Table 7.2: Imports at Ayia Irini. The percentages reported in this Table represent proportions of imported fabric groups in the overall imported assemblage only, and not the overall assemblage (see note 1; see also Gorogianni and Abell, forthcoming, table 2)

	Crete	Southern Cyclades	Other Cyclades	Aegina	Southeast Aegean	Other/ Unknown	Mainland
IV	60%	11%	5%	5%	0%	1%	17%
V	39%	22%	8%	10%	5%	3%	13%
VI	34%	14%	8%	19%	5%	1%	22%
VII	20%	9%	11%	10%	0%	9%	40%

men and women; she bases her arguments on the existence of evidence for Cretan technologies, such as the upright loom, cooking habits that include tripod cooking pots, and the potter's wheel, all technologies that can be connected to the presence of non-elite women from Crete (Abell 2014b).

The first generation of settlers is not represented in the cemeteries of the site, as there are no cemeteries or burials dated to the earliest sub-phase of Period IV. Nevertheless, a portion of the population of the subsequent generations was interred in cemeteries outside the fortification wall, and their graves provide much food for thought concerning socio-economic differentiation and the overall prosperity of the settlement. The twenty-five graves that were excavated in the cemeteries of Period IV belonged mostly to children and infants, with only a few adult burials (Overbeck 1989a, 184).[4] The occupants of these graves were probably deposited in cists or jars (and some of them were associated with stone platforms) in a contracted position (even though some of the infants and small children could have been extended), but there

---

[4] Information about the age and sex of the interred individuals is based on a recent re-examination of the skeletal material by Lynne Schepartz and Anastasia Papathanasiou (Schepartz and Papathanasiou in progress). The demographic data referred to here are slightly different from G.F. Overbeck's (Overbeck 1984a; 1989a) which were based on the unpublished results of Angel's initial examination.

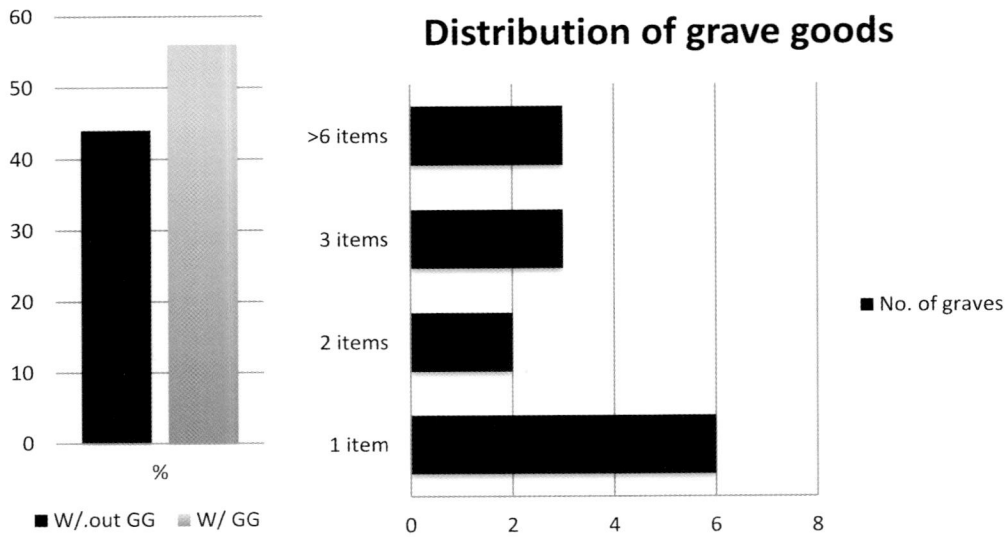

Fig. 7.3: Distribution of grave goods in Period IV graves.

was no preferred orientation in the deposition of the bodies (Overbeck 1989a, 184). All of these features betray similarities to, but also significant differences from, the mortuary traditions of the Cyclades, East Attica, and the coastal areas of mainland Greece during the Early Bronze Age, as well as of contemporary cemeteries on the Greek mainland.[5]

Any extrapolation about socio-political complexity based on mortuary data that represents only a subset of the total population is obviously fraught with difficulties that must not be overlooked.[6] Yet a coarse look into the distribution of grave goods shows that there are signs of incipient conspicuous consumption (Figs. 7.3–7.5). About half of the graves (48%) were devoid of burial goods and these (except one) were invariably associated with foetuses or newborns. Six graves (24%) contained one

---

[5] The similarities and differences of the Ayia Irini graves from the Cycladic and mainland burials have been summarized by G. F. Overbeck (see Overbeck 1989a, 204–205). Features, such as the presence of stone platforms, inhumation, the positioning of the dead, and spatial clustering of graves, represent continuity with earlier Cycladic ways of dealing with the dead (Doumas 1977; Sampson 1985). The use of terracotta containers is very common in Crete and Greek mainland (especially in the context of tumuli), but encountered only rarely in the Cyclades (burials from Phylakopi I–iii (Dawkins and Droop 1911, 6–9) and Paros (Rubenson 1917), which have been dated either to the end of the EC or MBA (Overbeck and Overbeck 1979, 114–117, 119; Barber 1983. Interesting parallels in terms of architectural details and the general placement of these graves outside the fortification wall can be drawn with the MH Shaft Grave on Aegina (Kilian-Dirlmeier 1997, 2003).

[6] The graves represent admittedly a very small proportion of the population, and a highly selective group of people. If we adopt Broodbank's estimates for Chalandriani (Broodbank 1989, 324–325, table 1), if the settlement was used for 100 years as was probably the case for Ayia Irini IV, a population of 30 families or 150 people would have produced around 600 graves.

7. Social complexity in Late Middle Bronze Age and Early Late Bronze Age Cyclades 131

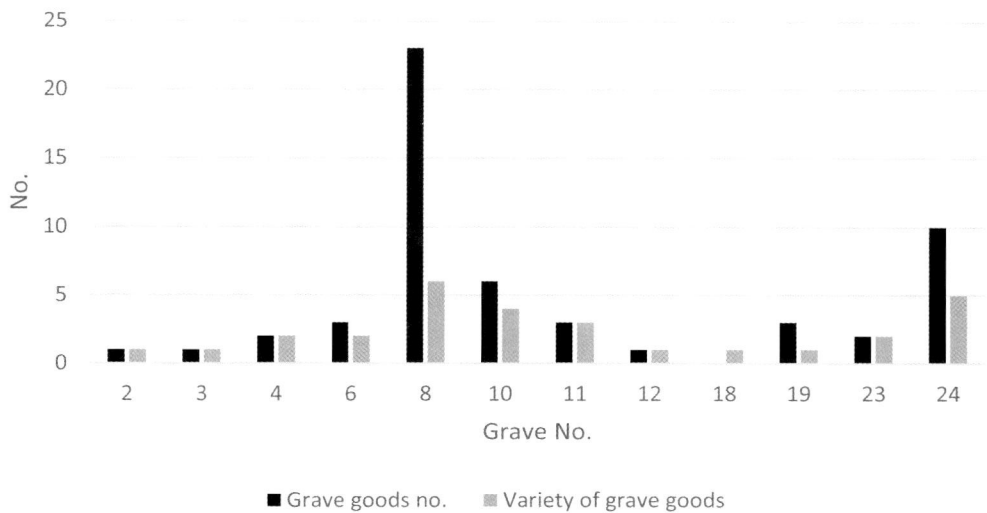

Fig. 7.4: Variety of grave goods in Period IV graves.

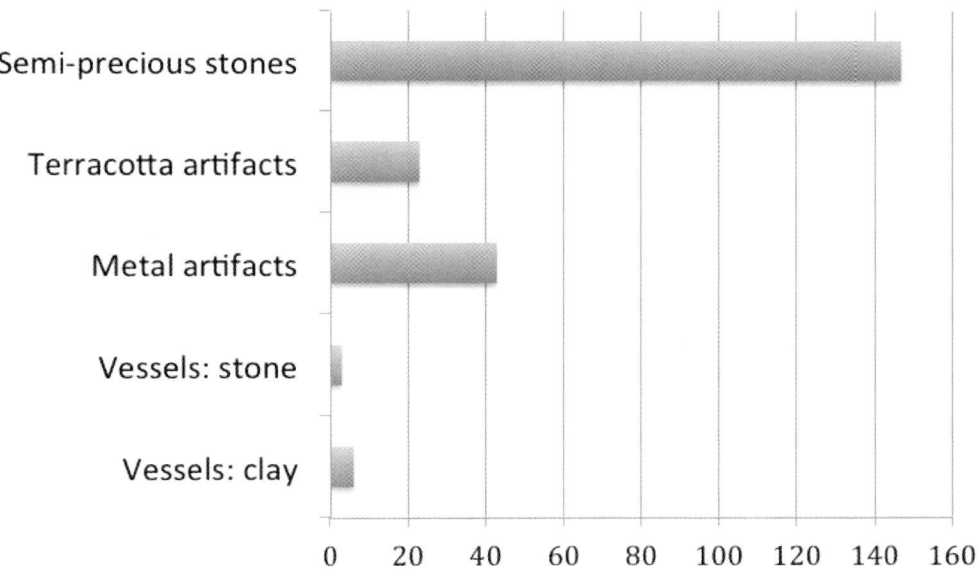

Fig. 7.5: Presence/absence of different grave goods in Period IV graves.

burial gift, and another five (20%) contained two or three gifts. Also, there are three graves that, comparatively, could be considered "rich": Graves 8 and 10 in the West Cemetery North and Grave 24 in the East Cemetery (Fig. 7.6).

Grave 8 (Overbeck 1989a, 190–192) is a multiple burial of eight adults and subadults, whose interments were placed in a large pithos encased in a built platform (C); they

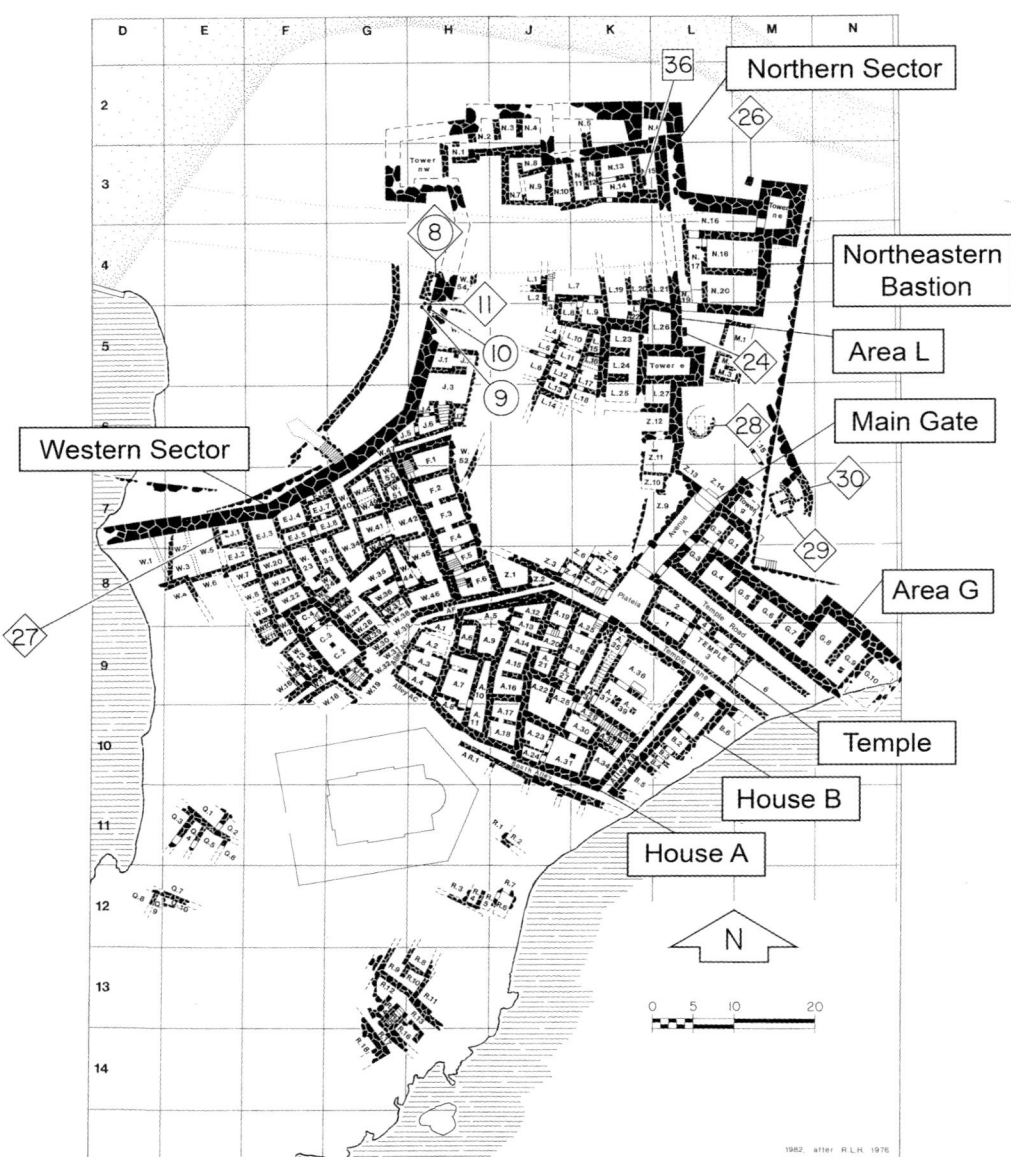

Fig. 7.6: Plan of the site during the main phase = ? and graves mentioned in the text (after Schofield 2011, pl. 2 and Overbeck 1989b, pl. 1). Graves marked with a square are simple burials, with circle are simple burials, and diamonds are built tombs (by M. Bebber).

collectively "owned" the largest and most diverse assemblage of burial goods (Tables 7.3–7.4; Figs. 7.6–7.8). Grave 10 (Overbeck 1989a, 193) was also a jar burial of a child similarly encased in a platform (D) along with two other graves (9 and 11) (Table 7.3; Figs. 7.6–7.7 and 7.9–7.10). Platform D was an addition to the south side of Platform C,

7. Social complexity in Late Middle Bronze Age and Early Late Bronze Age Cyclades

Table 7.3: Information about the age and sex of the interred individuals

Grave	No. burials	Occupants	Type of burial	Platform	Cemetery	Date
8	8	• 4 adults (1 female, 2 possible females, and 1 of indeterminate sex), • a young adult • an adolescent of indeterminate sex, • a toddler • a foetus	Pithos	C	WCN	IVc
9	1	• preterm foetus	Jar	D	WCN	IVc
10	1	• 8-year old child	Jar	D	WCN	IVc
11	2	• 2 toddlers	Cist	D	WCN	IVc
24	3	• 8–9 year-old female child, • an adolescent • a young adult of indeterminate sex	Cist		EC	IV

Based on a recent re-examination of the skeletal material by Lynne Schepartz and Anastasia Papathanasiou (Schepartz and Papathanasiou in prep.)

Table 7.4: Charts of grave goods in Period IV graves

Grave	Date	Vessels Pots	Pins	Necklaces	Beads	Rings	Diadem	Whorls	Seal stone	Metal: misc	Misc. Figurine
2	IVb	0	1								
3	IVb	1									
4	IVb	1				1					
6	IVc	1				5					
8	IVc	16	2	1	3	1				1	
10	IVc	1	2		6	4					
11	IVc	0				2			2		1
12	IVb/c	1									
18	IVb/c	1									
19	IV	2									
23	IV	2								1	
24	IV	6		2	?		1	22			
Totals (by category)		32	57								1

perhaps establishing a link between the occupants of Graves 9, 10, and 11 and the group buried in Grave 8. The East Cemetery (Fig. 7.6) is located on the other side of the settlement, and contains Grave 24 (Overbeck 1989a, 198–199), a large and deep cist grave in which three individuals were interred together with 10 burial gifts

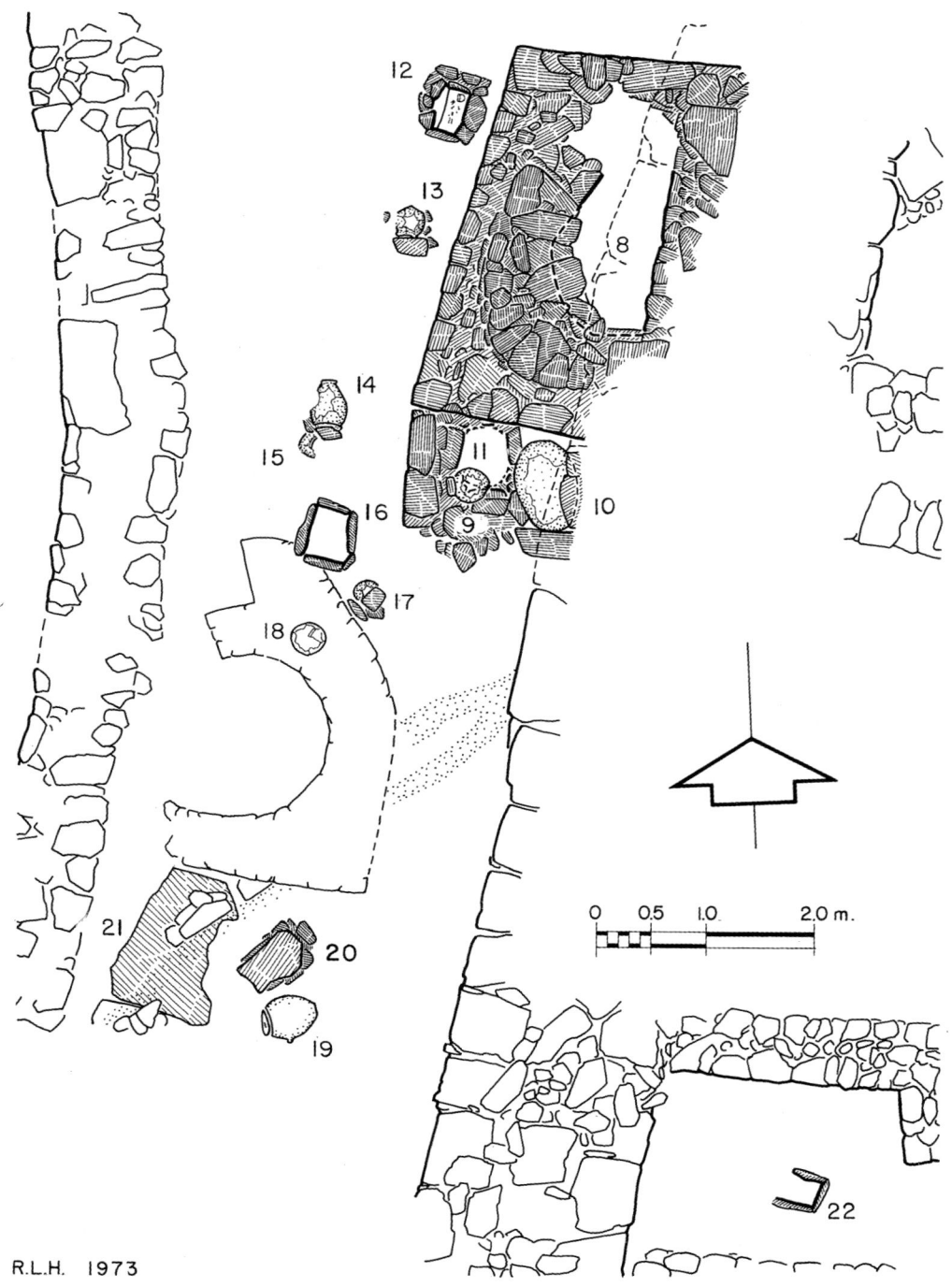

Fig. 7.7: West Cemetery North (Overbeck 1989b, pl. 20).

7. Social complexity in Late Middle Bronze Age and Early Late Bronze Age Cyclades   135

Fig. 7.8: Grave 8 select contents (Overbeck 1989b, pls. 92–94).

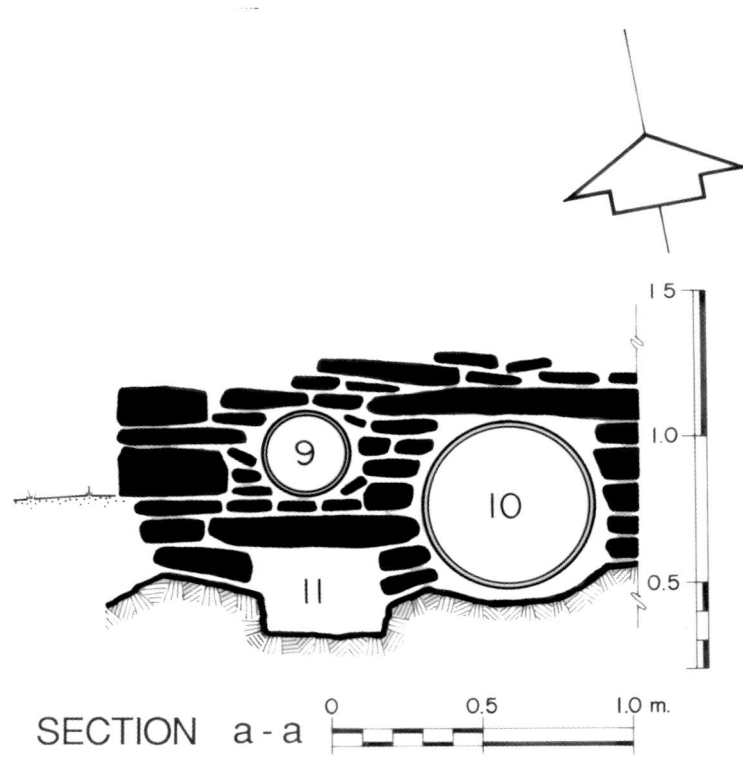

Fig. 7.9: Grave 10 in relation to Graves 9 and 11 in Platform D (Overbeck 1989b, pl. 22).

(Tables 7.3–7.4; Fig. 7.11), including a golden diadem decorated using openwork and dot repoussée techniques (Overbeck 1984a).

If the grave goods are any indication for social differentiation, some interesting observations can be made. First, the 'rich' graves, *i.e.*, Graves 8, 10, and 24, are rich not only in the number of artifacts but also variety (Figs. 7.3 and 7.4). The graves as a whole (Tables 7.3–7.4) contain a high proportion of articles for personal adornment, *i.e.*, pins, whorls, rings, beads, and even a diadem. Moreover, the grave goods betray an element of conspicuous consumption, since metal artifacts and beads make up the most numerous categories of grave goods (Fig. 7.5).

Nevertheless, the distribution of metal artifacts was not focused only on the 'rich graves'. Metal artifacts (both in precious metals and in lead and bronze) were the most widespread burial gifts, appearing in seven out of 12 graves that contained offerings, after terracotta objects (nine out of 12, excluding the burial containers or their lids); in comparison, fewer than half of the graves contained stone artefacts (five out of 12), such as stone vessels. The wide distribution of metal grave goods

Fig. 7.10: Select contents from Grave 10 (Overbeck 1989b, pl. 96).

provides additional evidence for the involvement of the settlement in the metals trade, to which the prosperity and the Aegean connections of the site should probably be credited.[7]

---

[7] Lead-isotope analysis has established that a significant proportion of metal circulating in the Aegean originated from the area of Lavrion, as well as other metalliferous islands in the Western Cyclades, such as Kythnos and Seriphos (Kristiansen and Larsson 2005, 124; Gale and Stos-Gale 2008; Gale, Kayafa, and Stos-Gale 2009; Kayafa 2010). The favourable location of Ayia Irini opposite Lavrion and widespread evidence for metal processing from all phases of the settlements (Cummer and Schofield 1984; Davis 1986; Overbeck 1989b; Schofield 2011) support the identification of the settlement as a metal entrepôt, which perhaps also controlled the mines (Gale et al. 1984; see also Wiener 2007, 237).

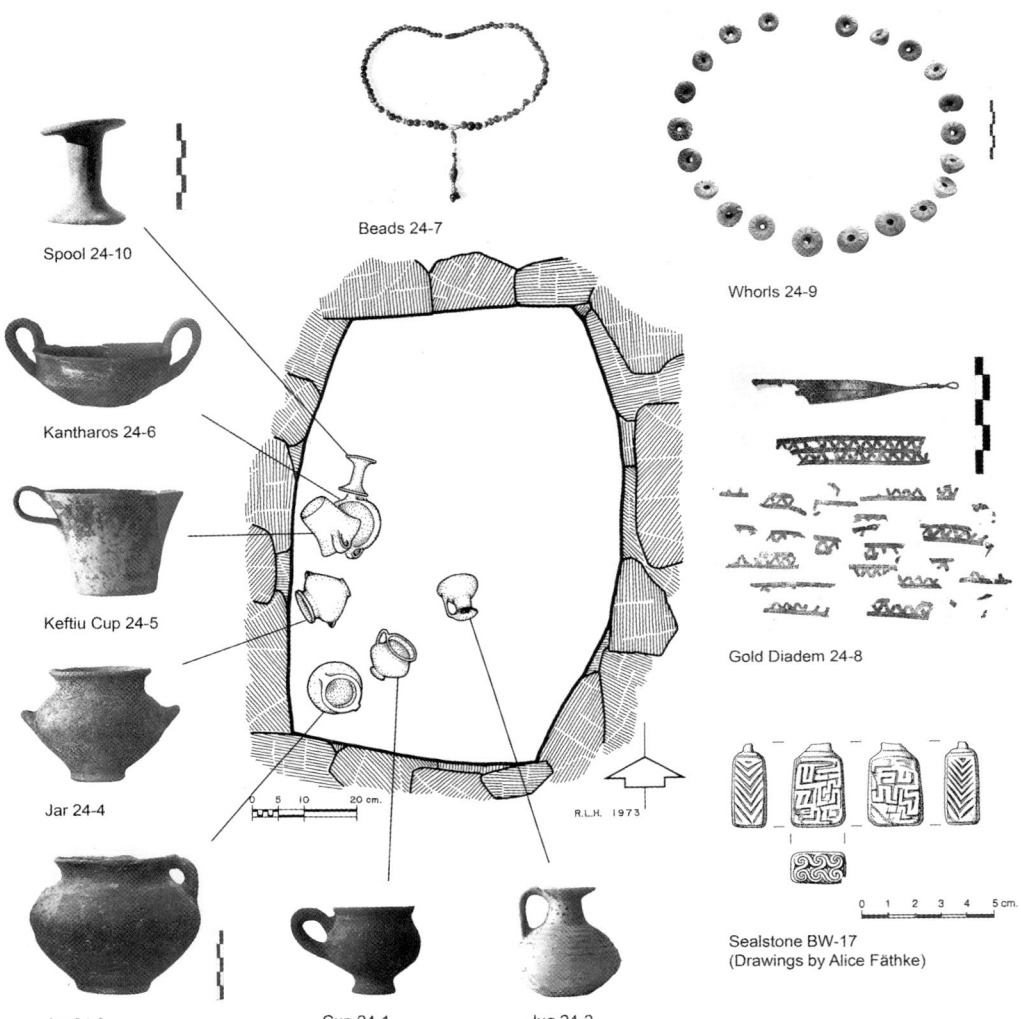

Fig. 7.11: Grave 24 in plan (Overbeck 1989b, pl. 22) with select contents (Overbeck 1989b, pls. 22, 103–104) (by M. Bebber).

Contextualizing these burials, which represent undoubtedly only a limited subset of the general population, the unusual character of this assemblage is striking, consisting mostly of extramural foetuses and child burials. In general, foetuses, neonates, and children belong to a category that is sometimes discriminated against in mortuary contexts, perhaps because of their undeveloped or underdeveloped ties to the wider social group at the time of death (Young and Papadatou 1997; Waterman and Thomas 2011). These undeveloped ties to the social network made the death of a foetus, a neonate or a young child largely a family affair (instead of a community-wide one), a death whose memory and commemoration would not outlast the death of their parents. Such an explanation seems to resonate with the general pattern of burials on the mainland from the period contemporary with the cemeteries at Ayia Irini; burials of young children and infants tend to occur intramurally (as do those of adults in the early MH) and such burials tend to be not well provided with burial gifts (Nordquist 1987; 1990; 2002; Aravantinos and Psaraki 2010; Milka 2010; Voutsaki et al. 2013), indicating a lack of investment in the funeral and in the commemorative exercise more abstractly (at least on behalf of the wider social group). Yet, the burials of children and foetuses at Ayia Irini occur extramurally (except one, which is a curious exception), and at least half of them are furnished with gifts (beyond the lid and pot in which they were interred, in the case of jar burials). Well-furnished child burials cross-culturally are relatively rare and when found are "typically interpreted as a sign of ascribed status or emerging class structure, and burials that treat children similarly to adults suggest that they were recognized as valued members of their communities" (Waterman and Thomas 2011, 165). Therefore, it seems that the mortuary investment for the Ayia Irini juveniles is notable considering the general patterns in the Aegean and among other human populations, perhaps indicating a fledging ranking system and/or an ideology of personhood, which recognized children as valuable members of the Ayia Irini community worth investing in and commemorating.

Thus, within the span of three or four generations, the Ayia Irini community was transformed from the start up, migrant group that chose the island to set up an emporium to take advantage of the increased trade and exchange activity structured around the metal resources of Lavrion, to a rather prosperous village-size settlement that underlined its prosperity with conspicuous consumption practices in commemorative rituals for the youngest members of the community.

Period V

The next period in the sequence, Period V (Table 7.1), has been highlighted as a very important phase in the development of the settlement, since the existing close connection with Crete and the rest of the Aegean intensified and prosperity continued. This prosperity is likely to have contributed significantly to a rise in population over time (a rise which should probably be attributed not only to the growth of the resident community but also to a trickle of immigration) that probably became in itself a multiplier of prosperity, expressed in the enlargement of the town, the intensification of its connections to the Aegean world, and the expression of a local identity through the medium of material culture that was as much locally situated as cosmopolitan (Gorogianni forthcoming).

The most striking and best-preserved vestige of the period is the new fortification wall (Fig. 7.12). The fortification wall was built of locally quarried boulders of blue marble and schist and featured a curtain wall, which has been estimated to have been at least 5 m high or more, and rectangular towers, which were probably higher than the wall itself (Davis 1986, 101). The new enceinte skirted the north part of the site, though there are strong indications that the site was fortified on all four sides (Caskey 1978, 760; Davis 1986, 102; Mourtzas and Kolaiti 1998, 680–681). Judging from the expansion of the site to the north, it has been suggested that the new wall

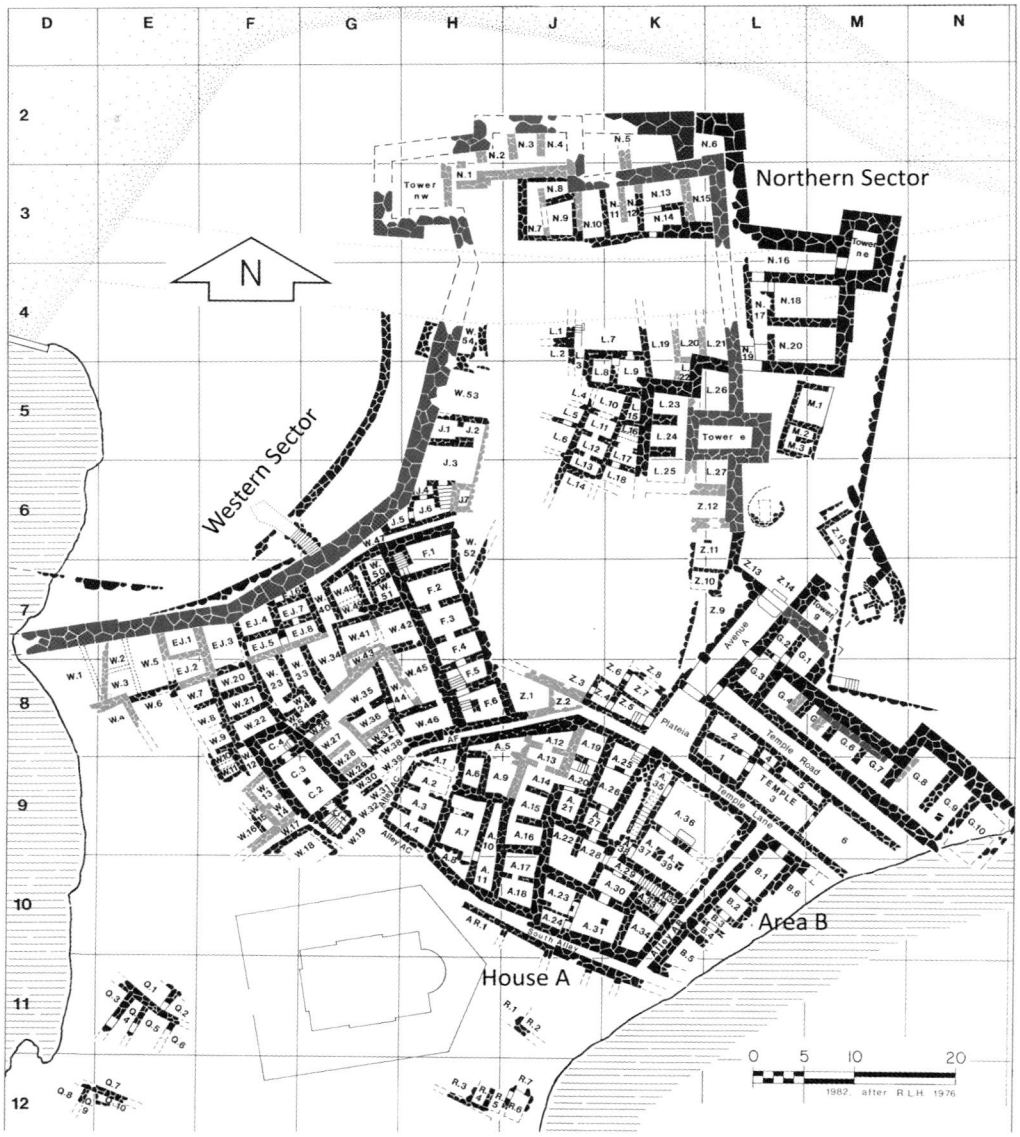

Fig. 7.12: Period V architectural remains (by R. D. Fitzsimons).

enlarged the site by one third (Davis 1986, 102). The new town was probably as large as 1.2 ha (Gorogianni 2016), including the part of the site that is visible today and the submerged area around it, and probably accommodated a much larger population than its predecessor. It is hard to say exactly how much bigger this population was (or, alternately, how dense habitation was within the confines of the fortification wall) especially because the fortification wall's fortuitous fate of good preservation is not shared by the rest of the built landscape of this period, which has been obscured by the later settlement (Fig. 7.12). Nevertheless, it is fairly certain that the walls of Ayia Irini protected the vast majority of the population living on the island (at least its north) at the time, since surface surveys have revealed the existence of a nucleated settlement pattern for the MBA and LBA periods, similar to Melos, with very few loci of probably seasonal occupation beyond the confines of the wall (Davis and Cherry 1990, 187–188; Cherry et al. 1991, 229–230).

The community that lived behind the wall does not manifest significant differentiation, at least in architecture. The (admittedly) limited architectural evidence for private dwellings does not betray major investment in those buildings. Wherever the plans of buildings can be retrieved, they seem to conform to a local type with axially arranged spaces built using local raw materials, schist and blue marble (*e.g.*, Rooms N.1 through N.4). Even House A, which during later periods is a structure interpreted as the house of a leader or Big Man, seems to have had a very unassuming predecessor(s) during Period V (Cummer and Schofield 1984, 30–31; Davis 1986, 73 ff., 102). The limited evidence for investment in architecture (beyond the fortification wall) that could signal conspicuous consumption is a curious phenomenon in itself, especially in light of the ceramic evidence (see below), which betrays far-reaching connections with the rest of the Aegean world. If this lack is not an accident of preservation, it may mean that the agents who were active in the trade and exchange of metals predominantly and pottery secondarily, were not seeking to distinguish themselves architecturally.

The same disappointing evidentiary picture is replicated in the case of the graves (Fig. 7.6). There are only three graves belonging to this phase, Graves 26, 27, and the conjectured intramural burial 36, which of course makes all generalizing statements extremely tenuous. Graves 26 and 27 (Fig. 7.6) are cist graves, which perhaps indicates adherence to local (and mainland) tradition and cultural continuity with the previous period. However, Grave 27, an intramural infant (?) burial, and the conjectured Grave 36 in room N. 15 (Davis 1986, 52) may also signify a possible break with tradition or social change, since both are intramural burials of infants that stand in stark contrast to the practices of the previous period. As for Grave 26, the tomb is a large, well-built rectangular cist that hosted one adult male burial with no associated grave goods, a condition almost certainly arising from the fact that it was found disturbed.

If the built landscape is disappointing, the same cannot be said for Period V movable material culture. From a ceramic point of view, Ayia Irini continues to be well connected to the rest of the Aegean (Table 7.2). The connections with Crete, especially north-central Crete, seem strong (Gorogianni and Abell forthcoming) and material culture reflects these affinities in the local production of Minoanizing shapes (Davis 1986, 85). Moreover, local production seems to make use of Minoan technologies, such as the potter's wheel (Davis and Lewis 1985; Georgiou 1986; Lewis 1986; Gorogianni et al. 2016a), the vertical warp-weighted loom (Cutler 2011; 2012; 2016), and the Linear A script (Caskey 1964, 325–326; 1966, 365–366; Karnava 2008, 381–383).

The wheel and the warp weighted loom may have been introduced in Period IV, but it is in Period V that we see evidence for local craftsmen and women making confident use of the new technologies. For example, a new study of the employment of the potter's wheel in local workshops (Gorogianni et al. 2016a) shows that, during Period V potters use this Cretan technological practice for a variety of shapes, both small and open, and also large and closed, a trend largely dissimilar to what Berg suggests for Phylakopi (Berg 2007a; 2007b). This boom in the use of this technology betrays a high level of confidence and expertise in a local potting community that was composed of immigrant craftspeople trained within communities of potters on Crete and the rest of the Aegean. The resident potters made artifacts that stand as examples of the cultural entanglement between Crete and Cycladic/mainland traditions (Gorogianni 2016). A similar conclusion can be drawn from the evidence for the introduction and use of Linear A. Three of the objects recovered from contexts from the Northern Sector (Davis 1986, 41–42 (U-40), 47 (U-128 and U-129); Karnava 2008, 381–383) prove local knowledge of the script and its use for the purposes of a local and independent administrative centre (Karnava 2008, 384).

Bringing all these strands of evidence together, one may safely claim that the community of Period V was certainly larger than the community bounded by the previous fortification wall during Period IV. The fragmentary nature of the evidence from the period and current status of research do not allow us at present to speak of ranking or socio-political differentiation among these residents. The absence of evidence for marked differentiation across the site (*e.g.*, no discernible spatial concentrations of imports) and the contrast between investment in public projects (*i.e.*, the building of the fortification wall) and disinterest in conspicuous consumption at the private level, at least as displayed in their buildings (*i.e.*, no evidence for Minoan style architecture), are both notable, and could be related to a socio-political ethos of relative transegalitarianism. On the other hand, the execution of a project of the magnitude of the fortification wall definitely makes it reasonable to infer a high degree of organization and *ad hoc* leadership that would enable the planning and completion of the project, but was not expressed in the material culture. The presence of individuals with leadership qualities, perhaps independent entrepreneurs (Knapp and Cherry 1994, 142–146), is also supported by the types of evidence that argue for the active participation in the pan-Aegean networks of exchange, not only as a consumer of imports but also as an independent local administrative centre supported by the presence of record keeping devices, such as the Minoan script.

Period VI and VII: Competing social groups during the main phase of the site

The beginning of the Late Bronze Age (Table 7.1) coincides with another expansion of the site, this time an internal one, as the settlement underwent a major programme of building and urban planning that targeted the area within the Period V fortification wall (Schofield 1998; 2011, 1). The building programme, whether centrally organized or not, included House A (Cummer and Schofield 1984), House B (Abell 2014a), House C (Schofield 2011, 135–157), House F (Schofield 2011, 3–28), structures in Area L (Caskey 1964, 322; 1971, 383), and the Northeast Bastion and tower (Gorogianni 2008, 304–308; Fitzsimons and Gorogianni forthcoming) (Fig. 7.6). The building programme, which was executed gradually during Period VI (and continued with repairs, rebuilding and urban in-filling during the next period), resulted in a town with paved streets and squares, covered drains, and free standing houses with associated courtyards (Schofield 1998), occupied by ca. 280–335 people (Gorogianni 2016, endnote 6).

Communities of this size have the potential to be ranked but not hierarchically organized, as face-to-face communication and mutual dependence for survival would have been prohibitive for the emergence of complex structures in decision making (Johnson 1982; Upham 1990; Feinman *et al.* 2000). Nevertheless, the settlement preserves traces of "expressed" socio-political differentiation, which is perhaps more evident than in the previous periods in several artifactual categories. The mortuary evidence is fragmentary yet suggestive. Even though the cemeteries for the general population corresponding to this period (or the previous one for that matter) have not been discovered (or did not exist), there are the two graves, 29 and 30, of Period VI, as well as another tomb, 28 of Period VII, in the vicinity of the main gate of the town (Fig. 7.6). These graves perhaps belonged to a group or groups of individuals attempting to place one or multiple ancestors in a place of mortuary prominence, underlining or legitimizing the group's status in contemporary Keian society (cf. Kilian-Dirlmeier 1997; 2003). All graves belong to the large rectangular built type, were found robbed (probably in antiquity), and are placed in the area right outside the 'Main Gate' of the site, a location which undoubtedly enhanced their visibility and hence the impact of this commemorative enterprise (Fig. 7.6).

Grave 29 (Figs. 7.6 and 7.13) is a rectangular tomb featuring two compartments separated by a partition wall, of which the northern compartment was probably used as an entrance and the southern for the burial chamber (Overbeck 1984a, 116–117; Caskey 1971, 381–382). Even though this tomb was robbed, the southern compartment included ten ceramic vases, including two imitation stone vessels. Grave 30 (Fig. 7.6), also robbed and heavily damaged, was a "more or less rectangular" tomb built earlier than Grave 29, since the latter used one of its walls as a buttress (Overbeck

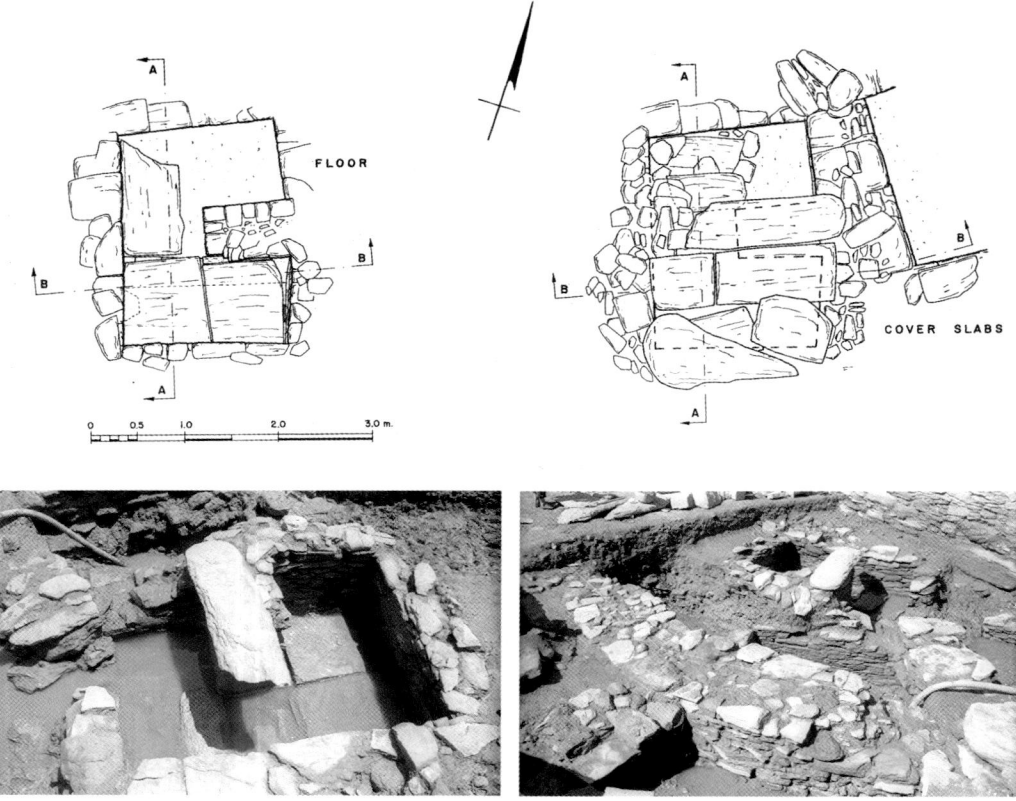

Fig. 7.13: Grave 29 (Caskey, 1971, fig. 12 and pl. 77 a and d).

1984a, 117). Both tombs might have been bounded by a curving enclosure wall preserved in remnants, which perhaps held in place a tumulus. Last but not least, Grave 28 (Period VII, Figs. 7.6 and 7.14) was a small tumulus delineated on its edges by a circular row of upright slabs (Overbeck 1984a, 116; Caskey 1971, 378–379). The tumulus concealed a shaft grave, probably dating to Period VII, and held one adult male, according to Angel. The tomb had been robbed in antiquity but some vases found outside the grave probably belonged to it. These tombs suggest that during the main phases of the site, social differentiation had reached a crucial point that allowed for the distinction of leaders who became, after their deaths, points of reference for their families and/or associated groups, as well as perhaps for the entire community, in a campaign of power legitimization.

Additional traces of socio-political differentiation can be identified in differential consumption practices (Miller 1995; Miracle and Milner 2002) of groups occupying different areas of the site. In this regard much has been gained by investigating the

7. Social complexity in Late Middle Bronze Age and Early Late Bronze Age Cyclades 145

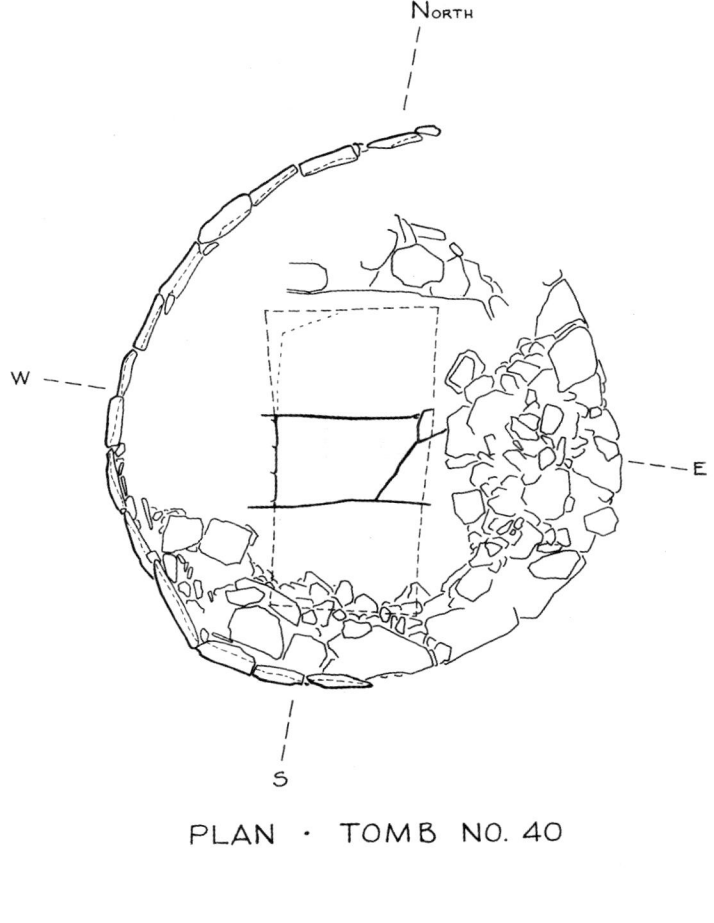

Fig. 7.14: Grave 28 (Caskey, 1971, fig. 11).

Northern Sector, especially the Northeast Bastion (Fig. 7.6; Fitzsimons and Gorogianni forthcoming). The Bastion was a complex which came into existence early in Period VI when the fortification system that had been established in Period V was modified to extend to the east and include one more tower and a Bastion, which was situated in a premier position overlooking the main gate to the south.

The Northeast Bastion had two floors, which seem to have had almost identical interior arrangements, consisting of a corridor, which runs north–south, a switchback staircase and two rather large rectangular rooms (Fig. 7.6). On the first floor, the northernmost of the rooms, N.18, contained several large storage vessels, suggesting that this room functioned as the primary storage facility for the bastion, whereas the southern room, N.20 probably functioned as a kitchen. The second floor of the building was accessible through the staircase (illuminated by a window or service entrance of sorts over a paved landing), but probably also through entrances on the same floor level. The upper floor featured two large formal rooms, adorned with two separate iconographic programmes of wall paintings (Morgan 1998; forthcoming a), stone paved floors, and possible pier-and-window partitions.

Caskey, in the preliminary report from 1971, though he remarked on the elegance of the second floor, hypothesized that the Northeast Bastion probably served as barracks for soldiers defending the walls of the settlement, solely because the bastion was incorporated into the defensive system of the town (Caskey 1971, 376). These remarks, of course, were of a preliminary nature since neither the assemblages nor the stratigraphy had received systematic and detailed study until recently by the authors with a collaborating team of specialists, as well as Lyvia Morgan (Gorogianni and Fitzsimons in progress; Morgan forthcoming a, b).

Careful study brought to the fore several interesting aspects of the assemblage. On the one hand, the ceramic repertoire contained a multitude of vessels that were connected to dining (eating, drinking, and pouring), food preparation, and transport and storage for both the short and long terms, as well as miscellaneous purposes (Gorogianni 2016). The wide variety of shapes seems to delineate the entire process of food preparation and consumption, which starts from the unassuming cellar, passes through the kitchen, and culminates in a dining area. On the other hand, in a site where almost every other building of Period VI/VII preserved evidence for industries (Schofield 1990, 209), such as metalworking, pigment-grinding, antler-working, lapidary activity, manufacture of aromatics, and textiles, evidence for such industries was surprisingly nearly absent from the Northeast Bastion.[8] This absence suggests that this complex was not a typical example of domestic quarters (often characterized by multi-functionality), but that it was a space of specialized use. Moreover, the study of the architecture of the Northeast Bastion (Fitzsimons and Gorogianni forthcoming) showed that this addition was constructed to function as an elite marker, since it represented a significant departure from the local architectural idiom and incorporated Minoan elements that were used in Minoan formal contexts, such as Minoan dining halls (Graham 1961; Driessen 1982; Letesson 2013). Furthermore, the impressive array of wall-paintings led Morgan, based on the thematic affinities between iconography and room usage, to conclude independently that it was probably a dining room (Morgan 1998; forthcoming a; see also Shank 2008).

Nevertheless, this identification for the function of this complex raises certain contradictions and interpretive conundrums to be resolved. The very existence

---

[8] Note here that in an investigation of the distribution of equipment involved in textile production, Davis presents a couple of items in the area of the Northeastern Bastion (Davis 1984b, fig. 3). Careful study of the assemblages showed that the item he notes were found outside the walls of the bastion and the figure is the product of his means of visualizing his results.

of a formal dining room (the first one identified on the site), according to anthropological literature on feasting, presupposes that the owners or rightful users of this facility organized events that served to reproduce or challenge social ordering (Dietler 1990; 2001; Dietler and Hayden 2001a; Bray 2003a; 2003b; Cook and Glowacki 2003; Bendall 2004; Hamilakis 2008; and other papers in Dietler and Hayden 2001b; Bray 2003c). Since Schofield has interpreted House A as Ayia Irini's "Mansion" or "house of the leader" (Cummer and Schofield 1984, 1), should we infer that the residents of House A and leaders of the town were also the owners/users of the Northeast Bastion facility? One sticking point, however, is that both the Northeast Bastion and the first phase of House A were built at the same time; if the Northeast Bastion belonged to the House A social group, one would expect a closer spatial relationship.

On the other hand, the supposition of ownership or management by a different group is hindered by the fact that the Northeast Bastion seems to be integrally incorporated into the expansion of the fortification wall during early Period VI. If the Northeast Bastion project was a private commission, then it follows that the expansion of the fortification wall was not a community-wide enterprise organized by a central authority, whatever that may have been. Therefore, if the purpose of the Period VI expansion was solely or primarily the strengthening of the fortification for defence, it is hard to imagine that it might have been a private project.

The architecture of the Northeast Bastion complex incorporates elements that may indicate that defence was probably not the primary consideration during the planning and subsequent construction. These elements include the window or service access at the south end of the corridor/staircase N.19/N.17, about 1 m from the contemporary ground level (Fig. 7.6), as well as the windows reconstructed on the upper storey of N.18 (east wall) and N.20 (east and south walls) on the basis of the painted plasters, an arrangement that would have been very similar to the West House of Akrotiri (Morgan forthcoming a). These two elements make it unlikely that the complex had a purely, or even primarily, defensive function. This proposition is further supported by evidence from the Western Sector, where, as Schofield suggests, the fortification wall ceased to serve its original purpose, *i.e.*, the defence of the town, after the end of Period V, yet it continued to function as a boundary, and, therefore, was repaired and refaced in places (Schofield 2011, 1 *et passim*).

Therefore, it is reasonable to assume that the Northeast Bastion was built at the beginning of Period VI by a group of elite occupants of the Northern Sector (or of the buildings in the yet unstudied Area L which might have been connected to the bastion). This group built the Northeast Bastion as a formal space for feasting, a space dedicated to showcasing luxury, wealth and exotic connections with the outside world, and to the negotiation of power on a local and perhaps even regional level.

In the area of House A during the same time, the Period VI house includes no preserved unit that could be interpreted as having a similar function, that is, a formal space for feasting, although it is possible that evidence for such a facility might have been obscured by use of the rooms during subsequent phases. Within the eastern part of House A (Figs. 7.15–7.16), however, the inspiration for the formal rooms is clearly to be sought in Crete. Rooms of wider dimensions than those of the local axial type,[9] such in the Northeast Bastion, may be indications that Minoan architectural principles were being emulated (cf. Whitelaw 2005, 56). Indeed, the suite in the eastern part of House A (rooms 35 to 39, Figs. 7.15–7.16), which was used contemporaneously with the Northeast Bastion (Cummer and Schofield 1984, 31–32), conforms to these Cretan architectural principles (Cummer and Schofield 1984, 6–10 and pl. 4b).

The use of the Northeast Bastion complex seems to have been relatively short-lived. Analysis of the stratigraphy shows that it was destroyed sometime in the very early Period VII (Table 7.1) and that its ruins were left standing and deteriorating for at least a century, into Mycenaean times. At the same time, House A seems to have undergone a phase of expansion that almost doubled its size (Cummer and Schofield 1984, 32–33). In addition, the new extension, especially on the eastern part of the house, seems to follow models that are encountered in the earlier Northeast Bastion (Fitzsimons and Gorogianni forthcoming). The new expansion of House A included (Figs. 7.15–7.16):

- a switch-back staircase (29/33) which gave access to the second storey of the building;
- a kitchen in the basement (30) which also gave access to space (31) as well as to rooms 22 and 28, which were magazines for storage of dry goods;
- a sequence of formal rooms on the ground floor of the house, such as the so-called Frescoed Parlour above room 31, which was decorated with the Blue Bird Fresco (Abramovitz *et al.* 1973, 286–293), and the columned hall with their associated courtyards (Cummer and Schofield 1984, 13–17 and pl. 4.c, d).

It is very possible that this arrangement reflects the presence of another dining room complex following closely the local prototype in the Northeastern Bastion (which had in turn followed Minoan prototypes), and which probably postdated or overlapped only the end of the bastion's use-life. If this reconstruction is correct, competition may be inferred between a group in the Northern Sector and one in House A, as well as perhaps another one based in House J of the Western Sector (Schofield 2011, 77–84). This competition probably escalated towards the end of Period VI and resulted in the construction of an addition to House A that would have served the needs of that group in terms of hosting and, by extension, negotiating

---

[9] Rooms of wide proportions necessitated different roofing solutions, at least wider than the local standard repeated in buildings throughout the site (*e.g.*, House F, Area G, Rooms N.2–4, and the western wing of House A).

Fig. 7.15: House A: Restored basement level plan of the eastern half House A (Cummer and Schofield 1984, pl. 9).

their position in the local socio-political landscape. This process of negotiation was clearly more successful for the occupants of House A, since House A outlived the Northeast Bastion and showed itself, in the words of Elizabeth Schofield, as a "microcosm of a Minoan palace" (Cummer and Schofield 1984, 1) at least during the phase before its destruction by the earthquake in mid-Period VII and based on the current evidence.

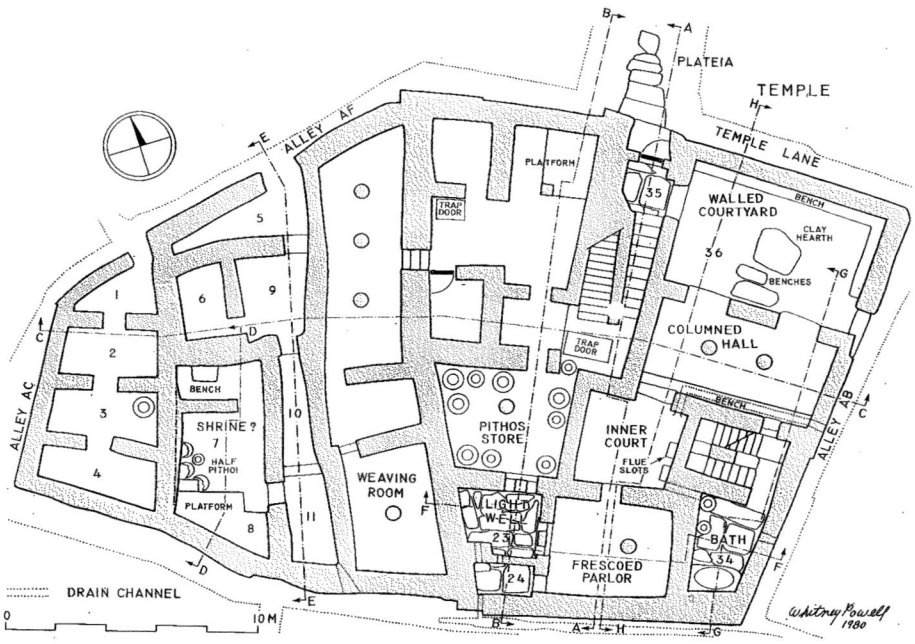

Fig. 7.16: Restored ground level plan of the eastern half of House A (Cummer and Schofield 1984, pl. 25b).

Conclusion

The community at Ayia Irini began with the small group of settlers who chose the site to establish an emporium. This was by all indications a mixed population, men and women, probably originating from Central Greece, Aegina, and Crete. Among the settlers, some level of cooperation, organization, and leadership enabled the fortification of the town, even though such group leadership was probably *ad hoc* and based on individual ability since in communities of this scale – about 200 people towards the end of the period – face-to-face interaction and wider participation in decision making was probably the norm. This does not mean, however, that the community lacked traces of inequality. Especially towards the end of Period IV, one can argue on the basis of the graves that there is evidence of conspicuous consumption and a desire for differentiation among the families of the community, some of whom chose an unusually high (even cross-culturally) degree of investment in the commemoration of foetuses and children, *i.e.*, members of the community with undeveloped social ties. These members of the community and a few adults were given a burial (if the present picture is not an accident of preservation) and about half of them received burial gifts sometimes of significant value. The treatment of non-adult burials as adult ones shows a developed ideology of personhood and a desire for differentiation (Waterman and Thomas 2011, 165).

The prosperity expressed in the graves of Period IV, especially the widespread distribution of metal finds, seems to have continued in the following period. This prosperity probably became a pole of attraction for new immigrants, as well as a prime mover behind the local rise in population. Population certainly grew and so did the town with the construction of the new enceinte to accommodate new needs. The construction of the wall necessitated the emergence of leadership that probably did not evolve into a hierarchical structure. The extant assemblage of Period V does not support the existence of one ruling family that, after the building of the fortification, was the notional socio-political centre of the community and its link to hierarchies elsewhere. On the contrary, imports do not seem to be concentrated in a particular part of the town and architectural conspicuous consumption at the private level is notably absent. Nevertheless, we can infer the presence of individuals with leadership qualities based on evidence that suggests the engagement of the site in the networks of exchange and the general culture of the Aegean, not only as a consumer of imports but also as an independent local administrative centre. The overall picture is consonant with a community of independent entrepreneurs made up of old and new immigrants attracted to the site because of its coveted location and active participation in the metals' trade and in commercial activities.

It is perhaps the descendants of the successful entrepreneurial families that in Period VI started showcasing their success in material terms, a process that is mirrored in the opposite coast of Lavrion in Tumulus V (Servais and Servais-Soyez 1984, 61–66). Even though imports, Minoan features, and Minoan architectural tropes are not concentrated in one quarter, as at Phylakopi (Whitelaw 2005), there are signs of social differentiation among groups living in different parts of the site. A comparison between the architecture of House F, built in the local architectural idiom of axially arranged spaces, and the architecture of buildings like House A, the Northeast Bastion and House J, which seem to have been built according to Minoan prototypes, shows that not every family at the site faired equally well. However, the very fact that we find multiple 'poles' of elite consumption perhaps indicates that the socio-political landscape of Ayia Irini, at least in Period VI, was not hierarchically ordered but one characterized by negotiation. Power must have been contested, especially during Period VI, among different families or groups as they tried to promote themselves by constructing buildings, organizing events (such as feasts), and using material culture that referenced their connections with the world beyond, as well as establishing conspicuous memorials to specific members of the community.

This process of negotiation seems to have been much more successful for the social group of House A, since in the following period the house expanded dramatically and became the biggest structure at Ayia Irini. This building housed a number of different functions, similar to the Minoan palaces, and seems to have the single largest concentration of lead weights at the site (regardless of periods) (Petruso 1992, pls. 2–3), which speaks to the importance of its inhabitants in commercial dealings. There is no doubt that in Period VII the people who lived in House A sat at the top of the local social pyramid. Yet, the cautionary tale here is that this was not the case in the previous periods. If indeed, Ayia Irini had a special relationship with Crete and its palatial societies, as the material culture suggests, it does not seem have been a microcosm of these palatial societies, equally hierarchical in organization. On the contrary, it seems to have been a haven full of independent entrepreneurs (Knapp and Cherry 1994, 142–146) exploiting the opportunities of the region during the MBA and early LBA.

Acknowledgements

We would like to thank Sofia Voutsaki and Corien Wiersma for the invitation to and hospitality during the conference "Explaining Change in Aegean Prehistory From the Early Bronze III to the Late Bronze I." We would also like to thank Jack Davis, Jerry Rutter, Natalie Abell, Carol Hershenson, and Brian Trail for reading the text and offering their insightful comments.

Bibliography

Abell, N. D. 2014a. *Reconsidering a Cultural Crossroads: A Diachronic Analysis of Ceramic Production, Consumption, and Exchange Patterns at Bronze Ayia Irini, Kea, Greece*. Ph.D. dissertation, University of Cincinnati.
Abell, N. D. 2014b. "Migration, Mobility, and Craftspeople in the Aegean Bronze Age: A Case Study from Ayia Irini on the Island of Kea." *World Archaeology* 46, 551–568.
Abramovitz, K., L. J. Majewski, and M. Reich. 1973. "Frescoes from Ayia Irini, Keos, Part I." *Hesperia* 42, 284–300.
Agouridis, C. 1997. "Sea Routes and Navigation in the Third Millennium Aegean." *Oxford Journal of Archaeology* 16, 1–24.
Aravantinos, V., and K. Psaraki. 2010. "The Middle Helladic Cemeteries of Thebes. General Review and Remarks in the Light of New Investigations and Finds." In *Mesohelladika. The Greek Mainland in the Middle Bronze Age*, Bulletin de Correspondance Hellénique Supplement 52, edited by A. Philippa-Touchais, G. Touchais, S. Voutsaki, and J. Wright, 377–395. Athens, De Boccard.
Barber, R. L. N. 1983. "The Definition of the Middle Cycladic Period." *American Journal of Archaeology* 87, 76–81.
Bendall, L. M. 2004. "Fit for a King? Hierarchy, Exclusion, Aspiration and Desire in the Social Structure of Mycenaean Banqueting." In *Food, Cuisine and Society in Prehistoric Greece, Sheffield Studies in Aegean Archaeology* 5, edited by P. Halstead and J. C. Barrett, 105–135. Oxford, Oxbow Books.
Berg, I. 2007a. *Negotiating Island Identities: The Active Use of Pottery in the Middle and Late Bronze Age Cyclades*, Gorgias Dissertations 31. Piscataway, Gorgias Press.
Berg, I. 2007b. "Meaning in the Making: The Potter's Wheel at Phylakopi, Melos (Greece)." *Journal of Anthropological Archaeology* 26, 234–252.
Bikaki, A. H. 1984. *Ayia Irini: The Potter's Marks* (Keos IV). Mainz am Rhein, Von Zabern.
Branigan, K. 1981. "Minoan Colonialism." *Annual of the British School at Athens* 76, 23–33.
Branigan, K. 1984. "Minoan Community Colonies in the Aegean." In *The Minoan Thalassocracy. Myth and Reality. Proceedings of the Third International Symposium at the Swedish Institute in Athens, 31 May–5 June 1982*, edited by R. Hägg and N. Marinatos, 49–53. Stockholm, P. Åström.
Bray, T. L. 2003a. "The Commensal Politics of Early States and Empires." In *The Archaeology and Politics of Food and Feasting in Early States and Empires*, edited by T. L. Bray, 1–13. New York, Kluwer Academic/Plenum.
Bray, T. L. 2003b. "To Dine Splendidly." In *The Archaeology and Politics of Food and Feasting in Early States and Empires*, edited by T. L. Bray, 93–142. New York, Kluwer Academic/Plenum.
Bray, T. L., ed. 2003c. *The Archaeology and Politics of Food and Feasting in Early States and Empires*. New York, Kluwer Academic/Plenum.

Broodbank, C. 1989. "The Longboat and Society in the Cyclades in the Keros-Syros Culture." *American Journal of Archaeology* 93, 319–337.

Broodbank, C. 1993. "Ulysses without Sails: Trade, Distance, Knowledge and Power in the Early Cyclades." *World Archaeology* 24, 315–331.

Broodbank, C. 2000. *An Archaeology of the Early Cyclades*. Cambridge, Cambridge University Press.

Broodbank, C. 2004. "Minoanisation." *Proceedings of the Cambridge Philological Society* 50, 46–91.

Broodbank, C. 2013. *The Making of the Middle Sea: A History of the Mediterranean from the Beginning to the Emergence of the Classical World*. Oxford and New York, Oxford University Press.

Broodbank, C., and E. Kiriatzi. 2007. "The First 'Minoans' of Kythera Revisited: Technology, Demography and Landscape in the Prepalatial Aegean." *American Journal of Archaeology* 111, 241–274.

Brumfiel, E. M., and J. W. Fox, eds. 1994. *Factional Competition and Political Development in the New World*. Cambridge, Cambridge University Press.

Caskey, J. L. 1964. "Excavations in Keos, 1963." *Hesperia* 33, 314–335.

Caskey, J. L. 1966. "Excavations in Keos, 1964–1965." *Hesperia* 35, 363–376.

Caskey, J. L. 1971. "Investigations in Keos. Part I: Excavations and Explorations, 1966–1970." *Hesperia* 40, 359–396.

Caskey, J. L. 1978. "Αγία Ειρήνη, Κέα – 1974." *Επετηρίς της Εταιρείας Κυκλαδικών Μελετών Ι'* 1974–1978, 755–766.

Caskey, M. E., J. L. Caskey, S. Bouzaki, and I. Maniatis. 1986. *Ayia Irini: The Temple at Ayia Irini. Part I: The Statues*. Keos II II. Mainz am Rhein, Philipp von Zabern.

Chapman, R. 2003. *Archaeologies of Complexity*. London and New York, Routledge.

Cherry, J. F., J. L. Davis, and E. Mantzourani, eds. 1991. *Landscape Archaeology as Long-Term History. Northern Keos in the Cycladic Islands From Earliest Settlement to Modern Times*, UCLA Monograph 16. Los Angeles, UCLA Institute of Archaeology.

Coleman, J. E. 1977. *Kephala: A Late Neolithic Settlement and Cemetery (Keos I)*. Princeton, American School of Classical Studies.

Cook, A. G., and M. Glowacki. 2003. "Pots, Politics, and Power." In *The Archaeology and Politics of Food and Feasting in Early States and Empires*, edited by T. L. Bray, 173–202. New York, Kluwer Academic/Plenum.

Crego, D. M. 2010. "Ayia Irini IV: A Distribution Center for the Middle Helladic World?" In *Mesohelladika. The Greek Mainland in the Middle Bronze Age, Bulletin de Correspondance Hellénique Supplement 52*, edited by A. Philippa-Touchais, G. Touchais, S. Voutsaki, and J. Wright, 841–845. Athens, De Boccard.

Cummer, W. W., and E. Schofield. 1984. *Ayia Irini: House A*. Keos 3. Mainz am Rhein, Philipp von Zabern.

Cutler, J. 2016. "Fashioning Identity: Weaving Technology, Dress and Cultural Change in the Middle and Late Bronze Age Southern Aegean." In *Beyond Thalassocracies. Understanding Processes of Minoanisation and Mycenaeanisation in the Aegean*, edited by E. Gorogianni, P. Pavúk, and L. Girella, 172–85. Oxford, Oxbow Books.

Cutler, J. 2011. *Crafting Minoanisation: Textiles, Crafts Production and Social Dynamics in the Bronze Age Southern Aegean*. Ph.D. dissertation, University College London.

Cutler, J. 2012. "Ariadne's Thread: The Adoption of Cretan Weaving Technology in the Wider Southern Aegean in the Mid-Second Millennium BC." In *KOSMOS. Jewellery, Adornment and Textiles in the Aegean Bronze Age*, Aegaeum 31, edited by M. L. B. Nosch and R. Laffineur, 145–154. Liège, Université de Liège, Histoire de l'art et archéologie de la Grèce antique.

Davis, J. L. 1979. "Minos and Dexithea: Crete and the Cyclades in the Later Bronze Age." In *Papers in Cycladic Prehistory*, UCLA Monograph 14, edited by J. L. Davis and J. F. Cherry, 143–157. Los Angeles, UCLA Institute of Archaeology.

Davis, J. L. 1984a. "A Cycladic Figure in Chicago and the Nonfuneral Use of Cycladic Marble Figures." In *Cycladica. Studies in Memory of N. P. Goulandris. Proceedings of the Seventh British Museum Classical Colloquium, June 1983*, edited by J. L. Fitton, 15–23. London, British Museum Press.

Davis, J. L. 1984b. "Cultural Innovation and the Minoan Thalassocracy at Ayia Irini, Keos." In *The Minoan Thalassocracy. Myth and Reality. Proceedings of the Third International Symposium at the Swedish Institute in Athens, 31 May-5 June 1982*, edited by R. Hägg and N. Marinatos, 159-165. Stockholm, P. Åström.

Davis, J. L. 1986. *Ayia Irini: Period V*. Keos 5. Mainz am Rhein, Philipp von Zabern.

Davis, J. L., and J. F. Cherry. 1990. "Spatial and Temporal Uniformitarianism in Late Cycladic I: Perspectives from Kea and Milos on the Prehistory of Akrotiri." In *Thera and the Aegean World III. Vol. 1: Archaeology. Proceedings of the Third International Congress, Santorini, Greece, 3-9 September 1989*, edited by D. A. Hardy, C. G. Doumas, J. A. Sakellarakis, and P. M. Warren, 185-200. London, Thera Foundation.

Davis, J. L., and E. Gorogianni. 2008. "Potsherds from the Edge: Defining the Limits of Minoanized Areas of the Aegean." In *Horizon. A Colloquium on the Prehistory of the Cyclades, Cambridge 25-28 March 2004. McDonald Institute Monographs*, edited by N. Brodie, J. Doole, and G. Gavalas, 379-388. Cambridge, McDonald Institute for Archaeological Research.

Davis, J. L., and H. B. Lewis. 1985. "Mechanization of Pottery Production: A Case Study from the Cycladic Islands." In *Prehistoric Production and Exchange: The Aegean and Eastern Mediterranean*, UCLA Monograph 24, edited by A. B. Knapp and T. Stech, 79-92. Los Angeles and Berkeley, University of California Press.

Davis, J. L., E. Schofield, R. Torrence, and D. F. Williams. 1983. "Keos and the Eastern Aegean: The Cretan Connection." *Hesperia* 52, 361-366.

Dawkins, R. M., and J. P. Droop. 1911. "The Excavations at Phylakopi in Melos." *The Annual of the British School at Athens* 17, 1-22.

Dawson, H. S. 2013. *Mediterranean Voyages: The Archaeology of Island Colonisation and Abandonment*. Walnut Creek, Left Coast Press.

Dietler, M. 1990. "Driven by Drink: The Role of Drinking in the Political Economy and the Case of Early Iron Age France." *Journal of Anthropological Archaeology* 9, 352-406.

Dietler, M. 2001. "Theorizing the Feast: Rituals of Consumption, Commensal Politics, and Power in African Contexts." In *Feasts: Archaeological and Ethnographic Perspectives on Food, Politics, and Power*, edited by M. Dietler and B. Hayden, 65-114. Washington, Smithsonian Institution Press.

Dietler, M. 2005. "The Archaeology of Colonization and the Colonization of Archaeology: Theoretical Challenges from an Ancient Mediterranean Colonial Encounter." In *The Archaeology of Colonial Encounters: Comparative Perspectives*, edited by G. J. Stein, 33-68. Santa Fe and Oxford, School of American Research Press; James Currey.

Dietler, M., and B. Hayden. 2001a. "Digesting the Feast – Good to Eat, Good to Drink, Good to Think: An Introduction." In *Feasts: Archaeological and Ethnographic Perspectives on Food, Politics, and Power*, edited by M. Dietler and B. Hayden, 1-20. Washington, Smithsonian Institution Press.

Dietler, M., and B. Hayden, eds. 2001b. *Feasts: Archaeological and Ethnographic Perspectives on Food, Politics, and Power*. Washington, Smithsonian Institution Press.

Donner, W. 1988. "Context and Community: Equality and Social Change in a Polynesian Outlier." In *Rules, Decisions, and Inequality in Egalitarian Societies*, edited by J. G. Flanagan and S. Rayner, 145-163. Aldershot, Avebury.

Doumas, C. G. 1977. *Early Bronze Age Burial Habits in the Cyclades*, Studies In Mediterranean Arachaeology 48. Göteborg, P. Åström.

Driessen, J. M. 1982. "The Minoan Hall in Domestic Architecture on Crete: To Be in Vogue in Late Minoan IA?" *Acta Archaeologica Lovanensia* 21, 27-92.

Ehrenreich, R. M., C. L. Crumley, and J. E. Levy, eds. 1995. *Heterarchy and the Analysis of Complex Societies*, Archeological Papers of the American Anthropological Association 6. Arlington, American Anthropological Association.

Feinman, G. M., K. Lightfoot, and S. Upham. 2000. "Political Hierarchies and Organizational Strategies in the Puebloan Southwest." *American Antiquity* 65, 449-470.

Fitzsimons, R. D., and E. Gorogianni., forthcoming. "Dining on the Fringe? A Possible Minoan-Style Banquet Hall at Ayia Irini, Kea, and the Minoanisation of the Aegean Islands." In *Minoan Architecture and Urbanism: New Perspectives on an Ancient Built Environment*, edited by Q. Letesson and C. Knappett. Oxford, Oxford University Press.

Gale, N. H., M. Kayafa, and Z. Stos-Gale. 2009. "Further Evidence for Bronze Age Production of Copper from Ores in the Lavrion Ore District, Attica, Greece." In *Proceedings of the 2nd International Conference "Archaeometallurgy in Europe," Aquileia, Italy 17-21 June 2007*, 158–176. Milan, Associazione Italiana di Metallurgia.

Gale, N. H., and Z. Stos-Gale. 2008. "Changing Patterns in Prehistoric Cycladic Metallurgy." In *Horizon. A Colloquium on the Prehistory of the Cyclades, Cambridge 25-28 March 2004*, McDonald Institute Monographs, edited by N. Brodie, J. Doole, and G. Gavalas, 387–408. Cambridge, McDonald Institute for Archaeological Research.

Gale, N. H., Z. Stos-Gale, and J. L. Davis. 1984. "The Provenance of Lead Used at Ayia Irini, Keos." *Hesperia* 53, 389–406.

Georgiou, H. 1986. *Ayia Irini: Specialized Domestic and Industrial Pottery*. Keos 6. Mainz on Rhine, Philipp von Zabern.

Gorogianni, E. 2008. *Creation Stories: The Archaeological Site of Ayia Irini, Kea and the Production of Archaeological Knowledge*. Ph.D. dissertation, University of Cincinnati.

Gorogianni, E. 2011. "Herrscher der Inseln. Anatomie einer Seefahrergesellschaft". In *Kykladen. Lebenswelten einer frühgriechischen Kultur. Katalog zur Ausstellung im Schloss Karlsruhe vom 17.Dez. 2011 bis 22. April 2012*, edited by Badisches Landesmuseum Karlsruhe, 50–57. Darmstadt, Badisches Landesmuseum.

Gorogianni, E. 2013. "Site in Transition: John L. Caskey, Ayia Irini and Archaeological Practice in Greek Archaeology." *Aegean Archaeology* 10 (2009–2010), 1–16.

Gorogianni, E. 2016. "Keian, Kei-noanised, Kei-cenaeanised? Interregional Contact and Identity in Ayia Irini, Kea." In *Beyond Thalassocracies. Understanding Processes of Minoanisation and Mycenaeanisation in the Aegean*, edited by E. Gorogianni, P. Pavúk, and L. Girella, 136–54. Oxford, Oxbow Books.

Gorogianni, E., and N. D. Abell forthcoming. "Insularity and Cosmopolitanism in Ayia Irini, Kea." In *Island, Mainland, Coastland & Hinterland Ceramic Perspectives on Connectivity in the Ancient Mediterranean, Conference at the University of Amsterdam, February 1-3, 2013*, edited by J. Hilditch, A. Kotsonas, C. Beestman-Kruijshaar, M. Revello Lami, S. Rückl, and S. Ximeri. Amsterdam, Amsterdam University Press.

Gorogianni, E., N. D. Abell, and J. Hilditch. 2016a. "Reconsidering Technological Transmission: The Introduction of the Potter's Wheel at Ayia Irini, Kea, Greece." *American Journal of Archaeology* 120, 195–220.

Gorogianni, E., P. Pavúk, and L. Girella, eds. 2016b. *Beyond Thalassocracies. Understanding Processes of Minoanisation and Mycenaeanisation in the Aegean*. Oxford, Oxbow Books.

Graham, J. W. 1961. "The Minoan Banquet Hall." *American Journal of Archaeology* 65, 165–172.

Hamilakis, Y. 2008. "Time, Performance, and the Production of a Mnemonic Record: From Feasting to an Archaeology of Eating and Drinking." In *Dais: The Aegean Feast. Proceedings of the 12th International Aegean Conference/12e Rencontre égéenne internationale, University of Melbourne, Centre for Classics and Archaeology, 25-29 March 2008*, Aegaeum 29, edited by L. A. Hitchcock, R. Laffineur, and J. L. Crowley, 3–19. Liège and Austin, Histoire de l'art et archéologie de la Grèce antique and University of Texas at Austin, Program in Aegean Scripts and Prehistory.

Hodos, T. 2006. *Local Responses to Colonization in the Iron Age Mediterranean*. London and New York, Routledge.

Johnson, G. A. 1982. "Organizational Structure and Scalar Stress." In *Theory and Explanation in Archaeology*, edited by C. Renfrew, M. J. Rowlands, and B. A. Seagraves, 389–412. New York, Academic Press.

Karnava, A. 2008. "Written and Stamped Records in the Late Bronze Age Cyclades: The Sea Journeys of an Administration." In *Horizon. A Colloquium on the Prehistory of the Cyclades, Cambridge 25-28 March 2004*, McDonald Institute Monographs, edited by N. Brodie, J. Doole, and G. Gavalas, 377–386. Cambridge, McDonald Institute for Archaeological Research.

Kayafa, M. 2010. "Middle Helladic Metallurgy and Metalworking: Review of the Archaeological and Archaeometric Evidence from the Peloponnese." In *Mesohelladika. The Greek Mainland in the Middle Bronze Age*, Bulletin de Correspondance Hellénique Supplement 52, edited by A. Philippa-Touchais, G. Touchais, S. Voutsaki, and J. Wright, 701–711. Athens, De Boccard.

Keene, A. S. 1991. "Cohesion and Contradiction in the Communal Mode of Production: The Lessons of the Kibbutz." In *Between Bands and States*, edited by S. A. Gregg, 376–394. Carbondale, Center for Archaeological Investigations, Southern Illinois University.

Kilian-Dirlmeier, I. 1997. *Das mittelbronzezeitliche Schachtgrab von Ägina. Kataloge vor- und frühgeschichtlicher Altertümer 27*, Alt-Ägina 4.3. Mainz am Rhein, Philipp von Zabern.

Kilian-Dirlmeier, I. 2003. "The MH Shaft-grave at Kolonna, Aegina." In Αργοσαρωνικός: Πρακτικά 1ου Διεθνούς Συνεδρίου Ιστορίας και Αρχαιολογίας του Αργοσαρωνικού, Πόρος, 26-29 Ιουνίου 1998, edited by E. Konsolaki-Giannopoulou, Volume Α΄: Η Προϊστορική Περίοδος, 29–32. Athens, Municipality of Poros.

Knapp, A. B., and J. F. Cherry. 1994. "Production and Exchange in the Bronze Age Mediterranean." In *Provenience Studies and Bronze Age Cyprus: Production, Exchange, and Politico-Economic Change*, Monographs in World Archaeology 21, 123–155. Madison, Prehistory Press.

Knappett, C., and I. Nikolakopoulou. 2005. "Exchange and Affiliation Networks in the MBA Southern Aegean: Crete, Akrotiri and Miletus." In *Emporia: Aegeans in the Central and Eastern Mediterranean. Proceedings of the 10th International Aegean Conference/10e Rencontre égéenne internationale, Athens, Italian School of Archaeology, 14-18 April 2004*, Aegaeum 25, edited by R. Laffineur and E. Greco, 175–184. Liège and Austin, Université de Liège, Histoire de l'art et archéologie de la Grèce antique and University of Texas at Austin, Program in Aegean Scripts and Prehistory.

Knappett, C., and I. Nikolakopoulou. 2008. "Colonialism without Colonies? A Bronze Age Case Study from Akrotiri, Thera." *Hesperia* 77, 1–42.

Kristiansen, K., and T. B. Larsson. 2005. *The Rise of Bronze Age Society: Travels, Transmissions and Transformations*. Cambridge, Cambridge University Press.

Letesson, Q. 2013. "Minoan Halls: A Syntactical Genealogy." *American Journal of Archaeology* 117, 303–351.

Lewis, H. B. 1986. "Appendix 1: Pottery Techniques and Surface Treatments." In *Ayia Irini: Period V (Keos V)*, edited by J. L. Davis, 108–109. Mainz am Rhein, Philipp von Zabern.

Malkin, I. 1998. *The Returns of Odysseus: Colonization and Ethnicity*. Berkeley, University of California Press.

Manning, S. W. 2010. "Chronology and Terminology". In *The Oxford Handbook of the Bronze Age Aegean (ca. 3000-1000 BC)*, edited by E.H. Cline, 11–28. Oxford, Oxford University Press.

Milka, E. 2010. "Burials upon the Ruins of Abandoned Houses in the Middle Helladic Argolid." In *Mesohelladika. The Greek Mainland in the Middle Bronze Age*, Bulletin de Correspondance Hellénique Supplement 52, edited by A. Philippa-Touchais, G. Touchais, S. Voutsaki, and J. Wright, 347–355. Athens, De Boccard.

Miller, D., ed. 1995. *Acknowledging Consumption: A Review of New Studies*. New York, Routledge.

Miracle, P., and N. Milner, eds. 2002. *Consuming Passions and Patterns of Consumption*. Cambridge, Cambridge University Press.

Morgan, L. forthcoming a. *The Ayia Irini Wall Paintings: Social Context and the Miniature Frieze*. Keos 11. Philadelphia, Institute of Aegean Prehistory Academic Press.

Morgan, L. forthcoming b. "Inspiration and Innovation: The Creation of Wall Paintings in the Absence of a Pictorial Pottery Tradition at Ayia Irini, Kea." In *Paintbrushes*, edited by A. Vlachopoulos. Athens, Melissa.

Morgan, L. 1998. "The Wall Paintings of the North-East Bastion at Ayia Irini, Kea." In *Kea-Kythnos. History and Archaeology. Proceedings of an International Symposium Kea-Kythnos. 22-25 June 1994*, Meletimata 27, edited by L. G. Mendoni and A. Mazarakis-Ainian, 201–210. Paris and Athens, De Boccard; Research Centre for Greek and Roman Antiquity, National Hellenic Research Foundation.

Mourtzas, N., and E. Kolaiti. 1998. "Αλληλεπίδραση Γεωλογικών και Αρχαιολογικών Παραγόντων Εξέλιξη των Προϊστορικών και Ιστορικών Οικισμών και Κατασκευών σε Σχέση με τις Μεταβολές του Επιπέδου της Θάλασσας στις Ακτές της Νήσου Κέας." In *Kea-Kythnos: History and Archaeology Proceedings of an International Symposium Kea-Kythnos. 22-25 June 1994*, Meletimata 27, edited by L. G. Mendoni and A. Mazarakis-Ainian, 679–693. Paris and Athens, De Boccard; Research Centre for Greek and Roman Antiquity, National Hellenic Research Foundation.

Nordquist, G. 1987. *A Middle Helladic Village. Asine in the Argolid*, Uppsala Studies in Ancient Mediterranean and Near Eastern Civilisations 16. Uppsala, Boreas.

Nordquist, G. 1990. "Middle Helladic Burial Rites: Some Speculations." In *Celebrations of Death and Divinity in the Bronze Age Argolid: Proceedings of the Sixth International Symposium at the Swedish Institute at Athens, 11–13 June, 1988*, ActaAth 4°, 40, edited by R. Hägg and G. Nordquist, 35–41. Stockholm, Swedish Institute of Athens.

Nordquist, G. 2002. "Intra- and Extramural, Single and Collective, Burials in the Middle and Late Helladic Periods." In *New Research on Old Material from Asine and Berbati in Celebration of the Fiftieth Anniversary of the Swedish Institute at Athens*, ActaAth 8°, 17, edited by B. Wells, 23–29. Stockholm, Swedish Institute of Athens.

Overbeck, G. F. 1984a. "The Development of Grave Types at Ayia Irini, Kea." In *The Prehistoric Cyclades: Contributions to a Workshop on Cycladic Chronology (in Memoriam: John Langdon Caskey, 1908-1981)*, edited by J. A. MacGillivray and R. L. N. Barber, 114–118. Edinburgh, University of Edinburgh.

Overbeck, G. F. 1989a. "The Cemeteries and the Graves." In *Ayia Irini: Period IV. Part 1: The Stratigraphy and the Find Deposits (Keos VII)*, edited by J. C. Overbeck, 184–205. Mainz am Rhein, Philipp von Zabern.

Overbeck, J. C. 1982. "The Hub of Commerce: Keos and Middle Helladic Greece." *Temple University Aegean Symposium* 7, 38–49.

Overbeck, J. C. 1984b. "Stratigraphy and Ceramic Sequence in Middle Cycladic Ayia Irini." In *The Prehistoric Cyclades: Contributions to a Workshop on Cycladic Chronology (in Memoriam: John Langdon Caskey, 1908-1981)*, edited by J. A. MacGillivray and R. L. N. Barber, 108–113. Edinburgh, University of Edinburgh.

Overbeck, J. C. 1989b. *Ayia Irini: Period IV. Part 1: The Stratigraphy and the Find Deposits (Keos VII)*. Mainz am Rhein, Philipp von Zabern.

Overbeck, J. C., and D. M. Crego. 2008. "The Commercial Foundation and Development of Ayia Irini IV (Kea)." In *Horizon. A Colloquium on the Prehistory of the Cyclades, Cambridge 25-28 March 2004*, McDonald Institute Monographs, edited by N. Brodie, J. Doole, G. Gavalas, and C. Renfrew, 305–309. Cambridge, McDonald Institute for Archaeological Research.

Overbeck, J. C., and G. F. Overbeck. 1979. "Consistency and Diversity in the Middle Cycladic Era." In *Papers in Cycladic Prehistory*, UCLA Monograph 14, edited by J. L. Davis and J. F. Cherry, 106–119. Los Angeles, UCLA Institute of Archaeology.

Petruso, C. 1992. *Ayia Irini: The Balance Weights. An Analysis of Weight Measurement in Prehistoric Crete and the Cycladic Islands (Keos VIII)*. Mainz am Rhein, Philipp von Zabern.

Rubenson, O. 1917. "Die prähistorischen und frühgeschichtlichen Funde auf dem Burghügel von Paros." *Attenische Mitteilungen* 42, 1–98.

Sampson, A. 1985. *Μάνικα. Μιά Πρωτοελλαδική Πόλη στη Χαλκίδα I*. Athens, Society for Euboean Studies.

Schofield, E. 1982. "The Western Cyclades and Crete: A 'Special Relationship.'" *Oxford Journal of Archaeology* 1, 9–25.

Schofield, E. 1990. "Evidence for Household Industries on Thera and Kea." In *Thera and the Aegean World III. Vol. 1: Archaeology. Proceedings of the Third International Congress, Santorini, Greece, 3–9*

September 1989, edited by D. A. Hardy, C. G. Doumas, J. A. Sakellarakis, and P. M. Warren, 201–211. London, Thera Foundation.

Schofield, E. 1998. "Town Planning at Ayia Irini, Kea." In *Kea-Kythnos: History and Archaeology. Proceedings of an International Symposium Kea-Kythnos. 22-25 June 1994,* Meletimata 27, edited by L. G. Mendoni and A. Mazarakis-Ainian, 117–122. Paris and Athens, De Boccard; Research Centre for Greek and Roman Antiquity, National Hellenic Research Foundation.

Schofield, E. 2011. *Ayia Irini: The Western Sector* (Keos X). Mainz am Rhein, Philipp von Zabern.

Servais, J., and B. Servais-Soyez. 1984. "La tholos 'oblongue' (Tombe IV) et le tumulus (Tombe V) sur le Vélatouri." In *Thorikos VIII, 1972-1976*, 15–71. Brussels, Belgian Archaeological School in Greece.

Shank, E. 2008. "Decorated Dining Halls." In *Dais: The Aegean Feast. Proceedings of the 12th International Aegean Conference / 12e Rencontre égéenne internationale, University of Melbourne, Centre for Classics and Archaeology, 25-29 March 2008,* Aegaeum 29, 97–103. Liège and Austin, University of Liège, Department of Art History and Archaeology of Ancient Greece and University of Texas at Austin, Program in Aegean Scripts and Prehistory.

Upham, S. 1990. *The Evolution of Political Systems. Sociopolitics in Small-scale Sedentary Societies.* Cambridge, Cambridge University Press.

Voutsaki, S., E. Milka, S. Triantafyllou, and C. Zerner. 2013. "Middle Helladic Lerna: Diet, Economy, Society." In *Diet, Economy and Society in the Ancient Greek World. Towards a Better Integration of Archaeology and Science*, Pharos Supplement 1, edited by S. Voutsaki and S.M. Valamoti, 133–147. Leuven, Peeters.

Wason, P. K. 1994. *The Archaeology of Rank.* New Studies in Archaeology. Cambridge, Cambridge University Press.

Waterman, A. J., and J. T. Thomas. 2011. "When the Bough Breaks: Childhood Mortality and Burial Practice in Late Neolithic Atlantic Europe." *Oxford Journal of Archaeology* 30, 165–183.

Whitelaw, T. M. 2004. "Alternate Pathways to Social Complexity in the Southern Aegean." In *Emergence of Civilisation Revisited*, Sheffield Studies in Aegean Archaeology 6, edited by J. C. Barrett and P. Halstead. Oxford, Oxbow Books.

Whitelaw, T. M. 2005. "A Tale of Three Cities: Chronology and Minoanisation at Phylakopi in Melos." In *Autochthon. Papers Presented to O. T. P. K. Dickinson on the Occasion of his Retirement*, British Archaeological Report, S1432, edited by A. Dakouri-Hild and S. Sherratt, 37–69. Oxford, Archaeopress.

Wiener, M. H. 2007. "Neopalatial Knossos: Rule and Role." In *Krinoi kai Limenes: Studies in Honor of Joseph and Maria Shaw*, Prehistory Monographs 22, edited by P. P. Betancourt, M. C. Nelson, and H. Williams, 231–242. Philadelphia, Institute of Aegean Prehistory Academic Press.

Wiener, M. H. 2013. "Realities of Power: The Minoan Thalassocracy in Historical Perspective." In *Amilla: The Quest for Excellence: Studies Presented to Guenter Kopcke in Celebration of his 75th Birthday*, Prehistory Monographs 43, edited by R.B. Koehl, 149–173. Philadelphia, Institute of Aegean Prehistory Academic Press.

Wilson, D. E. 1999. *Ayia Irini: Periods I-III. The Neolithic and Early Bronze Age Settlements*, Keos IX. Mainz am Rhein, Philipp von Zabern.

Young, B., and D. Papadatou. 1997. "Childhood Death and Bereavement Across Cultures." In *Death and Bereavement Across Cultures*, edited by C. M. Parkes, P. Languani, and B. Young, 191–205. London, Routledge.

Chapter 8

Long-term developments in southern mainland settlement systems from Early Helladic to Late Helladic times as seen through the lens of regional survey

John Bintliff

The emergence of corporate communities – City states

I would like to begin this chapter with some preparatory discussion of settlement dynamics, relevant to the later prehistoric Aegean. Many early farming societies show face-to-face social life controlled by village fissioning, as has been argued for earlier Neolithic Greece (Perlès 2001). Such small communities of less than 200 members must intermarry, so economic property is spread over many neighbouring settlements (Bintliff 1999). Neolithic Greece is dominated by autonomous face-to-face, sustainable village settlement. According to Perlès' convincing analysis, most of this long era sees a dense network of socially-harmonious villages. However, cross cultural historical geography and social anthropology show that agglomerations of more than 500–600 people, in contrast, tend to show "emergent complexity" (Freeman 1968) and frequently develop city-state behaviours in the direction of civil society (Bintliff 2000; 2012). When communities expand to this threshold and over, they show internalisation of communal life and are free to favour high endogamy, while many properties typical for the city-state appear. For example, Kolonna Bronze Age town on Aegina at around 4 ha (see Gauß and Lindblom, this volume) probably falls also into the demographic size to suit such a corporate community or small city-state. It also belongs to a group of nucleated and widely-networked centres common on other Aegean islands from the Middle into Late Bronze Age.

All this brings into clearer focus a comparison we can make with the Archaic to Classical *polis* or city-state of the historical Aegean. Of the 700–800 minimum city-states of the Classical Aegean for which data are available, 80% have populations of 2000–4000 people and maximal territories of 5–6 km radius (Ruschenbush 1985;

Hansen 2004). They were rightly dubbed "village-states" by Kirsten (*Dorfstaaten*) in his classic study (Kirsten 1956).

For my paper for the *Mesohelladika* conference (Bintliff 2010) I had systematically re-analysed the Neolithic to Mycenaean settlement patterns of southern mainland Greece as revealed through intensive survey, on the basis of the Oropus survey, the Boeotia survey, the Methana survey, the Nemea survey, the Berbati survey, the Argolid survey, the Laconia survey and the Asea survey.

What *was* surprising in this overview was that the range of settlement sizes and the variety of their spatial grouping are rather comparable across the *Neolithic* and the *Early Helladic* eras. Typical are small villages of 1–2 ha or less, separated in fertile areas by a few kilometres, and south of Thessaly, often associated with dispersed farm/hamlet sites. Rarely, a village may achieve 4–5 ha or more ("proto-poleis"), whilst also rarely, small or large nucleations can evidence signs of special monumental buildings of a public or maybe elite character. For example in the Argolid (Jameson *et al.* 1994), a dense Final Neolithic–EH landscape with four villages (two being 5 ha or more) several kilometres apart, is associated with many dispersed hamlet-farms.

What was *not* surprising from this overview was the confirmation that MH settlement patterns and overall population show strong thinning out of occupation, rather than a process of nucleation following abandonment of most of the dispersed settlements of the EH era. This would agree with the indications in later EBA times throughout the south Aegean of large-scale catastrophic disruption to human society, which seems particularly on the mainland to have created a longer-lived period of decline and then stagnation in early MBA times.

For example, again using the Argolid Survey data, the MH era sees a drastic collapse to two small villages and a farm/hamlet but spaced several kilometres apart. In the southern mainland MH period in fact, the overall impression is of similarity to the earlier periods, in that the key element is a chain of nucleated villages or hamlets separated by a few kilometres, although a thinning out can be argued in most regions. The second striking difference is the loss of most of the surrounding smaller rural sites.

With the LH comes a fuller network of villages and a minor recovery of smaller rural sites. Thus in the Argolid once more, the LH landscape is composed of several villages (some four to five being 5 ha or more), at several kilometres interval, along with dispersed hamlets and farms back to EH levels of density. On Methana, once again after an EH pattern of four villages with numerous dispersed hamlets and farms, which contracts during MH times to three village/hamlets, the LH era witnesses three villages-hamlets now accompanied by a slight number of smaller rural sites. We can repeat such sequences more widely across southern mainland Greece, which brings into greater highlight the core regions of Mycenaean development within which several more elaborate centres arise with mansion or palace facilities, intimately related to state formation (such as the Sparta Plain, the Argos Plain, the Iolkos region of Thessaly, Western Messenia).

But it is more significant to highlight the empirical observation that the overall pattern of settlement in Southern Greece from intensive and extensive surveys for the LH era remains similar to earlier periods, typified by networks of moderately-spaced rural villages or hamlets and variable numbers of lesser satellite sites. Rarely in space and in number there arise out of this 'normal pattern' unusually-elaborate, high-ranking central-places.

A preliminary conclusion

From the start of the Neolithic, the mainland landscape was one of intensely-interacting *villages*, in which emergent complexity was always a possible outcome. The permanent necessity for district social clusters of interacting settlements, given the extreme rareness of communities large enough to be mostly self-sufficient in biological terms – "small worlds" or achieved city-states – created arenas in which the mobilisation of manpower for military purposes, of agricultural and other surpluses for economic purposes, and participants for large-scale cult activities (such as have been hypothesized for the EH Corridor Houses, and are known from the Linear B texts to have been a significant activity coordinated by the LH palaces), were greatly facilitated. In this we may identify at least *one of the mechanisms* through which Bronze Age territorial states were formed. Aspiring "men of renown" (to borrow Jim Wright's (2004) term) might mobilize influence and resources across these networks as a basis for more personal clientship power. For an illustrative ethnographic parallel, Lehmann (2004) has plotted endogamous and exogamous marriage networks around a traditional Palestinian village in a ten kilometre radius (Fig. 8.1).

A second mechanism is this: once some villages expand into the 500–600+ corporate community size, they should have overcome social stress through horizontal differentiation (such as an enlargement of the kinship groups argued to be typical for MH I–II into extended clans argued by Voutsaki and Wiersma for the MH III–LH I era (this volume)), and/or by vertical differentiation (Big Men, chiefs) which has definitely occurred in exceptional places already in MH I–II, but which becomes widespread only from the MH III–LH I era. Such proto-poleis can exercise a gravity-influence on smaller surrounding settlements, but their internal politics have also emerged into greater complexity, with a potential for infinite expansion in regional political power. They replace their former role as partners in equal marriage networks, by forming attractors for marriage alliances with now subordinate satellite communities, although their endogamous rates remain dominant.

For a worked parallel, Figure 8.2 shows reconstructed inter-village marriage clusters around larger settlements in Early Iron Age Palestine, as a basis for the creation of small statelets (Lehmann 2004).

Bronze Age Boeotia

This province offers some interesting contrasts in its Bronze Age settlement trajectory to the North-Eastern Peloponnese, the heartland of the Mycenaean civilisation. Our survey evidence from the long-running Boeotia Project indicates a dominance of

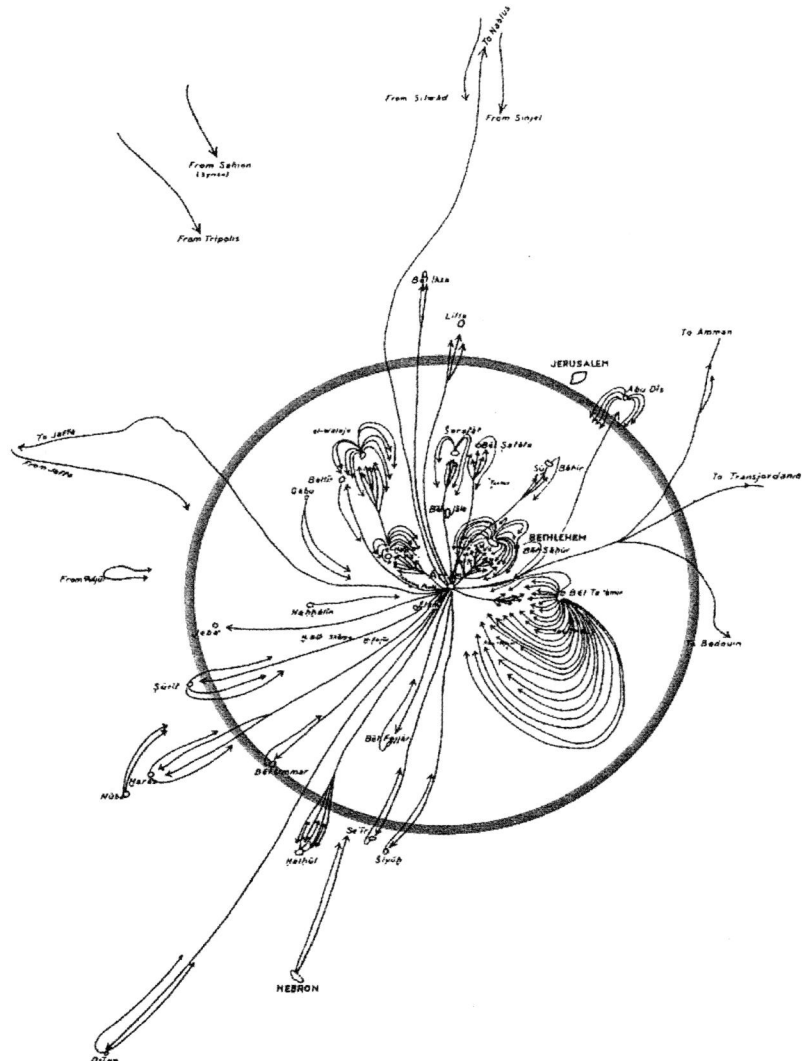

Fig. 8.1: A map of marriage patterns around the Early Modern period village of Artas, Palestine (from Lehmann 2004).

village settlement over the landscape, at far from high population levels from the Neolithic up till the end of the Mycenaean era. Let's make a quick tour of the evidence from our different study areas (Fig. 8.3).[1]

First off, the ancient city of *Koroneia*: an urban surface survey. Bronze Age activity at the later city-site is at most at hamlet level throughout.

---

[1] The ceramic specialists are Oliver Dickinson and Kalliope Sarri, our GIS map-maker Emeri Farinetti.

8. Long-term developments in southern mainland settlement systems 163

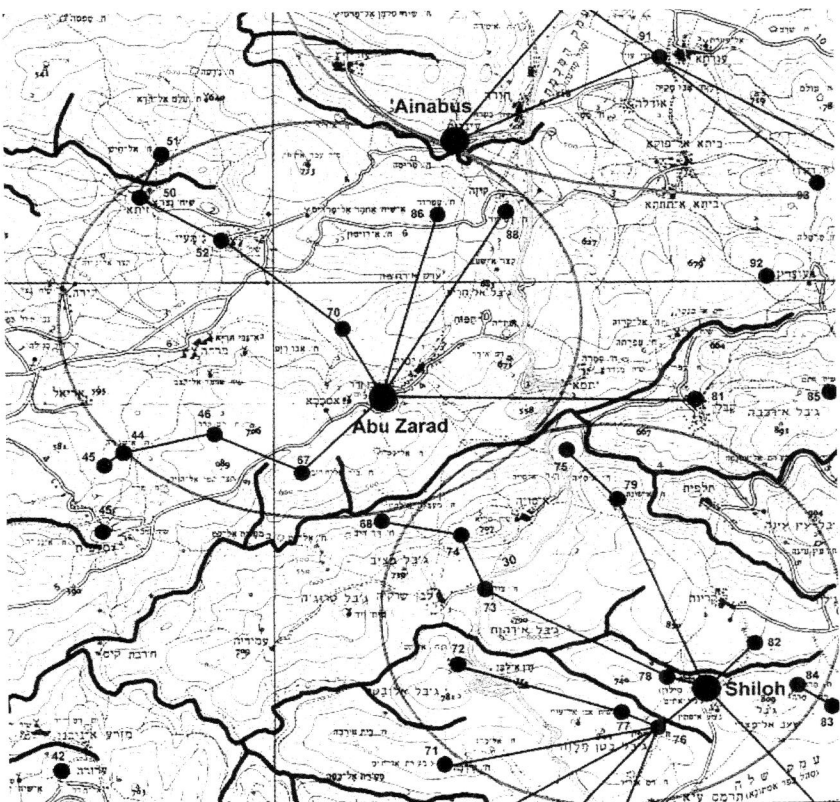

Fig. 8.2: An hypothetical marriage network centering on emergent Iron Age statelets in Palestine (from Lehmann 2004).

Tanagra urban survey: the later city site forms a prehistoric hamlet in all Bronze Age periods. From the Tanagra rural survey MH sherd finds are limited to the city-site village and a nearby village. By the MH–LH transitional period we have the same but with a small rural focus added. Finally for the mature LH period we find just the city-site village and small-scale rural activity.

The urban and rural survey at ancient *Hyettos* city: shows for the transitional Final Neolithic-EH and mature EH eras, a village at the later city-site, scattered farms and a possible hamlet. By MH times we have the city-site village, the hamlet and scattered rural activity. By LH times perhaps the city-site village has grown into a large village or proto-polis, the nearby hamlet has become a village, finally we have some scattered rural activity.

In the *S.W Boeotia* district (the rural area between Haliartos and Thespiai cities in Figure 8.3), hamlets and villages form the largest foci in the surveyed areas, for example in the Valley of the Muses. Here one village dominates each Bronze Age phase (cf. Bintliff 1996), with just a few prehistoric rural sites amongst the 90 mapped for all periods.

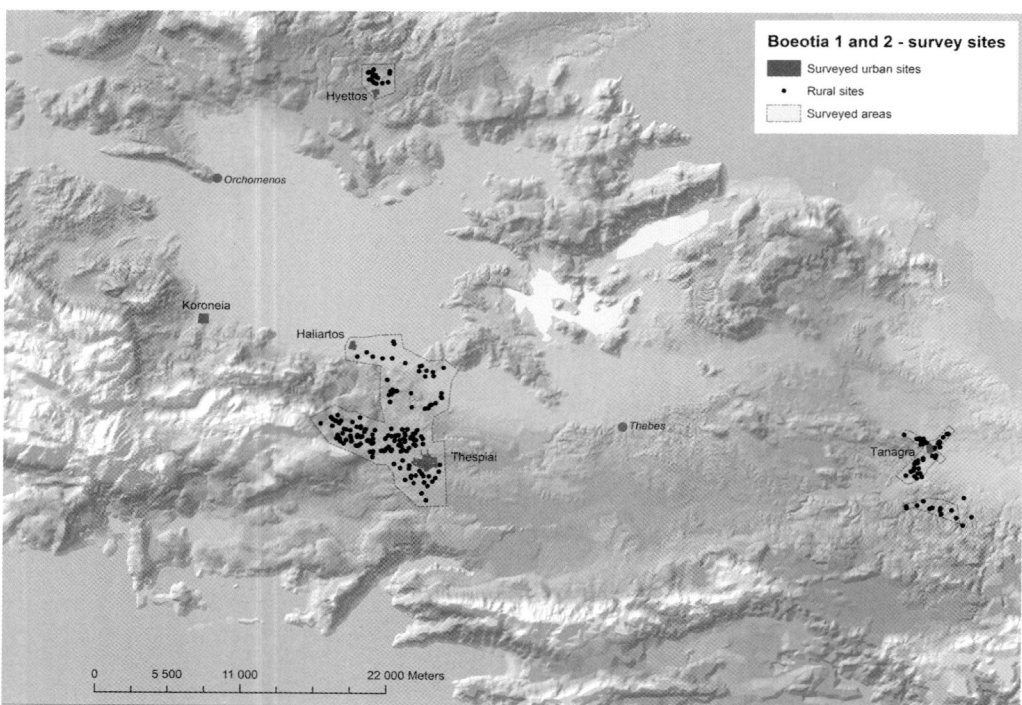

Fig. 8.3: Location of the surveyed ancient towns and landscapes by the Boeotia Project, 1979–2011 (from Farinetti 2011). The prehistoric centres of Thebes and Orchomenos are also indicated.

From the *Thespiae City* urban and hinterland survey (for the latter see Bintliff *et al.* 2007): beginning with the EH era, we reconstruct a core hamlet at the city-site, another a few kilometres distant, and widespread farms. By the MH period we reconstruct two close hamlets at the city-site, continued occupation at the distant hamlet and rare dispersed rural activity, and for the LH era a dispersed hamlet at the city-site, continuation at the other hamlet and some wider small-scale rural activity.

Given the generally modest density and scale of settlement throughout the Bronze Age within the widely distributed survey areas we have just covered in Boeotia, we may reasonably ask how the clearly immensely important palatial centre at Bronze Age Thebes (Dakouri-Hild 2010a) was sustained. To its north and south Thebes dominated a truly massive area of fertile dry-farmed land, its lower and upper plains (Farinetti 2011). Yet known sites of the MBA (mapped in Farinetti *op.cit.*), although admittedly for the territory of Thebes we largely lack intensive survey data, are relatively thin, consistent with our intensive survey windows. In the LBA, this map gets denser but is still only modestly populated, also agreeing with our intensive survey windows. The existence of secondary-centres such as Eutresis, between our Thespiae survey district and Thebes, does not boost Mycenaean demography significantly, since despite its 21 ha enceinte, the excavator could only identify contemporary occupation in a mere 3.5 ha of the site (Goldman 1931).

Since the Linear B texts make it likely that the Thebes palace controlled most of Central and Eastern Boeotia (Dakouri-Hild 2010b), we must assume that it compensated for modest population density and food surplusses by the sheer size of the region it dominated, together with the remarkable fertility of its own immediate hinterland. In contrast, the Pylos Project team in Messenia (cf. Bennet 1999) has suggested that the region around the emergent Mycenaean palace-town was remarkably dense with later MH to LH foci.

A second LBA landscape which appears heavily populated and intensively exploited, possibly to the point of marginal long-term sustainability, is the Plain of Argos (Bintliff 1977; 1989; Marzolff 2004). In fact I wonder if the wider palatial collapse occurring in the final LBA was perhaps partly driven by stress in such high-population zones.

The contrast between the "busy countrysides" (to steal a phrase from David Pettegrew) of the Mycenaean Argos Plain and the Pylos region, and the giant but only modestly populated territory dominated by Boeotian Thebes, should draw our attention to the spectacular activity of Thebes' likely rival, the west Boeotian Bronze Age centre of Orchomenos. Its immediate hinterland was beset by Lake Copais, the Kephissos Valley prone to floods, and much poor hill country (Farinetti 2011). But the Mycenaean dynasty at Orchomenos had pretensions, shown symbolically by the construction of the only Boeotian tholos tomb (the "Treasury of Minyas"), and one which directly imitated those at Mycenae, if not the Treasury of Atreus itself (Mee and Cavanagh 1990; see also Alcock and Cherry 2009).

By draining a major part of Copais in the Late Helladic III period for the production of massive food surplusses (Knauss 1987, Iakovidis 2001; the AROURA Mycenaean fields project, cf. http://www.umbc.edu/aroura/), did the Orchomenos rulers aim to elevate their resources and supporting manpower to those of Thebes or the centres in the Argive Plain and on the Pylos plateaux?

Conclusions

This chapter has brought together landscape archaeology and anthropological theory in an attempt to probe deeper into the social mechanisms and divergent historical and regional trajectories which underlay the rise and unfolding of Mycenaean civilisation on the southern mainland of Greece.

Bibliography

Alcock, S. E., and J. F. Cherry. 2006. "'No Greater Marvel': A Bronze Age Classic at Orchomenos". In *The Classical Traditions of Greece and Rome*, edited by J. I. Porter, 69–86. Princeton, Princeton University Press.

Bennet, J. 1999. "The Mycenaean Conceptualization of Space or Pylian Geography (... Yet Again!)." In *Floreant Studia Mycenaea*, edited by S. Deger-Jalkotzky, S. Hiller and O. Panagl, 131–157. Vienna, Austrian Academy of Sciences.

Bintliff, J. L. 1977. *Natural Environment and Human Settlement in Prehistoric Greece*, British Archaeological Report S28. Oxford, British Archaeological Reports.

Bintliff, J. L. 1989. "Cemetery Populations, Carrying Capacities and the Individual in History." In *Burial Archaeology*, edited by C. A. Roberts, F. Lee and J. L. Bintliff, 85–104. Oxford, British Archaeological Report 211. Oxford, British Archaeological Reports.

Bintliff, J. L. 1996. "The Archaeological Survey of the Valley of the Muses and its Significance for Boeotian History." In *La Montagne des Muses*, edited by A. Hurst and A. Schachter, 193–224. Geneva, Librairie Droz.

Bintliff, J.L. 1999. "Chapter 13: Settlement and Territory." In *The Routledge Companion Encyclopedia of Archaeology*, edited by G. Barker, 505–545. London, Routledge.

Bintliff, J. L. 2000. "Settlement and Territory: A Socio-Ecological Approach to the Evolution of Settlement Systems." In *Human Ecodynamics*, edited by G. Bailey, R. Charles and N. Winder, 21–30. Oxford, Oxbow Books.

Bintliff, J. L., P. Howard, and A. M. Snodgrass, eds. 2007. *Testing the Hinterland: The Work of the Boeotia Survey (1989-1991) in the Southern Approaches to the City of Thespiai*. MacDonald Institute Monographs. Cambridge, University of Cambridge.

Bintliff, J. L. 2010. "The Middle Bronze Age through the Surface Survey Record of the Greek Mainland: Demographic and Sociopolitical Insights". In *Mesohelladika. The Greek Mainland in the Middle Bronze Age*, Bulletin de Correspondance Hellénique Supplement 52, edited by A. Philippa-Touchais, G. Touchais, S. Voutsaki, and J. Wright, 755–763. Athens, De Boccard.

Bintliff, J. L. 2012. *The Complete Archaeology of Greece, from Hunter-Gatherers to the Twentieth Century AD*. Oxford-New York, Blackwell-Wiley.

Dakouri-Hild, A. 2010a. "Thebes." In *The Oxford Handbook of the Bronze Age Aegean*, edited by E. H. Cline, 690–711. Oxford, Oxford University Press.

Dakouri-Hild, A. 2010b. "Boeotia." In *The Oxford Handbook of the Bronze Age Aegean*, edited by E. H. Cline, 614–630. Oxford, Oxford University Press.

Farinetti, E. 2011. *Boeotian Landscapes: A GIS-Based Study for the Reconstruction and Interpretation of the Archaeological Datasets of Ancient Boeotia* British Archaeological Report S2195. Oxford, Archaeopress.

Freeman, S. T. 1968. "Corporate Village Organisation in the Sierra Ministra." *Man* 3, 477–484.

Goldman, H. 1931. *Excavations at Eutresis in Boeotia, Conducted by the Fogg Art Museum of Harvard University in Cooperation with the American School of Classical Studies at Athens, Greece*. Cambridge MA, Harvard University Press.

Hansen, M. H. 2004. "The Concept of the Consumption City Applied to the Greek Polis." In *Once Again: Studies in the Ancient Greek Polis*, edited by T. H. Nielsen, 9–47. Stuttgart, Franz Steiner.

Iakovidis, S. 2001. *Gla and the Kopais in the 13th Century B.C.* Athens, Library of the Archaeological Society at Athens No. 221.

Jameson, M. H., C. N. Runnels, and T. H. van Andel, eds. 1994. *A Greek Countryside. The Southern Argolid from Prehistory to the Present Day*. Stanford, California, Stanford University Press.

Kirsten, E. 1956. *Die Griechische Polis als historisch-geographisches Problem des Mittelmeerraumes* Colloquium Geographicum 5. Bonn, Ferd, Dümmler.

Knauss, J. 1987. *Die Melioration des Kopaisbeckens durch die Minyer im 2. Jt. v. Chr. Kopais 2*. Munich, Technical University of Munich.

Lehmann, G. 2004. "Reconstructing the Social Landscape of Early Israel: Rural Marriage Alliances in the Central Hill Country." *Tel Aviv* 31, 141–193.

Marzolff, P. 2004. "Das Zweifache Rätsel Tiryns." In *Macht der Architektur - Architektur der Macht*, edited by E.-L. Schwandner and K. Rheidt, 79–91. Mainz am Rhein, Philipp von Zabern.

Mee, C., and W. Cavanagh. 1990. "The Spatial Distribution of Mycenaean Tombs." *Annual of the British School at Athens* 85, 225–243.

Perlès, C. 2001. *The Early Neolithic in Greece*. Cambridge, Cambridge University Press.

Ruschenbusch, E. 1985. "Die Zahl der griechischen Staaten und Arealgrösse und Bürgerzahl der 'Normalpolis'." *Zeitschrift für Papyrologie und Epigraphik* 59, 253–263.

Wright, J. C. 2004. "Comparative Settlement Patterns during the Bronze Age in the Northeastern Peloponnese." In *Side-by-Side Survey. Comparative Regional Studies in the Mediterranean World*, edited by S. E. Alcock and J. F. Cherry, 114–131. Oxford, Oxbow Books.

Chapter 9

Middle Helladic reflections

John F. Cherry

"May you live in interesting times" goes the ancient (allegedly Chinese) curse. For nearly all of us, the most interesting times are naturally those in which we ourselves live, irrespective of how peaceful or chaotic they may be. But when we look in the rearview mirror and consider times well before our own, some periods appear seductively more interesting than others. In Aegean prehistory, one need only scan the standard textbooks to gain a sense of what some of these are: the so-called "international spirit" of the mid-third millennium; the apparent "promise" of the sociopolitical systems underlying the EH II "Corridor Houses"; the intense period of state formation on Crete between 2200 and 1900 BC; the Shaft Grave phenomenon; the cataclysm that destroyed Thera; the end of the Bronze Age; and so on. But within such quasi-historical narrative accounts, the end of the third millennium and the first several centuries of the second millennium BC on the Greek mainland are conspicuous by their absence. These were, apparently, simply not "interesting times". Emily Vermeule perhaps put it the most bluntly. In her *Greece in the Bronze Age* (1964) – the textbook, let's remember, from which an entire generation of students learned about Aegean prehistory – she began her chapter on "The Opening of the Middle Bronze Age" with these words:

> "The period 2200 to 1900 B.C. is framed by two major intrusions into Greece of similar invaders: the Patterned-ware people and the Minyans. These three centuries are not very interesting in Greece...". (Vermeule 1964, 66)

Half a century later, things look very different. Not least because of the efforts of the senior editor of this volume, the late EBA and MBA on the Greek mainland within the past decade or more have become the locus of targeted fieldwork efforts, the re-study or final publication of legacy datasets, the application of several new and promising types of scientific analysis, and a marked increase in the number of articles, book chapters, monographs, and congresses. Arguably, the starting point of this renaissance was Jeremy Rutter's characteristically thorough and thoughtful synthetic review of the evidence as it stood at the turn of the twenty-first century (Rutter 2001, an updated version of an article that first appeared in 1993). Soon after came the 2004 International Workshop in Salzburg on "Middle Helladic Pottery and Synchronisms" (Felten *et al.*

2007), two decades on from the Athens Workshop on Middle Bronze Age Pottery that led to the establishment of the specialized, limited circulation MBA journal *Hydra*. Two years later the massive 2006 Athens international conference on "The Greek mainland in the Middle Bronze Age" took place. This resulted in perhaps the largest Supplement ever published by the *bulletin de correspondance hellénique*: 1046 pages, weighing in at 6 lb (2.7 kg), with four co-editors, six major sections, and some 70 communications by 130 individual contributing authors – a monumental contribution to Aegean prehistory if ever there was one (Philippa-Touchais *et al.* 2010). Doctoral dissertations have also begun to be undertaken that deal with these centuries (*e.g.*, Spencer 2007; Wiersma 2013; Milka, forthcoming). A major impetus for much of this renewed interest and research, manifestly, was the five-year Middle Helladic Argolid Project (directed by Sofia Voutsaki at the Groningen Institute of Archaeology, and funded by the Netherlands Organization for Scientific Research), whose research goals and methods were set out at an early stage in an admirable paper published – appropriately – in the *Festschrift* for Oliver Dickinson, the *doyen* of Middle Helladic studies (Voutsaki 2005). The fruits of this project have begun to appear in many papers over the past few years, and they are frequently cited in most of the chapters of this book.

Now, additionally, we have the conference held in Groningen in October 2013, of which this volume represents the proceedings, aimed at explaining "processes of social, economic, and cultural change from the Early Bronze Age III to the Late Bronze Age I period (ca. 2200–1600 BC) in the southern Aegean, but with special emphasis on the southern mainland." Middle Helladic studies could truly be characterized as on a roll. But, equally, we can ask: after the massive unburdening of data and ideas and approaches to be found in the proceedings of the 2006 conference, what are the unresolved questions and research issues still to be tackled? Are we going about things the right way? And what progress does the present volume offer?

* * * * *

The EH III–LH I period suffers from being, as it were, trapped. It is book-ended "between two peaks of economic prosperity, social differentiation and cultural connectivity, the Early Helladic and Mycenaean periods", as Voutsaki and Milka (Chapter 6) put it. Likewise, the MH specialist can be forgiven for experiencing pangs of jealousy when the seemingly drab and uneventful centuries from 2200 to 1800 BC on the Greek mainland are set side-by-side with the incorrigibly more glamorous societies of Minoan Crete, which developed at breakneck speed over this same time-span, starting in EM III–MM IA, and resulting in the first palatial states outside of the eastern Mediterranean (Cherry 2010). This is what has always made the MH period the poor step-child of the Aegean Bronze Age.

It shows in the descriptive vocabulary bandied about to characterize the MH period (or, more broadly, EH III to MH I–II), even given the shortage of adequate soundly-based systematic analyses of empirical data. Thus, the period is often treated as beginning with a "crisis" – although a crisis in, or of, or caused by what is still very far from adequately understood. Communities "are considered fairly simple, homogenous, and introverted" (Wiersma and Voutsaki, this volume, introduction). Summarizing evidence from Dickinson's *The Origins of Mycenaean Civilisation* (1977), Voutsaki (2005, 134) wrote:

> "The MH period is characterized by depopulation, relative material poverty, and the absence of overt social differentiation, especially during the earlier and middle phases ... There is no pronounced site hierarchy, nor do houses within a settlement vary significantly in terms of architecture, size, or contents ... [The dead] usually received no offerings, but were at times accompanied by one or two vases, or a few simple ornaments made of bone, stone, or paste. Metal finds are quite rare, and precious metals (gold, silver) virtually absent. During this period, the southern mainland was culturally rather isolated."

Dickinson's book was foundational for this field, not only in providing the first thorough synthesis of the period, but also in focusing on how we might understand the social and political changes on the mainland towards the end of the MBA. Interestingly, he has twice revisited and updated his views, once in his 1989 paper for the Aegaeum *Transition* conference, and then again in his keynote lecture to the 2006 Athens conference (Dickinson 1989; 2010). Over the span of 35 years, and notwithstanding many new discoveries and publications, he has not changed his mind that MH Greece before its final phase was "technologically limited, underdeveloped, poor"; he has "no impression of increasing momentum, but rather ... of negative feedback, of stasis if not stagnation"; "the mainland was the 'Third World' of the Aegean region" (Dickinson 2010, 16–17).

Such gloomy and unflattering language is prompted in large part, I believe, by the feeling that EH III and earlier MH society was somehow a "failure", because it did not succeed in capitalizing on the alleged "promise" of EH II. This seems to me to be the wrong way of thinking about things. If we find the society and culture of the MBA mainland unexciting and disappointing, this is our problem, not that of the communities in question. Those largely village-based communities were actually quite successful, in that they found the means of social reproduction and interaction that allowed them to persist for centuries. As a matter of fact, social life on the Greek mainland had been structured as a landscape of villages, hamlets, and farmsteads (in differing proportions, to be sure, from one period or region to another: see Bintliff, Chapter 8; also 2010) ever since the coming of agro-pastoral economies to Greece in the Neolithic, and EH III–MH is no different. EH II seems "special" and full of "promise" primarily because, among the huge numbers of EH II sites now known from all over the mainland, a modest quantity (mainly those with "corridor houses") have been variously argued to show signs of administration, storage, redistribution, communal feasting events (Pullen, Chapter 4; also 2011a), and some measure of social differentiation – all features characteristic of Mycenaean palatial states centuries later. Consequently, MH is "disappointing" only because – with the hindsight that archaeology always offers – *we know what happened next.* This implies that we think we know what *should* have happened next; yet such a view invokes a dubious teleological view of unilinear social evolution, leading inexorably to states. If the EH II communities centred around sites with corridor houses were (as some believe: *e.g.* Pullen 2011b) organized as some form of small-scale chiefdom, then the expectable outcome, as with most chiefdoms, would be cycling, inherent instability, and collapse – if, in fact, chiefdoms are as prevalent in the archaeological record as many have supposed (Pauketat 2007). On this reading, EH III – early MH society represents not some tentative recovery from a "crisis" caused by who knows what (probably *not* an invasion of Vermeule's Painted Pot People), but rather a reversion to earlier and rather simpler forms of social organization that, in the long run, were more stable.

Whether one agrees with such suggestions or not, there can be no question but that the chapters in this volume shrive themselves of neo-evolutionary value-judgments, and aim to evaluate the evidence we have on a site-by-site basis, wherever possible employing new analytical techniques. That is admirable and is bearing dividends, and will continue to do so in future. At the same time, we need to beware of the impulse to re-instate the EH III and MH I–II periods to a position of explanatory importance they probably do not deserve. This volume's co-editors asked me whether we should perhaps "reconsider our ideas of EH III communities being poor, unorganized, undifferentiated and isolated" – and that may indeed be a worthwhile question. But I also think that we should be very wary of scouring the archaeological record for the "seeds" of what actually did happen in LH I and later. This is what Cyprian Broodbank (2008, 283), in a memorable phrase, termed "the tremendous temptations of retrojection". In the rather different context of explaining early second millennium state formation on Crete, I have for decades argued that a satisfactory explanation will not emerge from simply citing antecedent circumstances as causative (*e.g.* Cherry 1983; 2010). Collingwood, in his *The Idea of History* (1946), long ago explained why this could not work; and yet this is the dominant mode of explanation adopted by most of the scholars contributing to a recent volume on Minoan state formation with the telling title *Back to the Beginning* (Schoep *et al.* 2012). None of the arguments in that book, nor any new data, have shaken my conviction that on Crete the processes leading to the formation of states soon after 2000 BC did not get seriously underway much before EM III–MM IA, and that they happened with great rapidity; attempts to push the origins of Minoan states well back into the early third millennium, or in fact even earlier, seem poorly substantiated and even unhelpful.

Could something similar also be the case for mainland societies? To be sure, the new, finer-grained studies that have become available during the past decade are suggesting that the EH III–LH I period was far from static or stagnant – although, actually, why should we ever have supposed that to be the case? Things are most unlikely to have been literally 'the same' from one site to another, or from one generation to the next. The more closely we look, the more likely it is that subtle differences and distinctions will become apparent, as measured by, for example, the relative proportions of different forms of burial, or gendered differences in diet and health status. In this regard, an important and very welcome development is the push to improve chronological resolution by targeted programmes of high-precision ^{14}C dating, for example on human bone from Argos (Voutsaki *et al.* 2006), Asine (Voutsaki *et al.* 2009), and Lerna (Voutsaki *et al.* 2009; Lindblom and Manning 2011), as well as at Kolonna on Aegina on its long, continuous stratigraphic sequence running from the Late Neolithic to LH IIIA, with eight ceramic and settlement phases spanning EH III to LH I (Wild *et al.* 2010). Nevertheless, the picture that is emerging suggests that those changes we can detect during this era have little discernible directionality – presumably what Dickinson (2010, 17) had in mind in saying he had no impression of "increasing momentum" – and only in the late period (*i.e.*, MH III and LH I) do we see some marked and significant changes. To me, this indicates that early Mycenaean state formation may also have been quite rapid, just as seems to have been the case in Crete. Voutsaki and Milka (in Chapter 6) conclude that "the developments in the earlier part of the period do not set in motion an evolutionary process of growing complexity" and are doubtful about "a process of gradual and incremental growth". But here they are writing solely about Lerna, which may not be representative of the wider picture (since, after growth and prosperity in early MH, this site seems to have declined in the later part of the period and become relatively obscure by Mycenaean times). This serves to underscore the fact that we need many more careful studies at a far greater sample of sites before it will be possible to make soundly-based generalizations about the rise of complexity on the mainland.

Explaining processes of social, economic and cultural change is a worthy ambition. To do so, however, requires us to be explicit about what we mean by 'change' and how we plan to measure it in the archaeological record, as well as having the requisite tools to calibrate rates of change. The Middle Helladic Argolid Project's approach to the analysis of funerary data is exemplary in this respect. It examines individual axes of variation with quantifiable metrics – variation between individual burials, and within/between groupings of burials and cemeteries; proportional representation by age and sex; variable incidence of pathologies and occupational stresses manifested in the skeletal data; differences in diet, as revealed by dental microwear analysis and stable isotope analysis; and so on – and then considers the extent to which these co-vary and indicate corresponding changes through time (Voutsaki and Valamoti 2013). But even such careful analyses will generate only coarse data if their results cannot be placed against a precise temporal framework. That is why the programmes of ^{14}C analysis, noted above, are so important, and why (coupled with sets of such dates) the wide-scale comparative classification of pre-Mycenaean pottery shapes proposed by Gauß and Lindblom (this volume) might be worth the huge effort involved. Too little attention has been paid to the *pace* of change. As one of Jeremy Rutter's (2009) more amusing article titles puts it, "How about the pace of change, for a change of pace?". Data of adequate quality to precisely calibrate the pace of change have so far been lacking. And yet the rate of change (or perhaps even disparate *rates* of change in different variables) will surely have a major impact on the types of explanatory models we put forward to account for social, economic and cultural change.

* * * * *

Even though we are now in the sixth or seventh generation of Aegean prehistory as a discipline, we regularly lament gaps and deficiencies in the data for virtually every period. Nowhere is this more apparent than for the Middle Helladic. For one thing, the evidence is very uneven in its spatial distribution: the majority of the "good" sites (if by "good" we mean extensively excavated settlement sites with usefully long stratigraphic sequences) are notably concentrated in the northeast Peloponnese and especially around the Argive Plain. It is no surprise that most of the contributions to the present book focus mainly on just a few sites in this area, with some extension to important sites nearby, such as Tsoungiza to the north or Kolonna and Ayia Irini to the east. That is fine if one is interested primarily in the processes of sociocultural change leading to political centralization at sites such as Mycenae or Tiryns – but what about the rest of the central and southern Greek mainland during these centuries? There is the obvious danger of treating conclusions, drawn from a few sites in a region where the evidence is superior, as indicative of the nature of MH society and social change on a far wider scale. Even in the case of Lerna, whose material has long led it to be considered as the "type site" for the MH mainland (cf. Rutter 2007), Voutsaki and Milka (this volume), as already noted, rightly caution that it seems to have followed a different social trajectory than other sites in the Argolid, and so should not be regarded as representative of that region, let alone of the entire southern mainland.

Another difficulty with our MH evidence is that most of the handful of key sites have not yielded up their data readily. Stratigraphic complexity, the sheer abundance of material, and the fact that they were often excavated long ago have conspired to leave most of them in an only partially published state. Take Lerna, again, as a case in point. The focus of frenetic, wide-scale excavation for half a dozen years by Jack Caskey beginning in 1952, this site is still slouching towards adequate final publication, more than 60 years later. Aside from studies on the fauna and human osteology published reasonably promptly after the conclusion of fieldwork (but now inevitably both looking very dated in their approach), we still have only monographs covering Neolithic pottery; the architecture, stratigraphy and pottery of Lerna III; the pottery of Lerna IV; and (just two years ago) the settlement and architecture of Lerna IV. While there have been numerous shorter studies over the years of individual categories of material (the recent examination by the Middle Helladic Argolid Project team of a range of evidence from Lerna's EH III–LH I periods being especially noteworthy), much of the site, including its MH and Mycenaean phases, languishes unpublished, except in preliminary reports. Furthermore, as was the regular practice at the time, large (but unquantified) amounts of pottery deemed to be unimportant were discarded, so that the assemblages over which ceramic experts have struggled for so many years are not only an incomplete sample, but one that is biased, and to an unknown degree. (I was reminded of this same problem daily while working on the Northern Keos survey with Jack Davis in the 1980s, for which we made use of the *apothiki* at Ayia Irini, the site to which Caskey turned soon after Lerna; its front door was approached via a footpath that passed a veritable mountain of ceramic discards.) Caskey fell prey to the temptation of foregoing the hard slog of publication for the excitement of fresh excavation elsewhere (he dug at Ayia Irini 1960–1971), though in this he was hardly unique: it is a problem endemic in Aegean prehistory, and indeed much more widely.

The fact is (as my colleague Jack Davis remarked to me recently) that there are really rather too few EH III–LH I settlement contexts that provide reliable data in quantity – at least, ones we know of, or that have been adequately published. The consequence is that MH is a field prone to overly wide generalization on the basis of a restricted database, or (to put it a little differently) to joining up the dots in many different ways, all somewhat speculative. In this regard, the *Mesohelladika* conference (Philippa-Touchais *et al.* 2010) has been enormously valuable in collating reports on MH sites from all over the mainland and greatly expanding the basis for discussion. As the co-editors of the conference volume themselves put it (Philippa-Touchais *et al.* 2010, 1038):

> "The papers have opened our eyes to settlement around the Saronic Gulf, throughout Attika, in Lokris and Thessaly, throughout the Corinthian Gulf and its opening to the West, in the southwestern Peloponnesos, in relationship to the Cycladic islands and those of the northeast Aegean, and of course in relation to Crete."

It remains to be seen how these much-needed wider perspectives will impact research in the future and lead to more nuanced understandings of this period.

Another obvious way to ameliorate over-reliance on a narrow sample of sites, however, is to make greater use of archaeological survey data, something that is not a feature of any of the chapters in the present book, except in Bintliff's brief contribution (this volume). The wave of new regional survey fieldwork in Greece began in the mid-1970s, too late to be available for the synthetic overviews of this period by Colin Renfrew in *The Emergence of Civilisation* (1972), or Oliver Dickinson in *The Origins of Mycenaean Civilisation* (1977); but since then there have taken place countless such surveys, some of them published well and in considerable detail. Enough of them were providing information by the early 1990s, when Rutter was preparing his magisterial review of the prepalatial Bronze Age of the southern and central Greek mainland, that he was able to allot considerable space and attention to "surface survey, particularly of the systematic and intensive variety" as an integral part of his treatment of the evidence on a regional scale (Rutter 2001, 97–108, fig. 1 and table 1). He provided what was, for its time, a clear-headed discussion of some of the strengths (*e.g.* far larger numbers of sites within a given area; the regional perspective) and weaknesses (*e.g.* imprecise dating; problems with defining "sites"; demonstrating site contemporaneity; and so on) of survey data. He rightly predicted a "flood of interregional comparative studies that is bound to result from the publication of vast quantities of information of a fundamentally different character than has hitherto been available" (Rutter 2001, 102), also warning of the difficulties likely to be encountered when comparing data from surveys whose field methods and strategies have varied considerably.

He was correct on both counts: much more data has poured in over the subsequent quarter-century, and inevitable problems have emerged in trying to handle these often disparate datasets side-by-side (Alcock and Cherry 2004). Nonetheless, although it might be pretentious to speak of this as an opportunity for "big data" analysis, the sheer quantity of evidence from so many projects in so many different regions of Greece gives some substance to the broad-scale patterns that seem to emerge. Even in the 16 surveys earlier summarized by Rutter (2001, table 1), nine of them indicated a clear down-turn in site numbers between EH and MH. At the other end of the chronological spectrum, survey data collated by Cavanagh (1995, table 2) showed that all of the projects in his census revealed an increase in site numbers from MH to LH ranging from one-fold to seven-fold. The careful, detailed analysis of survey data from the northeastern Peloponnesos, published by Wright (2004) in the *Side-by-Side Survey* volume, and which attempts a much more nuanced breakdown of site numbers in every period from EH I to LH IIIC, overwhelmingly demonstrates a sharp downturn between EH III and LH I/II, even if (as is to be expected) the details vary from one project to another. Since these several studies were undertaken, intensive surveys of various kinds have continued in many parts of the central and southern Greek mainland, and it is my impression that comparable patterns have been revealed in these projects too – to give just one example from a project in which I am currently involved, no later EH or MH finds whatsoever have yet turned up in the survey of the Mazi plain in northwest Attica.

Charting and accounting for these regional patterns is surely central to understanding social and political change on the mainland from EH III to LH I, but it is not something I have space to explore here. It does now seem very clear that the downturn in settlement numbers in EH III and MH I–II was not the consequence of nucleation following the abandonment of the many dispersed hamlets and farms that seem to characterize Late/Final Neolithic and EH I–II landscapes, but rather a thinning of occupation (and thus, evidently, a fall in overall population) that resulted in the MH pattern of fairly widely-spaced villages, very few of them large. As Bintliff (2010, 758–759; Chapter 8) has argued, we have to assume that the exigencies of long-term reproduction for these smallish communities must have necessitated participation in social networks of mate-exchange, so that we should envisage for MH "a mosaic of overlapping clusters of socially-integrated villages". An intriguing further suggestion is that the goblets and jugs which are a prominent feature of MH ceramic assemblages, especially when found in what seem to be single episodes of discard or in paired groups (Nordquist 1999), might index small-scale commensal, reciprocal feasting "as social lubricant facilitating inter-community interactions in village-focussed societies" (Bintliff 2010, 759; cf. Pullen, Chapter 4). This seems distinct from the much larger-scale and more lavish type of feasting for which there are, perhaps, signs at certain places in the EH II world (Pullen 2011a) and clear evidence in Mycenaean and Minoan palatial societies (Wright 2004a), where commensality takes the form of social display manipulated by elites to extend or maintain their social and political influence over large portions of the population. Nordquist (1999, 573) plausibly suggests that the bigger sets of drinking vessels associated with some rich late MH graves might represent an intermediate stage. In any event, it does seem likely that such practices, and changes in them, underlie the processes that Voutsaki (2005, 137, 140–141) believes are captured in the MH mortuary data, leading from *kinship* as the chief criterion of social categorization, to *social status*, promoted for example by conspicuous consumption at death and by feasting.

It is, however, at the regional level, across clusters of villages locked in social interaction, that emergent leaders – whatever we choose to call them: organizers of factions; aspiring Big Men; heads of kin groups with prestige acquired through personal skills; perhaps simply "men of renown" (Wright 2004b) – would have found their arenas for aggrandizement. That is, it would be through these networks that they would build personal power and gain social dependents, by mobilizing resources and influence (Wright 1995; 2001). Once power begins to accrue around a person or faction at a single village it imbalances the entire network and subverts the prevailing ethos of (more or less) egalitarianism, undercutting formerly equal partners in marriage networks and rendering some satellite communities subordinate (Bintliff, this volume). Moreover, as Dickinson (2010, 15) pointed out in summarizing Wright's views on MH society and its transformation through factionalism into early Mycenaean society, "another interesting thing about factions is that they can have members in different communities, and so can compete for members and prominence within a whole region ..." Complex systems (including societies) have "emergent properties" that arise from the re-arrangement of existing components into new patterns that can do new things; these social re-organizations that took place within and between communities during later MH must be one part of our explanation for the developments of the early Mycenaean era.

The point I am emphasizing is that good data at the *regional* level will be fundamental to building persuasive models of sociopolitical change in EH III–LH I, and that requires an ongoing commitment to intensive survey. One might suppose that the situation in the northeastern Peloponnese and especially in the Argolid is already well served, considering the large amounts of fieldwork that have taken place there (see Cherry and Davis 2001, fig. 10.4). But in reality there are many gaps in what we know of settlement and land-use in the immediate environs and hinterlands of the major centres of the Argive Plain. In the conclusion to his study of comparative settlement patterns during the Bronze Age in the northeastern Peloponnese, Wright (2004b, 128) reeled off a string of a dozen such important areas that still lack systematic survey. He went on to say:

> "That the majority of those on this list comprise the immediate territories of the major centres is a concern, because until we understand in detail the changing nature of land-use and settlement in them, we will be hindered in any attempt to explain the processes by which major centres emerge – how they exploit local resources, the geographic dimensions of their demographic expansion, and the nature of their relations with their neighbours – and how they function during the acme of their development."

* * * * *

9. Middle Helladic reflections

By coincidence, as I write in August 2015, a major international conference is taking place at the American School of Classical Studies to celebrate 100 years since Carl Blegen's excavations in 1915–1916 at Korakou, a hill overlooking the Corinthian Gulf and Lechaion harbour. It was on the basis of the stratigraphy of this site and the pottery finds from it, as is well known, that Blegen formulated the tripartite EH–MH–LH chronological division of the Bronze Age on the Greek mainland, a "Helladic" system designed to run parallel with the Minoan one developed by Sir Arthur Evans (Wace and Blegen 1916–1918; Blegen 1921). Obviously, the broad, bald system proposed by Wace and Blegen has been under continuous and ever-more-detailed refinement, in face of the vast and unremitting torrent of new Bronze Age pottery finds that has poured in throughout the twentieth and into the twenty-first century; individual scholars have carved out entire careers based on expertise in particular corners of the Helladic ceramic repertoire. Still, an outsider might well wonder whether, after a century of studies by an army of scholars, we do not by now have the classification and chronology of Helladic pottery more or less under control. But apparently not, so far as MH is concerned. I mentioned earlier the apparent necessity for a major international conference on 'Middle Helladic Pottery and Synchronisms' (Felten *et al.* 2007) which was exclusively about, well, the classification and chronology of MH pottery. Perhaps in reaction, the co-editors of the *Mesohelladika* conference not long afterwards actually seemed pleased that less than a dozen of their 70 papers focused on ceramic studies, noting that "if the conference had taken place 10 or 15 years before, without doubt many more papers would have addressed these themes, because at that time they monopolized our interests" (Philippa-Touchais *et al.* 2010, 1037–1038). Yet now here we are again, in this latest book to focus on the Middle Helladic, with two chapters about pottery classification (and others, of course, in which pottery chronology is an important underlying component). I am not primarily an Aegean ceramic specialist (let alone a MH expert), but a few comments are in order.

Chapter 1 in this volume, by Gauß and Lindblom, is a bold-faced proposal to start all over again, after a century of research, with the classification of late EBA to early LBA ceramics. Reading their call for "a standardized terminology with transparent equivalencies in English, Greek, German and French", I was reminded of a moment I witnessed many years ago, as a student participant in the 2nd International Thera Congress, where a brains-trust of senior scholars (Philip Betancourt, Christos Doumas, and Peter Warren were among them) were huddled in a corner over a bottle of wine after the end of the day's paper sessions, trying to reach agreement on descriptive terminology for ceramic shapes in multiple languages. Nothing came of it, so far as I am aware. But, even so, if a "false-mouthed amphora" in Greek is the equivalent of a "stirrup-jar" in English, then what exactly is the distinction between an amphora and a jar? Gauß and Lindblom's taxonomy (Figs. 1.5–1.8) seems admirably level-headed, even scientific. But if reaching clearly-defined ceramic shapes is merely a matter of specifying "splitting points", at which every vessel has to be assigned at the next level to one among a range of well-defined classificatory possibilities, then classification itself could become a purely computer-driven process – provided that shape variables, such as rim profile, are sufficiently precisely defined and well discriminated from each other. Such "expert systems" have indeed been proposed (*e.g.*, Vitali 1989), but have not had much success. Presumably, they would not do well with a shape example such as the EH III "ouzo cup", which (for reasons unspecified, except that it is presumed to be a drinking vessel, and therefore open to the mouth) is classified as an open shape, even though it violates the clearly-specified rule that open vessels have a larger rim diameter than height. It would also be interesting to see whether a purely automated classification algorithm would end up with the same sets of forms and shapes for MH goblets as Gauß and Lindblom's 62B, 61B and 60B. These are already entirely recognizable shapes (some with well-established names: 62B = Lianokladhi goblet), with distinct geographical and temporal distributions, which may indeed also even reflect socially significant changes in drinking practices. This we already know: so it is fair to ask what the proposed new classificatory system will add.

As a graduate student long ago, I recall a particularly illuminating seminar on archaeological taxonomy and chronology; as an exercise, we were all given the self-same assemblage of Sassanian pottery to classify. The results were wildly disparate among the students, because of course classification is driven by research questions, and there can be no such thing as a neutral or impartial or absolute classification. I have considerable sympathy with Gauß and Lindblom's frustration that they cannot readily compare ceramics from Kolonna and Lerna, and that trying to examine continuities or disruptions in ceramic traditions between Lerna III and IV, or IV and V, are made exceedingly difficult by the normal practice (at least, at such big and complex sites) of assigning the study of materials from different phases to different scholars, who inevitably parse the material in different ways that best suit the characteristics of materials from "their" phase. The examples of classificatory mismatches they adduce (an EH III unpainted tankard from Kolonna, a decorated MH bowl from Kolonna, and how these would be treated under the Lerna IV or V system) are indeed telling.

Nonetheless, I believe that this "new resource" may not be successful in the long run, for several reasons. One is that the needs of these two individual researchers are unlikely to align with those of all scholars working on ceramics of this period. A second is my conviction that any classification system implies research questions, and not all MH scholars, obviously, will have the same questions in mind. A third is that ceramics are very complicated, and there is a multitude of variables we need to take into consideration, all of which co-vary in extremely complex ways: paste, temper, ware, shape, form, decoration, function, context, and so on. To expect to be able to capture this variation in a single, universally applicable taxonomy seems naïve. Even were that not the case, the proposed project seems – to say the least – rather ambitious, with hundreds of sites and many thousands of pots implicated, and thus likely to extend well beyond the life-span of its proposers.

Jeremy Rutter's brief proposal (this volume) is rather different. His idea does not concern ceramic taxonomy, but cultural phasing, which is another thing altogether.

Everyone can agree that there is a major caesura at the end of EH II, and the emergence of a very different kind of society in the period defined ceramically as EH III. If we wish now to refer to that as "Middle Bronze Age A", as Rutter suggests, that's fine – although its ceramic definition by what we will still refer to as EH III, or Protominyan, or Kolonna phases D and E will remain rather confusing. The contributions to this book make it clear that there are indeed significant differences in the sociocultural constitution of mainland societies in the ceramic phases EH III, MH I–II, and MH III–LH I, and so it may be helpful to recognize these via a meta-taxonomy. The obvious parallel here is Nikolaos Platon's proposal, many years ago, to divide the Minoan sequence into Prepalatial, Protopalatial, and Neopalatial periods, which also do not map neatly onto the established Minoan pottery sequence. "Slicing and dicing" can take place in more than one way.

Nonetheless, such tripartite classifications come with considerable intellectual baggage, reaching back 150 years. We should perhaps remember that Sir Arthur Evans split up the sequence at Knossos into three parts, each itself divided into three, at a very early stage of his excavations at the site. The working title of what would later become his monumental work *The Palace of Minos* was "Nine Minoan Periods" (cf. Evans 1906). In this tripartite division, he was clearly influenced by his father John Evans and the spirit of 19th-century geological classificatory schemes, and of course by the Three-Age system of Stone-Bronze-Iron introduced by nineteenth-century Scandinavian archaeologists (Trigger 2006). There is, of course, no obvious reason why any sequence of cultural change should fall neatly into three-part divisions. While almost everything of course has a beginning, a middle, and an end, or a birth, florescence, and death, an obvious danger here is the risk of treating human cultures in terms of inappropriate metaphors of biological evolution. Rutter's proposed classification cannot be faulted on this ground, since his MBA-A, MBA-B, MBA-C sequence in fact represents, if anything, a crescendo of development leading on to the mature Mycenaean civilisation. It remains to be seen if his proposal will catch on. But I am all for schemes that direct our attention to wider societal changes that may cross-cut the detailed ceramic classifications we need to use to track them.

* * * * *

I conclude with a few comments on three concepts that crop up in various places throughout these chapters: monumentality, urbanism, and nomadism. My cautionary tone may be out of keeping with the positive nature of the contributions to this volume, but I do think there are some things that need to be said.

First, the use of the term "monumental". As Weiberg very reasonably defines it in this volume:

> "Monumentality is obviously a very relative concept. It can be measured in many ways, such as the work hours needed to accomplish the structures, the elaboration of the details, the durability over time, as well as of course in the actual size of the structures (cf. Fitzsimons 2011). Clearly, features defined as monumental in some contexts, would not be so in others.

In this respect, monumentality is highly contextual and a framework for extraordinary accomplishments within specific settings."

This definition would certainly apply to, for example, the Cyclopean walls of Mycenae and Tiryns, the Lion Gate at Mycenae, the Late Mycenaean tholos tombs, the check-dam at Tiryns, and other such instances. But do the defensive walls, or the "Corridor Houses", of EH II also really qualify as "monumental", as Voutsaki and Wiersma (this volume, Introduction), Weiberg (this volume, Chapter 3), Wiersma (this volume, Chapter 5), and Bintliff (this volume, Chapter 8) all suggest? Just being a bit bigger or fancier than whatever is the norm in any given period is surely not enough, *ipso facto*, to qualify something as monumental. As Renfrew asked in his *The Emergence of Civilisation* (1972, 236–244, figs. 14.5–14.8), what, in Greece, is truly monumental, in the face of Egyptian and Near Eastern pyramids, ziggurats, and massive walled cities? Later papers by Branigan (2004) and Whitelaw (2004) toned down this contrast, demonstrating that many Middle and Late Bronze Age settlements in Anatolia and the Levant, at least, are of a comparable scale to those on Crete during the same periods; but something of Renfrew's point nonetheless still stands.

There is perhaps an inevitable tendency for archaeologists to want to aggrandize their own site or culture/period of interest, and Minoan archaeology seems particularly prone it. For example, the editors of the *Back to the Beginning* volume (Schoep *et al.* 2012) chose for their front-cover image a photo of the northwest corner of the EM III Northwest Terrace System at Knossos, as an example of monumentalization in action on the eve of state emergence. I do not mean to appear facetious, but I am struck by the fact that a terracing wall of nearly this size exists in my own back yard, for which the word 'monumental' certainly does not come to mind. Similarly, the excavator of Myrtos Pyrgos, Gerald Cadogan, described the interesting late Prepalatial communal tomb of Phase II at that site as "a planned monumental mortuary complex" (Cadogan 2011, 106). Writing about this tomb recently, I realized that it is in fact slightly smaller than the office in which I was then sitting to type, and that the so-called "monumental processional way" leading to the tomb is the same length (15 m) as the approach to the front door of my own house. Some reality checks are in order. I don't think we can simply assert whatever we like, because it's claimed to be all a relative matter. A fine instance of such tendencies to aggrandizement is Piet de Jong's oft-reproduced water-colour reconstruction of the Throne Room of the Palace of Nestor at Pylos. Axonometric architectural analysis shows its perspective to be more or less that of a small animal crouching in an extreme corner of the room, and those who have visited the site may share my own impression of it as one that is quite modest in scale – for a throne-room, after all. Loose usage of the word "monumental" is commonplace, yet it has consequences. It may be, for instance, that one reason why EH III and MH seem less "interesting" is that they are "non-monumental" periods (to quote from the title of Weiberg this volume) – but that makes sense only if we accept the existence of "monumental" structures in EH II.

And this leads me briefly to a second, and related, issue, one that again implicates the use of freighted terminology. Are any sites of the Aegean Bronze

Age appropriately characterized as "urban"? Or "proto-urban"? Or a "proto-*polis*" (as in Bintliff this volume)? Of course, this term too is comparative: even the city of Rome at its height is utterly dwarfed by modern Tokyo or Mexico City, while no settlement anywhere in the prehistoric Aegean remotely approached the size of ancient Rome. Writing about urbanism in prehistory has tended to be vague and ambiguous, even muddled, ever since Gordon Childe's classic 1950 article on "the urban revolution" (which, in fact, is mainly concerned with the characteristics of state-level societies, not cities). In the Aegean, the introduction by Renfrew of the murky term "proto-urban" added only fuzziness, and led on to peculiar studies such as "Stages of Urban Transformation in the Early Helladic Period" (Konsola 1986) – for me, a non-subject, since I do not believe that *any* EBA settlement, anywhere in the Aegean, could possibly be considered to be a "city". Simply applying labels, or searching for universal definitions, offers no explanatory power and distracts us from studying the varied factors that resulted in population aggregation in nucleated centres: what made people come together, and what were the opportunities and challenges when they did so? The *processes* resulting in the reorganization of smaller-scale social units into more complex configurations lie at the heart of the emergence of complex societies in the prehistoric Aegean, and we would do better to focus on them, rather than descriptive terminology.

Lastly, although I hate to take issue with such a distinguished scholar and also a good friend, I must record the fact that I have little sympathy with Rutter's suggestions (this volume) that the EH III period "at least in the Peloponnese, may have been populated largely by mobile groups who only gradually and rather irregularly became sedentary over a period of some half-a-dozen generations" in the Corinthia and the Argolid. As I write, hundreds of thousands of refugees from Syria, Afghanistan, and many other countries are pouring across the borders of the European Union, creating a political and, indeed, an existential crisis. Who are we to say that migration has not been an equally potent factor in the past? After years of disinterest under the New Archaeology, migration has once again become a topic attracting archaeological interest (*e.g.* van Dommelen 2014).

Yet Rutter's conjecture, if I understand it correctly, rests almost entirely on the idea that the buildings of the EH III phase at Lerna are somewhat flimsy, and thus must be "those of a previously mobile population who were settling down in a single location". Other features of EH III are then adduced as further evidence for such a presumption, such as the lack of evidence for funerary behaviour, as well as interregional and intercultural exchanges. But societies do not flip at will, and casually, between sedentary and nomadic stances. To be nomadic implies a dependence on pastoralism, and what we know from both ethnography and archaeology shows that this is, in fact, a quite specialized adaptation, generally possible only in symbiosis with sedentary, often fully urban, agriculturalists (Cherry 1988). It is no coincidence that pastoral societies in the ancient Near East emerged only after settled, agriculturally-based societies were in place. If Rutter's idea were correct, we ought to be able to identify "nomadic" societies (whatever that might mean – and the detection of pastoral nomadism in the archaeological record is notoriously difficult) in Boeotia in the period prior to EH III, presumably in interaction with settled agriculturalists; I am not aware of any data that would point to such a scenario. As with almost everything Rutter writes, this is a suggestion that makes us think anew about the details in the data, and how we can best make sense of them. Nonetheless, I find it hard to accept the basic premise that "nomads" migrated from Boeotia to the northwest Peloponnese towards the end of the third millennium BC.

* * * * *

But I do not wish to end on a cautionary or critical note, so let me return to my beginning. The renaissance of interest in studies of the EH III to LH I period that has taken place over the past dozen years or more is, within the wider scope of Aegean prehistory as a whole, greatly to be welcomed. There has been much excellent new fieldwork, analysis and publication. I sense that the various contributions in the present volume will likewise help sustain the momentum and assist in moving this field forward to new levels of understanding of life on the mainland of Greece in the late third and early second millennia BC, and of how and why the Mycenaean civilisation came into being.

Bibliography

Bintliff, J. 2010. "The Middle Bronze Age Through the Surface Survey Record of the Greek Mainland: Demographic and Sociopolitical Insights." In *Mesohelladika. The Greek Mainland in the Middle Bronze Age*, Bulletin de Correspondance Hellénique Supplement 52, edited by A. Philippa-Touchais, G. Touchais, S. Voutsaki, and J. Wright, 755–763. Athens, De Boccard.

Blegen, C. W. 1921. *Korakou. A Prehistoric Settlement Near Corinth*. Boston, American School of Classical Studies at Athens.

Branigan, K. 2004. "Aspects of Minoan Urbanism." In *Urbanism in the Aegean Bronze Age*, Sheffield Studies in Aegean Archaeology, edited by K. Branigan, 38–50. Sheffield, Continuum.

Broodbank, C. 2008. "Long after Hippos, Well Before Palaces: A Commentary on the Cultures and Contexts of Neolithic Crete." In *Escaping the Labyrinth: The Cretan Neolithic in Context*, edited by V. Isaakidou and P. Tomkins, 273–290. Oxford, Oxbow Books.

Cadogan, G. 2011. "A Power House of the Dead: The Functions and Long Life of the Tomb at Myrtos-Pyrgos." In *Prehistoric Crete: Regional and Diachronic Studies on Mortuary Systems*, edited by J. M. A. Murphy, 103–117. Philadelphia, Institute of Aegean Prehistory Academic Press.

Cavanagh, W. 1995. "The Development of Mycenaean Settlement in Laconia." In *Politeia. Society and State in the Aegean Bronze Age*, Aegaeum 12, edited by R. Laffineur and W.-D. Niemeier, 81–88. Liège, University of Liège; Austin, University of Texas.

Cherry, J. F. 1983. "Evolution, Revolution, and the Origins of Complex Society in Minoan Crete." In *Minoan Society*, edited by O. Kryszkowska and L. Nixon, 33–45. Bristol, Bristol Classical Press.

Cherry, J. F. 1988. "Pastoralism and the Role of Animals in the Pre- and Proto-historic Economies of the Aegean." In *Pastoral Economies in Classical Antiquity*, Cambridge Philological Society Supplementary Volume 14, edited by C. R. Whittaker, 6–34. Cambridge, Cambridge Philological Society.

Cherry, J. F. 2010. "Sorting Out Crete's Prepalatial Off-Island Interactions." In *Archaic State Interaction: The Eastern Mediterranean in the Bronze Age*, edited by W. A. Parkinson and M. L. Galaty, 107–140. Santa Fe, School for Advanced Research Press.

Childe, V. G. 1950. "The Urban Revolution." *Town Planning Review* 21.1, 3–17.
Collingwood, R. G. 1946. *The Idea of History*. Oxford, Clarendon Press.
Dickinson, O. T. P. K. 1977. *The Origins of Mycenaean Civilisation*. Studies in Mediterranean Archaeology 49. Göteborg, P. Åström.
Dickinson, O. T. P. K. 1989. "The Origins of Mycenaean Civilisation Revisited." In Transition. *Le monde égéen du Bronze Moyen au Bronze Récent. Actes de la 2ᵉ Rencontre égéenne internationale de l'université de Liège (18-20 avril 1988)*, Aegaeum 3, edited by R. Laffineur, 131–136. Liège, University of Liège, Department of Art History and Archaeology of Ancient Greece.
Dickinson, O. T. P. K. 2010. "The 'Third World' of the Aegean? Middle Helladic Greece Revisited." In *Mesohelladika. The Greek Mainland in the Middle Bronze Age,* Bulletin de Correspondance Hellénique Supplement 52, edited by A. Philippa-Touchais, G. Touchais, S. Voutsaki, and J. Wright, 13–27. Athens, De Boccard.
Evans, A. J. 1906. *Essai de classification des époques de la civilisation minoenne: Résumé d'un discours fait au congrés d'archéologie à Athènes*. London, Quaritch.
Felten, F., W. Gauß, and R. Smetana, eds. 2007. *Middle Helladic Pottery and Synchronisms. Proceedings of the International Workshop held at Salzburg October 31st-November 2nd, 2004*, Ägina-Kolonna Forschungen und Ergebnisse I/Österreichische Akademie der Wissenschaften Denkschriften der Gesamtakademie 42. Vienna, Austrian Academy of Sciences.
Fitzsimmons, R. D. 2011. "Monumental Architecture and the Construction of the Mycenaean State." In *State Formation in Italy and Greece: Questioning the Neoevolutionist Paradigm*, edited by N. Terrenato and D.C. Haggis, 75–118. Oxford, Oxbow Books.
Konsola, D. 1986. "Stages of Urban Transformation in the Early Helladic Period." In *Early Helladic Architecture and Urbanization: Proceedings of a Seminar Held at the Swedish Institute in Athens, June 8, 1985*, Studies in Mediterranean Archaeology 76, edited by R. Hägg and D. Konsola, 9–19. Göteborg, P. Åström.
Lindblom, M., and S. W. Manning. 2011. "The Chronology of the Lerna Shaft Graves." In *Our Cups Are Full: Pottery and Society in the Aegean Bronze Age. Papers Presented to Jeremy B. Rutter on the Occasion of his 65th Birthday*, British Archaeological Report S2227, edited by W. Gauß, M. Lindblom, R. A. K. Smith and J. C. Wright, 140–153. Oxford, Archaeopress.
Milka, E. Forthcoming. *Diversity and Change in Middle Helladic Mortuary Practices: a Comparison of Lerna and Asine*. PhD Dissertation, University of Groningen.
Nordquist, G. 1999. "Pairing of Pots in the Middle Helladic Period." In *MELETEMATA: Studies in Aegean Archaeology presented to Malcolm H. Wiener as he enters his 65th year*, Aegaeum 20, edited by P. P. Betancourt, V. Karageorghis, R. Laffineur, and W.-D. Niemeier, vol. 2, 569–573. Liège/Austin, University of Texas at Austin.
Pauketat. T. R. 2007. *Chiefdoms and Other Archeological Delusions*, Lanham, AltaMira Press.
Philippa-Touchais, A., G. Touchais, S. Voutsaki, and J. Wright, eds. 2010. *Mesohelladika. The Greek Mainland in the Middle Bronze Age*, Bulletin de Correspondance Hellénique Supplement 52. Athens, De Boccard.
Pullen, D. J. 2011a. "Picking out Pots in Patterns: Feasting in Early Helladic Greece." In *Our Cups Are Full: Pottery and Society in the Aegean Bronze Age. Papers presented to Jeremy B. Rutter on the Occasion of his 65th Birthday*, British Archaeological Report S2227, edited by W. Gauß, M. Lindblom, R. A. K. Smith and J. C. Wright, 217–226. Oxford, Archaeopress.
Pullen, D. J. 2011b. "Redistribution in Aegean Palatial Societies. Before the Palaces: Redistribution and Chiefdoms in Mainland Greece", *American Journal of Archaeology* 115.2, 185–195.
Rutter, J. B. 2001. "Review of Aegean Prehistory II: The Prepalatial Bronze Age of the Southern and Central Greek Mainland and Addendum: 1993–1999." In *Aegean Prehistory: A Review*, edited by T. Cullen, 95–155. Boston, Archaeological Institute of America.
Rutter, J. B. 2007. "Reconceptualizing the Middle Helladic 'Typesite' from a Ceramic Perspective: Is 'Bigger' Really 'Better'?" In *Middle Helladic Pottery and Synchronisms. Proceedings of the International Workshop held at Salzburg October 31st-November 2nd, 2004*, Ägina-Kolonna Forschungen und

Ergebnisse I/Österreichische Akademie der Wissenschaften Denkschriften der Gesamtakademie 42, edited by F. Felten, W. Gauß, and R. Smetana, 35–44. Vienna, Austrian Academy of Sciences.

Rutter, J. B. 2009. "How about the Pace of Change for a Change of Pace?" In *Tree-rings, Kings, and Old World Archaeology and Environment: Papers Presented in Honor of Peter Ian Kuniholm*, edited by S. W. Manning and M. J. Bruce, 189–194. Oxford, Oxbow Books.

Schoep, I., P. Tomkins, and J. Driessen, eds. 2012. *Back to the Beginning: Reassessing Social and Political Complexity on Crete during the Early and Middle Bronze Age.* Oxford, Oxbow Books.

Spencer, L. 2007. *Pottery Technology and Socio-Economic Diversity on the Early Helladic III to Middle Helladic II Greek Mainland.* PhD dissertation, University of London.

Trigger, B. G. 2006. *A History of Archaeological Thought* (2nd edn). Cambridge and New York, Cambridge University Press.

Van Dommelen, P., ed. 2014. Mobility and Migration. *World Archaeology* 46.4.

Vermeule, E. 1964. *Greece in the Bronze Age.* Chicago and London, University of Chicago Press.

Vitali, V. 1989. "Archaeometric Provenance Studies: An Expert System Approach." *Journal of Archaeological Science* 16.4, 383–391.

Voutsaki, S. 2005. "Social and Cultural Change in the Middle Helladic Period: Presentation of a New Project." In *Autochthon. Papers Presented to O.T.P.K. Dickinson on the Occasion of his Retirement*, British Archaeological Report S1432, edited by A. Dakouri-Hild and S. Sherratt, 134–143. Oxford, Archaeopress.

Voutsaki, S., S. Dietz, and A. J. Nijboer. 2009. "Radiocarbon Analysis and the History of the East Cemetery, Asine." *Opuscula: Annual of the Swedish Institutes in Athens and Rome* 2, 31–52.

Voutsaki, S., A. J. Nijboer, and C. Zerner. 2009. "Middle Helladic Lerna: Relative and Absolute Chronologies." In *Tree-rings, Kings, and Old World Archaeology and Environment: Papers Presented in Honor of Peter Ian Kuniholm*, edited by S. W. Manning and M. J. Bruce, 151–161. Oxford, Oxbow Books.

Voutsaki, S., A. J. Nijboer, A. Philippa-Touchais, G. Touchais, and S. Triantaphyllou. 2006. "Analyses of Middle Helladic Skeletal Material from Aspis, Argos, 1: Radiocarbon Analysis of Human Remains." *Bulletin de Correspondance Hellénique* 130.2, 613–625.

Voutsaki, S., and S. M. Valamoti, eds. 2013. *Diet, Economy and Society in the Ancient Greek World*, Pharos Supplement 1. Leuven, Peeters.

Wace, A. J. B., and C. W. Blegen. 1916–18. "The Pre-Mycenaean Pottery of the Greek Mainland." *Annual of the British School at Athens* 22, 175–189.

Whitelaw, T. M. 2004. "From Sites to Communities: Defining the Human Dimensions of Minoan Urbanism." In *Urbanism in the Aegean Bronze Age*, Sheffield Studies in Aegean Archaeology, edited by K. Branigan, 15–37. Sheffield, Continuum.

Wiersma, C. W. 2014. *Building the Bronze Age. Architectural and Social Change on the Greek Mainland During Early Helladic III, Middle Helladic and Late Helladic I.* Oxford, Archaeopress Archaeology.

Wild, E. M., W. Gauß, G. Forstenpointner, M. Lindblom, R. Smetana, P. Steier, U. Thanheiser, and F. Weninger. 2010. "^{14}C Dating of the Early to Late Bronze Age Stratigraphic Sequence of Aegina Kolonna, Greece." *Nuclear Instruments and Methods in Physics Research* B 268, 1013–1021.

Wright, J. C. 1995. "From Chief to King in Mycenaean Society." In *The Role of the Ruler in the Prehistoric Aegean*, Aegaeum 11, edited by P. Rehak, 63–80. Liège, University of Liège; Austin, University of Texas at Austin.

Wright, J. C. 2001. "Factions and the Origins of Leadership and Identity in Mycenaean Society." *Bulletin of the Institute of Classical Studies* 45, 182.

Wright, J. C., ed. 2004a. *The Mycenaean Feast.* Princeton, American School of Classical Studies at Athens.

Wright, J. C. 2004b. "Comparative Settlement Patterns during the Bronze Age in the Northeastern Peloponnesos." In *Side-by-Side Survey: Comparative Regional Studies in the Mediterranean World*, edited by S. E. Alcock and J. F. Cherry, 114–131. Oxford, Oxbow Books.